Praise for *How to Read a Poem*

"In short, reading Hirsch's *How to Read a Poem* is like a very long evening with a learned and perceptive friend who keeps leaping to his bookshelf for more and better illustrations, and finding ever more connections and revelations"
—*Newsday*

"Edward Hirsch is a passionate and careful reader, and the best parts of his book are his rapturously analytic readings of great poems.... [Hirsch provides] exactly the tools a reader needs in order to read poetry in a fully emotional and intelligent way."
—*The Boston Phoenix Literary Supplement*

"If you are pretty sure you don't like poetry, this is the book that is bound to change your mind. Hirsch demonstrates to one and all that the reading of poems is one of the supreme pleasures in life." —*Charles Simic*

"If you begin with his straightforward book, you may be led to a life of reading poetry, and reading about it. Hirsch is particularly good because he so respects the mystery [of poetry]. A lovely book, full of joy and wisdom."
—*The Baltimore Sun*

"In his latest volume, Hirsch writes about what poetry is, why it matters, and how we can open up our imaginations so that its message can reach us and make a difference. In a reading of verse from around the world, including works by Stevens, Baudelaire, Plath, and Neruda, Hirsch discovers the meaning of their words and ideas and brings their sublime message home." —*The American Poet*

"Readers will be delighted by Hirsch's intelligent enthusiasm and, in a time when too many are 'prisoners of the contemporary,' by his extraordinary conversancy with poetry of all tongues and ages." —*Richard Wilbur*

"Hirsch's contribution is significant, [grounded] in the obvious pleasure he has experienced through words. . . . Who could resist the wiles of this poetry broker—a writer rapidly becoming the baby boomers' pre-eminent man of letters?"   —*Detroit Free Press* (starred review)

"This book is the product of a lifetime of passionate reflection. Edward Hirsch has written a book that does for poetry what Robert Hughes did for modern art in *The Shock of the New,* and what Cornel West does for multiculturalism in *Race Matters.* Hirsch writes about political suffering, word magic and sensuous splendor, and the urge for human song. *How to Read a Poem* is a wonderful book for laureate and layman both."
                                                                    —Garrett Hongo

"Laudable . . . The answer Hirsch gives to the question of *How to Read a Poem* is: Ecstatically."   —*The Boston Book Review*

"Hirsch, a truly gifted poet and scholar, brings the full heat of his literary passion to this enlightening and deeply moving journey into the heart of poetry. . . . Hirsch offers many soul-touching examples over the course of his poetic, erudite, and generously self-disclosing celebration of poetry from the days of Ovid to the present. As Hirsch deftly analyzes the nature of lyric poems, dramatic monologues, elegies, and odes, he conducts close readings of the work of a stellar group of poets only he would select. . . . Hirsch's magnificent text is supported by an extensive glossary and superb international reading list."   —*Booklist*

"In a book of compelling, engaging prose, one of our country's most distinguished poets connects us knowingly to his craft—helps us to appreciate the magic of language as it grows within us, and shapes our way of seeing and hearing others and our understanding of the world."
                                                                    —Robert Coles

How to Read a Poem

HOW TO
READ
A POEM

And Fall in Love with Poetry

Edward Hirsch

A DoubleTakeBook
published by the Center for Documentary Studies
in association with

A Harvest Book
Harcourt, Inc.
San Diego   New York   London

Requests for permission to make copies of any part
of the work should be mailed to the following address:
Permissions Department, Harcourt, Inc.,
6277 Sea Harbor Drive, Orlando, Florida 32887-6777.

Library of Congress Cataloging-in-Publication Data
Hirsch, Edward. How to read a poem: and fall in love
with poetry/Edward Hirsch.—1st ed. p.   cm.
Includes bibliographical references and index.
ISBN 0-15-100419-6
ISBN 0-15-600566-2 (pbk.)
1. Poetics.   2. Poetry—Explication.
3. Poetry—History and criticism.   I. Title.
PN1042.H48   1999
808.1—dc21   98-50065

Text set in Bembo
Design by Lydia D'moch

Printed in the United States of America
First Harvest edition
A C E D B

DoubleTakeBooks publishes the works of writers and photographers
who seek to render the world as it is and as it might be, artists who
recognize the power of narrative to communicate, reveal, and
transform. These publications have been made possible by the
generous support of the Lyndhurst Foundation.

Center for Documentary Studies at Duke University
1317 West Pettigrew Street
Durham, North Carolina 27705

Permissions acknowledgments appear on pages 347–48,
which constitutes a continuation of the copyright page.

for Richard Howard,
adept of the world of reading

I dreamed that I floated at will in the great Ether, and I saw this world floating also not far off, but diminished to the size of an apple. Then an angel took it in his hand and brought it to me and said, "This must thou eat." And I ate the world.

—*Ralph Waldo Emerson*

Acknowledgments

This is a book of acknowledgments because it recognizes at every point that others have come before us, that poems breathe deeper meaning into our lives, and that we in turn breathe deeper life into poems. The word "knowledge" is hidden in the word "acknowledge," and this book suggests that poetry is a way of knowing, of honoring our solitudes and recognizing our interdependencies. It is a way of being simultaneously alone and together through art.

I am eager to avow my debt to Robert Coles, whose wide-ranging sympathies are a model of humane responsiveness, and to the other editors of *DoubleTake* magazine, where some of these pieces first appeared, including "How to Read These Poems," from which everything flowed. Rob Odom's encouragement in particular has been a sustained delight to me. It was Rob who first brought me to Iris Tillman Hill and Double-Take Books.

This book was conceived as a whole, but some of its individual chapters appeared as ongoing columns in *American Poetry Review* and gained from the enthusiasm and attentiveness of Stephen Berg. The chapter on epiphanies appeared in the *Sewanee Review.*

My special thanks to the poets Michael Collier, Nicholas Christopher, Garrett Hongo, Philip Levine, Gerald Stern, Adam Zagajewski, and S. X. Rosenstock for enabling conversations about poetry. I have been fortunate to have the collaborative help of the poet Averill Curdy in preparing the glossary and bibliography. I have been deepened immeasurably by my friendship with the fiction writer William Maxwell, whose intelligence is so rapturous and whose rapture is so intelligent.

I am lucky to have a fine agent in Liz Darhansoff. I consider myself especially lucky to have such an excellent instigating editor in André Bernard at Harcourt Brace. He is a model of editorial élan and rigor.

Thanks to my many friends in Inprint, Inc. in Houston who encouraged me to take up the subject of how to read a poem and to explicate my passions. Thanks, too, to the many young poets in the Creative

Writing Program at the University of Houston whose apprenticeship to our art has taught me so much about schooling our hearts through poetry.

This book is dedicated to the poet Richard Howard, the most enabling of friends, the most enthralled and omnivorous of readers.

My deep love goes out to my wife, Janet Landay, and to our son, Gabriel Hirsch, beloved sources.

Contents

Preface

This is a book about reading poetry. It is also a book of readings. I have gathered together many poems I have loved over the years, and I have tried to let them show me how they should be read. I let the poems themselves act as my Virgilian guides. I have called often on the poets, my beloved immortals, to testify about poetry.

My idea is to present certain emblematic poems I care about deeply and to offer strategies for reading these poems. My readings are meant to be instructive and suggestive, not definitive, since poems are endlessly interpretable. There is always something about them that evades the understanding, and I have tried to remain aware that, as Paul Valéry has put it, "The power of verse is derived from an indefinable harmony between what it *says* and what it *is*. Indefinable is essential to the definition."

Still, there are definite things that can be said about particular poems and I have tried to say some of them. I consider these poems emblematic because they suggest something crucial about the nature of poetry itself. I have trusted the individual poems to lead me to what those things are, to illuminate poetry. The lyric poem is the most intimate and volatile form of literary discourse and I have done my best to honor that intimacy, that volatility—the urgency that comes to me as poetry. I have listened hard and let the poems inhabit me. This book is a record of my initiations, encounters, responses, experiences. It is a record of my exaltations.

This is also a book of invitations and interactions, and I have sought to guide readers through the domain of my chosen art form. I have focused on the act of reading itself, on letting poems inhabit the reader's consciousness, the reader's body. I often move out from the individual poem to say something about the nature of poetic form or about the history of the particular form the poet employs or about where the poem stands in the body of the poet's overall work. I speak of poems, of poets, both familiar and unknown. I chart the course of certain themes. Many subjects come into my purview, many more evade me, but always the individual poem stands as my touchstone, my talisman, my naked truth.

"Learn about pines from the pine, and about bamboo from the bamboo," the seventeenth-century master of haiku, Matsuo Bashō, wrote in a series of insightful reflections on poetry. I would extend Bashō's wisdom about nature, and about the poetry of nature in particular, to include the particular nature of poetry: learn about poetry from the poem...

In this book I'd like to make poems as available and accessible, as passionate and disturbing, as I feel them to be. Poetry is a form of necessary speech. People who care about it know that poems have magical potency. But now there are many people who have become so estranged from the devices and techniques of poetry, from poetic thinking, that they no longer recognize what they are reading. Reading poetry is endangered, I suppose, because reading itself is endangered in our culture now. I need not cite the statistics. And yet at least in poetry the problem is not a new one. It seems to me that there will always be terminally middle-aged thinkers like Cicero who convince themselves that poetry is dispensable and art is unnecessary. Seneca reports in the *Epistles* (49.5) that "Cicero said that even if his lifetime were to be doubled he would still not have time to waste on reading the lyric poets." Cicero's hostile indifference, so characteristic of politicians, should not be taken as an indictment of lyric poetry (the *Greek Anthology* survives Cicero's indifference) but as testimony to Cicero's own pedestrian mode of thinking. In America the old line repeats itself with a kind of tired regularity, and every few years some Cicero or other decides that poetry is dead. It is not. When Plato suggested banning the poets from the Republic he showed much better sense, for he recognized the revolutionary power of poetic thinking. He understood it well because he employed it so successfully himself. That's because he is the philosopher most given to transport.

"Tell me a story of deep delight," Robert Penn Warren writes at the end of *Audubon: A Vision*. In this book I have tried to tell such a story. In the first chapter I lay out some of the tenets of the exchange between reader and writer in a poem textualized between speech and song. I do some necessary groundwork and distinguish some key terms, key features, of lyric poetry. I offer a kind of road map, an overview, that will resonate through subsequent chapters and, I hope, enable readers to experience poems more fully, more deeply, and more thoughtfully, though I believe that in the end poems strike something deeper than thought itself. Thereafter, I tend always to focus on unpacking individual poems, letting the issues of poetry emerge in the process. And I keep finding metaphors for the mutuality of the relationship between writer and reader.

Throughout this book I am enacting the role of the reader and hope you will unite with me. I seek to guide others as I myself have been guided by various strong readers through the sometimes challenging devices and difficulties, the splendid elaborations of poetry. One seeks to become the kind of reader who enters an area of expertise and yet still remains open to the spacious unfolding—the shining body—of the poem itself. It is the technical accomplishment—the actual physical body—of the poem that delivers our ecstatic response to it. This book is designed to give the reader the deepest access to all the ways of a poem's working. I'd like to believe that the ongoing initiation into art deepens our capacity for experiencing ourselves as well as others, thereby deepening our capacity for personhood, our achievement of humanity.

The nature of the poems I write about in this book has certainly affected the way in which I write about them. I have tried to be as clear as possible, to sound what James Wright calls "the pure clear word," but I have also tried to give my prose the wings that poetry deserves. I have sought to restore the aura of sacred practice that accompanies true poetic creation, to honor both the rational and the irrational elements in poetry. I would restore the burden of the mystery. I would illuminate an experience that takes us to the very heart of being.

1

Message in a Bottle

Heartland

Read these poems to yourself in the middle of the night. Turn on a single lamp and read them while you're alone in an otherwise dark room or while someone else sleeps next to you. Read them when you're wide awake in the early morning, fully alert. Say them over to yourself in a place where silence reigns and the din of the culture—the constant buzzing noise that surrounds us—has momentarily stopped. These poems have come from a great distance to find you. I think of Malebranche's maxim, "Attentiveness is the natural prayer of the soul." This maxim, beloved by Simone Weil and Paul Celan, quoted by Walter Benjamin in his magisterial essay on Franz Kafka, can stand as a writer's credo. It also serves for readers. Paul Celan said:

> A poem, as a manifestation of language and thus essentially dialogue, can be a message in a bottle, sent out in the—not always greatly hopeful—belief that somewhere and sometime it could wash up on land, on heartland perhaps. Poems in this sense, too, are under way: they are making toward something.

Imagine you have gone down to the shore and there, amidst the other debris—the seaweed and rotten wood, the crushed cans and dead fish— you find an unlikely looking bottle from the past. You bring it home and discover a message inside. This letter, so strange and disturbing, seems to have been making its way toward someone for a long time, and now that someone turns out to be you. The great Russian poet Osip Mandelstam, destroyed in a Stalinist camp, identified this experience. "Why shouldn't the poet turn to his friends, to those who are naturally close to him?" he asked in "On the Addressee." But of course those friends aren't necessarily the people around him in daily life. They may be the friends he only hopes exist, or will exist, the ones his words are seeking. Mandelstam wrote:

> At a critical moment, a seafarer tosses a sealed bottle into the ocean waves, containing his name and a message detailing his fate. Wandering along the dunes many years later, I happen upon it in the sand. I read the message, note the date, the last will and testament of one who has passed on. I have the right to do so. I have not opened someone else's mail. The message in the bottle was addressed to its finder. I found it. That means, I have become its secret addressee.

Thus it is for all of us who read poems, who become the secret addressees of literary texts. I am at home in the middle of the night and suddenly hear myself being called, as if by name. I go over and take down the book—the message in the bottle—because tonight I am its recipient, its posterity, its heartland.

To the Reader Setting Out

The reader of poetry is a kind of pilgrim setting out, setting forth. The reader is what Wallace Stevens calls "the scholar of one candle." Reading poetry is an adventure in renewal, a creative act, a perpetual beginning, a rebirth of wonder. "Beginning is not only a kind of action," Edward Said writes in *Beginnings*, "it is also a frame of mind, a kind of work, an attitude, a consciousness." I love the frame of mind, the playful work and working playfulness, the form of consciousness—the dreamy attentiveness—that come with the reading of poetry.

Reading is a point of departure, an inaugural, an initiation. Open the Deathbed Edition of *Leaves of Grass* (1891–1892) and you immediately encounter a series of "Inscriptions," twenty-six poems that Walt Whitman wrote over a period of three decades to inscribe a beginning, to introduce and inaugurate his major work, the one book he had been writing all his life. Beginning my own book on the risks and thralls, the particular enchantments, of reading poetry, I keep thinking of Whitman's six-line poem "Beginning My Studies."

> Beginning my studies the first step pleas'd me so much,
> The mere fact consciousness, these forms, the power of motion,
> The least insect or animal, the senses, eyesight, love,
> The first step I say awed me and pleas'd me so much,
> I have hardly gone and hardly wish'd to go any farther,
> But stop and loiter all the time to sing it in ecstatic songs.

I relish the way that Whitman lingers in this one-sentence poem over the very first step of studying, the mere fact—the miracle—of consciousness itself, the joy of encountering "these forms," the empowering sense of expectation and renewal, the whole world blooming at hand, the awakened mental state that takes us through our senses from the least insect to the highest power of love. We can scarcely turn the page, so much do we linger with pleasure over the ecstatic beginning. We are instructed by Whitman in the joy of starting out that the deepest spirit of poetry is awe.

Poetry is a way of inscribing that feeling of awe. I don't think we should underestimate the capacity for tenderness that poetry opens within us. Another one of the "Inscriptions" is a two-line poem that Whitman wrote in 1860. Called simply "To You," it consists in its entirety of two rhetorical questions:

> Stranger, if you passing meet me and desire to speak to me,
>   why should you not speak to me?
> And why should I not speak to you?

It seems entirely self-evident to Whitman that two strangers who pass each other on the road ought to be able to loiter and speak, to connect. Strangers who communicate might well become friends. Whitman refuses to be bound, to be circumscribed, by any hierarchical or class distinctions. One notices how naturally he addresses the poem not to the people around him, whom he already knows, but to the "stranger," to the future reader, to you and me, to each of us who would pause with him in the open air. Let there be an easy flow—an affectionate commerce—between us.

Here is one last "Inscription," the very next poem in *Leaves of Grass*. It's called "Thou Reader" and was written twenty-one years after "To You."

Thou reader throbbest life and pride and love the same as I,
Therefore for thee the following chants.

I am completely taken by the way that Whitman always addresses the reader as an equal, as one who has the same strange throb of life he has, the same pulsing emotions. There's a desperate American friendliness to the way he repeatedly dedicates his poems to strangers, to readers and poets to come, to outsiders everywhere. Whoever you are, he would embrace you. I love the deep affection and even need with which Whitman dedicates and sends forth his poems to the individual reader. He leaves each of us a gift. *To you,* he says, *the following chants.*

In the Beginning Is the Relation

The message in the bottle is a lyric poem and thus a special kind of communiqué. It speaks out of a solitude to a solitude; it begins and ends in silence. We are not in truth conversing by the side of the road. Rather, something has been written; something is being read. Language has become strange in this urgent and oddly self-conscious way of speaking across time. The poem has been (silently) en route—sometimes for centuries—and now it has signaled me precisely because I am willing to call upon and listen to it. Reading poetry is an act of reciprocity, and one of the great tasks of the lyric is to bring us into right relationship to each other. The relationship between writer and reader is by definition removed and mediated through a text, a body of words. It is a particular kind of exchange between two people not physically present to each other. The lyric poem is a highly concentrated and passionate form of communication between strangers—an immediate, intense, and unsettling form of literary discourse. Reading poetry is a way of connecting—

through the medium of language—more deeply with yourself even as you connect more deeply with another. The poem delivers on our spiritual lives precisely because it simultaneously gives us the gift of intimacy and interiority, privacy and participation.

Poetry is a voicing, a calling forth, and the lyric poem exists somewhere in the region—the register—between speech and song. The words are waiting to be vocalized. The greatest poets have always recognized the oral dimensions of their medium. For most of human history poetry has been an oral art. It retains vestiges of that orality always. Writing is not speech. It is graphic inscription, it is visual emblem, it is a chain of signs on the page. Nonetheless: "I made it out of a mouthful of air," W. B. Yeats boasted in an early poem. As, indeed, he did. As every poet does. So, too, does the reader make, or remake, the poem out of a mouthful of air, out of breath. When I recite a poem I reinhabit it, I bring the words off the page into my own mouth, my own body. I become its speaker and let its verbal music move through me as if the poem is a score and I am its instrumentalist, its performer. I let its heartbeat pulse through me as embodied experience, as experience embedded in the sensuality of sounds. The poem implies mutual participation in language, and for me, that participation mystique is at the heart of the lyric exchange.

Many poets have embraced the New Testament idea that "In the beginning was the Word," but I prefer Martin Buber's notion in *I and Thou* that "In the beginning is the relation." The relation precedes the Word because it is authored by the human. The lyric poem may seek the divine but it does so through the medium of a certain kind of human interaction. The secular can be made sacred through the body of the poem. I understand the relationship between the poet, the poem, and the reader not as a static entity but as a dynamic unfolding. An emerging sacramental event. A relation between an I and a You. A relational process.

Stored Magic

What kind of exchange are we dealing with? The lyric poem seeks to mesmerize time. It crosses frontiers and outwits the temporal. It seeks to defy death, coming to disturb and console you. ("These Songs are not meant to be understood, you understand," John Berryman wrote in one of his last Dream Songs: "They are only meant to terrify & comfort.")

The poet is incited to create a work that can outdistance time and surmount distance, that can bridge the gulf—the chasm—between people otherwise unknown to each other. It can survive changes of language and in language, changes in social norms and customs, the ravages of history. Here is Robert Graves in *The White Goddess*:

> True poetic practice implies a mind so miraculously attuned and illuminated that it can form words, by a chain of more-than-coincidences, into a living entity—a poem that goes about on its own (for centuries after the author's death, perhaps) affecting readers with its stored magic.

I believe such stored magic can author in the reader an equivalent capacity for creative wonder, creative response to a living entity. (Graves means his statement literally.) The reader completes the poem, in the process bringing to it his or her own past experiences. You are reading poetry—I mean really reading it—when you feel encountered and changed by a poem, when you feel its seismic vibrations, the sounding of your depths. "There is no place that does not see you," Rainer Maria Rilke writes at the earth-shattering conclusion of his poem "Archaic Torso of Apollo": "You must change your life."

The Immense Intimacy, the Intimate Immensity

The profound intimacy of lyric poetry makes it perilous because it gets so far under the skin, into the skin. "For poems are not, as people think, simply emotions (one has emotions early enough)—they are experiences," Rilke wrote in a famous passage from *The Notebooks of Malte Laurids Brigge*. I am convinced the kind of experience—the kind of knowledge—one gets from poetry cannot be duplicated elsewhere. The spiritual life wants articulation—it wants embodiment in language. The physical life wants the spirit. I know this because I hear it in the words, because when I liberate the message in the bottle a physical—a spiritual—urgency pulses through the arranged text. It is as if the spirit grows in my hands. Or the words rise in the air. "Roots and wings," the Spanish poet Juan Ramón Jiménez writes, "But let the wings take root and the roots fly."

There are people who defend themselves against being "carried away" by poetry, thus depriving themselves of an essential aspect of the experience. But there are others who welcome the transport poetry provides. They welcome it repeatedly. They desire it so much they start to crave it daily, nightly, nearly abject in their desire, seeking it out the way hungry people seek food. It is spiritual sustenance to them. Bread and wine. A way of transformative thinking. A method of transfiguration. There are those who honor the reality of roots and wings in words, but also want the wings to take root, to grow into the earth, and the roots to take flight, to ascend. They need such falling and rising, such metaphoric thinking. They are so taken by the ecstatic experience—the overwhelming intensity—of reading poems they have to respond in kind. And these people become poets.

Emily Dickinson is one of my models of a poet who responded completely to what she read. Here is her compelling test of poetry:

> If I read a book [and] it makes my whole body so cold no fire can ever warm me I know *that* is poetry. If I feel physically as if the top of my head were taken off, I know *that* is poetry. These are the only way I know. Is there any other way.

Dickinson recognizes true poetry by the extremity—the actual physical intensity—of her response to it. It's striking that she doesn't say she knows poetry because of any intrinsic qualities of poetry itself. Rather, she recognizes it by contact; she knows it by what it does to her, and she trusts her own response. Of course, only the strongest poetry could effect such a response. Her aesthetic is clear: always she wants to be surprised, to be stunned, by what one of her poems calls "Bolts of Melody."

Dickinson had a voracious appetite for reading poetry. She read it with tremendous hunger and thirst—poetry was sustenance to her. Much has been made of her reclusion, but, as her biographer Richard Sewall suggests, "She saw herself as a poet in the company of the Poets—and, functioning as she did mostly on her own, read them (among other reasons) for company." He also points to Dickinson's various metaphors for the poets she read. She called them "the dearest ones of time, the strongest friends of the soul," her "Kinsmen of the Shelf," her "enthralling friends, the immortalities." She spoke of the poet's "venerable

Hand" that warmed her own. Dickinson was a model of poetic responsiveness because she read with her whole being.

One of the books Emily Dickinson marked up, Ik Marvel's *Reveries of a Bachelor* (1850), recommends that people read for "soul-culture." I like that dated nineteenth-century phrase because it points to the depth that can be shared by the community of solitaries who read poetry. I, too, read for soul-culture—the culture of the soul. That's why the intensity of engagement I have with certain poems, certain poets, is so extreme. Reading poetry is for me an act of the most immense intimacy, of intimate immensity. I am shocked by what I see in the poem but also by what the poem finds in me. It activates my secret world, commands my inner life. I cannot get access to that inner life any other way than through the power of the words themselves. The words pressure me into a response, and the rhythm of the poem carries me to another plane of time, outside of time.

Rhythm can hypnotize and alliteration can be almost hypnotic. A few lines from Tennyson's *The Princess* can still send me into a kind of trance:

> The moan of doves in immemorial elms
> And murmurings of innumerable bees.

And I can still get lost when Hart Crane links the motion of a boat with an address to his lover in part 2 of "Voyages":

> And onward, as bells off San Salvador
> Salute the crocus lustres of the stars,
> In these poinsettia meadows of her tides,—
> Adagios of islands, O my Prodigal,
> Complete the dark confessions her veins spell.

The words move ahead of the thought in poetry. The imagination loves reverie, the daydreaming capacity of the mind set in motion by words, by images.

As a reader, the hold of the poem over me can be almost embarrassing because it is so childlike, because I need it so much to give me access to my own interior realms. It plunges me into the depths (and poetry is the literature of depths) and gives a tremendous sense of another world growing within. ("There is another world and it is in this one," Paul Éluard wrote.) I need the poem to enchant me, to shock me awake, to shift my waking consciousness and open the world to me, to open me up to the world—to the word—in a new way. I am pried open. The spiritual desire for poetry can be overwhelming, so much do I need it to experience and name my own perilous depths and vast spaces, my own well-being. And yet the work of art is beyond existential embarrassment. It is mute and plaintive in its calling out, its need for renewal. It needs a reader to possess it, to be possessed by it. Its very life depends upon it.

Mere Air, These Words, but Delicious to Hear

I remember once walking through a museum in Athens and coming across a tall-stemmed cup from ancient Greece that has Sappho saying, "Mere air, these words, but delicious to hear." The phrase inscribed into the cup, translated onto a museum label, stopped me cold. I paused for a long time to drink in the strange truth that all the sublimity of poetry comes down in the end to mere air and nothing more, to the sound of these words and no others, which are nonetheless delicious and enchanting to hear. Sappho's lines (or the lines attributed to her) also have a lapidary quality. The phrase has an elegance suitable for writing, for inscription on a cup or in stone. Writing fixes the evanescence of sound. It holds it against death.

The sound of the words is the first primitive pleasure in poetry. "In poetry," Wallace Stevens asserted, "you must love the words, the ideas and images and rhythms with all your capacity to love anything at all" ("Adagia"). Stevens lists the love of the words as the first condition of a capacity to love anything in poetry at all because it is the words that make things happen. There are times when I read a poem and can feel the syllables coming alive in my mouth, the letters enunciated in the syllables, the syllables coming together as words, the words forming into a phrase, the phrase finding a rhythm in the line, in the lines, in the shape of the words crossing the lines into a sentence, into sentences. I feel the words creating a rhythm, a music, a spell, a mood, a shape, a form. I hear the words coming off the page into my own mouth—in transit, in action. I generate—I re-create—the words incantatory, the words liberated and self-reflexive. Words rising from the body, out of the body. An act of language paying attention to itself. An act of the mind.

"Mere air, these words, but delicious to hear." In poetry the words enact—they make manifest—what they describe. This is what Gerard Manley Hopkins calls "the roll, the rise, the carol, the creation." Indeed, one hears in Hopkins's very phrase the trills or rolled consonants of the letter *r* reverberating through all four words, the voiced vowels, the *r-o-l* of "roll" echoing in the back of "*carol*," the alliterative *c*s building a cadence, hammering it in, even as the one-syllable words create a rolling, rising effect that is slowed down by the rhythm of the multisyllabic words, the caroling creation. The pleasure all this creates in the mouth is intense. "The world is charged with the grandeur of God." I read Hopkins's poems and feel the deep joy of the sounds creating themselves ("What is all this juice and all this joy?"), the nearly buckling strain of so much drenched spirit, "the achieve of, the mastery of the thing!"

The poem is an act beyond paraphrase because what is being said is always inseparable from the way it is being said. Osip Mandelstam suggested that if a poem can be paraphrased, then the sheets haven't been rumpled, poetry hasn't spent the night. The words are an (erotic) visitation, a means to an end, but also an end in and of themselves. The poet is first of all a language worker. A maker. A shaper of language. With Heinrich Heine, the linguist Edward Sapir affirmed in his book *Language,* "one is under the illusion that the universe speaks German." With Shakespeare, one is under the impression that it speaks English. This is at the heart of the Orphic calling of the poet: to make it seem as if the very universe speaks and reveals itself through the mother tongue.

In Plain American Which Cats and Dogs Can Read!

The lyric poem walks the line between speaking and singing. (It also walks the line between the conventions of poetry and the conventions of grammar.) Poetry is not speech exactly—verbal art is deliberately different than the way that people actually talk—and yet it is always in relationship to speech, to the spoken word. "It has to be living, to learn the speech of the place," as Wallace Stevens puts it in his poem "Of Modern Poetry." W. B. Yeats called a poem "an elaboration of the rhythms of common speech and their association with profound feeling" ("Modern Poetry"). W. H. Auden said: "In English verse, even in Shakespeare's grandest rhetorical passages, the ear is always aware of its relation to everyday speech" ("Writing"). I'm reminded of the many poems in the American vernacular—from Walt Whitman to William Carlos Williams ("The Horse Show"), Frank O'Hara ("Having a Coke with You"), and Gwendolyn Brooks ("We Real Cool")—that give the sensation of someone speaking in a texturized version of American English, that create the impression of letters written, as Marianne Moore joyfully puts it, "not in Spanish, not in Greek, not in Latin, not in shorthand, / but in plain American which cats and dogs can read!" A demotic linguistic vitality—what Williams calls "the speech of Polish mothers"—is one of the pleasures of the American project in poetry.

Here is the opening of Randall Jarrell's poem "Next Day":

Moving from Cheer to Joy, from Joy to All,
I take a box
And add it to my wild rice, my Cornish game hens.
The slacked or shorted, basketed, identical
Food-gathering flocks
Are selves I overlook. Wisdom, said William James,

Is learning what to overlook. And I am wise
If that is wisdom.

One hears in this poem the plaintive, intelligent voice of a suburban housewife who knows she has become invisible, who wants only to be *seen* and heard. What particularly marks the poem as a verbal construct is the self-conscious treatment of the words themselves, the way the words behave in rhythmic lines and shapely stanzas. There's the delightful pun on the names of household detergents, the play off "hens" and "flocks," the acute way the woman sums up her companions in the supermarket, how she pivots on the word "overlook" and ruefully quotes William James's pragmatic American notion of "wisdom." I've always been touched by the way Jarrell animates the woman's voice in this poem, how he inscribes his own voice into her voice and captures the reality of someone who is exceptional, commonplace, solitary.

Give a Common Word the Spell

The medium of poetry is language, our common property. It belongs to no one and to everyone. Poetry never entirely loses sight of how the language is being used, fulfilled, debased. We ought to speak more often of the *precision* of poetry, which restores the innocence of language, which makes the language visible again. Language is an impure medium. Speech is public property and words are the soiled products, not of nature, but of society, which circulates and uses them for a thousand different ends.

Poetry charts the changes in language, but it never merely reproduces or recapitulates what it finds. The lyric poem defamiliarizes words, it wrenches them from familiar or habitual contexts, it puts a spell on them. The lyric is cognate with those childish forms, the riddle and the nursery rhyme, with whatever form of verbal art turns language inside out and draws attention to its categories. As the eighteenth-century English poet Christopher Smart put it, freely translating from Horace's *Art of Poetry*:

> It is exceedingly well
> To give a common word the *spell*
> To greet you as intirely new.

The poem refreshes language, it estranges and makes it new. ("But if the work be new, / So shou'd the song be too," Smart writes.) There is a nice pun on the word *spell* in Smart's Horatian passage since, as tribal peoples everywhere have believed, the act of putting words in a certain rhythmic order has magical potency. That power can only be released when the spell is chanted aloud. I'm reminded, too, that the Latin word *carmen,* which means "song" or "poem," has attracted English poets since Sidney because of its closeness to the word *charm,* and, in fact, in the older Latin texts it also means a magic formula, an incantation meant to make things happen, to cause action (Andrew Welsh, *Roots of Lyric*). And a charm is only effective when it is spoken or sung, incanted.

The lyric poem separates and uproots words from the daily flux and flow of living speech but it also delivers them back—spelled, changed, charmed—to the domain of other people. As Octavio Paz puts it in *The Bow and the Lyre:*

> Two opposing forces inhabit the poem: one of elevation or up-rooting, which pulls the word from the language: the other of gravity, which makes it return. The poem is an original and unique creation, but it is also reading and recitation: participation. The poet creates it; the people, by recitation, re-create it. Poet and reader are two moments of a single reality.

Metaphor: A Poet is a Nightingale

The transaction between the poet and the reader, those two instances of one reality, depends upon figurative language—figures of speech, figures of thought. Poetry evokes a language that moves beyond the literal and, consequently, a mode of thinking that moves beyond the literal. "There are many other things I have found myself saying about poetry," Robert Frost confesses in "The Constant Symbol," "but chiefest of these is that it is metaphor, saying one thing and meaning another, saying one thing in terms of another, the pleasure of ulteriority." Poetry is made of metaphor. It is a collision, a collusion, a compression of two unlike things: A is B. The term *metaphor* comes from the Latin *metaphora,* which in turn derives from the Greek *metapherein,* meaning "to transfer," and, indeed, a metaphor transfers the connotations or elements of one thing (or idea) to another. It is a transfer of energies, a mode of interpenetration, a matter of identity and difference. Each of these propositions about the poem depends upon a metaphor: *The poem is a capsule where we wrap up our punishable secrets* (William Carlos Williams). *A poem is a well-wrought urn* (Cleanth Brooks), *a verbal icon* (W. K. Wimsatt). *A poem is a walk* (A. R. Ammons); *a poem is a meteor* (Wallace Stevens). *A poem might be called a pseudo-person. Like a person it is unique and addresses the reader personally* (W. H. Auden). A poem is a hand, a hook, a prayer. It is a soul in action.

    When Paul Celan wrote, "A poem . . . can be a message in a bottle," he didn't think literally that he would be dropping his poems into the Seine (though he was writing them from Paris) and that someone might find them floating ashore on the banks of the Chicago River (though I

Stevens

was living in Chicago when I first read him). What did he mean then? This book tries to tease out the implications.

The language of poetry, Shelley claims in his *Defence of Poetry*, "is vitally metaphorical; that is, it marks the before unapprehended relations of things and perpetuates their apprehension." Shelley is suggesting that the poet creates relations between things unrecognized before, and that new metaphors create new thoughts and thus revitalize language. In his fine book *Poetic Diction*, Owen Barfield remarks that he would like to change one detail in Shelley's phrase, to alter "before unapprehended relations" to "forgotten relations." That's because poetry delivers back an archaic knowledge, an ancient and vitally metaphorical way of thinking, now mostly lost. The poet, by creating anew, is also likely to be "restoring something old."

The oldest English poetry, for example (the Anglo-Saxon *Beowulf* and poems written in other old Germanic languages), has a number of poetic tropes that enable the poet to describe things at an angle, without naming them, and thus invite the listener to imaginatively construct them. The most widespread are known as *kennings;* these occur in compounds, such as calling the sea *swanrad* ("swan-road") or *winegeard* ("home of the winds"). The word *ken,* meaning "to know," is still used in Scottish dialects, and indeed such figurative language is a way of knowing.

What especially concerns me here is how the reader actively participates in the making of meaning through metaphor, in thinking through the relation of unlike things. How do we apprehend these previously unapprehended or forgotten relations: in ironic tension, in exact correspondence, in fusion? The meaning emerges as part of a collaboration between writer and reader. Out of this interactive process comes the determination to what extent a metaphor *works,* where it breaks down, to what extent a poem can be a message in a bottle, or a machine made out of words (Williams), or a derangement of the senses (Rimbaud); to what extent "a book is a cubic piece of burning, smoking conscience—and nothing else" (Boris Pasternak); to what extent, as Shelley writes,

A poet is a nightingale, who sits in darkness and sings to cheer its own solitude with sweet sounds; his auditors are as men entranced by the melody of an unseen musician, who feel that they are moved and softened, yet know not whence or why.

The singing of a nightingale becomes a metaphor for writing poetry here, and listening to that bird (that natural music) becomes a metaphor for reading it. One of the premises of Shelley's metaphor is that the poet "sings" in "solitude" without any consideration for an audience and that the audience—"his auditors"—responds to the work of an "unseen musician." They can't actually *see* him because they are physically removed from each other. And yet they are brought into mysterious (visionary) relation.

The philosopher Ted Cohen suggests that one of the main points of metaphor is "the achievement of intimacy." Cohen argues in "Metaphor and the Cultivation of Intimacy" that the maker and the appreciator of a metaphor are brought into deeper relationship with one other. That's because the speaker issues a concealed invitation through metaphor which the listener makes a special effort to accept and interpret. Such a "transaction constitutes the acknowledgment of a community." This notion perfectly describes how the poet enlists the reader's intellectual and emotive involvement and how the reader actively participates in making meaning in poetry. Through this dynamic and creative exchange the poem ultimately engages us in something deeper than intellect and emotion. And through this ongoing process the reader becomes more deeply initiated into the sacred mysteries of poetry.

Epic, Drama, Lyric: Be Plural Like the Universe!

There is a lively history of poetry, and poetry keeps engaging, fulfilling, and transgressing that history. Each of us becomes a more effective and responsive reader as we learn more about poetry's past and its forms. Literary works have conventionally been divided into three generic types or classes, dependent upon who is supposedly speaking:

> *epic or narrative:* in which the narrator speaks in the first person,
>   then lets the characters speak for themselves;
> *drama:* in which the characters do all the talking;
> *lyric:* uttered through the first person.

This useful but flawed textbook division evolved from Aristotle's fundamental distinction between three generic categories of poetic literature:

epic, drama, and lyric. All were radically presentational: recited, spoken, chanted, sung. "Like all well-conceived classifications," the Portuguese poet Fernando Pessoa writes in "Toward Explaining Heteronymy,"

> this one is useful and clear; like all classifications, it is false. The genres do not separate out with such essential facility, and, if we closely analyze what they are made of, we shall find that from lyric poetry to dramatic there is one continuous gradation. In effect, and going right to the origins of dramatic poetry— Aeschylus, for instance—it will be nearer the truth to say that what we encounter is lyric poetry put into the mouths of different characters.

Pessoa himself wrote poems under three different "heteronyms," creating three distinct bodies of work, all distinguished, under the signature of three different fictive "authors." He also wrote poems under his own name—equally dramatic, equally personal. I think we ought to take to heart his Whitmanesque motto, "Be plural like the universe!"

Aristotle's traditional groupings more or less held until the eighteenth century, but since then the epic and the novel, the drama, and the lyric have continually shadowed and shaded each other. They have blurred, transmuted, crossed boundaries. Readers experience how the narrative or storylike element drives lyric poems; how the musical element, the rhythm of emotions, charges narrative poems; how the element of dramatic projection empowers many narratives, many lyrics. These varieties are continuous, like the universe. All have their origin in religious practice and ritual.

Poetry never loses its sense of sacred mystery. Poetry emerged with the chant and the dance. As Sapir puts it, "Poetry everywhere is inseparable in its origins from the singing voice and the measure of the dance" (*Language*). Written poetry is for the most part no longer part of a communal religious practice. It is the medium of individuals for individuals. I myself am mostly interested in the existential experience of *reading* poetry, in the kind of private exchange that takes place between writer and reader. I emphasize the magical effectiveness of words as words, but I'm also aware that poetry has a strong relation to music on one side and to painting on the other. It has a musical dimension, a pictorial element.

Poetry and music are sister arts. So are poetry and painting. It's as if the eye and the ear were related through poetry, as if they had become siblings, or lovers.

Harmonious Sisters, Voice, and Vers

The poem appeals to the ear. At one boundary we have the lyric as a poem dependent upon music for its full effectiveness. The word *lyric* derives from the Greek *lyra,* or "musical instrument." The Greeks spoke of lyrics as *ta mele,* "poems to be sung." The musical element is so intrinsic to poetry that the lyric never entirely forgets its origins in musical expression—in singing, chanting, recitation to musical accompaniment. The poet was once a performer, a bard, a scop, a troubadour. In the Renaissance the lyric was repeatedly associated with the lyre and the lute. Here is how Milton evokes the juncture of poetry and music in his poem "At a Solemn Musick":

> Blest pair of *Sirens,* pledges of Heav'ns joy,
> Sphear-born, harmonious sisters, Voice, and Vers,
> Wed your divine sounds, and mixt power employ

Of the nine celestial sirens assigned to the nine spheres of the universe, Milton is here specifying two—Polyhymnia, the muse of sacred song, and Erato, the muse of lyric poetry—and calling upon them to join together. Before the eighteenth century, writers or critics seemed to make little or no apparent distinction between melodic lyrics, such as Campion's ayres ("Whoever dreams of a poem where language begins to resemble music, thinks of him," Charles Simic writes) or the songs of Shakespeare's plays, and nonmusical written lyrics, such as Shakespeare's sonnets or Donne's love poems.

Yet it was during the Renaissance that English writers first began to write their lyrics for readers rather than composing them for musical performance. They began to shape their poems to a visual medium. The space for writing as writing, for the poem as something to be read, opened up, for a written poem, unlike an oral one, has a spatial dimension. It becomes a physical object on the page. It appeals to the inner ear, to unique experience. As the idea of the individual emerged during the Renaissance, so did the lyric poem take on fresh elements for expressing that newfound selfhood. The lyric became an instrument of greater inwardness. Later, that dimension of inwardness would start to feel like lyric poetry itself. And some poetry would start to aspire to the pure condition of music.

Winged Type

The poem appeals to the eye. It has a shapely dimension and thus relates to the plastic arts, especially painting. The poem is something to look at as well as recite. Think, for example, of e. e. cummings's typographical experiments or of John Hollander's inventive poems of visual display in *Types of Shape* or of Marianne Moore's symmetrical stanzas that look as if they were written on a typewriter. Moore's poems are written in crystalline syllabics. It is hard to imagine them handwritten. The words look as if they were scoured and dipped in acid, broken down into particles, into constituent parts, and then reconstructed, cleansed and molded, on the page.

The desire to bring together both literary and visual impulses in a shaped poem is apparently very ancient, as Dick Higgins demonstrates in his encyclopedic history and anthology *Pattern Poetry: Guide to an Unknown Literature.* Higgins points to a bewildering variety of early sources: pattern poems in Greek, Latin, and Hebrew, and in most of the modern European literatures; Chinese pattern texts; Sanskrit Citrakāvyas and other Indic texts. There are six surviving pattern poems from Hellenistic Greece: two shaped as altars, and one each as an egg, a syrinx, an ax, and a pair of wings. (These may have served a magical or talismanic function since they were religious expressions.) These in turn became the model for the 110 pre-1750 British pattern poems that survive. It is this tradition, for example, that stands behind George Herbert's two masterpieces from *The Temple* (1633), "The Altar" and "Easter Wings," where the lines, of varying lengths, give the poems a visual shape suggesting an altar and Easter wings respectively. The lines fit the form exactly and the emotional curve of the poem matches the articulation of the shape on the page. I adore Guillaume Apollinaire's *Calligrammes,* a term he coined early in the century for the kind of shaped poem he believed he had invented for modernism ("Moi aussi je suis peintre," he wrote), but in truth he was developing the latest avant-garde manifestation of what in Latin poetry was called *carmen figuratum* (figured poems).

Here is Apollinaire's poem "Il Pleut," first in the original and then in Roger Shattuck's linear translation:

Il Pleut

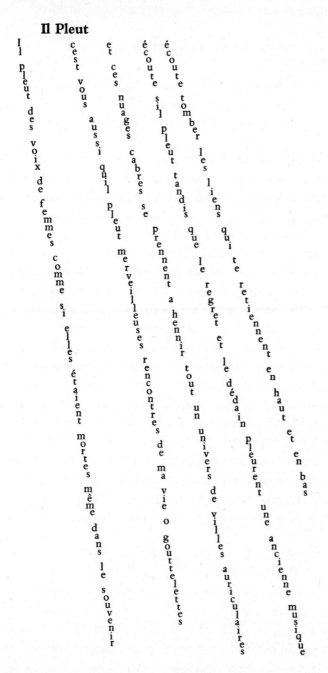

It's Raining

It's raining women's voices as if they had died even in memory
And it's raining you as well marvellous encounters of my life O
   little drops
Those rearing clouds begin to neigh a whole universe of
   auricular cities
Listen if it rains while regret and disdain weep to an ancient
   music
Listen to the bonds fall off which hold you above and below

The slanting lines of Apollinaire's poem create the sensation of rain running downward across a windowpane. Graphic form and verbal music come together as each long vertical line becomes a rhythmic unit of meaning. The sound of the unpunctuated lines in French creates an incantatory murmuring that evokes the sadness and melancholy of a rainy day in Paris. And yet, as Anne Hyde Greet and S. I. Lockerbie point out in their acute commentary on *Calligrammes,* there is a rich ambiguity of feeling in this poem that goes beyond a simple Verlainean melancholy. Whereas the first line associates the rain with a vanished happiness, the second and third lines associate it with the wide encounters—the opening outward—of the modern world. "Trickling raindrops may be expressive of sadness," they write, "but in the way they spread down and over the windowpane there is also a sense of adventure and exploration of space." Apollinaire thus concretizes in the light undulating lines the sense of an old life that is sadly passing even as a fresh world is opening up.

What especially compels me about the pictorial lyric, the lyrical emblem, is how the poem displays itself as a metaphor. It says, *I am something else.* The viewer interacts with the shape; the reader experiences the precise relationship between the subject and the object, the content and the form. The writer puts the rain down on the page, the reader lets it fall.

Out of the Cradle Endlessly Rocking

The poem would address an unseen listener, an unseen audience. It does so through the rhetoric of address since the message in the bottle seems to be speaking to the poet alone, or to a muse, a friend, a lover, an abstraction, an object in nature . . . It seems to be speaking to God or to no one. Rhetoric comes into play here, the radical of presentation, the rhythm of words creating a deep sensation in the reader. Rhythm would lift the poem off the page, it would bewitch the sounds of language, hypnotize the words into memorable phrases. Rhythm creates a pattern of yearning and expectation, of recurrence and difference. It is related to the pulse, the heartbeat, the way we breathe. It takes us into ourselves; it takes us out of ourselves. It differentiates us; it unites us to the cosmos.

Rhythm is a form cut into time, as Ezra Pound said in *ABC of Reading*. It is the combination in English of stressed and unstressed syllables that creates a feeling of fixity and flux, of surprise and inevitability. Rhythm is all about recurrence and change. It is poetry's way of charging the depths, hitting the fathomless. It is oceanic. I would say with Robert Graves that there is a rhythm of emotions that conditions the musical rhythms, that mental bracing and relaxing which comes to us through our sensuous impressions. It is the emotion—the very rhythm of the emotion—that determines the texture of the sounds.

I like to feel the sea drift, the liturgical cadence of the first stanza of Whitman's "Out of the Cradle Endlessly Rocking." It is one sentence and twenty-two lines long. It always carries me away.

Out of the cradle endlessly rocking,
Out of the mocking-bird's throat, the musical shuttle,
Out of the Ninth-month midnight,
Over the sterile sands the fields beyond, where the child
    leaving his bed wander'd alone, bareheaded, barefoot,
Down from the shower'd halo,
Up from the mystic play of shadows twining and twisting as if
    they were alive,
Out from the patches of briers and blackberries,
From the memories of the bird that chanted to me,
From your memories sad brother, from the fitful risings and
    fallings I heard,
From under that yellow half-moon late-risen and swollen as if
    with tears,
From those beginning notes of yearning and love there in the
    mist,
From the thousand responses of my heart never to cease,

From the myriad thence-arous'd words,
From the word stronger and more delicious than any,
From such as now they start the scene revisiting,
As a flock, twittering, rising, or overhead passing,
Borne hither, ere all eludes me, hurriedly,
A man, yet by these tears a little boy again,
Throwing myself on the sand, confronting the waves,
I, chanter of pains and joys, uniter of here and hereafter,
Taking all hints to use them, but swiftly leaping beyond them,
A reminiscence sing.

The incantatory power of this is tremendous as the repetitions loosen the intellect for reverie. It seems to me that Whitman creates here the very rhythm of a singular reminiscence emerging out of the depths of mind, out of the sea waves and the rocking cradle, out of all the undifferentiated sensations of infancy, out of the myriad memories of childhood, out of all possible experiences the formative event of a boy leaving the safety of his bed and walking the seashore alone, moving "Out," "Over," "Down," "Up," "From," exchanging the safety of the indoors for the peril of the outdoors, facing his own vague yearnings and the misty void, mixing his own tears and the salt spray of the ocean, listening to the birds, understanding the language—the calling—of one bird. He walks the shore on the edge of the world, the edge of the unknown. He has entered the space that Emerson calls "*I and the Abyss*," the space of the American sublime.

In this region: out of all potential words, these words alone; out of all potential memories, this memory alone. It is the emerging rhythm itself that creates the Proustian sensation of being in two places at once, "A man, yet by these tears a little boy again, / Throwing myself on the sand, confronting the waves." Whitman creates through the rhetorical rhythm of these lines the very urgency of fundamental memory triggered and issuing forth. He splits himself off and moves seamlessly between the third person and the first person. And as the bird chanted to him ("From the memories of the bird that chanted to me") so he chants to us ("I, chanter of pains and joys"). This is a poem of poetic vocation.

It is telling that Whitman builds to the self-command, "A reminiscence sing." He memorializes the memory in song. There is an element of lullaby in this poem, the lulling motion of the waves, the consoling sound of the sea. But this is a lullaby that wounds (as García Lorca said about Spanish lullabies), a lullaby of sadness that permeates the very universe itself, a lullaby that moves from chanting to singing. Paul Valéry calls the passage from prose to verse, from speech to song, from walking to dancing, "a moment that is at once action and dream." Whitman creates such a moment here. He would spin an enchantment beyond pain and joy, he would become the poetic shaman who authors that reminiscence *for* us, who magically summons up the experience *in* us.

The Wave Always Returns

Renewal is the "pivot of lyricism," as the Russian poet Marina Tsvetaeva says, comparing the lyrical element to the waves of the sea. "The wave always returns, and always returns as a different wave," she writes in her essay "Poets with History and Poets without History":

> The same water—a different wave.
> What matters is that it is a *wave*.
> What matters is that the wave *will return*.
> What matters is that it will *always* return *different*.
> What matters most of all: however different the returning wave,
>   it will always return as a wave of the *sea*.
> What is a wave? Composition and muscle. The same goes for
>   lyric poetry.

The poem is a muscular and composed thing. It moves like a wave and dissolves literalizations. We participate in its flow; we flow in its participation. We give ourselves up to its rhythm, to the process of individuation, the process of merging. When Tsvetaeva compares the lyrical element to the waves of the sea, I think of "Out of the Cradle Endlessly Rocking," I think of Wallace Stevens's seashore lyric "The Idea of Order at Key West," which leads to Elizabeth Bishop's "The End of March," Mark Strand's "The Idea," and Allen Grossman's "The Woman on the Bridge over the Chicago River." I think of Heraclitus's idea, expanded upon by Jung, that "It is delight...to souls to become wet." James Hillman explains in *The Dream and the Underworld* that "Water is the special element of reverie, the element of reflective images and their ceaseless, ungraspable flow. Moistening in dreams refers to the soul's delight in death, its delight in sinking away from fixations in literalized concerns."

The poem moves from the eye to the ear, to the inner ear, the inner eye. It drenches us in the particulars of our senses, it moves us through the articulations of touch, taste, and scent. It actualizes our senses until we start to feel an animal alertness opening up within us. It guides our reflections. It actualizes an intuition flowing deeper than intellect. ("Beneath my incredulity / All at once is flowing / Joy . . . Intuition weightless and ongoing/ Like stanzas in a book / Or golden scales in the melodic brook."—James Merrill, *Scripts for the Pageant*.) We use our senses in poetry, but it is a mistake to try to use our senses everywhere. The poem plunges us from the visible to the invisible, it plunges us into the domain of psyche, of soul. It takes us into the realm of the demonic. Goethe notes:

> In poetry, especially in that which is unconscious, before which reason and understanding fall short, and which, therefore, produces effects so far surpassing all conception, there is always something of the Demoniacal.
>
> *(Tuesday, March 8, 1831)*

We discover in poetry that we are participating in something which cannot be explained or apprehended by reason or understanding alone. We participate in the imaginary. We create a space for fantasy, we enter our dream life, dream time. We deepen our breathing, our mindfulness to being, our spiritual alertness.

Poetry is an animating force. It comes alive when the poet magically inscribes a wave and thereby creates a new thing, when the text immobilizes it, when the individual poem becomes part of the great sea, when the bottle washes ashore and the wanderer happens upon it, when the reader experiences its inexhaustible depths . . .

Help Me, O Heavenly Muse

Robert Graves writes in *On English Poetry*, "Henceforward, in using the word *Poetry* I mean both the controlled and uncontrollable parts of the art taken together, because each is helpless without the other." No one entirely understands the relationship in poetry between trance and craft, between conscious and unconscious elements, and, indeed, poets have been obsessed by the problem of what can and cannot be controlled in the making of art. This is especially instructive to readers who bring their own conscious purposes to poetry, their own unconscious mechanisms of displacement and identification, of sublimation, projection, condensation . . .

Sometimes the emphasis is put on conscious reason, on the conscious aspects of making. Paul Valéry spoke of "une ligne donné"—"the given line"—and suggested that everything else was labor, a matter of making. Baudelaire talked of "the labor by which a revery becomes a work of art." In his 1846 essay "The Philosophy of Composition," Edgar Allan Poe emphasized the conscious method of trial and error:

> Most writers—poets in especial—prefer having it understood that they compose by a species of fine frenzy—an ecstatic intuition—and would positively shudder at letting the public take a peep behind the scenes, at the elaborate and vacillating crudities of thought—at the true purposes seized only at the last moment—at the innumerable glimpses of idea that arrived not at the maturity of full view—at the fully matured fancies discarded in despair as unmanageable—at the cautious selections and rejections—at the painful erasures and interpolations—in a word, at the wheels and pinions—the tackle for scene-shifting—the step-ladders and demon-traps—the cock's leathers, the red paint and the black patches, which, in ninety-nine cases out of the hundred, constitute the properties of the literary *histrio*.

Here Poe is giving enormous preference—and theatrical privilege—to the nature of reason in the creative process.

But there is something else. It may be true that the poet is given only a single line but that line is nonetheless a gift from the unconscious, a hunch, an intuition, and a perception. The poet is one who often thinks by feeling. Remember the famous Cartesian cogito ("I think, therefore I am") and Paul Valéry's useful variation on Descartes, "Sometimes I think; and sometimes I *am*" (*Analects*). Inspiration is in-breathing, indwelling, and poetry can never be entirely willed—as Plato knew. It is often connected to passion, to mania, to childlike play, to the unconscious itself. Poets have always known they are trying to invoke for us something that can't be entirely controlled. This is the necessary touch of madness that Plato made so much of, the freedom that terrified him. Here is Socrates in the dialogue *Phaedrus*:

> There is a third form of possession or madness, of which the Muses are the source. This seizes a tender, virgin soul and stimulates it to rapt passionate expression, especially in lyric poetry, glorifying the countless mighty deeds of ancient times for the instruction of posterity. But if any man comes to the gates of poetry without the madness of the Muses, persuaded that skill alone will make him a good poet, then shall he and his works of sanity with him be brought to nought by the poetry of madness, and behold, their place is nowhere to be found.

In this view poetry is dangerous. It is allied closely to madness and is not entirely at the dispensation of the poet's conscious will or intellect. "Poetry is not like reasoning, a power to be exerted according to the determination of the will," Shelley writes in his romantic defense of poetry:

> A man cannot say, "I will compose poetry." The greatest poet even cannot say it for the mind in creation is as a fading coal which some invisible influence, like an inconstant wind, awakens to transitory brightness.

Whoever calls out "Help me, O Heavenly Muse," advertises a dependence on a force beyond the intellect. In general, the fierce power that sometimes comes through the work of the great poets of reason, from Samuel Johnson to Louise Bogan and J. V. Cunningham, comes from the deep undertow of the demoniacal that is fended off by the conscious activity of making. Visionary poets welcome the wind of madness—I think of Rimbaud and Shelley, of Hart Crane and Federico García Lorca—but part of their power comes from the fact that the sudden illumination is what the mathematician Henri Poincaré calls "a manifest sign of long, unconscious inner work," and that the wind is shaped to the exigencies of form. I have always liked the dictum of the baroque Jesuit poet Tommaso Ceva that poetry is "a dream dreamed in the presence of reason."

The poet would call the muse "Laura" or "Beatrice," the poet would name her "Mnemosyne" (personification of memory) or "Clio" (muse of history). The poet would borrow Freud's notion of the "uncanny," the unconscious, or Jung's collective unconscious, or Jacques Maritain's idea of creative intuition. The older poet advises the younger poet: mystery abides. So W. S. Merwin, for example, remembers his teacher John Berryman giving him advice in the years just after the Second World War:

> he suggested I pray to the Muse
> get down on my knees and pray
> right there in the corner and he
> said he meant it literally
> > *("Berryman")*

Berryman also said that

>   the great presence
> that permitted everything and transmuted it
> in poetry was passion
> passion was genius and he praised movement and invention
> > *("Berryman")*

A transfiguring passion. A force beyond the confines of the conscious self.

There is no true poetry without conscious craft, absorbed attention, absolute concentration. There is no true poetry without unconscious invention. The reader, too, enters into the relationship between the controlled and the uncontrollable aspects of the art. Shelley says that "Poetry redeems from decay the visitations of the divinity in man." The poem is a genie that comes out of the bottle to liberate the reader's imagination, the divinity within. The writer and the reader make meaning together. The poet who calls on help from the heavenly muse also does so on behalf of the imaginative reader.

It Is Something of an Accident That You
Are the Reader and I the Writer

Lyric poetry is a form of verbal materialism, an art of language, but it is much more than "the best words in the best order." It is language fulfilling itself, language compressed and raised to its highest power. Language in action against time, against death. There are times when I am awestruck by the way that poems incarnate the spirit—the spirits—and strike the bedrock of being. Other times I am struck by how little the poem has to go on, how inadequate its means. For what does the writer have but some black markings on a blank page to imagine a world? Hence these lines from the splendid Florentine poet Guido Cavalcanti:

> Noi siàn le triste penne isbigottite
> le cesoiuzze e'l coltellin dolente.

> We are the poor, bewildered quills,
> The little scissors and the grieving penknife.

Cavalcanti projects his own grievous feelings of imaginative inadequacy onto the writer's very tools (quills and the knives to sharpen them), the writer's diminutive instruments.

In *Six Memos for the Next Millennium*, Italo Calvino makes an insightful comment that enlarges on Cavalcanti's lines, creating a statement about the experience of literature itself:

> all "realities" and "fantasies" can take on form only by means of writing, in which outwardness and innerness, the world and I, experience and fantasy, appear composed of the same verbal material. The polymorphic visions of the eyes and the spirit are contained in uniform lines of small or capital letters, periods, commas, parentheses—pages of signs, packed as closely together as grains of sand, representing the many-sided spectacle of the world as a surface that is always the same and always different, like dunes shifted by the desert wind.

I am reminded by Calvino's description of the literal limits of art: that all the incitement and grace of literature has to take place in the lineup of written characters on the page.

"There is then creative reading as well as creative writing," Emerson says in "The American Scholar" in a statement that could be a credo for the reader of poems. Poetry alerts us to what is deepest in ourselves—it arouses a spiritual desire which it also gratifies. It attains what it avows. But it can only do so with the reader's imaginative collaboration and even complicity. The writer creates through words a felt world which only the reader can vivify and internalize. Writing is embodiment. Reading is contact. In the preface to *Obra poetica,* Jorge Luis Borges writes:

> The taste of the apple (states Berkeley) lies in the contact of the fruit with the palate, not in the fruit itself; in a similar way (I would say) poetry lies in the meeting of the poem and reader, not in the lines of symbols printed on the pages of a book. What is essential is the aesthetic act, the thrill, the almost physical emotion that comes with each reading.

Borges continues on to suggest that poetry can work its magic by fulfilling our profound need to "recover a past or prefigure a future."

Poetry depends on the mutuality of writer and reader. The symbols on the page alone are insufficient. Borges was a fabulist and in the foreword to his first book of poems he went even further to suggest that poetry goes beyond mutuality, beyond identification, into identity itself:

> If in the following pages there is some successful verse or other, may the reader forgive me the audacity of having written it before him. We are all one; our inconsequential minds are much alike, and circumstances so influence us that it is something of an accident that you are the reader and I the writer—the unsure, ardent writer—of my verses.

This is funny and brilliant and perhaps disingenuous, but there is also a truth in it which has to do with a common sensation of reading: the eerie feeling that we are composing what we are responding to. In *The Redress of Poetry* Seamus Heaney calls this "the fluid, exhilarating moment which lies at the heart of any memorable reading, the undisappointed joy of finding that everything holds up and answers the desire that it awakens." Poetry creates its own autonomous world, and what that world asks from us it also answers within us.

In *The Poetics of Space,* Gaston Bachelard says that "Poetry puts language in a state of emergence." It emerges at short range. Bachelard also quotes Pierre-Jean Jouve's statement that "Poetry is a soul inaugurating a form." The notion of the soul's inauguration of form suggests what Bachelard calls "supreme power" and "human dignity." I honor that dignity by recognizing the form it takes, the way it composes itself. Every work of art needs a respondent to complete it. It is only partially realized without that imaginative response. Jean-Paul Sartre puts the matter emphatically in *What Is Literature?:*

> The creative act is only an incomplete and abstract moment in the production of a work. If the author existed alone he would be able to write as much as he liked; the work as *object* would never see the light of day and he would either have to put down his pen or despair. But the operation of writing implies that of reading as its dialectical correlative and these two connected acts necessitate two distinct agents. It is the joint effort of author and reader which brings upon the scene that concrete and imaginary object which is the work of the mind. There is no art except for and by others.

The reader exists on the horizon of the poem. The message in the bottle may seem to be speaking to the poet alone, or to God, or to nobody, but the reader is the one who finds and overhears it, who unseals the bottle and lets the language emerge. The reader becomes the listener, letting the poem voice and rediscover itself as it is read.

The Shock, the Swoon, the Bliss

I take the poet as a maker who sends out a formal enticement, a provocation, a challenge. I encounter—I am encountered by—a work of art. For me, that encounter is active, inquisitive, relentless, disturbing, exuberant, daring, and beholden. Poets speak of the shock, the swoon, and the bliss of writing, but why not also speak of the shock, the swoon, and the bliss of reading?

2

A Made Thing

I have carried the message in the bottle home, but now I must decipher it as a linguistic event, as a rhythmic group of words packed in salt, as a last will and testament. What is it saying? Poetry is a soul-making activity, and the reader in part authors that activity by responding to the form of the poem, its way of shaping itself. I have the idea that a certain kind of exemplary poem teaches you how to read it. It carries its own encoded instructions, enacting its subject, pointing to its own operation. It enacts what it is about—a made thing that indicates the nature of its own making. Poems communicate before they are understood and the structure operates on, or inside, the reader even as the words infiltrate the consciousness. The form is the shape of the poem's understanding, its way of being in the world, and it is the form that structures our experience.

Poiēsis means "making" and, as the ancient Greeks recognized, the poet is first and foremost a maker. The Greeks saw no contradiction (and I don't think we should, either) between the truth that poetry is somehow or other inspired and, simultaneously, an art (*technē*), a craft requiring a blend of talent, training, and long practice. Open the *Princeton Encyclopedia of Poetry and Poetics* to the entry for "Poesie" and you discover that in the Renaissance the word *makers*, as in "courtly makers," was an exact equivalent for *poets*. The word *poem* became English in the sixteenth century and it has been with us ever since to designate a form of fabrication, a type of composition, a made thing.

I would also keep in mind the magical potency of the made thing. What Picasso said about painting being more than an aesthetic operation is equally true of poetry. He declared that art is "a form of magic designed as a mediator between this strange, hostile world and us, a way of seizing the power by giving form to our terrors as well as our desires."

Here are three poems—three messages—that have lodged in me as a reader, and that I, in turn, have found instructive and emblematic. They give form to our terrors and desires. And they have taught me how to interpret what I have encountered. They combine deep lyric feeling with an equally powerful organizing structure. The apologist for surrealism, André Breton, described poetry as "a room of marvels." But it is also a room with a design, a system. How does that design work? My notion is that it is possible to honor the reality of the poem by attending to its dynamic unfolding. It's worth trying to describe how deeply felt poems go about the business of creating meaning in and for us.

Here is Elizabeth Bishop's poem "One Art," from her last book of poems, *Geography III:*

The art of losing isn't hard to master;
so many things seemed filled with the intent
to be lost that their loss is no disaster.

Lose something every day. Accept the fluster
of lost door keys, the hour badly spent.
The art of losing isn't hard to master.

Then practice losing farther, losing faster:
places, and names, and where it was you meant
to travel. None of these will bring disaster.

I lost my mother's watch. And look! my last, or
next-to-last, of three loved houses went.
The art of losing isn't hard to master.

I lost two cities, lovely ones. And, vaster,
some realms I owned, two rivers, a continent.
I miss them, but it wasn't a disaster.

—Even losing you (the joking voice, a gesture
I love) I shan't have lied. It's evident
the art of losing's not too hard to master
though it may look like (*Write* it!) like disaster.

"One Art" is a kind of instruction manual on loss. It's infused with that
wry tonal irony so characteristic of Bishop's late poetry. The blank verse
is pitched at the level of speech ("Lose something every day") and the
language is natural sounding and deceptively informal, given the formal
requirements of the lyric. The poem is a villanelle—that defiant French
contraption with its roots in Italian folk song, which came into Amer-
ican poetry late in the nineteenth century. Like all villanelles, it has
nineteen lines divided into six stanzas—five tercets and one quatrain—
turning on two rhymes and built around two refrains. The first and third
lines rhyme throughout, as do the middle lines of each stanza. (The word
stanza means "room" in Italian, and the center rhymes help connect the
rooms of this lyric dwelling.) The first and third lines become the refrain
of alternate stanzas and the final two lines of the poem. As it turns and
returns, Bishop's verse becomes a model of stability and change, repeti-
tion and variation. The first line—"The art of losing isn't hard to mas-
ter"—repeats almost exactly throughout the poem, whereas the second
refrain never repeats in its initial form and modulates entirely around the
word "disaster." So, too, the poem combines feminine or multisyllabic
rhymes (such as "master" and "disaster") with masculine or one-syllable
rhymes (such as "spent" and "meant"), deftly varying its full or exact
rhymes with Dickinsonian half-rhymes (such as "fluster" and "master").
It also characteristically runs an enjambed line into an end-stopped one
(as in the fourth stanza: "And look! my last, or / next-to-last, of three
loved houses went"), thus creating a sense of qualification, of hesitating
forward movement and momentary rest. The momentum is chastened or
balanced by circularity, the circularity ruptured by a progressive move-
ment forward. This model of formal ingenuity deserves to stand with

such other exemplary modern villanelles as William Empson's "Villanelle" ("It is the pain, it is the pain, endures") and "Missing Dates"; W. H. Auden's "If I Could Tell You"; Dylan Thomas's "Do Not Go Gentle into that Good Night"; Theodore Roethke's "The Waking"; Weldon Kees's "Five Villanelles," especially the one beginning "The crack is moving down the wall"; and Donald Justice's "In Memory of the Unknown Poet, Robert Boardman Vaughn."

In the Vassar College library there are seventeen extant drafts of "One Art" written over a six-month period, and they reveal just how hard Bishop had to work to match and master an uncontrollable grief by structuring it into the almost mathematical equation of a villanelle. The poet Ellen Bryant Voigt, who has written well about the formal development of the different drafts, suggests that the process is summed up in the lines from Yeats's poem "Adam's Curse":

> A line will take us hours maybe;
> Yet if it does not seem a moment's thought,
> Our stitching and unstitching has been naught.

The making of Bishop's villanelle entailed a lifetime of deliberation, hours of stitching and unstitching, a long apprenticeship to the art of poetry, and an even longer apprenticeship to the art of loss, and yet the final product reads as if it had come together effortlessly in a moment's thought.

What especially intrigues me about "One Art" is how scrupulously Bishop has built a second structure into the villanelle form. She has reconfigured it so that the form itself becomes causal to the meaning. She starts small and continually enlarges the losses, beginning with inconsequential things—the door keys, the wasted hour—and moving up from there. The third stanza provides the essential clue as to how we are meant to read this poem. "Then practice losing farther, losing faster," she writes, signifying that the losses are going to progress, going farther, coming more quickly. It is worse to give up "places, and names, and where it was you meant / to travel" than to misplace keys or misspend an hour, though, as she hastens to add, it's still not a catastrophe. She then enlarges the terms by moving to the first poignant loss in the poem, the first thing that truly matters: "I lost my mother's watch." Now we are getting closer to home. "And look!" she exclaims, focusing the reader into an intimate listener, a confidant: "my last, or / next-to-last, of three loved houses went." It's characteristic of Bishop to diffuse the more melodramatic statement—"my last of three loved houses went"—by qualifying it for accuracy. The ethic of this poet is never to overstate the nature of the feeling, to be as precise as possible about the impact of loss. In the next stanza she enlarges that loss yet again, moving from the penultimate house to two beautiful cities and, even larger than that, some Shakespearean "realms," including a couple of splendid rivers and an entire continent where she once lived. We have completed an arc that moves from losing door keys to relinquishing a continent. And now for the first time in the poem, in the fifteenth line and the penultimate stanza, she acknowledges losing something she actually misses. "I miss them," she admits, immediately adding, "but it wasn't a disaster." Randall Jarrell once said about John Crowe Ransom:

> Most writers become over-rhetorical when they are insisting on more emotion than they actually feel or need to feel; Ransom is just the opposite. He is perpetually insisting, by his detached, mock-pedantic, wittily complicated tone, that he is not feeling much at all, not half so much as he really should be feeling.
>
> *("John Ransom's Poetry")*

And so it is with Elizabeth Bishop. And here we can see that the two refrain lines are working in tandem and counterpoint. Even as the speaker must acknowledge that the losses are cutting deeper and deeper, she also keeps insisting that they aren't disastrous. In this way the poet of understatement wittily resists the feeling of encroaching catastrophe. To modify something that Ezra Pound once said about a villanelle by Ernest Dowson, it seems to me that the losses are the emotional truth in this poem, which the intellect, through its various gyrations, struggles in vain to escape.

This brings us to the final stanza where, in an extraordinary turn, the lyric becomes a love poem. By the structural logic of the poem, the movement from the miniature to the gigantic, the loss of the beloved must necessarily be the greatest loss of all. "Even losing you," she says, momentarily turning and addressing her lover directly, then just as quickly pulling back, adding parenthetically "the joking voice, a gesture /

I love," thereby summoning and representing the beloved by two metonymic terms, "I shan't have lied."

> It's evident
> the art of losing's not too hard to master
> though it may look like (*Write* it!) like disaster.

The conclusion of the poem is the first acknowledgment, after everything that has come before, that this final loss actually feels disastrous. As the losses have accumulated throughout the poem, the defense mechanisms—the intellectual resistances—have stayed in place until in the end this poet of terrific understatement finally breaks down and admits that this signal loss feels catastrophic to her. William Maxwell once said that a writer gets two exclamation points in a lifetime, and Bishop has brilliantly used her quota here. At the point that she commands herself to "*Write* it!" one becomes aware that the activity of writing mirrors the psychological process of recognition. The repetition of the word *like* compounds the effect. By forcing herself to write it down she is forcing herself to admit and face it. Far from the villanelle being a form in which everything is already figured out and established, a container into which one pours previously worked-out thoughts and feelings, the form itself becomes a way for the writer to test and unearth those feelings in language. The process of recognition becomes the emotional discovery of this poem, the greater part of writing as well as reading it. The reader overhears what the poet is forcing herself to acknowledge. Thus the lyric psychologically enacts the experience of coming to terms with a universe of loss.

"Surely there is an element of mortal panic and fear underlying all works of art?" Elizabeth Bishop asked in her essay on Marianne Moore. "One Art" is a poem that summons such feelings even as it resists, contains, and tries not to succumb to them. That makes it all the more moving when the resistance finally caves in at the end.

Here is another poem of mortal panic and fear, Pablo Neruda's "Solo la muerte" ("Nothing but Death"), a lyric of radical overstatement from *Residencia en la tierra (Residence on Earth)* that desperately flings itself at human loss. Instead of trying to fend off the feeling, as Bishop does, Neruda invokes and summons it at every point.

There are cemeteries that are lonely,
graves full of bones that do not make a sound,
the heart moving through a tunnel,
in it darkness, darkness, darkness,
like a shipwreck we die going into ourselves,
as though we were drowning inside our hearts,
as though we lived falling out of the skin into the soul.

And there are corpses,
feet made of cold and sticky clay,
death is inside the bones,
like a barking where there are no dogs,
coming out from bells somewhere, from graves somewhere,
growing in the damp air like tears or rain.

Sometimes I see alone
coffins under sail,
embarking with the pale dead, with women that have dead hair,
with bakers who are as white as angels,
and pensive young girls married to notary publics,
caskets sailing up the vertical river of the dead,
the river of dark purple,
moving upstream with sails filled out by the sound of death,
filled by the sound of death which is silence.

Death arrives among all that sound
like a shoe with no foot in it, like a suit with no man in it,
comes and knocks, using a ring with no stone in it, with no
        finger in it,
comes and shouts with no mouth, with no tongue, with no
        throat.
Nevertheless its steps can be heard
and its clothing makes a hushed sound, like a tree.

I'm not sure, I understand only a little, I can hardly see,
but it seems to me that its singing has the color of damp violets,
of violets that are at home in the earth,
because the face of death is green,

and the look death gives is green,
with the penetrating dampness of a violet leaf
and the somber color of embittered winter.

But death also goes through the world dressed as a broom,
lapping the floor, looking for dead bodies,
death is inside the broom,
the broom is the tongue of death looking for corpses,
it is the needle of death looking for thread.

Death is inside the folding cots:
it spends its life sleeping on the slow mattresses,
in the black blankets, and suddenly breathes out:
it blows out a mournful sound that swells the sheets,
and the beds go sailing toward a port
where death is waiting, dressed like an admiral.

(translated by Robert Bly)

It seems to me that Neruda's poem has what García Lorca called "duende." The *duende* was traditionally an Andalusian trickster figure, much like the Yiddish dybbuk, but Lorca used it as a name for creative possession, for inspiration in the presence of death, for that scorched spirit that sometimes takes over in moments of artistic creation. It is an irrational power, something like a demonic religious enthusiasm. "All that has black sounds has duende," Lorca says in "Play and Theory of the Duende," and Neruda's poem is filled with such black sounds. It is a magnet for them. This lucid dream has a wild surreal associativeness, but it also has a relentless logic of its own. The spiritual problem is death—only death, a death that is everywhere. The technical problem, which is an index to the spiritual one, is how to write about it; that is, how to dramatize a ubiquitous presence, an omnivorous Something, which manifests itself as an absence, as Nothingness. The poet of Whitmanesque ambitions must find a way to present something that has as its sole purpose taking things away. Consequently, in "Nothing but Death" Neruda was forced, or forced himself, to invent an imaginative structure and develop an imagistic strategy for dramatizing and incarnating what he sees as the quintessence of death itself.

"There are cemeteries that are lonely, / graves full of bones that do not make a sound," Neruda asserts, thus beginning almost gothically by establishing the backdrop of the poem, but also projecting a human feeling—loneliness—into the graveyards. The cemeteries are lonely because they make us feel lonely, because the poet is overwhelmed by loneliness when he thinks of human beings reduced to silent piles of bones. The journey toward death, dying itself, is a necessarily inward experience ("like a shipwreck we die going into ourselves") but once death takes over, the subjects—and we are all subjects—turn into objects. There is an enormous abyss between subject and object. "And there are corpses, / feet made of cold and sticky clay." These in turn become part of what the poet envisions as the great procession of the dead—"Sometimes I see alone / coffins under sail"—that will include everyone, from the most romantically inclined ("pensive young girls") to their pragmatic, commonsensical husbands ("notary publics").

The first key to the weirdly logical nature of the imagery comes in these astonishing lines:

death is inside the bones,
like a barking where there are no dogs,
coming out from bells somewhere, from graves somewhere,
growing in the damp air like tears or rain.

Neruda presents the sound the animals make, the barking, but removes the origin of that sound, the dogs themselves. The sound seems all the more haunting since it comes from absent dogs in an indistinguishable place—a churchyard perhaps—and seeps, as if naturally, into the "air like tears," products of human grief, "or rain," a mere atmospheric condition. So, too, he paradoxically asserts that death has a sound, which is silence. The imagery goes into full operation in the fourth stanza:

Death arrives among all that sound
like a shoe with no foot in it, like a suit with no man in it,
comes and knocks, using a ring with no stone in it, with no
    finger in it,
comes and shouts with no mouth, with no tongue, with no
    throat.

In this sequence of images, Neruda repeatedly presents a human object but withdraws the human presence from it. He posits a shoe, but takes away the foot that wears it; he presents a suit, but withdraws the man who would inhabit it. Death comes and knocks, but it uses a ring without a stone or a finger. The progression—death shouts "with no mouth, with no tongue, with no throat"—mimics a process of taking a voice away in stages. These images all incarnate the paradox of a presence that is absence. "Nevertheless," he writes, using a logical proposition as in a poem by Donne or Marvell, "its steps can be heard / and its clothing makes a hushed sound, like a tree." Neruda has created an imagery for something which cannot be seen—something mysterious, indistinct, real.

Neruda is also thinking in similes here—that is, by comparing one thing with another: Death arrives amidst the loud racket *like* a shoe without a foot in it, *like* a suit without a man in it. All good similes depend upon a certain essential heterogeneity between the elements that are being compared. (Quintilian: "The more remote the simile is from the subject to which it is applied, the greater will be the impression of novelty and the unexpected which it produces.") The simile asserts a likeness between unlike things, it maintains their comparability, but it also draws attention to their differences, thereby affirming a state of division. It is left to the reader to decide how death exists inside the bones of corpses "like a barking where there are no dogs." This participatory dimension works brilliantly for the poet who is creating within us a sense of death's active and omnivorous power, its alien and alienating majesty. There is also a digressive impulse to similes that keeps extending the poem outward to take on new things, and Neruda builds on this tendency in order to suggest the power of death actively going through the world and sweeping things up, taking them away.

The great modernist writers, like Joyce or Eliot, often present us with an idea of the artist presiding over his creation like an objective, all-powerful god, but Neruda presents himself as writing from inside the experience of his own creation, trying to figure out what he is writing about, taking us through the logic of his thinking:

I'm not sure, I understand only a little, I can hardly see,
but it seems to me that its singing has the color of damp violets,
of violets that are at home in the earth,

He unpacks his own synesthetic image, trying to prove it, as it were, by placing death back into the green world, into the wintry natural realm.

And now it is as if he can say anything about death because death is everywhere. He associates wildly, almost comically, but always extending the imagery far enough for us to decipher and interpret it. Why does he say that death also goes through the world dressed as a broom? Because he pictures it lapping the floor, sweeping away the dead bodies, because it is inside a broom even as it is inside our bones, because the bristles of a broom are like a tongue, they are similar to a needle, because he is trying to incarnate images of an absence devouring everything in its path.

In the final stanza he literalizes the romantic connection between sleep and death. He sees death literally inside the beds where we sleep. All along it has been waiting for us to lie down for the last time so that our beds can become coffins and go sailing in a swelling procession into the otherworld, which is overseen by nothing else but death itself, an admiral. "Sola la muerte": only death, death alone, nothing but death. In this visionary poem Neruda has found a way to write about a mysterious presence that evades our understanding. We are mere *residents* on earth. The reader who uncorks the message in this particular bottle feels its surging waves of emotion, its strange playfulness, its dark undertow and sweeping oceanic power.

Here is the Czech poet Jiří Orten's poem "A Small Elegy." It is from his book *Elegies*, translated by Lyn Coffin:

My friends have left. Far away, my darling is asleep.
Outside, it's as dark as pitch.
I'm saying words to myself, words that are white
in the lamplight and when I'm half-asleep I begin
to think about my mother. Autumnal recollection.
Really, under the cover of winter, it's as if I know
everything—even what my mother is doing now.
She's at home in the kitchen. She has a small child's stove
toward which the wooden rocking horse can trot,
she has a small child's stove, the sort nobody uses today, but
she basks in its heat. Mother. My diminutive mom.
She sits quietly, hands folded, and thinks about

my father, who died years ago.
And then she is skinning fruit for me. I am
in the room. Sitting right next to her. You've got to see us,
God, you bully, who took so much. How
dark it is outside! What was I going to say?
Oh, yes, now I remember. Because
of all those hours I slept soundly, through calm
nights, because of all those loved ones who are deep
in dreams—Now, when everything's running short,
I can't stand being here by myself. The lamplight's too strong.
I am sowing grain on the headland.
I will not live long.

"We make out of the quarrel with others, rhetoric, but of the quarrel
with ourselves, poetry," W. B. Yeats asserts in *Per Amica Silentia Lunae*
(1917), and Orten's poem seems to inscribe that self-challenging notion
of the lyric. From the beginning, "A Small Elegy" dramatically estab-
lishes that the speaker—a stand-in for the poet—is by himself talking to
himself. He was with other people, but now he is completely alone, his
friends gone, his beloved sleeping elsewhere, unconscious, far away. The
speaker is the sole operating consciousness mourning in a world where
everyone else is asleep. Against the pitch-black darkness he starts saying
things to himself, using "white" words, which I take to mean words that
have a kind of unself-conscious purity about them. He daydreams about
his mother—an "autumnal recollection"—and that in turn moves him
back toward his childhood home where his mother seems still to preside,
although much diminished, over an outmoded world. She is smaller,
more vulnerable, someone to be protected. "Matku," he says tenderly in
Czech, "Mou maminku," "my little mommy," which the translator has
rendered as "my diminutive mom." He imagines that after all these years
she's still sitting there, quietly uncomplaining, thinking about his father
who died so long ago.

It is the next moment in the poem, when the tense radically changes,
that I find especially compelling. "And then she is skinning fruit for me,"
he says, "I am in / the room. Sitting right next to her." He doesn't say,
"And then she *was* skinning fruit for me," but instead finds himself cat-
apulted into the past as a living present. This is an instance of what Proust

calls "involuntary memory," when the entire world of the past comes flooding back. It is not something willfully recalled, but something that comes unbidden—suddenly, overwhelmingly present. He has been wrenched out of one time into another. The mysterious action of memory has restored his early life to him. "But he has not merely extracted from this gesture the lost reality of his grandmother," Beckett says about Proust's narrator, "he has recovered the lost reality of himself, the reality of his lost self" (*Proust*). And so it is with Orten.

The amplitude of his feeling is nearly unbearable and he starts shaking his fist at God, using a child's language, calling him a "bully" because now he is aware that God has taken away so much, because so much is lost. "How / dark it is outside!" he exclaims. And then he asks: "What was I going to say?" The sudden colliding of worlds, of the past and present, creates a gap or hole in his mind and thus in the text. He can't recall what he was going to say next because the experience is dislocating, the outer darkness bewildering. He has lost himself in time, which Beckett calls "that double-headed monster of damnation and salvation." And then he recovers: "Oh, yes, now I remember." And he proceeds to face what can no longer be evaded. There is ruthlessness in his logic. "Because / of all those hours I slept soundly, through calm / nights," he declares—that is, because of all those nights when he was safe and unconscious—"because of all those loved ones who are deep / in dreams"—that is, because of all those who are unconscious now, unaware of the peril that surrounds them—he realizes that time is running out and announces: "I can't stand being here by myself. The lamplight's too strong." Here the lamplight becomes the emblem of a consciousness that is too much to bear, an isolation that is killing:

I am sowing grain on the headland.
I will not live long.

The recognition here is that what he is planting is endangered, imperiled, vulnerable. What he plants he will not be able to protect. The sowing of grain on the headland is his last gesture, his way of putting a message in a bottle when he knows he won't last much longer. The poem concludes with a terrible recognition.

Jiří Orten belonged to a generation of poets who took Czech verse in a more inward direction. He did not shrink from his own subjectivity, from what he knew. "A Small Elegy" inscribes a sacred feeling, a tenderness so deep it feels almost otherworldly, a tenderness that seems always endangered, always threatened by a relentless worldliness, by temporality, by the march of history. It also inscribes the premonition of a death that was indeed coming for him. Orten died in a bizarre accident in Prague in the summer of 1941. One moment he was stepping off the curb to buy cigarettes from a local kiosk, the next he was hit and being dragged along the street by a speeding German car. He was refused admission to a nearby hospital because he was Jewish. Another admitted him, but it was too late. He died a few days later. He was only twenty-two years old. "A Small Elegy" seems to me a deeply unflinching poem. It is nearly unbearable. When I read it in the middle of the night, my impulse is to wake up everyone around me, everyone I love, before it is too late.

Ralph Waldo Emerson once said that poetry is "what will and must be spoken." It is a secret that can no longer be kept secret, a way of knowing. Perhaps poetry exists because it carries necessary human information that cannot be communicated in any other way. Some of that information is joyous, some a distress signal from afar that whispers in the inner ear. But, as Paul Valéry said about Pascal, "A distress that writes well is not so complete that it hasn't salvaged from the shipwreck." The poet is a maker who salvages from the shipwreck in a particular way. Writing poetry is a way of getting something right in language, of metaphoric or transformative thinking. Articulation gratifies, and the act of making is itself a great consolation. "The passions may be terrible," Denis Donoghue writes in *Ferocious Alphabets,* "but the syllables are a relief."

The poems I have chosen by Bishop, Neruda, and Orten—and I could easily have chosen other favorite poems by other poets as initiating readings—come to us mediated through different languages and different traditions; one is written in traditional form, two in free verse; one in English, one in Spanish, one in Czech. It goes without saying that each poem lives most fully in its native language. What these poems share as lyrics, however, is a mode of verbal behavior. Each of these writers has found a way to interrogate and transfigure a profound disquietude, to bring forth what otherwise might have evaded consciousness.

And each has made that coming into consciousness accessible to others by building it into the organic structure of the poem itself.

Whenever a poem enacts what it is about, it creates a way for itself to live dramatically inside the reader. It becomes an experience unto itself. The great individual poem is a last will and testament salvaged from the shipwreck, sealed in a bottle, and cast out on the waters. So take the time to go down to the dunes to see if you can find it. It is there. And when you do, bring it home because it is now yours. You are its secret addressee. This haunted and haunting message was meant for you. Listen to it. Turn on the lamp. Read this poem to yourself in the middle of the night.

3

A Hand, a Hook, a Prayer

One could write an essay on the theme of hands in poetry, as poetry. So much of postromantic lyric poetry in particular has been about connection and disconnection. About reaching out across a divide in an intimate gesture—sometimes desperate, sometimes futile—toward another person, a destined "you." Or it is about the inability, or refusal, to make such a gesture, turning inward instead toward a greater interiority, a deeper interiorization. The individual poem, especially the lyric of solitude, situates itself in distinct relationship to an imagined reader. It presupposes an encounter with a real reader somewhere in an indistinct future. And it sets itself up at a particular angle to the universe of other people.

Poets have often taken waving as an emblematic gesture of the poem itself: the lyric as greeting, the lyric as farewell. (I think of the fatal misunderstanding Stevie Smith anatomizes in "Not Waving but Drowning," the playful good-bye of Wallace Stevens's "Waving Adieu, Adieu, Adieu," what John Ashbery terms "the shield of a greeting" in "Self-Portrait in a Convex Mirror." I think of a bitterly cold Minneapolis morning in January 1972, when John Berryman climbed onto the metal railing of the Washington Avenue Bridge and made a gesture *as if waving* before plunging into the river to his death.) I find jaunty dignity in the poetic of a distance recognized, established, and maintained, in treating the poem as an act of waving, but I'm also struck by the urgency of poems that try to break down that distance, to push past it.

I want to look closely at three poems: one by John Keats that gestures toward and seeks connection; one by James Wright that finds a momentary human contact and communion; and one by Charles Baudelaire that shuns any such contact or affinity. I want to see what is being offered us and what is being withheld. Each of these poems seeks to go beyond the ambiguity of words to the certainty of touch.

There is great poignance in this quest for "contact," in the privileging of touch over sight, since in a poem touch must necessarily be metaphorical or symbolic. It cannot be literal, or literally realized.

In the first poem of *In Memoriam*, Tennyson asks who shall "reach a hand thro' time to catch / The far-off interest of tears?" It's a good question. Is the longing for direct contact enough? Can it suffice for a poet's hand to reach across time for a reader's hand? Each of the following poems raises the subject of our interconnectedness. And each summons up the desire for such connectedness (it is the desire of solitaries). The sweat of the poet's hand still clings to each of these poems, if we but let ourselves feel it.

Late in 1819, already dying of tuberculosis, Keats was working on a comic poem, a fairy tale. Charles Brown later reported in *The Life of John Keats* that the poem "was to be published under the feigned authorship of Lucy Vaughan Lloyd, and to bear the title *The Cap and Bells,* or, which [Keats] preferred, *The Jealousies.*" Keats never finished his comic poem but, suddenly, while he was working on it, he broke off writing— "Cupid I / Do thee defy"—and jotted down something else in a blank space on the manuscript. He wrote this untitled eight-line fragment:

> This living hand, now warm and capable
> Of earnest grasping, would, if it were cold
> And in the icy silence of the tomb,
> So haunt thy days and chill thy dreaming nights
> That thou would wish thine own heart dry of blood
> So in my veins red life might stream again,
> And thou be conscience-calmed—see here it is—
> I hold it towards you.

These were probably the last serious lines of poetry Keats wrote. Most scholars agree that he meant them for later use as part of a larger poem or play, but, nonetheless, this freestanding lyrical fragment seems so vital, so haunting, I don't see how anyone can safely ignore it. These lines were written by someone who knew, at the moment of writing, that the "warm" hand with which he could still touch you (the authoritative word "capable" hovers capably, both adjective and verb, at the end of the first line) will soon be "cold" and unable to grasp anyone, anything. He reaches out for contact because he can't stand it. He is distraught, enraged, terrified. He would prove to you he exists: "see here it is," he declares, interrupting himself, urgently holding out his hand. This is no sentimental gesture. He brings the future listener into direct focus. He turns that listener, that reader, from a more formal and distant "thou" to a closer and more intimate "you," even as the poem moves from the conditional future to the present tense. He knows he will soon be collaring someone from beyond the grave, but he can only enact that gesture, that grasping motion, while he is still alive. This lyric is a time bomb which the poet is setting to explode on contact, on reading.

The "I" and the "you" in this fragment are unspecified, indeterminate. The speaker could be addressing a private communiqué to someone he knows and possibly loves, say, Keats to Fanny Brawne. An unnamed character in a poem or play could be addressing another character in the same work. Or the poet could be projecting forward toward the reader. Criticism of Keats's work has concentrated on the great odes and been mostly silent about this short text, partially because of its ambiguous status (incomplete, fragmentary) between poem and play. But to read Keats's fragment meaningfully as drama we would have to be supplied with the name or identity of the speaker since in drama speakers are by definition identifiable. This is not the case in lyric. As Allen Grossman notes in *Summa Lyrica*, "The nature of the speaker in lyric is inferential or intuitive." The voice in lyric comes to us sponsored by the author, but unnamed in the lyric itself, and thus orphaned. I feel free to infer the speaker in the poem as a stand-in for Keats. And I hear the voice with the certainty that the person whose real voice animated the fictive one is now dead. If he could, Keats would have bridged in advance the gap—the impossible threshold—between the dead and the living. We know from his odes that he was obsessed by fusion experiences. But as it stands here, he cannot achieve one. Instead, he would cheat death by haunting the recipient's (the reader's) sleep, he would trouble your dreams, leave you so guilty, so stricken by loss you would wish to sacrifice yourself to bring him back to life, thus soothing your "conscience."

I have never been able to read the line "So in my veins red life might stream again" with any equanimity. The haunting, he seems to suggest, would be more terrible even than death and so you should actually give up your own life to resurrect him. The fury behind this idea is immense—the fury of the desire to live, the fury of the consciousness of death, the fury that some love might have assuaged all this suffering. The utter lack of love infuses the poem's tone. What ferocity drives it! Keats keeps the desperation going in this lyric, he embodies it in a Shakespearean rhetoric. That desperation gives voltage to the well-wrought lines, almost lifting them off the page, almost scorching them. I hear it in the beseeching, agonized, infuriated voice. I feel it incarnated in the physical image of his once-living hand.

To read Keats in good faith is to breathe in these devastated and devastating lines, to take up the offer of his flesh-and-blood hand. He holds that hand toward you in a fierce and plaintive gesture of poetry that tries to go beyond poetry. One imagines his hand moving furiously across the page and then suddenly stopping. The truth was intolerable. The reality that his actual hand would be replaced by these living lines of poetry seems to have given him no comfort. Still, these lines must carry as much of him as possible now; they are all that is left. The poet perceived this in advance. He gave his word for it. Take it up, as if you were taking his hand.

James Wright's poem "Hook" explores a moment of direct contact, of actual connection. It gestures toward the reader by recalling out of the distant past a fleeting but necessary encounter with another person, a stranger. It is written with that deceptively blunt and aggressive directness that characterizes so much of Wright's late work. Wright wrote an essay called "The Delicacy of Walt Whitman," and I find a similar delicacy, an unlikely almost Horatian lightness, in much of his own seemingly raw work. Here is "Hook":

> I was only a young man
> In those days. On that evening

The cold was so God damned
Bitter there was nothing.
Nothing. I was in trouble
With a woman, and there was nothing
There but me and dead snow.

I stood on the street corner
In Minneapolis, lashed
This way and that.
Wind rose from some pit,
Hunting me.
Another bus to Saint Paul
Would arrive in three hours,
If I was lucky.

Then the young Sioux
Loomed beside me, his scars
Were just my age.

Ain't got no bus here
A long time, he said.
You got enough money
To get home on?

What did they do
To your hand? I answered.
He raised up his hook into the terrible starlight
And slashed the wind.

Oh, that? he said.
I had a bad time with a woman. Here,
You take this.

Did you ever feel a man hold
Sixty-five cents
In a hook,

And place it
Gently
In your freezing hand?

I took it.
It wasn't the money I needed.
But I took it.

How do we account for a poem in the American vernacular that rises to this state of unlikely grandeur? "Hook" is a lyric of reminiscence that builds out of isolation into an epiphanic encounter. I want to linger over some of the details in the first part of the poem to show how emphatically everything reinforces a feeling of isolation turning into human recognition. The initial exposure to the wretched state of the speaker immediately announces that we are in the territory of a threshold experience. It cries out for transformation.

To begin: there is a free-floating sense of stasis in the first stanza. The speaker is not so much recalling a singular episode as establishing a state of being. "I was only a young man / In those days," he declares, summoning up a time when he was young, alone, inexperienced. The verb *was* is repeated five times in three sentences ("I was"; "The cold was"; "there was," etc.). It's as if a camera is zooming in for a close-up as we move from a larger period of time ("those days") to a particular evening to a street corner in Minneapolis. So, too, the word "nothing" is emphatically, even obsessively, repeated three times, a triple underlining—twice at the ends of lines where it gets special emphasis, and once as a one-word sentence. The feeling of being stranded and forlorn is intense.

The protagonist recalls that he was literally outside—an outsider—in cold darkness, which I take both as a place and a metaphoric state. The fact that he was "in trouble with a woman" engenders his suffering as male. He was exposed to the cold, unsheltered, exiled from whatever warmth and domestic comfort he associated with the feminine. There was nothing but him and dead snow. The sense of being damned is powerful. The motif of "God damned" bitter cold is picked up in the second stanza where he recalls being lashed about on an exposed corner as "Wind rose from some pit / Hunting me." He felt the icy inferno coming directly for him. It's crucial to Wright's poetics that these symbolic resonances are registered within a "realistic" framework; he has firmly established waiting on a corner for a bus to Saint Paul that is due in three hours. Yet those hours stretch out like an eternity—spatially, temporally. Everything here conspires to suggest a protagonist separated from the realm of other people, betwixt and between, in a liminal state. A marked Wordsworthian solitary damned to the city.

Notice the word *then* that serves as a turning point in the poem, as it often does in lyrics written in the epiphanic mode. He was alone, then suddenly another man "loomed" beside him, seemingly out of nowhere. The young Sioux simply appears, as if out of the underworld: an original American, an unlikely stranger, an older brother in suffering. The exactitude—"his scars / Were just my age"—establishes a keen likeness, an equation between one man's suffering and another's chronological time on earth. It centers the encounter. The man speaks in a raw vernacular. (Wright, who was so well-educated and learned himself, always seemed to sentimentalize the state of being undereducated in others, identifying emotionally with them as social misfits and outsiders.) He understands the protagonist isn't going anywhere for a while and asks if he has enough money to get "home," a word that resonates with a sense of lost comfort and safety. The question comes with the force of unexpected kindness and will hang there for a couple of stanzas. The conversation that follows exists in some other state of time.

The protagonist—I am tempted to call him a lost pilgrim—answers the question with another question about the Sioux's hand: our first recognition of his disability. The exchange burns at the heart of the poem, as the title makes clear. The meaning of that title has been suspended and only now comes into direct focus:

He raised up his hook into the terrible starlight
And slashed the wind.

This movement from darkness into light marks a poetic crossing, a sudden gesture of illumination that comes before speech, an answer to the answer. Notice the phrase "raised up," which carries religious overtones. The starlight is "terrible" because it flashes and glints off the hook (a mechanical device has replaced a living hand), but also because it casts shocking light on the cost of his suffering. He has paid with part of his body. The word "slashed" comes with a violent jolt.

Wright's delicate touch as a poet is suggested as we move from the apparent melodrama of "terrible starlight" to the odd understatement of the next stanza. "Oh, that? he said" (an offhand comment without the slightest trace of self-pity), "I had a bad time with a woman." And of course this acknowledgment of the cause of his suffering links him powerfully to the protagonist of the poem. He has already been where the protagonist seems to be going; he is a mirror to the future. Yet he doesn't dwell on what happened to him. The word *here* hangs at the end of the line ("I had a bad time with a woman. Here"), floating between two sentences, deemphasizing the bad time but emphasizing the key status of the moment itself. Then he offers change for the bus ride: "You take this." An offering.

In the next stanza, which is one sentence slowly drawn out across six short lines, the speaker turns abruptly to the reader with a question that further suspends the moment in time. The question has a rhetorical and possibly even belligerent edge as he turns to us—to you and me—in the present.

Did you ever feel a man hold
Sixty-five cents
In a hook,
And place it
Gently
In your freezing hand?

The stanza focuses on the moment itself. Word by word, it casts special light on the exchange. It implies that maybe we—the privileged ones—haven't ever had (or recognized) such a gift. Here the specificity of the "sixty-five cents" resounds with literal force so as to underline the understated tenderness of a man holding out an awkward number of coins in a hook and placing them (gently!) in "your freezing hand." The hook meets the numb hand: a gift in the coinage of the land from a more-experienced American Virgil to a less-experienced American Dante.

The final stanza makes absolutely clear that the gesture is not about commerce but communion:

I took it.
It wasn't the money I needed.
But I took it.

There is an emphatic tautness in the twice-repeated one-syllable word "took." Pause for a moment over the masterful use of sound in the phrase "took it," probably the harshest trochee in American poetry. The bitterness, the connotative power, is incredible, both as rhyme and as pure sound. Yet the bitterness feels redemptive (and this is one of Wright's great achievements) because of what is being recognized, acknowledged, accepted, "taken," both consciously and unconsciously. Maybe this has something to do with the position of the tongue in the mouth of the reader who says the phrase aloud—it moves behind the teeth, shoots back against the soft palate, then back to the teeth again. The sound all this makes, the feeling inside the mouth, is intense. For an instant it reduces the speaker to one who makes animal sounds. Repeat the phrase "I took it" aloud twice. Put in a disavowal about money, and it starts to have harsh sexual overtones. The vibration of the language inside the mouth enacts a certain kind of drama.

Wright has come a good distance from his earlier poems "In Terror of Hospital Bills" and "I Am a Sioux Brave, He Said in Minneapolis," both from *Shall We Gather at the River* (1968). The frightened speaker in "In Terror of Hospital Bills" wonders "what words to beg money with," and immediately summons up responses:

Pardon me, sir, could you?
Which way is Saint Paul?
I thirst.
I am a full-blooded Sioux Indian.

I understand these to be four different voices, each coming up with a line, a small con to bum money, to get by. Two approach with polite questions, two with bold declarations. The voices are disembodied, indeterminate. And there is a gap between the desperate motivation and what each speaker actually says. They are emblems of Wright's own shame, his sense of abandonment, the terror that he "will have to stalk timid strangers / On the whorehouse corners."

When the full-blooded Native American appears in the next poem, "I Am a Sioux Brave," he is described as "just plain drunk" and knows "no more than I do." The stranger can offer no native wisdom since he appears only as Wright's estranged and drunken double. But there had been a small sea change in Wright's work by the time of "Hook," which appears in *To a Blossoming Pear Tree* (1977). Does "Hook" dramatize the same encounter? If so, its tenor is completely different. The Sioux in Wright's later poem seems cold sober and knows more than the protagonist. Instead of a con, he comes with a gift, a coin, and "Hook" becomes a poem about unexpected kindness, about contact between strangers.

How powerful it becomes then in the title poem of *To a Blossoming Pear Tree*, the poem following "Hook," when the speaker refuses sex with an "ashamed" and "hopeless" old man who comes from nowhere out of the "unendurable snow" to stroke his face.

Give it to me, he begged.
I'll pay you anything.

I flinched. Both terrified,
We slunk away,
Each in his own way dodging
The cruel darts of the cold.

This is just the old man Wright was terrified of himself becoming in "In Terror of Hospital Bills." The shame and vulnerability of the old man "So near death / He was willing to take / Any love he could get" fills him with recognizable pain (a pain he identifies as "something human") and turns him longingly to the "pure delicate body" of a blossoming pear tree. What goes too far, what he cannot accept, in "To a Blossoming Pear Tree" goes just far enough in "Hook"—an engagement mixed with restraint (and restraint overcome)—and makes what he actually *takes* all the more extraordinary.

In many of Wright's best poems the speaker, a criminal outcast, escapes from the social realm of other people into the more consoling realm of nature. Think of the aboriginal encounter with the two Indian ponies in "A Blessing." Its final recognition is a late Wordsworthian epiphany:

Suddenly I realize
That if I stepped out of my body I would break
Into blossom.

This poem concludes with a lyrical release from selfhood into ecstasy. But instead of such a dissolution, "Hook" lingers over a moment of human connection. What is remarkable about this is that the epiphany brings the speaker into contact with another person. Such engagement is a rarity since, in poetry, epiphanies almost always have been solitary fusion experiences. But Wright here charges us with an instance of mutuality that becomes a metaphor for poetry itself. Think of the poem as a gift, a hook reaching out to a hand. You may not need the coins in the device, but you may need the contact, the words coming out of darkness and crossing a threshold to find you.

"We are on each other's hands / who care," John Berryman writes in *Homage to Mistress Bradstreet*, thereby articulating the caring and calling forth that is one of the basic premises of the lyric. Yet in our social contacts, in our daily rounds, we are often on each other's hands who could care less. Or so it seems. The question poses itself as how to keep alive an interior life in the face of our own and the world's corruptions. Baudelaire is one of the great laureates of this subject. He showed startling prescience about what modern urban life was becoming. He was, famously, a poet of spleen who introduced ugliness as a suitable subject for poetry. At the same time he brought his own subjectivity, his dandiacal manner, to the forefront of the lyric. It was a remarkable project. Disconnecting from the social realm in order to connect more fully with oneself, and using poetry to do so, is the subject of his prose poem "A une heure du matin" ("At One O'Clock in the Morning").

Alone, at last! Not a sound to be heard but the rumbling of some belated and decrepit cabs. For a few hours we shall have silence, if not repose. At last the tyranny of the human face has disappeared, and I myself shall be the only cause of my sufferings.

At last, then, I am allowed to refresh myself in a bath of darkness! First of all, a double turn of the lock. It seems to me that this twist of the key will increase my solitude and fortify the barricades which at this instant separate me from the world.

Horrible life! Horrible town! Let us recapitulate the day: seen several men of letters, one of whom asked me whether one could go to Russia by a land route (no doubt he took Russia to be an island); disputed generously with the editor of a review, who, to each of my objections, replied: "We represent the cause of decent people," which implies that all the other newspapers are edited by scoundrels; greeted some twenty persons, with fifteen of whom I am not acquainted; distributed handshakes in the same proportion, and this without having taken the precaution of buying gloves; to kill time, during a shower, went to see an acrobat, who asked me to design for her the costume of a *Venustra;* paid court to the director of a theater, who, while dismissing me, said to me: "Perhaps you would do well to apply to Z——; he is the clumsiest, the stupidest and the most celebrated of my authors; together with him, perhaps, you would get somewhere. Go to see him, and after that we'll see"; boasted (why?) of several vile actions which I have never committed, and faintheartedly denied some other misdeeds which I accomplished with joy, an error of bravado, an offence against human respect; refused a friend an easy service, and gave a written recommendation to a perfect clown; oh, isn't that enough?

Discontented with everyone and discontented with myself, I would gladly redeem myself and elate myself a little in the silence and solitude of night. Souls of those I have loved, souls of those I have sung, strengthen me, support me, rid me of lies and the corrupting vapours of the world; and you, O Lord God, grant me the grace to produce a few good verses, which shall prove to myself that I am not the lowest of men, that I am not inferior to those whom I despise.

(translated by Michael Hamburger)

A word about the form of this poem, which appeared in Baudelaire's book *Petits poèmes en prose.* The prose poem, that peculiar hybrid (the title is an oxymoron) has had a stronger history in France than in any other country because of the straitjacket of classical French versification. Baudelaire never made an exclusive commitment to prose poems since he wrote them intermittently and alongside his poems in vers libre. Nonetheless, one might say that he made the rebellion bloom against the French alexandrine which Rimbaud then turned into a full-scale revolt with *Illuminations*. Baudelaire was a master of the alexandrine who sought a liberation from it. He refused to be bound by traditional suppositions of an appropriate subject matter for poetry. He exploded overarching formal expectations even as he maintained a balletic sense of phrasing. Thus he had high ambitions for the medium of the prose poem and dreamed of creating "a poetic prose, musical without rhyme or rhythm, supple and jerky enough to adapt to the lyric movements of the soul, to the undulations of reverie, to the somersaults of conscience."

"At One O'Clock in the Morning" is one of Baudelaire's many poems that says "unhand me" to the world, that seeks a more authentic self, that follows "undulations of reverie" and "somersaults of conscience." I equate the world here with the cares of worldliness, as in Wordsworth's sonnet "The world is too much with us; late and soon." Everything in the first two paragraphs marks this as a prose poem moving in the direction of a visionary lyric, a poem that aspires to go through prose toward grace. For example, it begins with an outcry, a double exclamation—"Enfin! Seul!" which the translator renders as "Alone, at last!" This immediately separates the speaker from everyone else. Sound is repressed and the light of ordinary experience extinguished in "a bath of darkness." Refreshment beckons. The contacts of the day were so compromising that, in a comic touch which is also serious, he double bolts the door. Crucial to the visionary dimension is the feeling of an increased and fortified solitude, an absolute separation. That's why the poem must be set in the middle of the night when everyone else is seemingly asleep and the speaker can operate as a sole waking consciousness. We are about to move from one kind of experience (proselike, daylit) to another kind of experience (lyrical, night-bound).

The long middle paragraph that comprises the bulk of the poem recapitulates and summarizes the (nauseating) experiences of the day. The tone is acid, the revulsion complete. Every specific detail of social encounter dramatizes and reinforces the speaker's sense of being polluted by the unseemly business of the world, by the stupidity and cruelty of other people, by what Baudelaire elsewhere calls the "syphilization" of society. (Following the motif of hands, one notices the wry joke about distributing handshakes without taking the precaution of wearing gloves, as if one could actually pick up some filthy disease merely by passing contact with people in the "horrible town.")

Baudelaire, who has been called an "exquisite moralist," sees himself implicated in the gratuitous crimes of dailiness. His irony gives him no rest. His fulminating disgust is acted out in an onrushing catalog difficult to excerpt; and then this happened, he bursts out, and then that happened. The hustle-bustle of this paragraph charting another day in the city owes a great deal to the style and the social observations of the nineteenth-century French novel.

The list of the day's signal events is shocking. Even more shocking is the recognition that these events have become commonplace. What disgusts him is not just what has been done to him, but also what he has done to others. He is complicit, and this very complicity brings the catalog to a complete halt. He turns back to the night, to the present moment, appalled by himself. One now has a dramatic sense of the motivation that drove the opening of the poem, the wild fury that erupted and now circles back: "Discontented with everyone and discontented with myself."

One might say that the daylit middle of the poem is social and horizontal. It includes the reader ("Let us recapitulate the day"), whereas the conclusion of the poem is asocial and vertical, putting the reader in the position of hearing not so much the poet's conversation with himself as a prayer directed to almighty God. The quotidian world is suppressed as the speaker turns first to "Souls of those I have loved," then to "souls of those I have sung," and then, strengthened and cleansed, toward the Lord God himself. The tone is liturgical. He has separated himself from social space, social language, and now invokes religious space, transcendental language. He would replace the bedeviled social selves he has encountered during the day with the deeper souls of his beloved, souls of those he has praised. Strikingly, what he finally asks for is the grace of poetry itself, the inspiration of "a few good verses" which would somehow save him from his own world-weary disgust. He longs for proof of a spiritual life distant from the polluted ordinary realm, beyond corruption and worldliness. He calls for help to escape his own conscience. And poetry itself becomes the agent of a longed-for, redeeming purity. The messianic lyric which he is calling for has not yet been written. But it holds out a dream, a promise. The vocation of poetry becomes the out-stretched hand of transfiguration.

Walter Benjamin said that "Baudelaire envisaged readers to whom the reading of lyric poetry would present difficulties" ("On Some Motifs in Baudelaire"). The nineteenth-century poet anticipated readers too inat-tentive, too distracted, and too harried by modern life to engage the poem on its own terms. He railed against a world where inauthenticity reigned. Yet Baudelaire also dreamed of hospitable readers in the future (and we are those potential readers—that future is now) who would rec-ognize how poems speak from the ground floor of being. Reading po-etry is an encounter with one's depths. It is a participatory relationship, demanding intimacy with what the poet is asking for—deeper contact with another, deeper contact with oneself. No wonder, then, that Wal-lace Stevens said, "One reads poetry with one's nerves" ("Adagio"). One feels the beseeching desperation in Keats's fragment, the indictment of indifference that stands behind Wright's lyric of communion, the invita-tion to authenticity that bursts forth from Baudelaire's catalog of daily horrors. Each of these three poems charges us with its vital energy, its fu-rious electricity. It asks us to open up to its experience, it urges us toward a reckoning. Each asks us to be accountable to its dark wisdom. It incites us to listen, to change, to feel a living hand coming off a page. To take up the offer of these poems is to engage a solitude that would be trans-formed, a loneliness that would become holy, a desolate crying out that signals we are in the presence of the sacred.

4

Three Initiations

1

I was initiated into the poetry of trance on a rainy Saturday afternoon in mid–October 1958 (baseball season was over for the year) when I wandered down to the basement of our house to pick through some of my grandfather's forgotten books. I was eight years old. I vaguely remembered that my grandfather had copied poems into the inside cover of his favorite volumes, and I had decided to try to find one. (I didn't yet know that after his death his books had been given away to a local Jewish charity, and that his poems were thereby lost forever.) I opened a musty anthology of poetry to a section called "Night" and read a poem that immediately arrested me:

> The night is darkening round me,
> The wild winds coldly blow,
> But a tyrant spell has bound me
> And I cannot, cannot go.
>
> The giant trees are bending
> Their bare boughs weighed with snow,
> And the storm is fast descending
> And yet I cannot go.

Clouds beyond clouds above me,
Wastes beyond wastes below;
But nothing drear can move me;
I will not, cannot go.

There was no title or author's name attached to this songlike poem, and I somehow imagined that my grandfather must have written it. I read it right straight through, and its simple incremental rhythm seized me. I read it again slowly, pronouncing every word to myself, and suddenly I was in two places at once: I was standing next to a bookshelf in a small, one-windowed room in my parents' basement, and I was lost in the middle of a field somewhere in southern Latvia with a storm wildly brewing around me. I felt as though the words of the poem, like the storm itself, had cast a "tyrant spell" upon me. I couldn't move.

I can still feel the terrible immediacy of this poem written in the present tense. I couldn't tell if the poem was a charm inviting the storm into the world or a spell warding it off. I read stanza 1 and felt the dusk purpling around me, an icy wind blowing out of control, invisible hands holding me by the shoulders. I said, "And I *can*not, *can*not go." The repetitive stresses were like two blows to my chest.

I recited stanza 2 and felt the enormous weight of winter coming down. I could feel the giant trees giving way, their limbs burdened with snow. I was far from home. The storm was coming after me, but I couldn't bring myself to leave. I stubbornly repeated the refrain, "And yet I cannot go." The word "go," which rhymes with "snow," was like a door slamming in my head.

I said stanza 3 aloud and felt that I was standing in the middle of the world. I saw clouds stretching beyond clouds above me. They were layered all the way to heaven. I saw barren spaces stretching out endlessly below—the blasted country of hell. But I was firmly planted on the ground, a tree rooted to the earth. I took heart from the line "But nothing drear can move me." I recognized the word *drear* from Poe's "The Raven": "Once upon a midnight dreary . . ." I knew the double meaning of the word *move*. So the gloomy storm couldn't affect me or make me give way. I wouldn't budge. I asserted: "I *will* not, *can*not go."

I felt a deep resolve, and for a moment when I said it I remembered how I had stood on the hood of a car in the parking lot across the street from the hospital where my grandfather had gone to die. I started waving wildly, furiously, when I saw him standing at the window on the seventh floor. I remembered how he had pressed his lips to the glass and then touched the spot with his hand; it was the same way he used to kiss me on the upper arm at night and then seal the kiss with his fingertips. A gesture of unworldly tenderness.

And then I remembered how I had stood by the side of my grandfather's grave when they lowered him into the ground. I threw a shovel of dirt onto the coffin, like the other men. Some kindness had passed out of the world, but I wouldn't move away, I would never give him up. The storm was coming right for me, but suddenly I had the words for what I had felt then. I was determined by what I could not resist. I said, "I will not, cannot go."

I don't know how long I stood there on that rainy Saturday afternoon, lost in a book in the basement of my childhood house, in a cluttered Jewish cemetery on the south side of Chicago, in the middle of a field somewhere in Latvia, on an English moor. It would be years before I discovered I had been reading a lyric by Emily Brontë. I recognized the style as soon as I encountered "No Coward Soul Is Mine." I suppose that in some sense I never really shut that worn anthology of poetry again because it had opened up an unembarrassed space in me that would never be closed. I had stumbled into the sublime. I had been initiated into the poetry of awe.

Emily Brontë's poem, sometimes called "Spellbound," was written in November 1837, when she was nineteen years old. I was the same age when I rediscovered it in Auden and Pearson's anthology *Victorian and Edwardian Poets,* the fifth volume of their series Poets of the English Language, my college bible. I took it as a confessional lyric.

It was many more years before I discovered that in 1844 Emily Brontë had divided and transcribed her extant poems into two different notebooks: one contained thirty-one autobiographical lyrics; the other consisted of forty-five poems, including the one that had held me spellbound, that were part of the Gondal saga. Gondal was a mythical island in the North Pacific about which Emily and her younger sister Anne had written poems and stories since childhood. The speaker of the poem was not Emily Brontë proper, but Augusta Geraldine Almeda, the fatal heroine of Gondal. This created a subtle shift in emphasis. I still found the poem wild, melancholy, and elevating (to use Charlotte Brontë's words for her sister's poetry), but it made it easier for me to see it as a dramatic lyric, a made thing. Brontë's poem is so spellbinding precisely because of the pattern operating underneath it. It could move me to trance as a child because it rhythmically enacts the bondage it describes.

The poem that hit me so hard as I stood on the ground floor of my childhood consists of three simple rhyming quatrains (*abab*), each a sentence long. The language has dark sinews, but there's not a word a child can't understand. Brontë condenses into twelve lines the feeling of exposure to the elements, to dangerous natural forces, that she enlarges into epic scope in *Wuthering Heights*. We're on the edge of the wild moors (the fierce weather of Gondal is the same as Brontë's native Yorkshire); her world is pagan and merciless. I'm struck by the sensation that the poem combines an ecstatic energy with the eerie calm of acceptance.

The rhythm of the poem seems to me both stately and unremitting. Brontë creates this effect by manipulating the sense of time within and across the lines. Each of the lines is a phrasal and syntactic unit unto itself, yet also proceeds as an equal quarter partner in the stanza and the sentence. This creates an almost processional movement. For example, the character of the night getting darker, falling and surrounding the speaker, is enacted in the length of time it takes to say the first line:

> The night is darkening round me,

This is followed by the equally stressed, equally stressful, but foreshortened second line:

> The wild winds coldly blow,

The night is the active agent in the first line ("The night *is darkening* round me") and this creates a sense of the speaker's passivity before nature. The feeling is enhanced by the next line: the many uncontrollable winds "blow." The verb socks me with its power. It feels powerful because of its special placement at the close of the line and the emphatic stress it receives. The sense of inescapable movement is heightened by the repetition of sounds: the alliterative *w*s in "*w*ild *w*inds," the assonant long os in "coldly blow." The repeated blowing is also mimicked in the reversed o and l in the phrase "coldly blow." (The alliterations are picked up in the second line of the second stanza in those "bare boughs weighed with snow.") The emphatic consonance binds the line, the psyche, and brings us in range of the oldest Celtic poetries, the archaic powers of language. The word "blow" followed by "But" insists upon a pause between the two lines that prefigures an impending sense of paralysis. So, too, the rhythm is driving the lyric forward even as the intact and elongated third line,

But a tyrant spell has bound me,

creates a feeling of paralysis which is nailed down by the exact repetition of

And I cannot, cannot go.

The period gives the sentence, the stanza, a feeling of finality. And this is repeated at the close of the next two stations of the poem.

I had a strong sense of being tyrannically bound by these stanzas when I read them as a child, and I see now that that sense was also created by the firm pattern of rhymes. Throughout the poem, the first and third lines have feminine or multisyllabic rhymes. This gives off a powerful sense of handcuffing, of being handcuffed—as in "round me" and "bound me." The extended rhyme forces a linkage of words and lines—as in "bending" and "descending." Both give a powerful downward thrust to the second stanza. These rhymes alternate with the harsher and more taut one-syllable masculine rhymes that connect the even-numbered lines of the poem. These true or perfect rhymes have a terrific acoustic impact. They seal the verbal relationships and create the transformation in the lyric from initial unwillingness ("But a tyrant spell has bound me") to conscious submission ("I will not...go"). I also hear the echo, sometimes distant, of the consonant n reverberating all through the poem. It gives me the eerie feeling of being in a haunted chamber, that nature itself is a haunted chamber, and that we are somehow caught up and bound into it.

The spellbinding verbal force is also reinforced by the rhetoric and logic of argumentation ("Emily had a head for arguing," her sister Charlotte said), a structure so seamless it's easy to overlook. Each stanza begins with a proposition and then turns on a "but" or an "and yet." This effects the powerful feeling of duality—a dangerous storm is coming relentlessly forward from which one cannot flee. It's an exposure to which one ultimately submits.

The secret shifts in Emily Brontë's language enact a sense of transfiguration and dark initiation. I submitted to that power as a child and it became part of my birthright as a poet and as a reader of poetry. I can recite this poem aloud and once more become an eight-year-old boy giving myself up to the poetry of trance, ritualizing my grief. Emily Brontë's words enacted through form seem to me the bright sparks that fly from the soul of the writer to the soul of the reader. I will always be grateful to her for delivering up the wild moors inside me, for giving me my childhood grieving through her bardic craft.

2

Let the eighteenth-century poet Christopher Smart initiate you, as he initiated me, into the poetry of praise. Let him fill you up with his glorious humor and wild jubilation, his grave and comic mysticism, his religious awe. Let him animate your spirit with his animism. Here is the galvanizing passage about his cat Jeoffry:

> For I will consider my Cat Jeoffry.
> For he is the servant of the Living God duly and daily serving
>   him.
> For at the first glance of the glory of God in the East he
>   worships in his way.
> For is this done by wreathing his body seven times round with
>   elegant quickness.
> For then he leaps up to catch the musk, which is the blessing
>   of God upon his prayer.
> For he rolls upon prank to work it in.
> For having done duty and received blessing he begins to
>   consider himself.
> For this he performs in ten degrees.
> For first he looks upon his fore-paws to see if they are clean.

For secondly he kicks up behind to clear away there.

For thirdly he works it upon stretch with the fore-paws
extended.

For fourthly he sharpens his paws by wood.

For fifthly he washes himself.

For Sixthly he rolls upon wash.

For Seventhly he fleas himself, that he may not be interrupted
upon the beat.

For Eighthly he rubs himself against a post.

For Ninthly he looks up for his instructions.

For Tenthly he goes in quest of food.

For having consider'd God and himself he will consider his
neighbour.

For if he meets another cat he will kiss her in kindness.

For when he takes his prey he plays with it to give it chance.

For one mouse in seven escapes by his dallying.

For when his day's work is done his business more properly
begins.

For he keeps the Lord's watch in the night against the adversary.

For he counteracts the powers of darkness by his electrical skin
and glaring eyes.

For he counteracts the Devil, who is death, by brisking about
the life.

For in his morning orisons he loves the sun and the sun loves
him.

For he is of the tribe of Tiger.

For the Cherub Cat is a term of the Angel Tiger.

For he has the subtlety and hissing of a serpent, which in
goodness he suppresses.

For he will not do destruction, if he is well-fed, neither will he
spit without provocation.

For he purrs in thankfulness, when God tells him he's a good
Cat.

For he is an instrument for the children to learn benevolence
upon.

For every house is incomplete without him and a blessing is
lacking in the spirit.

For the Lord commanded Moses concerning the cats at the
    departure of the Children of Israel from Egypt.

For every family had one cat at least in the bag.

For the English Cats are the best in Europe.

For he is the cleanest in the use of his fore-paws of any
    quadrupede.

For the dexterity of his defence is an instance of the love of
    God to him exceedingly.

For he is the quickest to his mark of any creature.

For he is tenacious of his point.

For he is a mixture of gravity and waggery.

For he knows that God is his Saviour.

For there is nothing sweeter than his peace when at rest.

For there is nothing brisker than his life when in motion.

For he is of the Lord's poor and so indeed is he called by
    benevolence perpetually—Poor Jeoffry! poor Jeoffry! the
    rat has bit thy throat.

For I bless the name of the Lord Jesus that Jeoffry is better.

For the divine spirit comes about his body to sustain it in
    complete cat.

For his tongue is exceeding pure so that it has in purity what it
    wants in music.

For he is docile and can learn certain things.

For he can set up with gravity which is patience upon
    approbation.

For he can fetch and carry, which is patience in employment.

For he can jump over a stick which is patience upon proof
    positive.

For he can spraggle upon waggle at the word of command.

For he can jump from an eminence into his master's bosom.

For he can catch the cork and toss it again.

For he is hated by the hypocrite and miser.

For the former is afraid of detection.

For the latter refuses the charge.

For he camels his back to bear the first notion of business.

For he is good to think on, if a man would express himself
    neatly.

For he made a great figure in Egypt for his signal services.

For he killed the Ichneumon-rat very pernicious by land.

For his ears are so acute that they sting again.

For from this proceeds the passing quickness of his attention.

For by stroking of him I have found out electricity.

For I perceived God's light about him both wax and fire.

For the Electrical fire is the spiritual substance, which God
sends from heaven to sustain the bodies both of man and
beast.

For God has blessed him in the variety of his movements.

For, tho' he cannot fly, he is an excellent clamberer.

For his motions upon the face of the earth are more than any
other quadrupede.

For he can tread to all the measures upon the music.

For he can swim for life.

For he can creep.

This poem (or fragment) has enthralled me for thirty years. When I first started reading it as a teenager I wondered if I had stumbled into a brilliantly whacked-out version of the psalms. The poem felt ancient and biblical to me and also English and a couple of centuries old and also fresh and contemporary. I was entranced by its repetitions, its euphoric catalogs so giddy and excessive, so incantatory. I loved the poet's outlandish religious fervor and enthusiasm, which seemed funny, and more than a little desperate and dangerous. I felt smart and subversive reading him. I felt as if a prophet had walked out of the Hebrew Bible and focused all his attention on an English cat.

Anyone could see that the entire passage radiates with the joyful spirit of that cat, with what I wanted to call a *divine catfulness*. I liked everything Smart said about Jeoffry, beginning with his name. It's worth noting that, anthropologically speaking, we humanize animals by giving them names, but then use those designations to distance them a bit from our human neighbors. It's one more way of defining and organizing the natural and social worlds, thus distinguishing cats from kings. But Smart gave his cat the same name as a good friend, precisely because he treated him as an equal—not an inferior, not a pet—and gave him the same consideration he would have given a king. It's a way of talking back to power. Everything is given equal weight, equal status, in Smart's world because everything is infused with divinity. Everything is charged with a deeply animating force. The world shines out with radiant particularity. This is what Gerard Manley Hopkins meant by indwelling.

It's evident how scrupulously and even obsessively Smart observed Jeoffry day after day. His pleasure in Jeoffry's antics is palpable (he always gives him the benefit of the doubt), and he's terrifically alert to the way cats actually move and behave. Yet he also dissolves literalizations and immediately leaps beyond the empirical realm to consider Jeoffry's movements under the sign of eternity. The entire passage begins with an astounding claim:

> For I will consider my Cat Jeoffry.
> For he is the servant of the Living God duly and daily serving
>   him.
> For at the first glance of the glory of God in the East he
>   worships in his way.

A lot of weight is given here to the phrase "in his way" since Smart is going to interpret Jeoffry's natural movements as a form of prayer, a religious action. He is going to read and (playfully) overread what it means for Jeoffry to do the same things in the same order every day. I have always enjoyed the humorous mysticism of how Smart treats the way Jeoffry wreathes himself exactly seven times as a kind of mystic duty, like some primitive rite out of Stonehenge. He interprets the way Jeoffry jumps in the air as a blessing from God and then claims that Jeoffry's rolling around in the dirt is a prankish way of sealing in that blessing. The ten degrees so precisely defined, enumerated, and performed every day become a ritual of instruction. It's understood that Jeoffry praises God simply by doing what cats do, by being himself. He enacts the Lord's orders. Then he turns to the business of the world at large where he kisses neighboring cats, dallies with mice, and becomes an allegorical hero who fights off the powers of darkness with his "electrical skin and glaring eyes," counteracting the devil by prowling around the residence at night. This cat is no consort of witches. And he has a heroic almost biblical lineage ("For he is of the tribe of Tiger").

One of the astonishing things about Smart's poem is that it makes no relative truth claims. He was a democrat of details who lavished his attention equally on the smallest objects and the grandest ideas. He selected carefully, but then treated everything as a fact of equal value. Thus Jeoffry's ability to jump over a stick is given the same weight as his recognition of God as a Saviour. There's no apparent distinction made between things Smart knew were demonstrably true about Jeoffry ("For he is docile and can learn certain things") and things he might only have believed were true ("For the divine spirit comes about his body to sustain it in complete cat").

He was also eager to make the greatest spiritual claims on Jeoffry's behalf. Jeoffry is pagan ("For in his morning orisons he loves the sun and the sun loves him"), he has a Jewish heritage of exile ("For the Lord commanded Moses concerning the cats at the departure of the Children of Israel from Egypt"), and he becomes a blessed Christian sufferer ("For he is of the Lord's poor"). Smart also made no visible distinction between things he derived from history and mythology ("For he made a great figure in Egypt for his signal services") and things he learned from science ("For by stroking of him I have found out electricity"), just as he made no distinction between what he observed about one particular cat and what he made up about cats in general. (There's no evidence in Exodus, for example, that suggests the Lord included cats in his instructions to Moses.) Part of what makes Smart's poem so immensely pleasurable is how he wove together and juxtaposed different kinds and levels of information, infusing everything with his tenderness and good will, with the lavishness of his affections. The whole poem has the quality of comic holiness.

When I first read this poem three decades ago I intuited that the poet who wrote so ardently about his own cat was radically estranged from everyone else, even from daily life itself. He was so cut off from the ordinary world that everything about it appeared alien and magical to him. (Years later I recognized the same feeling, the same sense of an estranged and performing dailiness, when I came across the New York poet James Schuyler's long work "The Morning of the Poem.") The drowning man rejoices in the reliable oar. Smart was humorous, deadpan, watchful, and learned. Since his sincerity seemed to go hand in hand with his playfulness I decided that the poet, like his cat, was "a mixture of gravity and waggery." He was amusingly odd and deeply serious, like Stevie Smith—part Ogden Nash, part John Donne. He was irrepressible, he was unguarded, he was willing to play the holy fool, to proclaim that God was in his cat and therefore in everything else, too. He was writing from the far side of daily life where the world appears mysterious and unfamiliar, where everything trembles with divine presence, where every routine seems marvelous and every action is imbued with the sacred.

Christopher Smart's writing about his cat Jeoffry was not, as I had initially supposed, a complete poem unto itself, but an untitled fragment (B695–768) from his majestic and unfinished long sequence *Jubilate Agno*. Smart wrote the sequence from 1759–1763, the four-year period when he was unwillingly confined to Potter's madhouse, a private asylum at Bethnal Green. He had already been dismissed as an "uncured" lunatic from St. Luke's Hospital for the Insane. The main symptom of his disorder was a manic compulsion to pray in public, anytime, anyplace. *"For I blessed God in St James's Park till I routed all the company,"* the poet later explained (B89). Smart suffered terribly for his affliction. Samuel Johnson was one of the few who accepted Smart's religious mania on its own terms, saying, "He insisted on people praying with him; and I'd as lief pray with Kit Smart as any one else."

Smart wrote *Jubilate Agno* with scrupulous rigor by copying out one, two, or three pairs of verses every day, no more, no less. It was a ritual creation. He may never have expected to have the poem read or published, but seems to have known precisely what he was doing. We do not because only about a third of the original manuscript survived. The manuscript of disconnected fragments consists of three reconstructed double folios and ten single sheets; some contain verses beginning with the word *Let*, others with the word *For*. Astoundingly, it wasn't printed until 1939, when W. F. Stead published an annotated edition under a title of his own devising, *Rejoice in the Lamb: A Song from Bedlam*.

Stead believed the "Let" and "For" verses formed two separate but related poems. Fifteen years later W. H. Bond argued instead for a close interrelationship between the "Let" and "For" lines. He surmised on the basis of internal evidence that Smart intended to write matching pairs of verses, the first all beginning with the versicle "Let," the companion verses with the responsive "For." Smart was adapting the basic principles of Bishop Robert Lowth's *De sacra poesi Hebraeorum,* a course of lectures delivered before Oxford and published in Latin in 1753. (Smart called it one of the best performances of the century.)

Lowth argued for the antiphonal structure of Hebrew poetry. Smart would therefore have been modeling his work on the structure of the Psalms and other poetic books of the Bible. The main method was a responding parallelism. Here's an example from Psalm 95:

> Let us come before his presence with thanksgiving,
> and make a joyful noise unto him with psalms.
>   For the LORD *is* a great God, and a great King above
> all gods.

It seems likely then, as some scholars have since speculated, that Smart was trying to create a fresh liturgical service, a great canticle, "my MAGNIFICAT" he called it. A hypothetical chorus would then be singing the "Let" verses—

> Let Elizur rejoice with the Partridge, who is a prisoner
> of state and is proud of his keepers.

and a solo voice would then be singing the responsive "For" verses—

> *For I am not without authority in my jeopardy, which I*
> *derive inevitably from the glory of the name of the Lord.*
>   (B1)

The intended effect was a wonderfully various type of call-and-response method. Two different kinds of testimony were meant to echo and counterpoint each other, to bring the community and the individual into right relationship.

I find it a little heartbreaking then, and perhaps emblematic of Smart's isolated situation, that there are no corresponding "Let" verses for the dynamic passage about Jeoffry. It may be that they were lost, or it may be that Smart abandoned his schema. In any case, the liturgical performance of the group is gone, and so we have left only the free-floating testimony of the individual.

Smart took great authority from his jeopardy, from the prophetic power of his sentences, but he was also incredibly vulnerable ("*For they work me with their harping-irons, which is a barbarous instrument, because I am more unguarded than others,*" he confessed [B124]). He knew his strangeness ("*For I have seen the White Raven and Thomas Hall of Willingham and am my self a greater curiosity than both*" [B25]) and must at times have doubted his intelligibility. *Jubilate Agno* is filled with his esoteric knowledge of mystical traditions (his primary sources are cabala, hermeticism, and freemasonry) as well as his current reading in eighteenth-century science. He was also an accomplished classicist and a determined punster in four languages (English, Greek, Latin, and Hebrew). He puts me in mind of other major poets who followed him and relied on esoteric knowledge to create new scriptures, who also feared unintelligibility and put themselves in jeopardy for their reliance on occult traditions: William Blake and John Clare, W. B. Yeats, Hart Crane, Allen Ginsberg...

Despite the eccentric particularity of Smart's predicament, his position also seems almost paradigmatic of the situation of the Whitman-esque modern poet whose work is read rather than sung, who creates "*a psalm of my own composing*" (B32) and labors in isolation, who has lost the power to yoke the collective but nonetheless would speak for the benefit of that collective by inscribing a choral form for readers. Smart called what he did "punching," and clearly understood that the power of his incantations had to come off the page for readers:

> *For my talent is to give an impression upon words by punching, that when the reader casts his eye upon 'em, he takes up the image from the mould which I have made.*
>
> (B404)

The notion of "impression," as Smart's editors have pointed out, comes from the process of typefounding, and Smart uses it to impress upon us how he made words distinctive, how he inscribes the language with greater concreteness and concision, greater figural force, and how his tireless linguistic experiments were meant to explode with verbal and spiritual energy.

The fragment of *Jubilate Agno* about Jeoffry has its own quality of punching, its own sequentiality and logic. The formal method that Smart uses is called *anaphora,* from the Greek word for "a carrying up or back." Anaphora is the repetition of the same word or words at the beginning of successive sentences. Every line is a sentence, a complete unit, and this also gives the feeling that each line is an aphorism inscribed into a commonplace book. The length of the line extending past the Miltonic blank verse line also gives the utterance a prophetic feeling, a dreamlike quality, going beyond speech. Smart was, in fact, inventing free verse based on the cadences of the King James translation of the Bible and the original Hebrew texts. He was the precursor to Blake and Whitman, who would originate the same form with their free-verse chorales. All three poets are great democratic catalogers who rebelled against "authoritarian prosodies" (the phrase is Gaston Bachelard's), who understood the piling up of particulars as a joyous poetic activity, who claimed the world by chanting its various names and delivering canticles of blessing upon it, a poetry of happiness. The cataloging impulse almost always expresses, in Richard Wilbur's words, "a longing to possess the whole world, and to praise it." It was Whitman, but it could just as well have been Blake or Smart, who wrote: "I hear and behold God in every object."

The free-verse catalogs that I most value tend to be eccentric, particular, and inclusive. They have an odd intimacy, the quality of revelation. And they continually surprise us. What especially turns one's head in reading Smart's catalog is the seamless disjunctiveness between his sentences. Sometimes his observations are clearly meant to be progressive—

> *For he can set up with gravity . . .*
> *For he can fetch and carry . . .*
> *For he can jump over a stick . . .*
> *(B745–747)*

But other times he moves from one kind of utterance to another without any acknowledgment of difference—

> *For he is the quickest to his mark of any creature.*
> *For he is tenacious of his point.*
> *For he is a mixture of gravity and waggery.*
> *For he knows that God is his Saviour.*
> *(B734–737)*

Smart learned this strategy from the poets of the Hebrew Bible. Reading Robert Alter's chapter "The Dynamics of Parallelism" in his instructive book *The Art of Biblical Poetry*, I was recently reminded of the Russian formalist Viktor Shklovsky's notion in "Art as Technique" that "The perception of disharmony in a harmonious context is important in parallelism. The purpose of parallelism, like the general purpose of imagery, is to transfer the usual perception of an object into the sphere of a new perception—that is, to make a unique semantic modification." Shklovsky points to the dynamic transfer of power between unlike but parallel statements. The dislocation and resultant bliss one experiences in reading Smart is based on the scrupulous interchange of different kinds of propositions about reality. These empower each other. Thus an observation about Jeoffry's physical dexterity leads to a statement about his character which in turn leaps over into a claim about his spiritual knowledge. The effect is dizzying. Smart repeatedly goes up and down the ladder of meaning in this way. He makes it impossible to ignore our sense perceptions but equally impossible to employ them everywhere. Spirit infuses everything. He uses a method of dynamic parallelism to occult every sentence with a feeling of adoration.

Smart was the least jaded of poets. He never lost his sense of astonishment at the workings of the world, his sense of the deep mystery of being. He had a driving sincerity. I believe he believed everything he said. He would not be dissuaded from saying it, either, though his testimony imperiled him and placed him on the far margins of society. He was defenseless, but he had no choice. He wrote the way he had to write because the sacred was everywhere present for him. He crossed its threshold every day; he engaged the divine in every object. Therefore his natural impulse was to write a poetry of benediction. He would go on after *Jubilate Agno* to create his most sustained single work, *A Song to David*, his model of the perfect hero and "the best poet which ever lived." Here is stanza 50, which points to the transcendent virtue of praise itself:

PRAISE above all—for praise prevails;
Heap up the measure, load the scales,
    And good to goodness add:

The gen'rous soul her Saviour adds,
But peevish obloquy degrades;
    The Lord is great and glad.

Smart's dedication to a poetry of absolute praise made him incredibly vulnerable to the world. It also puts him at the heart of the English holy tradition. He looks forward to Blake and Hopkins, backward to Traherne and Vaughan, to the seventh-century poet Caedmon, who stands at the very top of English poetic tradition as the first Anglo-Saxon to compose Christian poetry in his own language. Bede tells the story of a voice that came to Caedmon in a dream and commanded him to sing about the beginning of created things: "Thereupon Caedmon began to sing verses which he had never heard before in praise of God the Creator." Caedmon's dream is a sign of poetic vocation; his hymn is a praise poem to the Lord, like the Latin canticle *Benedicite, omnia opera domini*.

Here are the first verses:

O all ye Works of the Lord, bless ye the Lord: praise him, and
    magnify him for ever.
O ye Angels of the Lord, bless ye the Lord: praise him, and
    magnify him for ever.
O ye Heavens, bless ye the Lord: praise him and magnify him
    for ever.

This catalog, like *Jubilate Agno,* goes on to embrace all the works of creation.

Smart clearly thought of himself as a Christian poet, but *Jubilate Agno* reaches even further back to earlier pre-Christian Celtic poetries because its hypnotic cadences summon up a pagan past, an animistic worldview which finds vital essence in everything mortal and divine, organic and inorganic. "*For EARTH which is an intelligence hath a voice and a propensity to speak in all her parts,*" Smart writes (B234). He tried to give choral voice to those many parts, all of which moved, to embrace the earth's great variousness. He was an alchemist of praise. Thinking about the language, the reverie, employed by alchemists, Gaston Bachelard writes in *The Poetics of Reverie*:

When the forces of matter must be awakened, praise is sovereign. Let us remember that praise has a magical action. That is evident in the psychology of men. It ought then to be the same in a psychology of matter which gives substances human forces and desires.

There is a dreamlike quality to Smart's lists because he is calling to the inside of matter, he is entering the mystery of a world riven with *anima*, with process, a world that awakens to the Orphic calling of the poet. The impulse is shamanistic. He would enchant objects, he would be a technician of the sacred. Here the passage about Jeoffry is especially telling because Smart shows how much he knows about him *as an animal*. He also knows the "mazes" of the hare, the "subtlety and industry" of the spider, the "piercer" of the flea. He identifies the mouse as "*a creature of great personal valour*" and understands how "*a LION roars HIMSELF complete from head to tail.*" Most of all he knows this: "*For the power of some animal is predominant in every language.*" It's as if every language has a totemic animal. Smart recognizes that power. His studious entry into the language of animals is a sign of his mystic, shamanistic ambition. As Mircea Eliade notes in *Shamanism,* his definitive work on the subject: "All over the world learning the language of animals...is equivalent to knowing the secrets of nature and hence being able to prophesy." Smart sought the power of nature manifested through language. He heard a spiritual music, and although it made him seem lunatic, he sealed his poetic vocation with the language of adoration.

Aristotle insightfully observed and argued that poetry has two essential forms: *praise* (which results in hymns and heroic poetry) and *blame* (which expresses itself as iambic satire). Early in this century the anthropologist of religion Jane Harrison noted that Aristotle could not have known that these two modes derived from two ritual forms: "The ritual of expulsion, riddance, cursing and finally purification issues in the literature of blame, the ritual of induction, of blessing, of magical fertilization in the literature of *praise*" (*Epilegomena to the Study of Greek Religion*). Both rituals reveal an "impulse towards life." I'm reminded of that formative moment in Genesis when Yahweh calls Abraham out of his homeland with a promise of greatness, a nation, and a blessing. "Be a blessing!"

Yahweh commands. That blessing, as Harold Bloom astutely interprets it, is the promise of more life, ever more life.

Praise is clearly inscribed in the Egyptian Pyramid Texts, the oldest lyrical fragments in existence; it is a defining motive in *The Iliad* (the praise poem of Achilles) and in Genesis (the praise poem of Yahweh). "Rühmen, das ists!" Rilke exclaims in the seventh sonnet to Orpheus. "To praise, that's it." Praise is what matters. Orpheus was called to praise, Rilke writes, "He was summoned for that, / and came to us like the ore from a stone's / silence." Smart thought much the same thing—"*For the story of Orpheus is of the truth*," he affirmed.

Praise lays claim to as much of the extant world as possible by uttering the names of things. It teaches us that "Exuberance is Beauty" (Blake), and it summons "the force that through the green fuse drives the flower" (Dylan Thomas). It would awaken matter and show us the true face of awe. It would transcend history and rename the world. As the West Indian poet Derek Walcott says in *The Antilles: Fragments of Epic Memory:*

> For every poet it is always morning in the world. History a forgotten insomniac night. History and elemental awe are always our early beginning, because the fate of poetry is to fall in love with the world, in spite of History.

Praise is a dream of transcending history, a motive from which one never fully recovers. It's a way of falling in love with the world again. It's a way of getting through grief to the other side. "I do what's in character," William Meredith writes in his elegy for John Berryman, "In Loving Memory of the Late Author of *Dream Songs*":

> I look for things
> to praise on the riverbanks and I praise them.
> We are all relics, of some great joy, wearing black.

I still remember the funny instilled joyousness I felt when I came across the title poem of Gerald Stern's book *Lucky Life* with its direct opening "Lucky life isn't one long string of horrors / and there are moments of peace, and pleasure, as I lie in between the blows," and its jubilant conclusion:

> Lucky life is like this. Lucky there is an ocean to come to.
> Lucky you can judge yourself in this water.
> Lucky the waves are cold enough to wash out the meanness.
> Lucky you can be purified over and over again.
> Lucky there is the same cleanliness for everyone.
> Lucky life is like that. Lucky life. Oh lucky life.
> Oh lucky lucky life. Lucky life.

"Lucky life" is a mantra here. Praise restores us to the world again, to our luckiness of being. That's why I thought of *Sonnets to Orpheus* and "Song of Myself," of the Canticles of Francis of Assisi and Adam's catalogs in Genesis, of Richard Wilbur's essay "Poetry and Happiness" and Stanley Kunitz's reminder that "the poem comes in the form of a blessing—*like rapture breaking through on the mind*," and even of a teenage boy encountering an untitled fragment from an eighteenth-century poem, when I came across W. H. Auden's statement in "Making, Knowing, and Judging":

> Whatever its actual content and overt interest, every poem is rooted in imaginative awe. Poetry can do a hundred and one things, delight, sadden, disturb, amuse, instruct—it may express every possible shade of emotion, and describe every conceivable kind of event, but there is only one thing that all poetry must do; it must praise all it can for being and for happening.

3

We live in a superficial, media-driven culture that often seems uncomfortable with true depths of feeling. Indeed, it seems as if our culture has become increasingly intolerant of that acute sorrow, that intense mental anguish and deep remorse which may be defined as grief. We want to medicate such sorrow away. We want to divide it into recognizable stages so that grief can be labeled, tamed, and put behind us. But poets have always celebrated grief as one of the deepest human emotions. To grieve is to lament, to let sorrow inhabit one's very being.

Robert Frost liked to distinguish between grievances (complaints) and griefs (sorrows). He even suggested that grievances, which are propagandistic, should be restricted to prose, "leaving poetry free to go its way in tears." Implicit in poetry is the notion that we are deepened by heartbreaks, that we are not so much diminished as enlarged by grief, by our refusal to vanish—to let others vanish—without leaving a verbal record. Poetry is a stubborn art. The poet is one who will not be reconciled, who is determined to leave a trace in words, to transform oceanic depths of feeling into the faithful nuances of art.

I was initiated into the poetry of grief—of raw, heroic, aboriginal grief—on a windy autumnal morning in late October 1968. I was eighteen years old. I knew I had found what I was unknowingly seeking on the day my freshman humanities teacher—a petite woman with an immense vocabulary, the only person I'd ever met who spoke in perfectly formed sentences—stood up in class and started talking about Achilles's desperate response to the death of his friend Patroclus. I felt something obscure opening inside me, I recognized some unknown, some unassuaged rage of feeling, a frenzied internal sobbing, a delirium of grief. I looked out the window and saw the mad leaves swirling and falling everywhere. I was transported.

Here is the passage in Richmond Lattimore's translation. It is from Book 18 of *The Iliad*. Nestor's son Antilochus has just given Achilles the message that his closest friend, his trusted ally and brother-in-arms, had been killed wearing Achilles's own armor. Now enemies were fighting over Patroclus's naked body:

> He spoke, and the black cloud of sorrow closed on
> Achilleus. In both hands he caught up the grimy dust, and
> poured it over his head and face, and fouled his handsome
> countenance, and the black ashes were scattered over his
> immortal tunic. And he himself, mightily in his might, in
> the dust lay at length, and took and tore at his hair with his
> hands, and defiled it.

My teacher must have gone on to talk about Achilles's feelings of guilt and shame, his deep sense of responsibility over his friend's death. This is a pivotal incident in *The Iliad* because it triggers Achilles's reentry into battle and therefore assures the destruction of Troy. It's the only way to account for his uncharacteristically savage revenge on Hector. But I couldn't follow closely what she was saying because some part of my mind was stuck on the primal image of Achilles smearing his face with dirt and tearing out his hair. I recognized the image from somewhere . . .

I found this passage so moving when I heard it read aloud in Lattimore's translation that I can only begin to imagine the impact and power that the dactylic hexameters of the ancient Greek must have had when a rhapsode recited them. It makes me feel bereft for the oral tradition poetry has lost. Nonetheless, years later I discovered this same passage recreated in Christopher Logue's free adaptation of Books 16–19 entitled *War Music,* and I was stunned by how effectively the translator captures Achilles' unbearable grief over the death of his friend. I still shudder over the description of Achilles hurling himself down to the ground. I feel it like a blow, as though someone has kicked me in the chest.

> Down on your knees, Achilles. Farther down.
> Now forward on your hands and put your face into the dirt,
> And scrub it to and fro.
> Grief has you by the hair with one
> And with the forceps of its other hand
> Uses your mouth to trowel the dogshit up;
> Watches you lift your arms to Heaven; and then
> Pounces and screws your nose into the filth.
> Gods have plucked drawstrings from your head,
> And from the template of your upper lip
> Modelled their bows.
> Not now. Not since
> Your grieving reaches out and pistol-whips
> That envied face, until
> Frightened to bear your black, backbreaking agony alone,
> You sank, throat back, thrown back, your voice
> Thrown out across the sea to reach your Source.

This passage is a crucial event in the larger epic, but it's also an embryonic lyric, like Helen's laments or the elegiac statements at Hector's funeral. The translator employs the directive voice of command, which gives a dramatic and even cinematic feeling to the scene—we can see what is happening—but also creates the sense of an enormous force overpowering Achilles. Logue punches the English monosyllables here, and he gets terrific effect from the jabbing short sentences. The command is so direct, the language so fierce and inescapable, one can only watch with fascinated horror as Achilles hurls himself down, first to the position of prayer, which can't help him, and then, even more abjectly, onto all fours, like an animal. Then he lies prostrate on the ground. Grief has taken him over so completely that it becomes a separate independent force, something that controls and dominates him from above. Each of its actions is decisive and seems almost self-consciously cruel, as if Grief is a person taking perverse pleasure in making Achilles suffer. We become voyeurs of his pain. The narrator is telling Achilles what is happening to him even as it is taking place, as if to say: Look, Achilles, first Grief is grabbing you by the hair with one hand and with the forceps (such a cool, clinical word) of its other hand using your mouth to trowel up nothing less than dogshit, then it stands by and watches indifferently while you cry out to deaf Heaven, and then it takes the opportunity of your weakness to pounce down and screw your nose into the filth. The cruelty of the way Grief exploits Achilles's vulnerability is almost unbearable.

In fact, the epic hero, the warrior, the griever is brought so far down by his grief that he becomes like a dead man himself. Many commentators have pointed out that Homer mingles the language of mourning with the language of death in this passage. Defiling one's head with dust is a sign of grief but also of death on the battlefield. The very next passage of the epic presents an image of lamenting women, another indication that Achilles has assumed the position of death. Patroclus had died wearing Achilles's armor, now Achilles would join Patroclus...

I'm struck by how effectively Logue moves between an Augustan language, which he apparently adapts and updates from Pope's translation of *The Iliad* ("Gods have plucked drawstrings from your head") and a harsh twentieth-century vernacular, which he seems to have learned from the English war poets, from Wilfred Owen, Siegfried Sassoon, Robert Graves, and Keith Douglas. This might have created an anachronistic feeling (one doesn't automatically think of Grief pistol-whipping Achilles as the natural idiom of *The Iliad*), but instead creates an eerie feeling of recurrence and timelessness. After all, the war poets were the true poetic heirs to this epic grief. I think of a grief so terrible it will always need voicing, so terrifying it will always seek expression, so primitive it will always throw itself back to an original source. And the language of this grief is formalized as poetry.

At eighteen I was riveted by sorrow, by the anguished poetry of loss, and was never afterward the same. "In every work of genius we recognize our own rejected thoughts," Emerson claimed, "they come back to us with a certain alienated majesty." It was as if a proto-lyric from Book 18 of *The Iliad* had opened up some grief inside me I didn't realize I had already experienced, as if I had recognized the alienated majesty of Achilles's feelings in advance.

It was sixteen years later that my closest friend died. He was thirty-seven; I was thirty-four. We had bonded immediately when we first met, and our friendship had soared during the years we taught together at a university in Detroit. Then one day I drove him to the hospital with an intense stomachache, and two days later he was diagnosed with terminal liver cancer. It seemed impossible that the most charmed and charming of all my friends, the one luckiest in his personality, could have turned into the unluckiest one of all. Over the course of a summer I watched him getting progressively thinner and thinner, getting more and more desperate. I watched him aging about fifty years; I watched him dying. On the day of his death I thought of the soul flying out of the body and remembered the image of Achilles dropping down to his knees and then scrubbing his face back and forth in the dirt, back and forth...

During the next year I found great consolation in many elegies, which do what Freud calls "the work of mourning," ritualizing grief and thereby making it more bearable. The great elegy touches the unfathomable and originates in unacceptable loss. It allows us to experience mortality. It turns loss into remembrance ("I put down these memorandums of my affections," John Clare wrote) and finds a way to deliver an inheritance. Here is a key stanza from Hart Crane's moving poem "Praise for an Urn," dedicated to the memory of Ernest Nelson:

His thoughts, delivered to me
From the white coverlet and pillow,
I see now, were inheritances—
Delicate riders of the storm.

The elegy opens up a space for retrospect ("I see now"), for over-whelming personal feeling, and it drives a wordless anguish toward verbal articulation.

It also establishes a precise relationship between the bereaved mourner and the beloved dead one. I felt the importance of this acutely because I understood that we have no adequate language for the kind of male friendship I had with Dennis Turner. There was such deep tenderness and sympathy between us—we played pickup basketball together and talked about Jacques Lacan, with whom he had studied; we talked about film noir, about our childhood girlfriends. . . . Our friendship was profound, but it was not heroic, it was not sexual, and it was not familial. "Friendship is the *anomalous* relation," David Halperin observes: "It exists outside the more thoroughly codified social networks forged by kinship and sexual ties; it is 'interstitial in the social structure' of most Western countries."

After my friend died I thought of the closing lines from Theodore Roethke's "Elegy for Jane" ("My Student, Thrown by a Horse"):

Over this damp grave I speak the words of my love:
I, with no rights in this matter,
Neither father nor lover.

There's a fine pun on the word "rights" (rites) here. I, too, felt I had no rights or rites in the matter. The anomaly of male friendship left me alone with my grief, and therefore it was only by immersing myself in many elegies—in Milton's "Lycidas," in Tennyson's *In Memoriam,* in Yeats's "In Memory of Major Robert Gregory"—that I could start to come to terms with what had happened. I was living in Detroit and thus found special consoling resonance in the elegiac poems written by the great poets of Detroit—in Philip Levine's deeply elegiac book for his family, *1933;* in Robert Hayden's overarching "Elegies for Paradise Valley" with their persistent *ubi sunt* theme (*Oh, where are they now?* these poems keep asking); in L. E. Sissman's ironic and heartbreaking book of self-elegies, *Dying: An Introduction,* which was folded into his collected poems, *Hello, Darkness.* I, too, was greeting the darkness and so I threw myself into books that were filled with an apocalyptic planetary grief such as Galway Kinnell's *The Book of Nightmares,* W. S. Merwin's *The*

Lice, and Stephen Berg's *Grief.* Requiems greeted me everywhere. "I have lost him," Achilles would confess to Patroclus's ghost. It was true; he had. One never doubts the intensity or the sincerity of that loss. One never doubts the true richness of feeling.

The sense of overwhelming personal loss that powers the poetry of lamentation seems to exist in all languages and in all poetries. One finds it in Hebrew, in Chinese, in Sanskrit, in Zulu. The Egyptian Pyramid Texts include species of the funeral song (elegy) as well as examples of songs of praise to the king (ode) and the invocation to the gods (hymn). The word *elegy* derives from the Greek *elegeia,* or "lament." It was among the first forms of the ancients, though in Greek literature it refers to a specific verse form as well as the emotions conveyed by it. It was always chanted aloud.

The Greek lyric, like the Hebrew and the Egyptian, like all poetry, has its roots in religion, and the earliest poems seem to have been composed for ritual occasions of celebration and mourning. Thus the poetry of lamentation and the poetry of praise seem to have arisen at the same time and may always have gone hand in hand. They are two aspects of sacred mystery. "Distinctly praise the years," Hart Crane writes in the last section of "For the Marriage of Faustus and Helen." "Only in the sphere of praise may Lamentation / walk," Rilke declares in the eighth sonnet to Orpheus.

We can only understand what we can name. Longinus calls sublimity "the echo of greatness of spirit." This is our joining with the great, and it has a quality of supreme feeling, of straining toward the outer limits, of rising to a threshold of greater consciousness. But what was for Longinus an experience of joy and exaltation has been for many moderns an experience of extreme aphasia and disorientation, of nausea and existential anguish. *Confusion* is the preeminent response to the incomprehensibility of the sublime, Schiller argues. "For every seeing soul, there are two absorbing facts," Emerson claims, "*I and the Abyss.*" The experience of looking over the edge of that abyss can be dizzying, especially when one locates the abyss as something that exists inside us. Poetry is the literature of dizzying heights and lowly depths, of inwardness plunged and brought back to earth.

I have sometimes felt the experience of poetry is so intrinsic to the language in which it is written that it can never be truly translated. And yet I cannot forget that one of my deepest initiations into poetry took place when I felt a terrifying rapture echoing down the centuries in the translated cadences of another language. I recognized at some level that Homer had achieved what Keats calls a power "to see as a God sees." He could speak the language of the gods which Santayana calls "the height of poetry." He could discover and embody one's own feelings writ large. I looked down from that height and experienced a hero pouring dust over his head and face, baptizing himself with black ashes.

I am grateful that *The Iliad* opened up a space in me that made it possible to name what I would feel. The overwhelming extremity of Achilles's grief over the death of his friend, which so troubled Plato because of its irrational and excessive nature, was precisely what cried out to me. I loved how unflinching it was. I recognized its demonic power, its outsize emotion and epic grief. I was wounded by its truth. And I was also healed by it.

5

At the White Heat

I want to look at a few poems that seem to me unflinching and even ruthlessly authentic. "Dare you see a soul *at the White Heat*?" Emily Dickinson asks. This is a recurrent dare in lyric poetry from Sappho to Christopher Smart, from Pindar to Hart Crane and Theodore Roethke. A good question in a prosaic world. It also suggests something of the risk attached to getting involved with poetry where one is repeatedly confronting the soul of others at the white heat and, much more dangerously, confronting one's own soul. The stakes are high: we not only "find ourselves" in poetry, we also lose ourselves to it.

Dickinson herself could never quite understand why the most intense human experiences had to be relegated to the margins of human society. I suspect she read poetry every day, and wrote it, because she needed a daily dose of the ecstasy poetry provides: "I find ecstasy in living," she wrote to Thomas Wentworth Higginson. I believe she understated the case. It's striking that Emerson, who knew himself to be a poet at heart ("I am born a poet, of a low class without doubt yet a poet. This is my nature and vocation"), treated literature largely as a stimulus for rapture and declared, "Life is an ecstasy." I have sometimes thought that Dickinson's life might have been different—and the history of American poetry profoundly changed—if she had sent her poems to Emerson rather than to Higginson. After all, we know how enthusiastically Emerson responded to Whitman. He almost certainly would have welcomed the extravagant Dickinsonian note:

> Take all away from me, but leave me Ecstasy,
> And I am richer then than all my Fellow Men—

Like Emerson, who called the poets "liberating gods," Dickinson understood that ecstasy finds a natural outlet in poetry, and she had a whole repertoire of capitalized poetic terms for rapturous experience. "Transport" was one of those terms ("To learn the Transport by the Pain" was one of the lessons she taught herself); "Joy" was another; "Exultation" was a third; yet a fourth was "Bliss." "I had a daily Bliss," she declares in one poem. She could never understand why an overwhelming bliss—what one of her poems calls "A perfect—paralyzing Bliss"—had to be abstemiously portioned out:

> Why Bliss so scantily disburse—
> Why Paradise defer—
> Why Floods be served to Us—in Bowls—
> I speculate no more—

In *The Pleasure of the Text,* his speculative book on the erotics of reading, Roland Barthes writes of "the asocial character of bliss" which occasions "the abrupt loss of sociality." I suggest that lyric poetry moves beyond speculation to give us the particulars of asocial bliss and despair. The Polish poet Wisława Szymborska might be speaking for any number of lyric poets, and perhaps for lyric poetry itself, when she confesses, "My identifying features / are rapture and despair." The experience of seeing a soul at its white heat is so discomfiting that it ruptures the carefully constructed societal frame and puts us in another relationship to the world. The poem of bliss scandalizes with its ability to indict the social realm for deferring paradise and serving up floods in bowls.

Here is a love poem by the Israeli poet Yehuda Amichai. "A Pity. We Were Such a Good Invention" first appeared in Amichai's book *Now in the Storm, Poems, 1963–1968.* I first discovered it twenty-five years ago in a cheap paperback edition of Amichai's *Selected Poems* published in a series of Modern European Poets. I quote it in Assia Gutmann's lively English version.

A Pity. We Were Such a Good Invention

They amputated
Your thighs off my hips.
As far as I'm concerned
They are all surgeons. All of them.

They dismantled us
Each from the other.
As far as I'm concerned
They are all engineers. All of them.

A pity. We were such a good
And loving invention.
An aeroplane made from a man and wife.
Wings and everything.
We hovered a little above the earth.

We even flew a little.

This poem is remarkable for its directness and profound simplicity, its unique mixture of the erotic and the political, its subtle tone of outrage and nostalgia. As a love poem it's worthy to stand beside John Donne's "The Good-Morrow" and "The Canonization." Donne was an early influence on Amichai, and this poem has some of the qualities, though presented retrospectively, of "For God's sake hold your tongue, and let me love."

I want to tease out a few of the implications of this affecting little poem I am reading from left to right rather than from right to left. But I note the greater terseness and compression of the Hebrew original which consists of the title and a mere thirty-five words, divided into eleven lines and three stanzas. By contrast, the English is practically discursive, since it contains more than twice as many words broken into fourteen lines and four stanzas. There is also something radically contemporaneous in the way Amichai uses biblical language for an apparently secular subject. It's characteristic of him to reverse terms and treat the religious idiom as secular and the erotic terms as sacred. As he puts it in "A Tourist,"

> Long ago Hebrew used to be
> God's slang in those streets.
> Now I use it to speak
> holy words of passion.

One kind of love poem: a declaration of holiness that puts the lovers beyond the social pale.

The opening gambit of Amichai's poem is the long two-part title. "A Pity. We Were Such a Good Invention" is summary (something has already happened, already ended) and immediately puts us in the range of the vernacular—the way a speaker might shake his head and say, "It's a pity that..." or "It's a pity because..." Benjamin and Barbara Harshav lose this quality when they render the title as one sentence, "Pity, We Were a Good Invention." It's as if pity were being addressed here. But the correct summary renders both a feeling (pathos) and a definition (what we were). Its understated emphasis—"we were such a good invention"—seems modest; after all, the poem isn't entitled, "A Tragedy. We Were a Fabulous Creation." But that modesty is deceptive. The title is addressed to the beloved as well as to an open readership, to anyone who will listen. It's wistful about what "we" were. But the poem itself is then ruthless about what "they" did.

The first two lines immediately rivet the feeling by addressing the lover directly. The wistfulness of the title completely gives way to an opening dramatic utterance—a horrifying first statement—that violently characterizes and even embodies the violence of what has been done to the lovers by "them." The image is nearly unbearable because so castrating:

> They amputated
> Your thighs from my hips.

The pronoun "they" seems to sum up all the implacable impersonal force of the collective. "They" are nameless in their inhuman treatment of the couple. We have an image of sexual union, of erotic connection, of two lovers surgically being separated from each other. The image is metonymic: "your thighs" and "my hips" stand in for the lovers. "Amputated" is the conclusive word here because it is so cutting, so violent and irreversible. No wonder the speaker decides (and he is careful to frame this as his own point of view) "They are all surgeons." Stephen Mitchell renders this more literally as "they're always / doctors." I like the word "always" because it suggests that what they *did* will forevermore define what they *are*. But I also prefer the acid sarcasm of calling the doctors "surgeons." These physicians, trained in the healing arts, are cold operators. No one is exempt. The speaker makes sure to include all of them, and the indictment is therefore large and socially inclusive.

The doctors become engineers in the second stanza as the speaker seeks to find another term for the ruthless efficiency of the intervening society. I note that engineers are those who apply scientific principles to practical ends of design and construction. Here they have efficiently, even scientifically, taken apart the lovers in a methodical misuse of their power. We have moved from an invasive surgery to a mechanical dismantling.

Against which: an airplane. This poem turns like a sonnet and the title takes on full significance as the speaker himself teases out the meaning of a good and now "loving" invention. Think of Adam and Eve brought together in an image of physical love, of two bodies merged to create a third thing, a new "invention." Here the lovers are not akin to "stiffe twin compasses," as in Donne's famous simile, but, appropriate to their century, "an airplane made from a man and wife." Amichai finds an image for the lovers, as Donne did, in terms of our modernity. He plays with that image and extends it a bit ("Wings and everything," wings and all), therefore moving it in the direction of the metaphysical conceit, which Eliot defines in his essay "The Metaphysical Poets" as the elaboration "of a figure of speech to the furthest stage to which ingenuity can carry it." But Amichai's ingenuity doesn't take him to the furthest or most extreme development—it is brought up short by the poignance of the memory. There is a sad, ironic, outraged, bitter, and wistful tone associated with the homely modern invention of a hovering aircraft.

It's worth pointing out that the narration of the poem reverses the actual chronological sequence of events reported. The poem starts off with the image of two lovers torn apart and concludes with the image of what they created together. It would be a different poem—and a less complex one—if it commenced with an image of two lovers as an airplane and concluded with its surgical dismantlement. The destroyers do not get the last word here. The final memory of the poem, understated and passionate, may be effectively poised against the violent and surgical destruction by the unspecified representatives of the social order. It stands in the speaker's mind as an image of radiance beyond time.

"Wings and everything." The wings serve as a wistful reminder of the power and damage of eros. When desire takes over the body, Sappho says, "It puts the heart in my chest on wings." As the poet and classicist Anne Carson explains in *Eros the Bittersweet:*

> Wings, in traditional poetry, are the mechanism by which Eros swoops upon the unsuspecting lover to wrest control of his person and personality. Wings are an instrument of damage and a symbol of irresistible power. When you fall in love, change sweeps through you on wings and you cannot help but lose your grip on that cherished entity, yourself.

Wings are the sign of a power that would make the lovers give up their reason, their reasons, and thus give up themselves. Wings are the signal of an uncontrollable force that would put them beyond the pale, above the earth.

"A Pity. We Were Such a Good Invention" ends with an image of flight. It's not a sensation of great height—this airplane only flies a little—but it does give a feeling of liftoff, of rising. There is a sense of the transcendental associated with the image of flight. I am reminded of how in his journals Emerson cites a woman who says that transcendentalism means going "*A little beyond.*" At the end of Amichai's poem we are left with the poignant sensation of two lovers who for a while hovered together over earthly ground, going a little beyond—in transport, in rapture, in bliss.

The scandal of poetry: sacred pleasure, the words of praise coming alive in your mouth, in your body, the euphoria of flight. It is always shocking, always transgressive, to call the words of passion holy. But poets will never be deterred from this intransigence. No governmental regulations, no religious strictures, can stop them from swooning in words (many have tried), from writing fierce devotional hymns to the beloved. The precise, extravagant, asocial, and testimonial lyrics continue without abatement from the Song of Songs to the automatic writings of the French surrealists. Rapture testifies. "Love poems were breaking out all over my body," Pablo Neruda said about writing his early book *Twenty Love Poems and a Song of Despair*. It's one of the characteristic claims of the lyric poet. "This is true bliss, and I confess / There is no other happiness," Thomas Carew concludes in "The Second Rapture."

Here is Paul Éluard's songlike poem "L'amoureuse" in Samuel Beckett's splendid translation from the French:

Lady Love
She is standing on my lids
And her hair is in my hair
She has the colour of my eye
She has the body of my hand
In my shade she is engulfed
As a stone against the sky

She will never close her eyes
And she does not let me sleep
And her dreams in the bright day
Make the suns evaporate
And me laugh cry and laugh
Speak when I have nothing to say

Éluard's poem exemplifies the radiant presence that seems to flood the fulfilled (and the fulfilling) love poem. That flooding is a possession so overwhelming that it must occasion a change in the speaker. Such transformation cries out to be voiced, and it motivates the poem in the direction of pure song. Note the progression in Éluard's lyric from love *is* ("She is standing on my lids") to love *has* ("She has the colour of my eye") to love *does* ("And she does not let me sleep") to love *makes* ("And her dreams in the bright day / Make the suns evaporate"). That visionary obliteration of the daylight world, the daylight mind, completely undoes the speaker and occasions a stunning joy, a giddy breakdown: "And me laugh cry and laugh..." I delight in the last line—"Speak when I have nothing to say"—that shows an interior restraint giving way. The speaker is so deliciously amazed and awestruck by what has happened to him that he breaks into involuntary speech. He bursts into song. And song is praise.

There seems to be a shadow of desire, a shadow of the beloved, hovering over every successful love poem. Love crops up so often in lyric poetry because it is the soul's primary way of going out to another, of freeing itself through another from the pressures and distractions of ordinary existence. It is the soul's preferred mode of attainment. "In other words," Joseph Brodsky writes in "Altra Ego," an essay that makes a careful distinction between the beloved and the Muse (the beloved dies, the Muse finds another mouthpiece in the next generation), "love is a metaphysical affair whose goal is either accomplishing or liberating one's soul: winnowing it from the chaff of existence. That is and always has been the core of lyric poetry."

I feel the shadow of the beloved looming over the love poem. The final loss and disappearance of that beloved leads to a poetry of abandonment and disconsolation (Philip Larkin's late dejected lyrics of lovelessness come to mind). When the beloved visits the poem we get a poetry of joyous presence, a poem that blots out the sun with brightness, like Éluard's. "The *brio* of the text," Roland Barthes writes, "is its *will to bliss*." There is a poetry fueled by an excess of that will, a poetry of the intensest memories and desires. It is unremitting and feeds off extravagance. The brio of this poetry—the love poem of attainment—is its relentless pursuit of vertiginous bliss.

Ethnographic examples abound of how repetitions induce transport and bliss: think of magic spells and erotic charms, obsessive chants, hypnotic incantations. "It must not be forgotten that for centuries poetry was used for purposes of enchantment," Paul Valéry reminds us. The devices of archaic poetry have always infused poetic forms, even (and perhaps especially) of the most cultivated and aristocratic kinds. There have always been poets who energize and ruffle the forms with repetitions so extravagant they incite an answering ecstasy. I am thinking of the erotic poem that hypnotizes words into repetitions eccentric and formal. The poem electrically charged into formal procedures. The poem of what Vladimir Nabokov calls "aesthetic bliss."

Here is Sonnet 31, a poem of relentless joy by the Italian poet Guittone d'Arezzo (1230–1294), first in the original Italian and then in Michael Spiller's literal translation:

Tuttor ch'eo dirò gioi, gioiva cosa,
intenderete che di voi favello,
che gioia sete di beltà gioiosa,
e gioia di piacer gioioso e bello:
　　e gioia in cui gioioso avenir posa
gioi d'adornezze e gioi di cor asnello,
gioia in cui viso è gioi tant'amorosa,
ched è gioiosa gioi mirare in ello.
　　Gioi di volere e gioi di pensamento
e gioi di dire e gioi di far gioioso,
e gioi d'onni gioioso movimento.
　　Perch'eo, gioiosa gioi, sì disioso
di voi mi trovo, che mai gioi non sento,
se'n vostra gioi il meo cor non riposo.

(Whenever I say "joy," you thing of joy, you will understand that I speak of you, for you are a joy of joyful beauty and a joy of joyful and fair pleasure;
　　and joy in which a joyful future is, joy from your beauties, joy from your slim body, joy in which so much loving joy is seen that it is a joyful joy to wonder at it.
　　Joy of will and joy of thought, and joy of speech and joy of making joy, and joy of every movement full of joy.
　　So I, my joyful joy, am so unsettled by you that I never feel joy unless my heart is quieted in your joy.)

Guittone d'Arezzo's poem is a rhapsodic sonnet. The sonnet form was invented in southern Italy around 1235 or so. Note how early Guittone was writing in the tradition. From its inception the fourteen-line rhyming poem has been particularly amenable to romantic pleading and learned argument, to forensic pattern, but this poem demonstrates that from the beginning it was also used to create a wild disturbance within the prescribed form. For example, it helps us to understand Petrarch, the greatest maker of sonnets who ever lived, if we think of a poetry so incited by desire that it tries to seduce and incite that same state in the beloved, and, by implication, in the reader.

Thinking about this sonnet I am reminded that Robert Graves playfully describes the symptoms of love as "a universal migraine, / A bright stain on the vision / Blotting out reason" ("Symptoms of Love"). In effect, Guittone uses a highly reasonable, a toughly reasoning, poetic form to blot out reason itself. Exuberant joy is irrational, and wild excitement creates an incoherence within the poem. This sonnet does frame a sort of argument from the initial "Whenever I say 'joy'" to the concluding "So I, my joyful joy . . ." But the speaking of joy is so loud in this poem, the sound of the word *joy* (*gioi*) rebounds through the poem with such ecstatic volubility, that the poem gives way to an overmastering emotion.

The whole poem consists of three sentences, and its rhythm is incantatory. Listen to the hypnotic rhyming words, the lining up of consonants (*l*s and *s*s and *n*s) and vowels (*a*s and *o*s), and you start to feel a poetic trance coming on: *cosa, favello, gioiosa, bello, posa, asnello, amorosa, ello, pensamento, gioioso, movimento, disioso, sento, riposo.* Speaking of Dante's use of terza rima, Osip Mandelstam said that Italian is like baby talk because everything rhymes with everything else. One starts to feel that here the joyous baby talk of desire threatens the container because it is irrational and scarcely containable.

From the Song of Songs to *Jubilate Agno* and "Song of Myself," the catalog has been used as a form of praise. The catalog of joys is a particularly Adamic way of naming and detailing that praise. "Energy is eternal delight," Blake teaches us. The catalog almost always stretches into long lines that go beyond the range of normal speech into prophetic utterance. For that reason the catalog of joys threatens to rupture the sonnet form in Guittone's poem. The catalog builds to such a high crescendo that the syntax starts to collapse and cause a complete meltdown of the dramatic utterance. The list culminates in the eleventh line—"e gioi d'onni gioioso movimento" ("and joy of every movement full of joy"). The poem takes a final turn, a last swerve, with the word "Perch'eo" in the next line, which brings itself back from a joyful incoherence, asserting the mind's determination to contain unbounded energy.

Guittone has generously given us in Sonnet 31 a poem of pure Mozartian joy. It is completely unabashed about itself, unashamed of its own joyousness. It dances and dances in the ear. It sings and stuns the mind with extravagant repetitions. The sound of joy repeating and repeating seems to career wildly ahead of the thought behind this poem, rushing ahead of the sense. It has a tickling uncontrolled energy. The escalating rhythms of the poem create a sensation of enchantment, a rhetoric of rapture. It lets itself go. And then it reels itself back from the brink in a moment of joy at last becalmed. Rhythm and pattern—insistent verbal repetitions—evoke sexual love in this poem, actual physical attainment. And here I am reminded that Barthes's word, "*jouissance,*" "bliss," also means "orgasm," *coming.*

Desire testifies. Joy declares itself. "Whenever I say 'joy,'" Guittone writes, "you will understand that I speak of you." Paul Éluard inscribes a moment of writing as speaking "when I have nothing to say." Petrarch points to "the sound of the sighs that nourished my heart." Shakespeare unlocks his "tongue-tied" speech that breaks loose in a "saucy bark" (Sonnet 80). René Char summarizes: "*The poem is the realized love of desire still desiring*" ("The Formal Share"). I am thinking of the love poem as a realized site of such desire still desiring, a place of attainment, "a room of marvels" (André Breton), a writing that requires a speech beyond speech, a saucy bark, or a loud song. There is a specialized version of the love poem that takes drastic measures to mesmerize time, to induce euphoria, that keeps opening up and turning back on itself to create a sensation of enchantment. This poetry takes rhythmic measure (and "measure" is one of the oldest terms for poetry) to imagine a world beyond measure.

There is a poetry driven to distraction by the unfathomable depths of desire. "Desire, yes, always," Breton writes. Such poetry will always outstrip causality and rise beyond ordinary logic. Time and again lyric poets have testified to a rapture incommensurate with common sense, with normative circumstance, with a regulating (and regulatory) social world. "What shall I do, by nature and trade / a singing creature," the

Russian poet Marina Tsvetaeva asks, "as I go over the bridge of my en-
chanted / visions, that cannot be weighed in a / world that deals only in
weights and measures?"

Tsvetaeva's bridge, like Hart Crane's, is a site of crossing into an
atemporal realm, and it makes her an outcast from a bewilderingly mate-
rial (and materialistic) socioeconomic world. "We are poets, which has
the sound of outcast," she writes. She wasn't posturing. (Tsvetaeva puts
it more shockingly when she declares that "All poets are Jews in a Chris-
tian world." Or, more literally, "All poets are kikes.") Being a poet (by
temperament and craft) certainly cost Tsvetaeva, whose "enchanted vi-
sions" isolated her so terribly from the practical world. Her exile was
doomed, her return to Russia suicidal. The last stanza of her poem "The
Poet" consists of two rhetorical questions fueled by desperation. She is
beside herself—and also proud:

> What shall I do, singer and first-born, in a
> world where the deepest black is grey,
> and inspiration is kept in a thermos?
> with all this immensity
> in a measured world?
> *(translated by Elaine Feinstein)*

Tsvetaeva's complaint of a surrounding world where inspiration is bot-
tled in a thermos is painfully reminiscent of Dickinson's bewilderment at
a society where floods are served up in bowls. In her memoir, "Mother
and Music," Tsvetaeva says that the reason there cannot be "too much"
of the lyrical is because the lyrical is itself the "too much." Immensity
declares itself as a fullness that overflows, as an overbrimming romantic
song, as an inner space breaking loose to obliterate temporal circum-
stance, as an asocial bliss. It puts language under stress and creates a deep
rupture in the social fabric. The poem of immensity is an act of *beyond-
ing,* and it re-creates a transcendental idiom. "A poet is carried far away
by speech," Tsvetaeva writes: "the way of comets / is the poet's way."

Here is a love poem by the most openhearted of French surrealist
poets, Robert Desnos, that seems to me entirely carried away by speech
toward a beloved other, taking the comet's path away from the daylight
mind and into the night mind, and thereby giving full-throated voice to

the immensity of desire. I first read this enchanted poem twenty-five years ago in William Kulik's volume of Desnos translations, *The Voice*. It has haunted me ever since.

The Voice of Robert Desnos
So like a flower and a current of air
the flow of water fleeting shadows
the smile glimpsed at midnight this excellent evening
so like every joy and every sadness
it is the midnight past lifting its naked body above belfries and
    poplars
I call to me those lost in the fields
old skeletons young oaks cut down
scraps of cloth rotting on the ground and linen drying in farm
    country
I call tornadoes and hurricanes
storms typhoons cyclones
tidal waves
earthquakes
I call the smoke of volcanoes and the smoke of cigarettes
the rings of smoke from expensive cigars
I call lovers and loved ones
I call the living and the dead
I call gravediggers I call assassins
I call hangmen pilots bricklayers architects
assassins
I call the flesh
I call the one I love
I call the one I love
I call the one I love
the jubilant midnight unfolds its satin wings
    and perches on my bed
the belfries and the poplars bend to my wish
the former collapse the latter bow down
those lost in the fields are found in finding me
the old skeletons are revived by my voice
the young oaks cut down are covered with foliage

the scraps of cloth rotting on the ground and in the earth
    snap to at the sound of my voice like a flag of rebellion
the linen drying in farm country clothes adorable women
    whom I do not adore
who come to me
obeying my voice, adoring
tornadoes revolve in my mouth
hurricanes if it is possible redden my lips
storms roar at my feet
typhoons if it is possible ruffle me
I get drunken kisses from the cyclones
the tidal waves come to die at my feet
the earthquakes do not shake me but fade completely
    at my command
the smoke of volcanoes clothes me with its vapors
and the smoke of cigarettes perfumes me
and the rings of cigar smoke crown me
loves and love so long hunted find refuge in me
lovers listen to my voice
the living and the dead yield to me and salute me
    the former coldly the latter warmly
the gravediggers abandon the hardly-dug graves
    and declare that I alone may command their nightly work
the assassins greet me
the hangmen invoke the revolution
invoke my voice
invoke my name
the pilots are guided by my eyes
the bricklayers are dizzied listening to me
the architects leave for the desert
the assassins bless me
flesh trembles when I call

the one I love is not listening
the one I love does not hear
the one I love does not answer.

(translated by William Kulik)

Reading Desnos's poem I am reminded of Keats's touchstone declaration, "I am certain of nothing but of the holiness of the Heart's affections and the truth of Imagination." What the heart holds most sacred in Desnos's poem is the unattainable beloved, a woman who takes on near-mythical proportions. What the imagination seizes as truth is a lost, dying, and murdered world apocalyptically summoned back and then persuasively transformed into a living realm of the poet's own devising. "The Imagination may be compared to Adam's dream," Keats goes on to say: "he awoke and found it truth." The imagination in Desnos's poem "speaks surrealistically," to use Breton's phrase, because Adam's dream is a poetic reverie of the night mind. He wakes not to the sunlit morning, but to the "jubilant midnight," triumphant hour of epiphany. He can only name and control what he discovers by recourse to an irrational or unconscious dream logic and language. Here Keats was again ahead of the surrealists: "I have never yet been able to perceive how any thing can be known for truth by consequitive reasoning."

The Orphic voice of desire in Desnos's poem charms the sleeping world into responding to it. It summons the force of "yesterday's midnight lifting its naked torso above belfries [a religious emblem] and poplars [a natural one]." Everything moves and flows in this poem in response to the voice itself, which is compared to a flower (blooming open and blossoming outward) and a current of air (the romantic breeze of inspiration that carries the breath into the universe). The Orphic voice is so ravenously driven by desire for the irretrievable beloved (Eurydice) that it defies space and time. It moves through a shadowy underworld ("the flow of water fleeting shadows") which it immediately claims and renames as an astonishing or excellent evening. It's noteworthy that the air is ghostly and filled with smoke ("I call the smoke of volcanoes and the smoke of cigarettes") that blots out the ordinary daylight world, replacing it with a mythical present ("the jubilant midnight unfolds its satin wings and perches on my bed"). The visionary voice instigates a force—a libidinized music—that re-creates the world to the heart's desire; it merges the miniature and the gigantic, subject and object, and it summons builders (bricklayers, architects) and destroyers (hangmen, assassins), lovers and loved ones, living and dead. Most of all, the voice defiantly sets itself against stasis, which is death, and creates a surplus of images that overflows writing.

The voice in Desnos's poem inscribes a profound longing and desire. I note that the very nature of voice in written poetry must be metaphorical, it cannot be literal. The material qualities and acoustic range of voice (tone, timbre, volume, register) can only be invoked, metaphorized, inscribed. "The desire for live voice dwells in all poets," Paul Zumthor writes in *Oral Poetry,* "but it is in exile in writing." And yet I'm not sure that this article of faith about the inscribed voice in exile entirely applies to Desnos, the prototypical surrealist talker, who could blur the boundary between speaking and writing by erasing the line between waking and dreaming. Here is Louis Aragon's vivid account of the poet putting himself into a self-induced hypnotic trance:

> In a café, amid the sound of voices, the bright light, the jostlings, Robert Desnos need only close his eyes, and he talks, and among the steins, the saucers, the whole ocean collapses with its prophetic racket and its vapours decorated with long oriflammes. However little those who interrogate this amazing sleeper incite him, prophecy, the tone of magic, of revelation, of revolution, the tone of the fanatic and the apostle, immediately appear. Under other conditions, Desnos, were he to cling to this delirium, would become the leader of a religion, the founder of a city, the tribune of a people in revolt.

Desnos could apparently simulate these trances ("Is simulating a thing any different from thinking it?" Aragon asked. "And what one thinks exists"). He could select details from his dreams and give prophetic frenzy a lineated structure on the page. "Thought takes place in the mouth," Tristan Tzara claims, but it also takes place in the shaping hand that gives form to the disturbance. (Aragon: "We saw, for example, a written image which first presented itself with the characteristic of the fortuitous, the arbitrary, reach our senses, lose its verbal aspect to assume those fixed phenomenological realities which we had always believed impossible to provoke.") Desnos himself would come to believe that poetry should be "delirious and lucid." In his late "Reflections on Poetry" he declared:

It seems to me that beyond Surrealism there is something very mysterious to be dealt with, that beyond automatism there is the intentional, that beyond poetry there is the poem, that beyond poetry received there is poetry imposed, that beyond free poetry there is the free poet.

Thinking about the nature of voice in "The Voice of Robert Desnos" I recall Sharon Cameron's formulation in *Lyric Time,* based primarily on reading Emily Dickinson, that "Lyric speech might be described as the way we would talk in dreams if we could convert the phantasmagoria there into words." The loss of literal voice in lyric is more than compensated for by a celebration of textuality, by the triumph of written imagination. ("The imagination is perhaps about to reclaim its rights," Breton proclaimed.) Desnos's verbal eroticism creates an aura of enchantment, a speech beyond speech, a prophetic language, and his strongly surrealist technique creates an access through the page to the back of the brain, to the unconscious mind. Like Whitman in his marvelous poem "The Sleepers" ("I wander all night in my vision," Whitman begins), Desnos has found a viable passageway to oracular experience and thus creates art over what otherwise cannot be said. Like Whitman, he thinks at dream speed and seems to let the night mind spiral out into the night itself.

Here is his late poem "The Voice":

A voice, a voice from so far away
It no longer makes the ears tingle.
A voice like a muffled drum
Still reaches us clearly.

Though it seems to come from the grave
It speaks only of summer and spring.
It floods the body with joy.
It lights the lips with a smile.

I listen. It is simply a human voice
Which passes over the noise of life and its battles
The crash of thunder and the murmur of gossip.

And you? Don't you hear it?
It says "The pain will soon be over"
It says "The happy season is near."

Don't you hear it?
                    (translated by William Kulik)

I hear in this poem Desnos's characteristic clairvoyance, his affirmative presence, his radiant desire to transfigure pain and prophesy happiness seemingly from beyond the grave. But I also hear the profound anxiety of that last twice-repeated question, "Don't you hear it?" The writer who wrote this knew that he was going to die. The poem was included in *Contrée,* the last book that Desnos published before he was arrested by the Gestapo.

In "The Voice of Robert Desnos" the poet gives us a voice so driven to distraction by desire that it can only express itself through what Roman Jakobson calls "the incantatory function of language." He creates an alternative world through the powers of incantation, and those incantations are delivered formally (not haphazardly). The repetition of the phrase "I call" (or as Bill Zavatsky translates it, "I'm calling") is meant to produce magical effects. Longinus treated anaphora—that is, the repetition of a word or phrase at the beginning of successive sentences—as an imitative action and a key feature of the sublime. Certainly that's true here as Desnos's voice crosses a threshold into a visionary world which it itself creates. The incantatory voice becomes the monument to a dream state, to a world outside the material one. And it is only reeled back to rude reality by the glaring absence and intractability of the beloved.

The Orphic voice is a sign of poetic vocation. Orphic ambition is given a precise name in this poem: "The Voice of Robert Desnos." It seems to me always a little ironic and (intentionally) funny when a poet narcissistically uses his or her own name in the title of a poem, drawing attention to the conventional divide between author and subject, writer and speaker. To do so is always to split oneself off, to say with Rimbaud, "Je est un autre": "I is another." (One of the most pleasurable instances of this I can think of is the Hungarian poet Attila József's love poem to himself; it's entitled "Attila József" and begins, "I really love you, / believe me. It is something I inherited / from my mother.") Desnos's particular form of playfulness is also oracular and testimonial. The voice has a life of its own, an independent existence, liberated from a historical body ("The Voice of..."), but it also has a claimant, the author. I feel in this poem some of the rhapsodic vehemence that concludes the poem, "No, Love Is Not Dead":

> ...I'm not Ronsard or Baudelaire.
> I'm Robert Desnos, who, because I knew
> and loved you,
> Is as good as they are.
> I'm Robert Desnos who wants to be remembered
> On this vile earth for nothing but his love for you.
> *(translated by William Kulik)*

The vatic voice breathes creation against what Desnos here calls "vile earth"—the destructive human world. That sense of disgust spills over into "The Voice of Robert Desnos." W. H. Auden once said that "All poets adore explosions, thunderstorms, tornadoes, conflagrations, ruins, scenes of spectacular carnage" ("The Poet and the City"). Desnos is a case in point as he calls up "tornadoes and hurricanes / storms typhoons cyclones / tidal waves / earthquakes..." It's as if he is fulfilling Tsvetaeva's claim that a poet is "an explosion, a breaking in." But I also note that Desnos calls down all those destructive forces against gravediggers and assassins, architects of death, murderers. He takes apocalyptic natural forces into his very mouth ("tornadoes revolve in my mouth / hurricanes if it is possible redden my lips"), thereby empowering his voice to blast open the old world and call a new order into being. He brings the forces of destruction to their knees ("the tidal waves come to die at my feet"). The prophetic imagination dispenses its own kingdom and creates a sanctuary for everyone, but especially for lovers who at last requite desire ("loves and love so long hunted find refuge in me").

It is crucial to remember that Desnos's poem was written in 1926 and published in his book *Les Ténèbres* (1927). Interposed between two world wars, it violently poses itself against all the devastating forces of history, against history itself. Indeed, it creates a mythical world where the forgotten are remembered and the murdered spring back to life, where the masters of death lay down their tools:

> the gravediggers abandon the hardly-dug graves
> and declare that I alone may command their nightly work
> the assassins greet me
> the hangmen invoke the revolution
> invoke my voice
> invoke my name

Desnos's narcissistic magic show is an act of intervention ("the assassins bless me") that abolishes the historical reign of death and replaces it with mad love. I hear a deeply joyous and wildly stubborn voice in this poem. It seems to me the same voice that affirms "'The pain will soon be over'" and "'The happy season is near.'" I feel as if I can recognize in that voice the person who would one day join the French Resistance to oppose fascist oppression, who refused to buckle under torture and give up the names of his fellow Resistance workers, who met with a group to study astrology and literature at Compiègne, whose last letter from a concentration camp promised "a love story in an entirely new genre," who is said to have floated through the ranks of the doomed prisoners at Buchenwald telling fortunes, encouraging people awaiting the gas chambers by opening their palms and predicting future happiness and long life.

It's stunning that in Desnos's apocalyptic poem the Orphic voice can get the entire world to respond and obey, but it cannot reach the beloved. When it invokes the actual flesh—the body—it starts to obsessively cry out. I hear this as an erotic charm, a magic spell repeated three times:

> I'm calling the one I love
> I'm calling the one I love
> I'm calling the one I love
> (translated by Bill Zaratsky)

The spell works wonders on everything else, including "adorable women whom I do not adore," but it cannot call forth the absent beloved. And so the flesh must finally tremble and the triple summoning must be echoed by the three refusals at the conclusion of the poem. The French repetitions are exact:

> celle que j'aime ne m'écoute pas
> celle que j'aime ne m'entend pas
> celle que j'aime ne me répond pas.

and here I prefer Bill Zavatsky's likeness:

> the one I love does not listen to me
> the one I love does not hear me
> the one I love does not answer me

The eroticized voice—the inscribed desire—is unending in this poem; it goes on generating itself even beyond the conclusion of the poem. Desnos has exalted the voice to mythic status—it goes on calling and calling and calling.

The poetry of love has always been enamored by comparisons, haunted by issues of similitude. It has always rejoiced in extravagant analogies. I think, for example, of how often the Song of Songs—the greatest love poem ever written—proclaims the imaginative powers of language in celebrating erotic love. The lovers vie with each other in their praise for each other. (Love poets have competed for the most extravagant comparisons ever since.) Hence the word *damah* ("to be like") occurs often, as does one of its conjunctions, *dimmah,* meaning "to liken, to compare" and also "to conjure up a mental image, to fantasize." The landscape itself becomes eroticized as sexuality is invoked through the metaphor of the garden and the vineyard, the mountain of myrrh and the hill of frankincense. ("Until the day break, and the shadows flee away, I will get me to the mountain of myrrh, and the hill of frankincense" [4:6].) The famous erotic similes and metaphors become a way of fantasizing a time when the lovers will lie together. Hence the movement from

> Let him kiss me with the kisses of his mouth:
> for thy love *is* better than wine.
>
> *(1:2)*

Make haste, my beloved, and be thou like to a roe
or to a young hart upon the mountain of spices.

(8:14)

Calling the lover to come away and be like a gazelle or like a young stag
upon spice-laden mountains is a way of celebrating the natural joyousness
of love, the unabashed pleasure and beauty of erotic fulfillment. It is a
way of having—*knowing*—the beloved.

I'm struck by the many great love poems that not only primarily use
comparisons to praise the beloved (everyone knows, or should know,
Robert Burns's perennially fresh "My love is like a red red rose / That's
newly sprung in June: / My love is like the melodie / That's sweetly
played in tune") but also ostentatiously flaunt their analogies, drawing at-
tention to the artificial process of figuration itself. "Shall I compare thee
to a summer's day?" Shakespeare famously asks in a sonnet that goes on
to develop and extend the analogy.

I was startled when I first came across this comparison from the
Song of Songs:

I have compared thee, O my love, to a company
of horses in Pharaoh's chariots.

(1:9)

The Hebraist actually reverses the order of this so a more literal transla-
tion than the King James version's would read:

To a mare among Pharaoh's chariots
I would liken you, my darling.

The medieval Jewish commentators elucidated the stratagem behind this
comparison. Since Pharaoh's chariots were drawn exclusively by stallions,
a mare in heat harnessed to one of Pharaoh's chariots could transform an
orderly procession of soldiers into a riot of plunging stallions. Robert
Alter, who has pointed out how frequently figuration is foregrounded in
the Song of Songs, explains the matter nicely when he suggests that

The lover speaks out of a keen awareness of the power of figurative language to break open closed frames of reference to make us see things with a shock of new recognition: the beloved in poem after poem is lovely, gentle, dovelike, fragrant, but the sexual attraction she exerts has an almost violent power to drive males to distraction, as the equine military image powerfully suggests.

Always in the shadow of the poem of bliss is the question of the concentrated image, the apt comparison, that will do justice to the subversive power of eros. There's the poet's traditional promise of making the beloved immortal: "Your name from hence immortal life shall have," Shakespeare promises in Sonnet 81. But Shakespeare rebelled, as true poetry must, when the Renaissance panegyric became heedless. He rebelled against the convention of flattering a typecast mistress in a clichéd language. There is a whole tradition of sentimental poems that stand behind the famous anti-Petrarchan Sonnet 130:

> My mistress' eyes are nothing like the sun;
> Coral is far more red than her lips' red;
> If snow be white, why then her breasts are dun;
> If hairs be wires, black wires grow on her head.
> I have seen roses damasked, red and white,
> But no such roses see I in her cheeks,
> And in some perfumes is there more delight
> Than in the breath that from my mistress reeks.
> I love to hear her speak, yet well I know
> That music hath a far more pleasing sound.
> I grant I never saw a goddess go;
> My mistress, when she walks, treads on the ground.
>   And yet, by heaven, I think my love as rare
>   As any she belied with false compare.

Here Shakespeare cuts and mocks the stock imagery of Elizabethan love poetry, deriding odious comparisons and banal flattery. The conventional typecast Elizabethan mistress had eyes brighter than the sun, lips "more red than any coral stone," proverbially snowy skin, blond tresses, rosy cheeks, sweet breath, etc. It's significant that some of the comparisons Shakespeare had himself perpetrated in his early poetry. So he is also turning the knife against his own earlier invidious hyperboles. He refuses the notion that he has to falsify the beloved into a goddess. The poem turns in the final two lines to swear "by heaven, I think my love as rare / As any she belied with false compare." The poet refuses here to compete through flattery. He points to the precious, extraordinary quality of his beloved but also to her uniqueness. He derides whatever analogy obscures rather than reveals the particularity of being. By questioning the very limits of "false compare," of metaphoric language, he invites us to as well, thereby regaining for poetry the precision and sincerity of true praise.

Every poem is shadowed by desire, but it is also shadowed by the problem of rendering desire in language. There is a place where similitude seems to break down because experience itself seems beyond compare. "We may compare life / to a shoe, or a laundromat, / or whatever," Attila József wryly observes: "Nonetheless, we love it / for reasons of our own." Analogies seem beside the point when it comes to our secret obsessive reasons for loving life. Of course, József's examples are comically pedestrian ("a shoe," "a laundromat") and arbitrary ("whatever"). As if our cherished lives could possibly be narrowed down and compared to something we buy in a store, something we wear daily, something we simply put on and take off, or to a place we go to clean our clothes. Yet at the conclusion of the poem József makes a related and comparable analogy with great poignance:

> Let us carefully save our
> true souls
> like our best suit of clothes
> to keep them spotless for the days of
> celebration.
> *(translated by John Bátki)*

The poet evokes the echo of communion days, of festive special occasions, jubilant holidays, communal celebrations. How tenderly József advises us to "save our true souls" (the religious overtones are powerful) for the sacred days ahead. Life may not be like a shoe or a laundromat, but our souls may be like a special article of clothing that we save for joyous days. This becomes a love poem to the liberation of the soul within the self.

There are ironic poems that first disentangle themselves from worn-out language, the shopworn sentimentalities, in order to restore innocence to the language, to reenchant and reintoxicate, and to call the words of passion holy. "You are beautiful, like prophecies," Amichai writes in "A Majestic Love Song," characteristically intermingling religious and erotic imagery, "And sad, like those which come true, / Calm, with the calmness afterward. / Black in the white loneliness of jasmine, / With sharpened fangs: she-wolf and queen."

Robert Desnos wrote of a magical world that obeys the poet's charms, but of an unattainable beloved he could not attract or reach. His quest for the Immortal Beloved shadows and fuels all his subsequent poetry, haunting the imagination. But now I want to counterpose that vision of the unattainable with one last poem where the lover is brought back from the past and repossessed in memory. The external world remains recalcitrant and even alien, but the inner world is completely fed. It finds its own way of fulfilling itself. The preferred method of transport for the euphoric imagination is the lyric poem.

Here is an overlooked poem, "One Night," that Constantine Cavafy wrote in Alexandria in July 1907. It's characteristic of the many frank, unflinching homoerotic love poems Cavafy wrote during the years he worked as a special clerk in the Irrigation Service (Third Circle) at the Ministry of Public Works. All these poems show the lyric poet's devotion to a sensual pleasure he would name sacred. They are transgressive, joyous, and remarkably free of guilt. I quote "One Night" in Edmund Keeley and Philip Sherrard's definitive translation from the Greek:

The room was cheap and sordid,
hidden above the suspect taverna.
From the window you could see the alley,
dirty and narrow. From below
came the voices of workmen
playing cards, enjoying themselves.

And there on that common, humble bed
I had love's body, had those intoxicating lips,
red and sensual,
red lips of such intoxication
that now as I write, after so many years,
in my lonely house, I'm drunk with passion again.

This poem was first titled "One of My Evenings," and then "One of My Nights," and finally, "One Night." The revisions demonstrate Cavafy's impulse toward the epigrammatic (an aristocratic form because it doesn't explain itself), but they also show him closely focusing the lens on a single (and singular) night. He also gives up the possessive ("my"), thereby making the title more definitive and impersonal. (Joseph Brodsky once observed that something deeply personal animated Cavafy's historical poems and something equally impersonal operated in his erotic poems of casual pickups and short-lived affairs.) The title "One Night" is casual, but there's something implacable in the poet's gaze, relentlessly focused on a long-ago night lifted out of time.

One can't help but notice that there are actually two nights dramatized in this poem. The first is the night of the passing sexual encounter itself. The second is the night years afterward when the speaker actively recalls and relives that first encounter. The brio of this text is to collapse those two nights into one through the experience of writing.

The poem is carefully divided into two equal parts. Cavafy tended to write in a stripped-down style without much ornament, but notice how artfully he sets the scene and creates a sense of the illicit, the secretive, the degraded. The room was *cheap* and *sordid,* it was *hidden* above the *suspect* taverna, and its window looked down on a *dirty* and *narrow* alley. The description is naturalistic, but all these words characterize the nature of the encounter (or appear to) by describing the clandestine setting. When Henry James describes a house he is also describing the inhabitants of that house—and that's (almost) true of Cavafy as well. It's also crucial that the room is situated *above* the workmen playing cards in the tavern below. The first movement of the poem ends with a sense of a working-class setting, of men released from work and pursuing an ordinary enjoyment.

There's a gap, an enormous chasm between the two stanzas, between the quotidian world below and the erotic world above. The second stanza unfolds in one beautifully modulated sentence as the poem exchanges a demotic for a pure Greek, a secular for a transcendental idiom. It's as if a camera moves in for a close-up as we get a last, stark detail that emphasizes the seedy external world. But it's a trigger to the epiphany. "The common, humble bed" turns into a site of ecstasy, and the poem immediately lifts beyond that earthly realm toward a platonic ideal. All the weight comes down on that shocking, wildly extravagant claim, "I had love's body." The phrase "love's body" is romantic, impersonal, and transcendent. And the statement is made with absolute certainty. Thus is the sordid transfigured into the sacred.

Recurrence incites and creates enchantment. The speaker imaginatively pitches himself into an erotic trance over "those intoxicating lips, / red and sensual, / red lips of such intoxication." The re-creation of the experience seems autoerotic; he is elating himself with the memory.

And he is doing so through the act of writing. As he asserts: "now as I write, after so many years, / in my lonely house, I'm drunk with passion again." Cavafy is creating a scenography of writing. He is staging a writing (who knows how many nights the poem actually took him to write?) so that the author and the speaker seem to collapse into one. He creates an emphatic immediacy of time ("now as I write") and place ("in my lonely house"). The house must be lonely because the writer has to be alone to engage the experience. He must also be in need of it. The loneliness is posed against the plenitude of the memory. Crucial to this poem is the speaker's sense of being in two places at once, of transporting himself backward in time, reliving the memory in writing about it, *by* writing about it. The poem hones in on the experience of writing as a way of having someone again, of cutting back through the bramble of years. The feeling lives inside the one who writes. He is solitary, aging, devoted, joyous, triumphant, and as ruthless in pursuit of the memory of love's body as he was of the original body itself. The memory of those intoxicating lips, of writing those intoxicating lips, overcomes him. The feeling erupts, the taker is taken back, and the transport is complete. "One Night" gives us the dizzying sensation of writing as a medium of attainment, as a way of getting drunk on passion again, thus destroying time.

"Some people will stay / pedestrians no matter what they ride, / horse, car, or airplane," Attila József observes. There are few things more discomfiting to hardened critical readers than a poem of naked and unembarrassed desire, a lyric of transport that formally delivers a soul at white heat, a body that flies a little, a voice that speaks when it has nothing to say, or collapses in a "joyful joy," or wings through the universe in a mad quest for the beloved, or releases itself to a drunken passion. Think of a poem that gushes in words and crosses a precarious and dangerous threshold. ("Unrestorable, unhaltable, / irretrievable—gush of verse," Tsvetaeva writes.) Such a poem indicts normative strictures and authors in the reader an equivalent desire for asocial bliss, an answering ecstasy.

T. S. Eliot is right, when he says in "The Three Voices of Poetry" that "a good love poem, though it may be addressed to one person, is always meant to be overheard by other people." (I can't agree with his next assumption that "Surely, the proper language of love—that is, of communication to the beloved and no one else, is prose." Why can't love also speak a transcendental idiom?) The love poem is the site of a specialized discourse, but it succeeds when it eventuates that discourse in a third party, the reader. "Reading," says Tsvetaeva, "is complicity in the creative process." Paul Valéry goes further than Eliot when he says:

> A poet's function—do not be startled by this remark—is not to experience the poetic state: that is a private affair. His function is to create it in others. The poet is recognized—or at least everyone recognizes his own poet—by the simple fact that he causes his reader to become "inspired."
>
> ("Poetry and Abstract Thought")

I am inspired by the lyric poem that initiates and instills a state of intoxication in the reader. We ought to speak of the poem that desires to sweep the reader away, to *take* the reader. Of reading as a form of sensual pleasure, a mode of possession, a method of travel. Of reading as a voluptuous and jubilant practice with its own ruthless will to the language of joy. Poetry is a devouring passion. Rapture testifies: I am reading my way into a state of enchantment and exultation, a state of bliss.

6

Five Acts

Act 1

Imagine that you have just settled down in your seat in a crowded theater. The houselights dim, the excited murmurs from the audience at last die down, and the final chords from the orchestra slowly fade out. Someone coughs. A hush comes over the audience as the curtain rises on a brightly lit stage that shows Tsarskoye Selo, the Tsar's village near St. Petersburg, circa 1911. You strain forward to listen as a statuesque young actress, Anna Gorenko (part classical Greek heroine, part modern Russian woman), steps forward to deliver the first dramatic speech of her career.

> I was helpless, my breasts were freezing.
> I walked one foot on tiptoe,
> I put my left glove on
> my right hand, like an idiot.
>
> There seemed to be so many steps then
> but I knew there were only three.
> Autumn whispered through the maples
> "Die, like me:
>
> that sick, truculent liar, Fate,
> has stripped me, for the hell of it."

"I've been flayed like you," I remember answering
as I left, "and I'll die when you do."

This is the song of our last meeting.
I looked back at the shape of the dark house.
Candles guttered in the bedroom window,
indifferent, yellow.

(version by Stephen Berg)

The opening soliloquy turns out, astonishingly, to be the dramatic ac-
count of a farewell meeting, a last good-bye. It has a title, "Song of the
Last Meeting," and it must dramatize the drastic burden of that en-
counter—the weight of irrevocable loss—entirely on its own since the
speech has been severed from its context in the larger play. That's be-
cause there is no play, no stage, no supporting cast, no collective audi-
ence to gasp at the witty Chekhovian dialogue showing us character in
action. What we're listening to instead, what each of us is in fact read-
ing, is a lyric poem. Four quatrains. A square of black marks surrounded
by white margins, white space.

These sixteen lines comprise one of the first poems in the first book,
Evening (1912), by Anna Akhmatova, née Anna Gorenko. Along with
the two books that followed it, *Rosary* (1914) and *White Flock* (1917),
Evening sounds a note that had not been heard in literature before and,
perhaps, has not been heard again. I hear that note whenever I recite this
poem aloud. It echoes down the century, surviving translation.

Every poem is a scene of language. It is a rite without a ceremony. To
set this particular scene, it is winter 1910–1911. Symbolism, the dominant
literary mode of the time, is in self-declared crisis. In the Bryullov read-
ing room in the Russian Museum in St. Petersburg a twenty-one-year-
old bohemian, a provincial girl with a pagan childhood who has been
writing poems from the time she was eleven years old (her father had
playfully called her "a decadent poetess" even before that) read the galleys
of Innokenty Annensky's posthumous book, *The Cypress Box*, and under-
stood something dramatic about poetry. Her husband, the faithful young
symbolist poet Nikolay Gumilyov ("as a boy he believed in symbolism as
people believe in God. It was an inviolable sacrament. But the closer he
approached symbolism... the more his faith faltered") traveled to Africa

for six months, and his spouse started writing the poems that would help bring Russian literature into the twentieth century. Acmeism and Futurism were both being hatched. When Serge Makovsky accepted some of these poems for the magazine *Apollo,* Anna Gorenko's father urged her "not to befoul a good respected name" and to take a pseudonym. Thus "Anna Akhmatova"—a name with five open *a*s and an exotic Tatar feeling—entered Russian literature at the top of the Russian alphabet.

It was Osip Mandelstam, the other great Acmeist poet, who first observed that the roots of Akhmatova's art are in the nineteenth-century Russian novel, in Tolstoy, Turgenev, Dostoevsky, and that her poetic form "was developed with a glance at psychological prose." Symbolism is indicted by this poetry. A dramatic clarity of expression stands against its moody vagueness and otherworldly mysticism. Look how swiftly Akhmatova sets the scene with tangible details and bold novelistic strokes. She also irrevocably marks that scene with her gender. Here a literal translation is helpful:

> So helplessly my chest grew cold
> But my steps were light.
> I put on my right hand
> My left-handed glove.
>   *(translated by Joanna Trzeciak)*

These lines are spare, concentrated, severe.

What seems characteristic of the dramatic lyric and not of the nineteenth-century novel is the process of terrific distillation operating here, a condensation so extreme it seems more reminiscent of Sappho than of Dostoevsky, more Li Po than Tolstoy. The speaker is narrator, observer, and actor all at once. She speaks with the rhythm of Russian verse, her words rhyme. She is not the author exactly ("When I state myself, as the Representative of the Verse—it does not mean—me—but a supposed person," Emily Dickinson explains), but she is not a full-fledged fictional construct either (as in, say, a dramatic monologue by Robert Browning). The sliding line between rhetorical projection and revealing self-confession may be characteristic and perhaps even constitutive of a certain first-person love poem.

I'm struck by the helpless sense of exposure in the first two lines, the terrible self-division, the paradox of a speaker declaring that her breast was cold but her footsteps light, suggesting both numbness and liberation, the fateful onrushing freedom of a woman riven in half. An element of mortal panic that seems palpable carries over to the next two lines, the next extraordinary gesture. Marina Tsvetaeva has given an insightful accounting of these two lines, and her enthusiasm seems an exemplum of poetic responsiveness, a model of how to read. She writes:

> When in the first poem of her first book, the young Akhmatova conveys the confusion of love in the lines:
>
> > I drew my left-hand glove
> > onto my right hand—
>
> she conveys at one blow all feminine and all lyric confusion (all the confusion of the empirical!), immortalising with one flourish of the pen that ancient nervous gesture of woman and of poet who at life's great moments forget right and left—not only of glove, but of hand, and of country of the world, suddenly losing all their certainty. Through a patent and even penetrating precision of detail, something bigger than an emotional state is affirmed and symbolised—a whole structure of the mind. (A poet lets go the pen, a woman lets go her lover's hand, and immediately they can't tell the left hand from the right.) In brief, from these two lines of Akhmatova's, a broad, abundant flow of associations comes into being, associations which spread like the circles from a flung pebble. The whole woman, the whole poet is in these two lines; the whole Akhmatova, unique, unrepeatable, inimitable. Before Akhmatova none of us portrayed a gesture like this. And no one did after her.
>
> *("Poets with History and Poets without History")*

We might say now that the gesture of putting the left glove on the right hand enacts a blur in the two spheres of the brain during a moment of crisis. It is a blotting out, a moment when the mind goes somewhere else. And that disturbing loss of equilibrium, that radical redefinition of time, that entry into an atemporal present, is one of the key features of lyric poetry.

There is a tragic, almost Greek, sense of fate operating in the next two linked stanzas, the main body of the poem. What appears to be many steps quickly narrows down to three fateful ones (a magic number) and autumn whispers to the heroine like a classical Greek chorus, "Die like me." Akhmatova's poem implies rather than tells a story. It inflects a plot with a beginning, middle, and end, but it never narrates a literal account of the final meeting itself, as in a novel or play. Instead of a dialogue between the lovers, for example, the poem delivers a conversational exchange with the wind. Autumn whispers to the speaker (in a voice that is both below speech and above it) and the speaker responds in kind. This creates an operatic overtone—love as an epic martyrdom—that plays over the scenario of parting lovers.

I want to linger over the strangeness of this conversation for a moment because it seems a moment characteristic of lyric poetry itself. We experience that peculiar moment not as comical but as fateful, hypnotic. There is something hallucinatory about it. Ruskin observes that the mind "unhinged by grief" (the phrase is his) projects irrational feelings onto nature, and that is true here as a panic of violent feelings externalizes itself into autumn. Here is Joanna Trzeciak's literal version:

> The whisper of autumn among the maples
> Asked: "Die like me!
>
> I am deceived by my dismal,
> Changeable, evil fate."
> I answered, "My dear, my dear!
> I am also. I will die with you..."

There is a purposeful confusion of gender in the Russian where the word "autumn" is feminine but the word "whisper" is masculine, and this clearly plays back to the parting lover. But something more compelling is also going on. Nature speaks with the accents of Shakespeare's Cleopatra—intimate, harsh, noble—almost offhandedly calling for a suicide pact. And Akhmatova's stand-in, equally regal and tough-minded, equally devastated, replies with a matching intimacy and rhetoric. She addresses fall as a lover. "My dear, my dear!" she exclaims, promising with a terrifying resignation, "I will die with you." This interaction is a symbolist strategy, but as opposed to the silent innuendos of symbolism ("the rose nods to the girl, the girl nods to the rose," Mandelstam mocked), this is nothing less than a high lyrical voicing, a prophetic speaking back. Nature and the poet are on intimate, equal terms. They speak with equivalent outraged voices.

Far from being an aberration, Akhmatova's strange conversational intimacy with the autumnal wind is one of her marked, perhaps unconscious ways of signaling a poetic vocation. "Human voices did not touch me, / it was the wind whose words I heard," she would write nearly thirty years later in a poem about her deep companionship with a silver willow from her childhood. I'm reminded how often in romantic poetry the wind is a sign of poetic inspiration—a creative and destructive inspiriting force. Think of Shelley's famous invocation, "O wild West Wind, thou breath of Autumn's being," and how he calls upon the wind to make him its natural instrument: "Make me thy lyre, even as the forest is." To invoke the wind is to constitute a relationship with it as a sentient being. Jonathan Culler is correct when he argues in his essay "Apostrophe" that "One who successfully invokes nature is one to whom nature might, in its turn, speak. He makes himself poet, visionary. Thus, invocation is a figure of vocation." But Akhmatova goes further than invocation when she successfully, even matter-of-factly extends a dialogic capacity to nature. These are the terms not of a realistic poet but of a theatrical, visionary one who would speak in a prophetic voice beyond the social or naturalistic realm. One might speculate that her suicide pact with nature signals an underlying ambition to become a vatic poet. She understands the wind's voice, its "words." Shelley calls out, "Be thou, Spirit fierce, / My spirit! Be thou me, impetuous one!" D. H. Lawrence testifies: "Not I, not I, but the wind that blows through me!" ("Song of a Man Who Has Come Through").

Akhmatova also expresses her own sense of poetic destiny in terms of the concept of fate. Autumn says, I have been lied to and stripped down by a changeable, evil fate (a natural process is hereby personified as an act of supreme cruelty) and the speaker implies that she, too, has suffered an equivalent fate. Autumn gives voice to the despair of a mutable nature, the speaker to a betrayed human nature. Their fates are exactly comparable. A sense of poetic destiny speaks in equally hyperbolic terms. "Lyrics have been so individualistic," Annensky announced in

1909, "that they now *need* a feminine musicality." Akhmatova stepped forward to fill what was perceived as a vacant chair. Speaking of the vacuum of women poets in Russian literature in 1910, she said, "Fate wanted it to be occupied by me." Fate may have left the season and the speaker bereft, but it had also instilled a compensatory music in the poet, who is an instrument.

"This is the song of the last meeting," Akhmatova writes. It is not an account, not even a speech, but a so-called "song." It hits a register above speech, beyond speech. Like a mad Orpheus already resigned to his tragic fate, her speaker remembers glancing back at a darkened house—the domestic site—and seeing candles burning in the bedroom window—the intimate marital site—with an indifferent yellow flame. She is unsheltered, doomed, changed, charged.

Akhmatova's first major poem inscribes a parting and creates a music of finality. It is also a poem of literary vocation, the opening salvo of an intoxicating and severe new voice in poetry. I hear in this poem the verbal music of a young woman who has boldly marched onto the stage. She would be Phaedre, she would be Lot's wife, she would be Cleopatra. She would speak in "Requiem" as the voice of an entire generation. Fate deemed it so. The curtain has gone up.

Act 2

"Everything written is as good as it is dramatic," Robert Frost declares in the preface to his verse play "A Way Out," thereby characterizing his own strong practice and making a key point by overstating the case. ("A least lyric alone may have a hard time," Frost acknowledges.) Poems become "dramatic," in Frost's sense of the term, when we get a sensation of someone speaking, when we hear a poem, in his words, "as sung or spoken by a person in a scene—in character, in a setting." (Conversely, plays become poemlike when we feel as if a given dramatic utterance has been formalized and become complete enough to stand on its own apart from the larger dramatic context. Think of Shakespeare's songs.)

It is sometimes said that the individual poem approaches drama when it presents a conflict, either within or outside the speaking self. But that is a weak way of putting it. Here is another way: we know we are in the presence of a dramatic poem when the intensity of the utterance is so great that it blots out any surrounding context or discourse. It is a dream that refigures reality. "In form, a poem looks very like a monologue; it *is* a monologue," Paul Goodman writes in his defense of poetry, *Speaking and Language*. "But a monologue is not the same as talking to oneself. It is more like a daydream."

In Sappho, in Catullus, in Blake, in Montale, the story exists for the daydream, for the song, and not the other way around. Ezra Pound defined the dramatic lyric in a 1908 letter to William Carlos Williams:

> To me the short so-called dramatic lyric—at any rate the sort of thing I do—is the poetic part of a drama the rest of which (to me the prose part) is left to the reader's imagination or implied or set in a short note. I catch the character I happen to be interested in at the moment he interests me, usually a moment of song, self-analysis, or sudden understanding or revelation.

Pound's idea was to hit a high moment when a psychic state triggers into revelation.

Akhmatova clearly understood how a short poem could yoke a ferocious conflict at a revelatory moment when she went for the jugular in "Song of the Last Meeting." Here's a tiny poem from the same period that shows her ruthless dramatic sense:

> Three things enchanted him:
> white peacocks, evensong,
> and faded maps of America.
> He couldn't stand bawling brats,
> or raspberry jam with his tea,
> or womanish hysteria.
> ...And he was tied to me.
> > *(translated by Stanley Kunitz*
> > *and Max Hayward)*

Akhmatova vehemently balances and poses the lover's three talismanic, romantic, and distant emblems of reverie (peacocks, evensong, faded maps of America) against three equally talismanic and harsh emblems of the domestic realm (crying children, raspberry jam with tea, female "hysteria"). These three enchanted sites of dream rhyme (that is, they are brought into precise relationship) with three disenchanted aspects of rude reality. And then the poet binds the two incompatibles, male and female, together with a clinching last line: "...And he was tied to me," or as D. M. Thomas translates it, "And he had married me." The binding is made more dramatic by the ellipsis, those three tiny dots at the beginning of the last line, which stand as a kind of chasm between the description and the recognition. The acknowledgment that the dreamer despises "womanish hysteria" (names have been called, battlelines drawn) creates a hole in the narrative, a gulf, a stunned silence. The ellipsis widens the space for reverie, it instills a moment when the mind goes trailing off before it is brought up short by the swift perception of doomed connection: "And he was tied to me." Reading this I feel as if the wedded couple are like one of John Donne's conceits—they are yoked by violence (and love) together. Something is going to explode. The lyrics start to pile up and reinforce each other in Akhmatova's early love poems so that the reader begins to infer a greater story, a larger dramatic construction. But each individual poem inscribes a ferocity.

Akhmatova's early love poems survive not because they are sentimental—they are not—but because they are unsparing and revelatory. There are those who distrust dramatic technique in poetry as artificial, but technique takes us not away from, but toward, authenticity in lyric. (Pound went so far as to call technique the test of a poet's "sincerity.") Form is enactment and revelation. So, too, we tend to talk about speakers in poems as if those speakers had independent lives and created the poems themselves, but, of course, it's the other way around; texts create speakers. They ventriloquize voices and formally inscribe them from beginning to end.

I'm struck, for example, that neither "Song of the Last Meeting" nor "Three Things Enchanted Him" takes the form of the classical lyric solo, the pronominal pattern of an "I" addressing a "you." That pattern can create a rich feeling of confessional intimacy by locating a listener who appears to be the only one addressed. (Think of how Wordsworth gestures to Coleridge "as if to thee alone.") By contrast, "Song of the Last Meeting" hits a register that seems more volatile and histrionic than conversational. It isolates the speaker and dislocates the listener within the poem. I would call it the intimate oracular. (Autumn whispers and pleads from above, "Die like me," and the speaker responds, "My dear...I will die with you.") The conclusion of the poem is by turns declamatory ("This is the song of the last meeting") and narrative ("I glanced at a dark house"). These lines seem pitched not to any particular listener or even audience but into the darkness of an empty theater toward a future reader.

So, too, "Three Things Enchanted Him" presents not an "I" and a "you," but an "I" and a "he," thus situating the speaker simultaneously inside and outside the scene—both a player and an observer. There is something definitive and absolute about the opening declaration: "Three things enchanted him." Just three, only three. It allows no breach or disagreement. How much more questionable it would seem if the speaker told the listener something he (supposedly) already knew, "Three things enchanted you..." As it is, there is also something impersonal, something implacable, about the final revelation. The ironic matter-of-factness of the recognition that fate has bound these two together is so potent that it can only terminate this short poem. It strikes like a blow to the head.

One might say that the individual lyric moves in the direction of the short story by introducing more and more narrative action into the poem. It moves in the direction of the one-act play and the short story by taking a glimpse at psychological prose and introducing more than one speaking character into a setting. (Frost's *North of Boston* is a spellbinding example.) When an entire poem is set in dialogue it becomes a ballad or a verse play. (There is no poetic equivalent to Beckett's "Act without Words.") Here is one more early poem by Akhmatova that shows the poet creating a scene:

I wrung my hands under my dark veil...
"Why are you pale, what makes you reckless?"
—Because I have made my loved one drunk
with an astringent sadness.

I'll never forget. He went out, reeling;
his mouth was twisted, desolate...
I ran downstairs, not touching the banisters,
and followed him as far as the gate.

And shouted, choking: "I meant it all
in fun. Don't leave me, or I'll die of pain."
He smiled at me—oh so calmly, terribly—
and said: "Why don't you get out of the rain?"
       (translated by Stanley Kunitz and Max Hayward)

"Dramatize, dramatize!" Frost directed the poet, and Akhmatova takes
the cue here in spades. One could almost direct this poem—or film it.
Notice the penetratingly swift progression: first the speaker's harsh en-
gendered distress ("I wrung my hands beneath the dark veil"), then the
voice of an unnamed interlocutor ("Why are you so pale today?"), then
the explanation, now unvoiced, declared by the speaker back to herself
("Because I gave him of bitter sadness / To drink, until he was drunk
with it"). The next stanza begins literally with a rhetorical question
("How shall I forget?") and then it launches into dramatizing, in mem-
ory, the drunken sadness of the man reeling out of the house in agony.
She races after him to the gate. The last stanza presents a dialogue trans-
acted by two people facing each other across a threshold that separates
everything inside from everything outside. Sam Driver's literal transla-
tion reads:

> Out of breath, I shouted: "It was all a joke,
> What happened. If you go, I shall die."
> He smiled calmly and terribly
> And said to me: "Don't stand in the wind."

She calls him back, theatrically, histrionically. There's a terse, affection-
ate, preternaturally calm and therefore terrible quality to his deceptive
reply, "Don't stand in the wind." The word "wind" here resonates with
all the visionary associations we've thus far brought to it. And so the
speaker is left with a painful choice: the inside or the outside, the social
or the asocial, the domestic or the poetic. And of course for a poet with
Akhmatova's vocation that is no choice at all. I'm reminded of the first
stanza of Yeats's poem "The Choice":

> The intellect of man is forced to choose
> Perfection of the life, or of the work,

And if it take the second must refuse
A heavenly mansion, raging in the dark.

The confrontation between the two lovers is left unresolved at the close of Akhmatova's poem. It is a memory that stops the speaker in her tracks. A flaring memory that almost stands out of time, like candles burning with an indifferent yellow flame in a bedroom window. And yet the choice is clear: the visionary poet is always one who would stand out in the wind. Whitman writes:

I swear I will never again mention love or death inside a
  house,
And I swear I will never translate myself at all, only to him or
  her who privately stays with me in the open air.

Act 3

There is an artistic impulse to wear a mask, to take on a persona (in Latin *persona* means the putting on of a mask by players in a drama). There is a need to speak in a voice other than one's natural or social voice, to strike a pose, play a role (we all play any number every day). To reveal a truth while (partially) concealing its source. To get access to that truth through another voice, another angle of vision. The lyric delivered at the pitch of the dramatic calls out to be recited aloud.

Testimonies abound over the past two centuries about the dialectic, the sliding boundary line, between the fictive and the real in poetry. We hit the paradox of a kind of truth that can only reveal itself through disguise. "Tell all the Truth but tell it slant," Emily Dickinson famously directed herself (number 1129). "I am a lie that tells the truth," Jean Cocteau confessed. W. B. Yeats established as the first principle of his work: "A poet writes always of his personal life, in his finest work out of its tragedy, whatever it be, remorse, lost love, or mere loneliness; he never speaks directly as to someone at the breakfast table, there is always a phantasmagoria." Yeats also said that he committed his emotion "to shepherds, herdsmen, camel-drivers, learned men, Milton's or Shelley's Platonist, that tower Palmer drew." He said, "Talk to me of originality and I will turn on you with rage. I am a crowd, I am a lonely man, I am nothing" ("A General Introduction for My Work").

In 1914 Ezra Pound explained his third book, *Personae* (1909), as a "search for oneself," for "sincere self-expression":

> I began this search for the real in a book called *Personae*, casting off, as it were, complete masks of the self in each poem. I continued in a long series of translations, which were but more elaborate masks.

The most elaborated modernist act of masking I can think of is the three distinct "heteronyms" that the Portuguese poet Fernando Pessoa adapted for his complete works. Each of his poems comes with the special stylistic imprint of a particular authorial intention. Each marks an aspect of Pessoa himself.

The self-conscious act of putting on a mask (and subsequently discarding it) reveals a deep anxiety about the self, about one's "true" identity. The strongly dramatic poem requires a high degree of impersonation and even of impersonality, as T. S. Eliot would have it, but, equally important, it is also a quest for identity. Poems are personlike, they are *pseudopersons*. Identity can only be established and elaborated in relationship to an audience. The speaking voice craves a listener. This is as characteristic of the dramatic lyric (the poem with an unnamed speaker, an "I," who stands in for the author) as it is for the dramatic monologue (a poem uttered by a speaker who is evidently not the author). The voice in Sylvia Plath's "Daddy" is as directive as the voice in T. S. Eliot's "The Love Song of J. Alfred Prufrock."

The "Middle Generation" of American poets—Robert Lowell, Randall Jarrell, Delmore Schwartz, Theodore Roethke, Elizabeth Bishop—all understood the power of the dramatic monologue to probe a selfhood. It's worth recalling the dramatic monologues in *The Mills of the Kavanaughs* that stand between Lowell's early work and the "confessional" poems of *Life Studies* which give the carefully fostered impression that we are getting the "real" Robert Lowell. I think of the purposefully sliding boundary line between the character of "Henry" and the author "John Berryman" in *The Dream Songs,* or of the continuity of voices between the housewife who speaks in Jarrell's "Next Day" and the man himself who shows up in "A Man Meets a Woman in the Street" ("Because, after all, it *is* my wife / In a new dress from Bergdorf's," he exclaims), or of how Weldon Kees invents the self-revealing character of "Robinson" to inscribe the existential dilemmas of American life at mid-century.

It's the multiple legacy of confessionalism to give us voices of deep extremity that are apparently personal (think of the lineage from Anne Sexton's *Live or Die* to Sharon Olds's *The Father* and Susan Hahn's *Confession*), that are seemingly invented (think of the movie figures in Nicholas Christopher's *Desperate Characters* or the freakish characters who inhabit Cynthia Macdonald's *Amputations*), and that are based on actual historical personages (think of Frank Bidart's "The War of Vaslav Nijinsky").

The issue of who is speaking in lyric, of the sincerity or authenticity of the speaker, has haunted English poetry for a couple of centuries now. It has led to the incorrigible postromantic feud between biographical and formalistic critical responses to literature. "With this key Shakespeare unlocked his heart," Wordsworth wrote of the sonnet; to which Browning replied, "Did Shakespeare? If so, the less Shakespeare he!" Similarly, in Latin America, the majority of poets who have written about Whitman (such as José Martí, the Cuban poet who introduced Whitman to Hispanic literature in 1877) have simply identified the hero of "Song of Myself"—a kosmos, one of the roughs—with the man who created him. Against which Jorge Luis Borges wrote that one of the persistent errors in thinking about Whitman "is the summary identifying of Whitman, the conscientious man of letters, with Whitman the semi-divine hero of *Leaves of Grass*."

Borges's sonnet about Whitman's dying days makes the issue palpable:

Camden, 1882
The fragrance of coffee and newspapers.
Sunday and its tedium. This morning,
On the uninvestigated page, that vain
Column of allegorical verses
By a happy colleague. The old man lies
Prostrate, pale, even white in his decent

Room, the room of a poor man. Needlessly
He glances at his face in the exhausted
Mirror. He thinks, without surprise now,
That face is me. One fumbling hand touches
The tangled beard, the devastated mouth.
The end is not far off. His voice declares:
I am almost gone. But my verses scan
Life and its splendor. I was Walt Whitman.
                    (translated by Richard Howard
                    and César Rennert)

"Yo fui Walt Whitman," the dying writer says in Borges's dramatic sonnet: "I was Walt Whitman."

The terms of the fictive and the confessional are too rigid, too absolute. Selfhood is always a constructive process in poetry. It is always something that the writer and the reader invent together. We tend to talk about speakers in poems as if they show up with full-blown identities. But speakers don't come to us with fully achieved selves at the beginnings of poems. (Hugh Kenner calls J. Alfred Prufrock "a name plus a voice.") Their identities are in process, their selves constructed out of words, line by line, stanza by stanza. The speaking voice constitutes a self by addressing others, and this is as true for the unidentified narrator in one of Emily Dickinson's poems as it is for the protagonist of one of Browning's dramatic monologues. (In *My Emily Dickinson,* Susan Howe writes: "Dickinson and Browning were both instinctive masters of the art of dramatic monologue. Their secretive natures knew soliloquy's power to conceal as it reveals messages. Anonymous shape-changer, she carried the concealing farther. Her poems are monologues without a named narrator, their supreme source is Shakespeare.") Both the monologue and the dramatic monologue imagine a speaker into being over the course of a poem. We see the speaker becoming a self before our very eyes. Indeed, we collaborate in the construction of that self. It is a participatory, imaginative achievement.

The move into personae seems to have a quality of animism. It actually embodies the displacement of the poet's self into another existence. It is replete with what, in a letter to his brothers, Keats famously called "Negative Capability."

Negative Capability, that is when man is capable of being in uncertainties, Mysteries, doubts, without any irritable reaching after fact and reason.

(December 21, 1817)

Remember, too, his galvanizing letter to Richard Woodhouse:

As to the poetical Character itself... it is not itself—it has no self—it is everything and nothing—It has no character—it enjoys light and shade; it lives in gusto, be it foul or fair, high or low, rich or poor, mean or elevated—It has as much delight in conceiving an Iago as an Imogen. What shocks the virtuous philosopher, delights the camelion Poet... A Poet is the most unpoetical of any thing in existence; because he has no Identity—he is continually in for—and filling some other Body—The Sun, the Moon, The Sea and Men and Women who are creatures of impulse are poetical and have about them an unchangeable attribute—the poet has none; no identity.

(October 27, 1818)

To fill the body of the sun and moon, to speak to the wind and to hear the wind talking back to you, through you, is to project psychic life into animate and inanimate nature alike. (I'm reminded of Mallarmé's idea to write a drama with only two characters, himself and the wind.) The romantic, symbolist, and modernist interest in masks is related to the simultaneous interest in archaic religions. To speak not just to the other but also from its vantage point is to harness something of its numinous, primitive power.

In his excellent book *The Gods Made Flesh: Metamorphosis and the Pursuit of Paganism,* Leonard Barkan suggests that the hold of Ovid's *Metamorphoses,* the bible of mythological stories, over the past centuries can be largely traced to the central paradox of the poem which "proves the natural world magical and the magical world natural." The poet has a protean self. Despite the radical inroads of science into our thinking over the past two centuries, many poets have not lost this delicious sense of paradox. Metamorphic transformation, the interpenetration of identities, is for many still at the heart of poetry.

Here is an early poem, "The Tree," from Pound's first book, *A Lume Spento* (1908), that enacts the animistic impulse. Pound placed it at the head of all post-1926 editions of *Personae,* his collected earlier poems, thus making it a kind of overture to his work. It is a program poem.

The Tree

I stood still and was a tree amid the wood,
Knowing the truth of things unseen before;
Of Daphne and the laurel bough
And that god-feasting couple old
That grew elm-oak amid the wold.
'Twas not until the gods had been
Kindly entreated, and been brought within
Unto the hearth of their heart's home
That they might do this wonder thing;
Nathless I have been a tree amid the wood
And many a new thing understood
That was rank folly to my head before.

This twelve-line poem has a kind of ongoing charm, despite its somewhat musty diction and dated Edwardian language. I suppose that is because it is about being charmed into another state of existence. I recall Pound's odd idea that "Greek myth arose when someone having passed through delightful psychic experience tried to communicate it to others and found it necessary to screen himself from persecution" (*The Spirit of Romance*). "The Tree" objectifies such a delightful psychic experience and shows Pound at his most Ovidian. The poet stands still and transforms himself into a tree, thereby coming to understand the myths of Daphne and of Baucis and Philemon (*Metamorphoses,* 1 and 8). What he now "sees" is how the gods changed human beings into organic life. Pound further elaborates his idea of myths of metamorphoses in *Pavannes and Divisions* (1918):

The first myths arose when a man walked sheer into "nonsense," that is to say, when some very vivid and undeniable adventure befell him, and he told someone else who called him a liar. Thereupon, after bitter experience, perceiving that no one could understand what he meant when he said that he "turned into a tree" he made a myth—a work of art that is—an impersonal or objective story woven out of his own emotion, as the nearest equation that he was capable of putting into words.

The uncanny experience of turning into a tree is, in Pound's terms, a kind of equation for a mood, for an inexplicable psychological state, and it becomes a way of bringing the gods "within / Unto the hearth of their heart's home." "The Tree" stands at the top of Pound's work because it enacts the central metamorphic act of poetry itself. The move into animism brings the gods home to the psyche. The move into personae also brings into psychic range all the historical figures who would animate Pound's early poetry, especially the Provençal poets who served as his primary "masks of the self."

"The Tree" marks one of Pound's first dramatized visionary episodes. These exalted moments of consciousness, of revelation and metamorphosis, recur throughout his work from "In a Station of the Metro" to *The Pisan Cantos*. Pound was always obsessed by what he called "the 'magic moment' or moment of metamorphosis," the "bust thru from quotidin into 'divine or permanent world.'" "The Tree" is an incipient attempt to embody such a state of dramatic ecstasy.

The true voice of feeling speaks in many registers. I am using Pound's poem as a kind of paradigm for the animism of the dramatic lyric when it moves into personae. The deep poem of personae speaks to oracular experience. It would inherit the power of the oracle. In "Song of Myself" Whitman writes:

Through me many long dumb voices,
Voices of the interminable generations of prisoners and slaves,
Voices of the diseas'd and despairing and of thieves and
    dwarfs,
Voices of cycles of preparation and accretion,
And of the threads that connect the stars, and of wombs and of
    the father-stuff,
And of the rights of them the others are down upon,
Of the deform'd, trivial, flat, foolish, despised,
Fog in the air, beetles rolling balls of dung.

I'm struck by how fluently Whitman moves in this catalog from down-trodden human beings to natural elements. He would be the vehicle of everything wounded and human as well as everything overlooked and in-human. He refuses social hierarchies and especially identifies with those on the lowest rung of the social ladder—prisoners, slaves, and thieves. He would be the voice of the sick, the degraded, the despised, the oppressed. But he is also going up and down the ladder of being, magically moving between the invisible threads that link the constellations and the lowliest "beetles rolling balls of dung." The Orphic poet would be the voice of everything that needs voicing, of whatever drives life. A profound demo-cratic impulse is hereby wedded to an archaic one, and the poem itself be-comes an act of animism, of the transmigration of souls.

Think for a moment of Wordsworth's poem "A Slumber Did My Spirit Seal" and how the personified spirit, engendered as a "she," "rolled round in earth's diurnal course, / With rocks, and stones, and trees." The rocks and stones betoken an extreme loss of human life, of humanity, and thus the impulse to animate them speaks to the far reaches of poetic imagination. That's why there are always so many rocks and stones rolling around poetry, from Ovid's *Metamorphoses* to Ponge's phenomenological poems to the abbreviated lyrics of the Deep Imagists who wanted, after all, to show the natural world saturated with psyche. ("Go inside a stone," Charles Simic writes, "That would be my way.")

Or consider this instance from Theodore Roethke's sequence "The Lost Son" when he suddenly calls out:

Voice, come out of the silence.
Say something.
Appear in the form of a spider
Or a moth beating the curtain.

And the voice comes back to him:

Dark hollows said, lee to the wind,
The moon said, back of an eel,
The salt said, look by the sea,

Your tears are not enough praise,
You will find no comfort here,
In the kingdom of bang and blab.

Grief is not praise and, strikingly, the sea refuses to comfort the human protagonist. And yet Roethke's psychological regression, like Keats's negative capability, instills the natural world with soul. The poet would be a vehicle for the oracular language of nature, the poem an act of shamanism.

The drama has its roots in ritual, and theater retains aspects of participation by a group in an established or collective ceremony. Poetry must now do without that sense of collective participation, but it would nonetheless yoke for itself some of that participatory magic. Thus the move into personae when it takes animistic form may be understood as a move past drama back into ceremony and festival, into ritual action. Many splendid poets of dramatic lyric—Christina Rossetti, Robert Graves, Theodore Roethke—would be the inheritors of a mystical power that derives from ritual itself. The move past theater in lyric poetry is at the highest level a move into sacred space, into sacred groves. It is an act of spiritual reenchantment. Listen to how Whitman testifies to a pagan holiness: "Divine I am inside and out," he writes, "and I make holy whatever I touch or am touch'd from." Whitman summons up for himself the prophetic powers of a lost poetic priesthood. He enters the new world with the authority of the most ancient poetic practice, reminding us that at its dramatic and spiritual peak the poem itself becomes a breakthrough into the divine.

Act 4

"Authors are actors, books are theatres," Wallace Stevens said ("Adagia"). What strange intertextual theaters they are. I love poems of self-manifestation, of incandescent histrionic power, and that's one of the reasons I'm called to the dramatic monologue when the speaker adopts the voice of a known figure from the past. I'm equally called to poems that take on the voice, the secret spirit, of an unknown or imaginary person. Both kinds of poems acknowledge our antecedents; they recognize that others have preceded us. The dramatic monologue displays a poetic intersubjectivity because it is always dependent upon another term. It is a poem of address.

The invisible but binding interrelationship between the poet and the speaker can be intensely moving and agonized. Poems are not found experiences; they are made things. (The found poem is the exception that proves the rule.) The dramatic monologue engages us in the very act of poetic making. It is shocking because it reminds us that no matter how natural sounding it is, the poem is always an artificial utterance.

There are poems that invite the reader into the process of sacred making. It is sometimes alleged that such poems are cool or "neoclassical" because they are so "literary," but I find they often have an intense emotional heat. Think, for example, of Cavafy's "The God Abandons Antony." It immediately sets up a triadic relationship between the poet, the anonymous protagonist (not a historical personage), and the historical figure of Mark Antony himself.

The God Abandons Antony

When suddenly, at midnight, you hear
an invisible procession going by
with exquisite music, voices,
don't mourn your luck that's failing now,
work gone wrong, your plans
all proving deceptive—don't mourn them uselessly.
As one long prepared, and graced with courage,
say goodbye to her, the Alexandria that is leaving.
Above all, don't fool yourself, don't say
it was a dream, your ears deceived you:
don't degrade yourself with empty hopes like these.
As one long prepared, and graced with courage,
as is right for you who were given this kind of city,
go firmly to the window
and listen with deep emotion, but not
with the whining, the pleas of a coward;
listen—your final delectation—to the voices,
to the exquisite music of that strange procession,
and say goodbye to her, to the Alexandria you are losing.
                    (translated by Edmund Keeley and Philip Sherrard)

Cavafy has filtered his own terrible sense of loss through the fictive voice of an unknown person who addresses Mark Antony at the grave, bewildered moment of final departure and onrushing death. The poem is directive: the speaker presumes to give Antony instructions (don't mourn your failing luck, don't deceive yourself with empty hopes, go to the window with resolve, etc.). It reminds him (twice) that he is "long prepared, and graced with courage," and it counsels him to deep stoic emotion, to a final pleasure, a last good-bye. In some sense Cavafy is talking to himself about how to say farewell to a cherished city at the proper moment. He is simultaneously addressing and teaching us by inscribing his idea of facing the music and leaving a beloved place.

Mark Antony believed he was under the special protection of the god Dionysus, but he was not, and the withdrawal of the god abandons Antony to a fate without any supernatural warrant. He is left in a *human* situation. The procession that suddenly weaves by Antony's window at midnight (the epiphanic hour of revelation) becomes a ritual procession. Cavafy is counseling Antony to a ritual good-bye, a formal gesture of celebration and mourning.

There is a strong interdependency of texts as well as voices operating in this poem. Cavafy took his title from Plutarch's *Life of Antony* and built the poem out of Plutarch's historical narration. (Plutarch describes a bacchanalia winding past Antony's house just before the fall of Alexandria and reads this as a sign of Antony's abandonment by Dionysus.) Cavafy also reads Plutarch through the powerful lens of Shakespeare's *Antony and Cleopatra* (act 4, scene 3). The Shakespearean inheritance doesn't lead Cavafy away from his personal feeling for Alexandria but toward that feeling, and the story becomes the vehicle of its dramatic expression. The poem itself enacts a ritual action.

The shifting borderline in poetry between imagination and reality, between historical personage and fictive reconstruction, between lying and telling the truth, induces an ontological queasiness in some readers. The puritanical distrust of high theatricality in contemporary poetry has seemed to me a particular limitation of our moment, part of the radical constriction of high culture in our times. It is certainly that, but after I read Jonas Barish's book *The Antitheatrical Prejudice*, I recognized that our lingering puritanism also has a long history and that our current idiom embodies, in

Barish's words, "the vestiges of a prejudice against the theater that goes back as far in European history as the theater itself can be traced."

It is apparently difficult for some readers to accept ductility as a feature of the poetic sensibility. "The poet is a sophist," Plato complains, "a maker of counterfeits that look like the truth." Against which: "What shocks the virtuous philosopher, delights the chameleon Poet." The transformative power of the dramatic poet resembles that of the empowered actor. Baudelaire claims:

> The poet enjoys the incomparable privilege of being, at will, both himself and other people. Like a wandering soul seeking a body, he can enter, whenever he wishes, into anyone's personality.... He takes as his own all the professions, rejoicings and miseries that circumstance brings to him.

Here is a poem by Delmore Schwartz that lands on Baudelaire himself. It enters his sensibility and (imaginatively) inhabits his body.

Baudelaire

When I fall asleep, and even during sleep,
I hear, quite distinctly, voices speaking
Whole phrases, commonplace and trivial,
Having no relation to my affairs.

Dear Mother, is any time left to us
In which to be happy? My debts are immense.
My bank account is subject to the court's judgment.
I know nothing. I cannot know anything.
I have lost the ability to make an effort.
But now as before my love for you increases.
You are always armed to stone me, always:
It is true. It dates from childhood.

For the first time in my long life
I am almost happy. The book, almost finished,
Almost seems good. It will endure, a monument
To my obsessions, my hatred, my disgust.

Debts and inquietude persist and weaken me.
Satan glides before me, saying sweetly:
"Rest for a day! You can rest and play today.
Tonight you will work." When night comes,
My mind, terrified by the arrears,
Bored by sadness, paralyzed by impotence,
Promises: "Tomorrow: I will tomorrow."
Tomorrow the same comedy enacts itself
With the same resolution, the same weakness.

I am sick of this life of furnished rooms.
I am sick of having colds and headaches:
You know my strange life. Every day brings
Its quota of wrath. You little know
A poet's life, dear Mother: I must write poems,
The most fatiguing of occupations.

I am sad this morning. Do not reproach me.
I write from a café near the post office,
Amid the click of billiard balls, the clatter of dishes,
The pounding of my heart. I have been asked to write
"A History of Caricature." I have been asked to write
"A History of Sculpture." Shall I write a history
Of the caricatures of the sculptures of you in my heart?

Although it costs you countless agony,
Although you cannot believe it necessary,
And doubt that the sum is accurate,
Please send me money enough for at least three weeks.

Schwartz's own obsessions are channeled through this fictive address
from Baudelaire to his mother. He knew from his own experiences of
madness what it meant to hear voices coming to you seemingly out of
nowhere, voices commanding sleep itself. The poet creates a convincing
scenography not of speaking but of letter writing ("I write from a café
near the post office") and thus we get the frisson of intimacy that comes
from reading a poet's letter to his mother. The device seems to give

Schwartz particular access to Baudelaire's inner life because the poem imagines Baudelaire at the moment when the aesthete must explain himself to his absent but disapproving parent. In the process, the poem characterizes the particular kind of warring intimacy between mother and son. ("But now as before my love for you increases. / You are always armed to stone me, always: / It is true. It dates from childhood.") The poem moves from the grandiloquent to the mundane and back again, and it shows the interface between the great work ("The book, almost finished, / Almost seems good") and the quotidian life ("I am sick of this life of furnished rooms"). The request for money to live "for at least three weeks" exposes Baudelaire to an appalling shame, and that's why it's so agonizing to read. Schwartz gets some of Baudelaire's power (he speaks convincingly, after all, as the creator of *Les Fleurs du mal*), but also his humiliation (he obviously knows all too well what it means to plead for money from a withholding parent). In the most specific way possible Schwartz creates a drama of the poet's life at the unhappy moment when he recognizes his embarrassing dependency upon the practical world. I love Schwartz, too, for his dramatic exaggerations, for acknowledging that writing poems is "the most fatiguing of occupations."

The poem written to or from the point of view of a previous writer enters into an oddly intersubjective field. It is a model of mutuality and presence because it shows us the poet's need for other material, even for guidance. There is something abject and beautiful about the way that Dante summons Virgil to his side to lead his pilgrim self through the inferno itself to the gateway of paradise, or the way that Blake summons Milton, Yeats summons Blake, Roethke summons Yeats ("I take this cadence from a man named Yeats. / I take it and I give it back again"). I'm struck by the way the young Ezra Pound entered poetry not alone but with a self-acknowledged dependence upon Cino da Pistoia, Arnaut Daniel, Pierre Vidal, Bertran de Born. He was transporting himself into the role of the Provençal poet, remaking the Provençal poet for the modern world.

The dramatic monologue, which takes us into a preexisting world, has a different relationship to time than the short lyric. We might say that time moves within its state of timelessness. The narrative poem borrows the novel's obligation to the facts and gives us a social realm. The dramatic poem is presentational of that realm. Both drama and narrative want to keep going, to expand and develop, to create fictive worlds for themselves. In contrast, the lyric calls for the greatest degree of concentration. It may be that the dramatic poem is forged on the crucible of condensation straining against expression, lyric time against narrative time.

There are moments in lyric poetry when the intersubjective pull is so strong that the poem expands into dialogue. Think of the difference between the highly theatrical dramatic monologues in Richard Howard's book *Untitled Subjects* and the bright pageantry that comprises his book *Two-Part Inventions*. Or think of how W. H. Auden shuffles forth from the otherworld to address JM and his companion across the Ouija board in James Merrill's epic trilogy. Auden is just one of the tutelary spirits who comprise the visionary chorus, visionary company, of *The Changing Light at Sandover.* To bring forth figures to speak from the otherworld is inevitably to enter into the range and territory of *The Divine Comedy.*

Pause for a moment to think of *The Waste Land*. Dante provided one of the key models for this poem of the living dead originally entitled *He Do the Police in Different Voices. The Waste Land* is an open structure of fragments, a poem without a fixed center, and it has no single interpretation or truth, no single narrator or narrative thread to hold it together. It disseminates the self. It contains scenes and vignettes from a wide variety of times and places: agitated scraps of conversations, parodies, intertextual allusions, unattributed and often broken quotations, a medley of radically shifting languages, a disturbing cacophony of voices. The result is a poem with the feeling of a nightmare. The poem arises out of what Eliot once called "some rude unknown psychic materials." In a psychoanalytic sense, the poem represents the psyche's disintegration and the reconstitution of a self. I see no contradiction between the personal elements in the poem—one of Eliot's friends called it "Tom's Autobiography"—and the immense panorama of other voices that animate it. Eliot is the least autonomous of poets. His work is abject with quotations which he then idealized as "tradition." It is one of the striking ironies of literary history that his work has been taken to authorize autonomous readings of poetry.

I want to summon up one final example of dramatic interdependency: *Homage to Mistress Bradstreet.* John Berryman's poem started out as fifty lines and ended as fifty-two stanzas, and it combines the concentration of an extended lyric with the amplitude and erudition of a historical romance. (Saul Bellow called it the equivalent of a five-hundred-page novel.) Berryman himself said that his model was *The Waste Land,* though the poem feels more like "The Wreck of the Deutschland" condensed from *The Adventures of Augie March.* Berryman had to invent a fluctuating language in this poem that could speak across the centuries, and he came up with a resourceful hybrid of the vernacular and the archaic, a diction floating wildly between the intimate colloquial and the elevated formal. The move into a speaker with a language that is not ordinary speech gives a particular kind of shine to the poem. But it also does more than that. The stylistic mannerism creates a way to render a deep state of psychological connection and unity, to get dramatic liftoff and ecstasy. The libidinal excitement is ensouled in the odd diction and grammatical reversals. Berryman's ruptured grammar, his particular style of pathos and desperation, becomes the only way that he can have Anne Bradstreet. The form transports him to her. I believe that through a Shakespearean inheritance Berryman found a quirky and brilliant language to address the problem which Anne Bradstreet faced and, in fact, which all American poets face: "the almost insuperable difficulty of writing high verse in a land that cared and cares so little for it."

I want to focus on that moment in the second section when the poem suddenly breaks loose into dialogue. The first section moves between novelistic discourse and dramatic soliloquy; it addresses the seventeenth-century poet and tries to physically summon her up out of the grave ("Out of maize & air / your body's made, and moves. I summon, see, / from the centuries it"). The poet calls upon Anne Bradstreet to speak for herself ("Versing, I shroud among the dynasties") and then interrupts her with his relevant and sometimes irreverent comments ("all this bald / abstract didactic rime I read appalled"). But at the end of the first movement, stanza 30, Anne Bradstreet says directly to the modern poet, "Kiss me" and "Talk to me."

The effect is riveting. One could surmise that Berryman's need for Anne Bradstreet was so great that he was forced to magically summon her to love him across the centuries. He literally, even demonically, would seduce her out of the dust. Thus her startling speech:

—Ravishing, ha, what crouches outside ought,
flamboyant, ill, angelic. Often, now,
I am afraid of you.
I am a sobersides; I know.
I *want* to take you for my lover.

I'm struck by the fact that Anne Bradstreet speaks one of Lise's lines from *Berryman's Sonnets*. This does more than make Anne Bradstreet's speech more "realistic"; it suggests that there may not be any ontological difference between the adulterous lover in the *Sonnets* and the fictive one in *Homage*. Berryman is so startled by Bradstreet's speech that his reply is unusually monosyllabic: "Do," he says to her. Here is their next exchange:

—I hear a madness. Harmless I to you
am not, not I?—No.
—I cannot but be. Sing a concord of our thought.

This call for concord, for communion, is so overwhelming to the poet that it ruptures the frame of the dialogue, and Bradstreet momentarily falls back. So much does he want her now that he gets desperate:

—Wan dolls in indigo on gold: refrain
my western lust. I am drowning in this past.
I lose sight of you
who mistress me from air.

Berryman continues on to make a confession to Mistress Bradstreet, his demon lover who is no more than air, a mouthful of words: "I am a man of griefs & fits / trying to be my friend."

This confessional moment of acknowledgment is terribly moving. The poet would befriend and comfort himself, if only he could. Out of this need, out of this quest to surmount his dissatisfactions and griefs, to heal his self-divisions, the poet turns for help to a poet from the past. He recognizes and acknowledges the depth of longing out of which art is created, and he turns outward to an imaginary beloved. It is a thrilling moment of poetry's self-awareness that it is being made. The poem becomes an act of sacred calling, sacred passion.

Act 5

The end is near. Soon the curtain will come down for the last time. Think of the last startling cycle of songs that Heine wrote from his "mattress-grave," of Whitman's Deathbed Edition. *The Cantos* have been abandoned. ("I cannot make it flow through...") *Tristia* has been sent, the *Sonnets to Orpheus* dictated, *The Bridge* completed, *The Dream Songs* finished. It is a time for late reckonings, for summary and divestiture, for lying down "in the foul rag-and-bone shop of the heart." It is the moment for Yeats's "The Circus Animals' Desertion" ("Maybe, at last, being but a broken man," he writes, "I must be satisfied with my heart"), for Stevens's "Final Soliloquy of the Interior Paramour" ("This is, therefore, the intensest rendezvous"), for Louise Bogan's "Song for the Last Act" ("Now that I have your heart by heart, I see").

Then there are the last poems themselves, the final final soliloquies, the ones literally hammered out from the edge of the grave. It is the hour for self-elegies, for the concluding glamours: Yeats's "The Black Tower" and Stevens's "Of Mere Being," Philip Larkin's desolate "Aubade" ("The mind blanks at the glare"), Sylvia Plath's crossover poem "Edge" ("The woman is perfected"). Sir Walter Raleigh is writing his own epitaph, "Even such is Time," on the night before his beheading in 1618; Chidiock Tichborne is rhyming the poem that came to be known as "Tichborne's Elegy" ("Written with his own hand in the tower before his execution"). It's June 14, 1837, and the hunchbacked Leopardi is dictating the radiant last lines of "*Il tramanto della luna*" ("The Setting of the Moon") within a few hours of his death:

> Vedova è insino al fine; ed alla notte
> Che l'altre etadi oscura,
> Segno poser gli Dei la sepoltura
>
> Widowed we shall remain until the end;
> And in the night to come
> The gods have raised a sign for us, the tomb.
> *(translated by Ottavio Mark Casale)*

"In this mortal frame of mine, which is made of a hundred bones and nine orifices, there is something, and this something can be called, for lack of a better name, a windswept spirit, for it is much like thin drapery that is torn and swept away by the slightest stirring of the wind. This something in me took to writing poetry years ago, merely to amuse itself at first, but finally making it its lifelong business." So Matsuo Bashō on writing poetry. Now it's the small hours of November 25, 1694, and the master, who is near death, is calling out to his disciple Donshū so he can dictate his last poem. The ink has been prepared. "I know this is no occasion for writing a hokku, as I am faced with death," Bashō would reflect aloud: "Yet poetry has been on my mind all through my life, which is now more than fifty years long." The poem is sometimes called "During Illness." Here is Robert Hass's rendering:

> Sick on a journey
> my dreams wander
> the withered fields.

This is a poem of the final journey: the helpless body collapsing; the dreaming mind, the windswept spirit, still trying to roam free, to soar over the now-withered fields.

Look closely into the poetry of our century and you find history warming up its sacrificial victims, preparing its martyrdoms: Osip Mandelstam, Miguel Hernández, César Vallejo ("I will die in Paris, on a rainy day," he prophesied, "On some day I can already remember"). Somewhere it is 1914 and Georg Trakl, a dispensing chemist in the Austrian army, has found the wherewithal to craft his magisterial poem "Grodek," the name of a town in Galicia, Poland, where the Austrians were defeated and he was left to care for ninety wounded men, most of whose sufferings he could not relieve, some of whom committed suicide in his presence. Soon he would follow with a self-administered overdose of cocaine. "O prouder grief!" Trakl cries out,

> You brazen altars,
> Today a great pain feeds the hot flame of the spirit,
> The grandsons yet unborn.
> *(translated by Michael Hamburger)*

The dream of the concluding poem. It is the sacrificial hour of abandonment and prayer, of ritualized grief before brazen altars, of the last determined quest for a consoling unity. These are threshold poems. That's why they so often begin with nightfall (Trakl writes: "At nightfall the autumn wind cries out / With deadly weapons and golden plains") and take place in the absolute field of night (Yeats's hour, like Cavafy's and Desnos's, was jubilant midnight). Just as often they conclude in the eerie blue light of dawn ("the cauldron of morning," as Plath called it). These poems take place at whatever moment evokes the transition between worlds. They have the gravity of a light forever changing, of visionary imagination. They are written in the presence of what Heidegger called "being-to-death." The poet is performing the last rites in advance of death, and thus the poem is delivered back to us with a certain formal sense of ceremonial procession.

Poems are presences. They ventriloquize voices. Many dramatic poems have the quality of soliloquy: the act of speaking to oneself in or as if in solitude. A final soliloquy is the last version of such a speech. In some sense, every poem is about time, but the final soliloquy is posed against death in a particular way. It is a boundary poem that inscribes a last wish about vanishing, a concluding trope of disappearance. It is furiously crafted against the contingencies of time. It had better be, for the poet is vanishing and human life must be breathed into the poem. There is no other way: the words are all. Such life can be instilled in poetry through style. Style both creates the surface and calls upon—calls up— the deep unconscious life.

Remember everything is at stake in this conclusive last utterance, this rising self-elegy, and yet no actor is getting ready to dramatize the words, no costumed thespian is preparing to strut across a scenic stage for an appreciative communal audience. This ritual enacts another kind of magical transference and imaginative exchange. There was a writer who became a book, there is a reader leaning over the page to decipher the letters, to meet the written characters...

The art of last things is an art pared away to what is absolutely essential, an art of making language at the edge of a void where everything is undone, unmade. Language was put to a grave test on October 31, 1944, when the Hungarian poet Miklós Radnóti somehow found it within himself to write the last of his four "Postcard" poems in the midst of a forced march westward across Hungary.

Postcard
4

I fell next to him. His body rolled over.
It was tight as a string before it snaps.
Shot in the back of the head—"This is how
you'll end." "Just lie quietly," I said to myself.
Patience flowers into death now.
"Der springt noch auf," I heard above me.
Dark filthy blood was drying on my ear.

> Szentskirályszabadja
> October 31, 1944
> *(translated by Steven Polgar,*
> *Stephen Berg, and S. J. Marks)*

Radnóti speaks to the unspeakable in these seven lines, to the horrific death he knew was coming. The poem inscribes a suffering unimaginably intense, a consciousness of death unbearably palpable. It is a poem nearly literally rising up from a mass grave. Near the town of Abda, sometime between November 6 and November 10, Radnóti was one of twenty-two prisoners murdered and tossed into a collective grave. He was thirty-five years old. After the war his widow had his body exhumed and his last poems were found in his field jacket, written in pencil in a small Serbian exercise book. They display the classical poise of an Orphic art that comes back from the underworld to give testimony.

All the poems written during Radnóti's internment appeared in a posthumous volume, *Clouded Sky* (1946), which is one of the pinnacles of Central European poetry in this century. I have sometimes wondered if Radnóti's commitment to classical values as well as his immense labor in translation (his 1942 volume *In the Footsteps of Orpheus* ranges across two thousand years of European poetry) was a way of keeping alive an ideal of Europe as a place of Enlightenment during a time when it had clearly become a site of barbarism.

Radnóti's poems are filled with disquieting premonitions of the horrors to come. Characterizing the times, he wrote, "I lived on this earth in an age / when man fell so low / he killed willingly, for pleasure, without orders." He was doom-ridden and had an uncanny sense of his own impending destruction. "I am the one they'll kill finally / because I myself never killed," he prophesied in 1939 for a new edition of *Steep Road*, the last individual collection of his poetry published while he was still alive. One high-water mark of his work is a series of eight eclogues, written in hexameters, that refashion the pastoral form to address an era when morality is turned upside down and right and wrong have changed places. He calls on the pastoral muse to assist him in trying to preserve the values of civilization. These poems sing to overcome terror, invoking the splendor of memory, the landscape of childhood, and the necessity of love at a time when "reason falls apart."

Radnóti's descriptive powers never faltered. Until the end, he was able to characterize with poignant accuracy the nightmare he experienced. I'm struck by the fact that he entitled his last poems "Postcards." Here the jauntiness of the title belies the gravity of the content. It's an offering characterized as much by what is left out as by what is put in, and its brevity (its self-acknowledged communicative inadequacy) speaks volumes to what must be left unsaid. The informality of the postcard (dashed off, superficial) is also belied by the scrupulousness with which Radnóti re-creates the scene with a few dramatic brushstrokes.

Radnóti's poem is not an exact transcription of experience but a made thing. It is not a work of reportage but of art, and therefore it enters art psyche, art time. It has the moonglow of a poem made halfway to Hades. There are minds that can split themselves off and still have utterance, minds that show uncanny stoicism on the edge of the grave. It takes a particular kind of involvement and detachment both to speak and to stand beside oneself, to engage oneself as an artist with a dead person lying next to you. I think of Wilfred Owen, Robert Graves, Siegfried Sassoon, or Keith Douglas.

There may be no name for the kind of speaker we have in a poem like Radnóti's last "Postcard." It doesn't seem entirely accurate to call him either a fictive construction or a mere witness, though he has elements of both. Rather, Radnóti's speaker is both completely personal and somehow beyond the personal, at once a historical self and a transcendental self. I would call him "transpersonal." Radnóti's classical training and his psychological insight come together here under the stimulus of his own finality, and he uses art to pull himself up to some higher level, to change consciousness. Maybe he dreamed that by imagining his own end he could somehow be saved from it.

The fourth "Postcard" begins drastically with two sharp staccato sentences that fuse together in one line broken in the middle: "I fell next to him. His body rolled over." The speaker has fallen out of time into the netherworld (no time for elaboration now) and immediately we're inside the experience of someone who has fallen, or been thrown down, next to a dead body. That body is compared to a string so taut it's about to snap. I can't stop thinking of him lying there next to someone who had been shot in the back of the head. Something has got to give, and Radnóti seems to be desperately trying to hold on to reason, to fend off madness, which terrified him. Remember his poem "Maybe...":

> But don't leave me, delicate mind!
>   Don't let me go crazy.
> Sweet wounded reason, don't
>   leave me now.
>
> Don't leave me. Let me die, without fear,
>   a clean lovely death,
> like Empedocles, who smiled as he fell
>   into the crater.
>   *(translated by Steven Polgar,*
>   *Stephen Berg, and S. J. Marks)*

These pleading lines echo as I listen to the voice in "Postcard" that comes to the still-living man with a flat warning, a matter-of-fact declaration: "This is how you'll end." A threat made good. The poet counsels himself to hold still, to accept what is happening to him. He says it aloud to calm himself, to enact it for us. There's a terrifying stoicism to the line "Patience flowers into death now." A blossoming into oblivion. Then he hears an unattributed voice floating over him in German, the language of death. There's remarkable richness in the phrase "Der springt noch auf," which means something like "Wait till you see this guy break open." It has a nasty colloquial edge. But the verb *aufspringen*, which means "to break or pop open," is usually used to describe a bud or a flower. It's an image of germination, and so perhaps there's a hidden tenderness here, as if the poet ventriloquized the German to say, "Wait till you see him blossom." He is breaking free of his fetters; and death has become a liberation. After this, the last statement of the poem (a memory made more forceful by the way the sentence and the line coincide) has an eerie calmness: "Dark filthy blood was drying on my ear." Radnóti was also thinking associatively here, and the sound of German links to the image of blood coagulating on his ear. The one who listens and observes is still alive, speaking from the earth.

I cling to the fact that a postcard is a message directed to another person. It has a particular reader in mind. But its openness suggests that it can be read by anyone. The poem in the guise of a postcard is a testimony back to life, a signal that Radnóti has pushed back the silence long enough to embody a final experience. This postcard peels off his body. He has taken us all the way into the shadowy hushed space of death itself.

There are elegies for the self—poems of self-commemoration—that move into lyric time, religious space. These poems are written from the far side of alienation, from the vanishing point of life, and thus they seek consolation in closing the circle. They are poems of the deepest initiated awe.

Think for a moment of the sixteenth-century anthology piece "Tichborne's Elegy." The title was supplied by an early publisher.

> My prime of youth is but a frost of cares,
> My feast of joy is but a dish of pain,
> My crop of corn is but a field of tares,
> And all my good is but vain hope of gain;
> The day is past, and yet I saw no sun,
> And now I live, and now my life is done.
>
> My tale was heard and yet it was not told,
> My fruit is fallen and yet my leaves are green,
> My youth is spent and yet I am not old,
> I saw the world and yet I was not seen;
> My thread is cut and yet it is not spun,
> And now I live, and now my life is done.

I sought my death and found it in my womb,
I looked for life and saw it was a shade,
I trod the earth and know it was my tomb,
And now I die, and now I was but made;
My glass is full, and now my glass is run,
And now I live, and now my life is done.

This simple three-part lyric monumentalizes a fleeting instant of con-sciousness, a springboard or threshold moment. It bears some similarity to other commemorative inscriptions scratched or carved into the walls of the Tower of London, but its dizzying circularity creates a different sense of time and space than other last statements ("Here was..."). Its in-cantatory structure and balanced repetitions make a different proposition about eternity. Reading it I'm reminded of Peter Sacks's claim in his fine book *The English Elegy* that "Repetition creates a sense of continuity, of an unbroken pattern such as one may oppose to the extreme discontinu-ity of death." The rhythm of lament expresses and controls the experi-ence of unbounded grief.

"Tichborne's Elegy" relies entirely on the language of paradox to create a sense of reconciliation between opposites. Its reiterations are a creative response to psychological trauma. Note the progression of tenses throughout the poem: how it begins in the present (stanza 1), moves to the past (stanza 2), and fuses past and present together (stanza 3). Note, too, that each refrain becomes more literal and thus brings the speaker closer to actual death. The poem presses back against that literalism by symbolically closing the circle: "I sought my death and found it in my womb." The Renaissance poet who wrote this shows his kinship with his pre-Christian Celtic inheritance now overlaid with a redemptive Chris-tian immortality.

"Tichborne's Elegy" ritualizes a moment of slippage between past and present, present and future, and thus between death and immortal-ity. Sharon Cameron points out that Tichborne's paradigmatic scheme looks very much like the one proposed by Emily Dickinson:

Behind Me—dips Eternity—
Before Me—Immortality—
Myself—the Term between—

The lyric poem itself becomes the term between, its form a consolation that would deliver us into a primal unity, a deep fusion experience of the world. The lyric delivered at the edge of the earth puts me in mind of the Sufi maxim, "The Beloved and I are one."

On February 5, 1963, just one week before her suicide, Sylvia Plath completed two poems. One of these is "Edge." "Edge" has that absolute certainty which we associate with poetry that has been dictated from the deepest sources. Contact has been made. The poem has a sense of recognition and inevitability so complete it suggests a dream life has been fulfilled.

Edge

The woman is perfected.
Her dead

Body wears the smile of accomplishment,
The illusion of a Greek necessity

Flows in the scrolls of her toga,
Her bare

Feet seem to be saying:
We have come so far, it is over.

Each dead child coiled, a white serpent,
One at each little

Pitcher of milk, now empty.
She has folded

Them back into her body as petals
Of a rose close when the garden

Stiffens and odors bleed
From the sweet, deep throats of the night flower.

The moon has nothing to be sad about,
Staring from her hood of bone.

She is used to this sort of thing.
Her blacks crackle and drag.

I still remember the mounting revulsion and horror, the near physical nausea, I felt when I first read this poem thirty years ago. I almost had to raise up an arm to fend off its harsh white light. I saw how the suicide imagined herself—she created a space which she would soon enter and occupy—and it terrified me. Suddenly, I could view my own body laid out dead. I saw the naked feet pointing upward on the metal table and felt the chill of the morgue. I recoiled from the lifeless object I'd become, from what I was forced to see and acknowledge. Such a shock of recognition opens up a grave region, a profound religious hush, within the reader.

There is something deeply eerie about the way Plath has split and textualized herself in this poem which hits the unconscious with an age-old horror. The fury of its self-estrangement, its self-detachment, is immense. It's a poem with a performing stoicism. A poem of easeful death. It also pushes back the silence in a way that's hard to get a grip on. Like other minimalist successes—a de Chirico painting, a Beckett one-act play, a Japanese scroll painting—it threatens to distill itself away from you. It shakes you off. No wonder then that most of Plath's commentators have turned away from it, averting their gaze. It's unbearable. An enormous artistic victory.

"Edge" looks dramatic on the page: the severe black lines surrounded by empty white space. The first line is utterly foreseen, propositional, indicative, implacable: "The woman is perfected." The narrative of the living body is over (it now "wears the smile of accomplishment") and the rest of the poem has the mystery and clarity of a mournful procession. Its language is stark, spare, stately: the language of essential things. There's purposefulness to the couplets in a poem filled with twinnings—the joining of life and death, of a mother gathering back her two children. The elasticity of short and long lines unfolding across the two-line stanzas gives the poem a dirgelike movement, the finality of a funeral. Each of the stanzas is enjambed until the final four lines of the poem, and this also creates a sense of movement within stasis. The language has the severity of "doing something" which we associate with ritual. "Edge" takes place not in narrative but in nonlinear time, timeless space. It has the character of the last act of a classical Greek tragedy.

Plath went to school on other poetry. She took from Robert Lowell the breakthrough fire of personal material, the fever of confession. She internalized the power of other modern poets who had used archaic methods to give their poems ritual power: Yeats, Graves, Lawrence, Roethke, Hughes. And she appropriated the uncanny gothic imagination of Emily Brontë and Mary Shelley: *Wuthering Heights* and *Frankenstein* were both books that circulated in her blood. That's how a so-called confessional poet could become a mythological one, a personal history transform itself under the sign of eternity.

The modern woman who has died in "Edge" is barefoot and dressed in a simple Greek toga, like a figure on a sarcophagus. She has become her own tragic and completed work: a corpse, a corpus. I have a sense that Plath is moving back through Christian into pre-Christian or pagan rites in this lyric stripped down to an elemental black and white. "Edge" was called "Nuns in Snow" in an early draft. Its title and some of its imagery arose when she was writing her earlier poem "Mystic." But the "Greek necessity" refers to Greek tragedy and the notion that suicide was an honorable release from dishonor. It returns one to the religious rites of death.

I find a dark tribalism in the way the dead woman clutches to her breasts her two dead children, each a coiled white serpent. Plath is thinking symbolically here: the whiteness appears as a sign of ritual purity, the serpent a consort of the great goddess who could induce trance and prophesy, who takes on pre-Christian power. (It was at a relatively late date that the serpent was reappropriated as a Christian emblem of evil.) Plath is also thinking metaphorically since each breast becomes a little "pitcher of milk, now empty." It's as if by folding her children back into her body (a terrifying reversal of childbirth) she is participating in a primitive vegetation rite.

She is also asserting an age-old mother right, an awesome maternal power. The Medusa element is shocking, and we should not shrink from the horror of the sacrifice being enacted here. We should also remember that there is catharsis in liturgy, in symbolic action. Perhaps the poet was acting out this sacrifice on a symbolic level precisely so that she wouldn't have to do it literally. She could not save herself, but she could spare her children.

The symbolic legacy of the dead woman in "Edge" is a thwarted personal inheritance, but also a trope of sexual and maternal power returned to the earth. She enacts a sacrifice that will bloom forth, like Whitman's lilacs, in the elegiac flowers of poetry. The last two couplets hit a complex register:

> The moon has nothing to be sad about,
> Staring from her hood of bone.

The moon's indifference is expressed colloquially, but her blank gaze is a bleak romantic image that goes up a linguistic notch. The pattern is repeated in the last two lines:

> She is used to this sort of thing.
> Her blacks crackle and drag.

The fact that this kind of sacrifice is now so common that the moon has become accustomed to it is expressed colloquially, but the final line hits a note that is below or above speech, and therefore visionary. The moon is engendered and hooded, she is wearing funeral attire, the clothes of mourning. She's a white figure in black robes. It's as if the moon is grieving despite herself, and this reluctant mourning, this form of animism gives the poem its final feeling of catharsis and incarnation, of a transcendent numinous power. "Edge" embodies a final desire to be completed, to be reborn into the deepest unity.

The curtain has at last come down. The play is over, the essential biography of the writer completed, the great work done. Eternal rest to the maker. But the lyric left behind proposes a legacy beyond death, an immortality. The dramatic poem has been generously crafted to give testimony, to enact and release itself inside of us, to be passed on, like manna.

7

Beyond Desolation

We treat poems as if they come to us dispassionately, whereas in truth many of the very greatest poems seem as if they were written in blood. They come from the deepest wellsprings of being. "I went with my very being toward language," Paul Celan said. That intense transformation of energy, that transubstantiation of mute feeling into words, is a key mark of poetry. The New Critics usefully taught us that the poem stands as an autonomous work of art, but they didn't indicate that it also breathes with the presence of its maker. To fully encounter a poem we must let its mysteries breathe through us. Then we can track its strategies and untangle its ironies, not merely as a game (though the ludic aspect of poetry is one of its great pleasures), but also as a form of necessary speech.

In a column entitled "My Favorite Poem" (1955), the Austrian poet Ingeborg Bachmann wrote:

> whoever writes poetry engraves forms in our memory, wonderful old words for stone or leaf, tied to or released by new words, new signs of reality. And I believe that whoever inscribes these forms also disappears into them with his own breath, which he offers as the unrequited proof of these forms' truth.

The poet disappears into the poem, which stands mute, like an idol, until the reader breathes life back into it. And only then does it shimmer again with imaginative presence.

The lyric poem breathes in the most intimate form of literary discourse. It is the social act of a solitary maker. I feel, in many of the poems I love best, as if I am in the presence of the heart's voice arguing with itself.

I find the very idea of language, of lyric poetry itself, immensely hopeful. That's why no poem is too despairing for me. Even when John Clare writes from an asylum

> I am—yet what I am, none cares or knows;
>   My friends forsake me like a memory lost:
> I am the self-consumer of my woes—
>   *("I am")*

he still situates the feeling in language. Despair is turning away from human commerce, it is silence.

"Poetry confronts in the most clear-eyed way just those emotions which consciousness wishes to slide by," C. K. Williams writes in *Poetry and Consciousness*. Poetry puts us on the hook—it makes us responsible for what we might otherwise evade in ourselves and in others. It gives us greater access to ourselves. Now I want to look at three poems on the far side of desolation—one by Robert Frost, one by Gerard Manley Hopkins, one by Nâzim Hikmet—to see how a seething, self-consuming woe is transmuted into an energetic work of art, and isolation is transformed into a relationship with a future reader. To read these poems is to become their recipients, to open up the space for their dark wisdom. Breathe into the idol—the page—and the dead letters spring alive again.

We were driving across central Iowa in a light snowfall. It was a late midwinter afternoon, a blue day in the heartland. I was trying to memorize one of my favorite poems, Robert Frost's "Desert Places," and so, as I stared out steadily at a ribbon of interstate stretching ahead of us, my wife opened a book of Frost's poems on her lap. It wasn't necessary. As soon as I started reciting the poem I realized that I already had it by heart. It's as if the words were engraved on the windshield in front of me, and I simply had to read them. I could see the shapely stanzas unscrolling before my inner eye. I suspect that most committed readers of poetry have experienced this odd pleasure—the shock of recognition—of a poem coming back to you phrase by phrase, line by line, stanza by stanza. Over the years I had returned so often to this lyric, in solitude, that the words had become part of me. Now, as the bruised air deepened into darkness and the snow covered the flat ground surrounding us for hundreds of miles, the words were rising out of me again, summoned into consciousness, as I recited them to someone else. They had been living in me all this time. Now they were voicing themselves in the wintry air.

Desert Places

Snow falling and night falling fast, oh, fast
In a field I looked into going past,
And the ground almost covered smooth in snow,
But a few weeds and stubble showing last.

The woods around it have it—it is theirs.
All animals are smothered in their lairs.
I am too absent-spirited to count;
The loneliness includes me unawares.

And lonely as it is, that loneliness
Will be more lonely ere it will be less—
A blanker whiteness of benighted snow
With no expression, nothing to express.

They cannot scare me with their empty spaces
Between stars—on stars where no human race is.
I have it in me so much nearer home
To scare myself with my own desert places.

This poem is fluent and spacious and yet also extremely tight and well-crafted. Each stanza is a block, a solid unit. The stanzas progress like stations on a journey. "A poem is a walk," A. R. Ammons contends in an essay, and "Desert Places" opens with the feeling of a solitary walk, with a lone figure in a cold landscape. The rhythm of the poem marks the rhythm of that walk. The rhymes are markers, deft and simple. One notes how the first two lines rhyme fully ("fast" / "past") while the third line strays off on its own ("snow") only to be reeled back by the conclusiveness of the fourth line rhyming with the first two ("last"). Each stanza gives a sense of fullness, of coming together and stopping. That wandering third line projects a sense of outward momentum. It also keeps the triple rhymes from seeming overdetermined or comical. And those triple rhymes—coming together with a full stop at the close of each stanza—help give the lyric its feeling of dark inevitability, chiseling it permanently into memory.

There is an oddly persistent popular image of Frost as a folksy, optimistic old gentleman farmer. To be fair, it's an image he proposed and fostered, but it doesn't have much to do with the true effect of his best poems, the real suggestions of danger that are shot through them. For one, there is a dialogue in much of his work between the inner and outer worlds, between inner and outer weather. ("That day she put our heads together, / Fate had her imagination about her," he writes in "Tree at My Window," "Your head so much concerned with outer, / Mine with inner, weather.") Often in his poems what is going on between the characters inside the confines of a house seems so claustrophobic that someone has to leave—think of "Home Burial" and how the woman rushes off at the close of the poem. She comes down the stairs and crosses the enclosure of the house in order to escape. By contrast, "Desert Places," as in Frost's more famous poem "Stopping by Woods on a Snowy Evening," begins outdoors, with a figure already exposed to the elements, to the lure of darkness. He has been away from home. The snow falling and the night falling in the first line are a subject rhyme, a double descent into darkness. The end of the initial line ("fast, oh, fast") rhythmically mimics the way night drops quickly over the fields. The speaker moving at the boundary of those fields looks into them and *sees* the world darkening, the earth obliterated except for a few scrawny markings. The first sentence rolling across the length of a quatrain has taken us to the mysterious borderline of the woods.

There is a powerful sense of stasis in the second stanza, as if the figure had paused in his walking. This particular stroll through nature comes upon a cold moment. Notice the passivity of the verbs: "The woods around it have it"—whatever that indeterminate "it" is feels like the subject of the poem—"it *is* theirs"; "the animals"—every single one of them—"*are* smothered in their lairs"; "I *am* too absent-spirited to count." The speaker recognizes and acknowledges that this vacancy of spirit is an outward sign—a manifestation—of his own inner weather. Counting stands for distinguishing things individually; not counting means leaving them to merge into the larger indistinguishable darkness. There is also a pun on the word "count," as in "I am too absent-spirited to matter." As it is defined here, the loneliness includes everyone and everything, though loneliness itself, as a feeling, can only be apprehended by a human being, an observer. Among other things, this four-stanza sixteen-line poem is about consciousness, about the inevitability of relinquishing and losing it.

The third stanza progresses like a syllogism—it seems to press home an argument. The speaker is not so much describing a scene as generalizing from that scene, making it emblematic. The snow falling has become a kind of dark Emersonian sign of obliteration. I like the echo of *b* sounds in "blanker whiteness" and "benighted snow." There is nobility in the word "benighted," which means both "overtaken by darkness or night," and "in moral or intellectual darkness." Both meanings apply. The speaker, like the pilgrim at the beginning of *The Divine Comedy,* has lost his way. He stands on the edge of a dark wood valiantly trying to give human meaning to a snowfall in a field which, as he well knows, has no human meaning. Indifferent weather, indifferent nature, indifferent earth—these have no facial expressions. They have nothing to tell us because they have no meaning at all, no interior feeling or life.

The concluding stanza makes a remarkable turn inward. It takes us right to the edge of oblivion—the vacant spaces—that so terrified Pascal. ("The eternal silence of these infinite spaces fills me with dread," *Pensées*). But Frost is an American Pascal bumping up against the void.

> They cannot scare me with their empty spaces
> Between stars—on stars where no human race is.

It's as if the unknown "they"—who are *they* but indeterminate forces or gods of desolation?—are actively trying to terrify him, but can't succeed because, as he almost boasts, he can frighten himself more than they can frighten him. There is a belligerent, even Hemingwayesque toughness operating here, a Yankee stoicism. There is also a touch of playfulness in the rhyme of one word ("spaces") with two words ("race is"), a ludic gesture in the face of hostile forces, in the face of oblivion. The enjambment after the word "spaces" also forces us to hesitate and hover over the spaces between stars. The last two lines are unremitting:

I have it in me so much nearer home
To scare myself with my own desert places.

The desert places become a sign of the speaker's inner descent, vacancy, void. He knows a desolation inside that can match and even outdo any desolation that exists apart from him. The word "home" seems especially charged since the dwelling cannot protect him from himself. The final phrase circles the poem back to its title, but with a new knowledge and meaning. I love "Desert Places" not only for its precision about loneliness, but also for its courage in facing an inner desolation greater than any external darkness. Frost has made a claim on the terrifying inner spaces, and he has given them a fresh name. That process of naming is an act of mastery.

"Desert Places" enacts a terrible and terrifying solitude, but I find that full-scale loneliness slightly belied by its clarifying articulation in language. By voicing the experience Frost makes it social, even as the reader it locates exists somewhere in the distance, in an unknown future. The speaker in this poem turns back from the lure of the woods—that final silence—to the realm of the human. The poet is a maker who has made something out of the expressionlessness of the world, out of a punishing inner desolation.

Years later, driving through the Midwest on a flat and darkening day, a day with its own encompassing emptiness, I find it consoling to let the words breathe through me toward another solitude, toward another person sitting next to me reading the words to herself, listening.

Gerard Manley Hopkins's untitled crisis lyric, "I wake and feel the fell of dark, not day," was one of the first poems in my experience to embody a sense of being spiritually lost, of an unrequited solitude, of an anxious and guilty loneliness. It was among the first poems that I practically wore out reading, that I recited to myself so many times I found I had pretty much memorized it without ever consciously trying. One might say that it memorized me. The sense of bewildering isolation, of a loneliness I could neither assuage nor fully comprehend, had sent me spinning into poetry as a teenager, and it was thrilling for me to encounter poems that fearlessly named and thus authorized that feeling. I found it consoling but also liberating to come across lyrics that articulated my own sense of distress better than I could. These poems valorized human feeling. They seemed to know me better than I knew myself.

Hopkins's poem is one of the "terrible sonnets," a group of six poems, beginning with "Carrion Comfort," that he wrote during a grave spiritual crisis in 1885. It has always struck me as one of the marvels of poetry that a fourteen-line poem written by a Jesuit priest emotionally shipwrecked in Ireland ("I am in Ireland now," he wrote in another poem, "now I am at a third / Remove") could speak so directly nearly a hundred years later to an American Jewish kid sitting in a dormitory room in a small college in the Midwest. No doubt there are many others in the past century who have been instructed by this and other kindred lyrics how to face despair without succumbing. We stumble upon these poems, but it feels as if they have come searching for us.

I wake and feel the fell of dark, not day.
What hours, O what black hours, we have spent
This night! what sights you, heart, saw; ways you went!
And more must, in yet longer light's delay.
   With witness I speak this. But where I say
Hours I mean years, mean life. And my lament
Is cries countless, cries like dead letters sent
To dearest him that lives alas! away.

   I am gall, I am heartburn. God's most deep decree
Bitter would have me taste: my taste was me;
Bones built in me, flesh filled, blood brimmed the curse.
   Selfyeast of spirit a dull dough sours. I see
The lost are like this, and their scourge to be
As I am mine, their sweating selves; but worse.

Hopkins's poem has the directness of a prayer. It is sounded from the depths, spoken from the dark night of the soul. As such it takes its place in a line of spiritual poems going back—through Christopher Smart, through George Herbert—at least to St. John of the Cross. These poems have a powerful religious feeling, but they are in no way institutional: they enact the self's solitary struggle with the soul.

Hopkins tended to push language to the breaking point, to see just how much stress poetic language could bear, and here he freights the words by working within the confines of a rhyming sonnet. The word *sonnet* derives from the Italian *sonetto,* meaning "a little sound, a little song." The stateliness of the fourteen-line form (there are three main versions in English: Shakespearean, Spenserian, and Petrarchan) belies the seeming modesty of the word's derivation. Hopkins invented a "curtal" or foreshortened sonnet, but he also liked to work, as here, with the Italian model. It is structurally divided into two parts: an octave (the first eight lines) and a sestet (the concluding six lines). The octave rhymes *abbaabba;* the sestet rhymes *cdecde.* (Hopkins tightens the second stanza even further by rhyming *cdccd.*) This poet liked to mark the two distinct parts of the poem with a white space between. That space—contentwise—is a chasm.

Given the passionate drama of Hopkins's poem, it should be evident that the elaboration and fulfillment of the sonnet form in no way mitigates the authenticity of the feeling. Hopkins's "terrible sonnets" came from a long way down to break a poetic silence that he had endured for two years. At least one of them, as he wrote to Robert Bridges, was written in blood. These poems indicate that for Hopkins, as for his beloved Greek poets, there was no contradiction between the initiating inspiration and the final realization of form, between the necessity of speech and the demands of poetic making. The form becomes a way for the poem to contain and release verbal energy. The words explode on impact.

This sonnet opens with immediate authority. "I wake," the speaker declares, but instead of waking to a rising daylight, as would be natural, he awakens to a fallen darkness. The first line coincides with the first sentence and stands as a unit unto itself. One can feel the strong iambic accents of the one-syllable words falling like blows—"I *wake* and *feel* the *fell* of *dark, not day.*" One almost tastes the alliterative repetition of consonants: the *f*s and *l*s in "*feel* the *fell*," the *d*s in "*dark, not day.*" The poem enacts the dramatic situation of a speaker stymied in the night, alone in outer darkness. Unable to sleep, he is an isolated consciousness.

The second line begins with rhetorical emphasis, with a dark underlining: "What hours, O what black hours," the speaker exclaims, "we have spent / This night!" One hovers over the enjambed word "spent"— a moment of mimesis—before following through to the first exclamation. There is a moment in reading the second line when one wonders precisely who that "we" refers to, but that is immediately cleared up in the third line ("What sights you, heart, saw; ways you went!") when the speaker addresses his own heart, which has seen so much, strayed so far. The speaker is split, riven. There is a play on the word "sights" since the heart can apparently "see" dreaded things precisely because the eye can see nothing. The second and third lines form an intact inner couplet. The fourth line—rhyming with the first—indicates that the heart, which I take as a metonym for the feeling self, is still in the midst of seeing, that is, perceiving, its own unspecified horrors in the darkness. "Eloquence is *heard;* poetry is *overheard,*" John Stuart Mill said, and the first quatrain puts the reader in the position of overhearing the speaker challenging himself.

The speaker turns outward in the second quatrain, as if standing on a stage and speaking into the darkness to an unseen audience, to an unknown thou: "With witness I speak this." He declares his speech a swearing forth: a sincere act of witness, a form of truth telling. Notice the emphasis on *say* at the close of the fifth line; it rhymes backward with the words *delay* and *day* in the first quatrain and forward with the word *away* in the last line. Similarly, the word *lament* rhymes forward to the word *sent* and backward to *spent* and *went.* This Italian pattern binds the two quatrains together and gives them a strong feeling of being enclosed, of forming one unit, intact.

How compelling that the speaker announces that he is himself allegorizing, that in this "saying" the hours stand for years and the years mean life itself. In a sense he reads the experience of the night and declares it as emblematic, as representing the state of his soul. This self-interpretation teaches us to read the darkness as an external sign of his inner turmoil, inner plight. So, too, he suggests that his singular "lament" actually consists of innumerable "cries," cries which he compares to "dead letters," that is, letters that are inert, a correspondence that will not spring alive.

Much ink has been spilled over the identity of "dearest him," though it seems to me that the identity of that male recipient—if we may call him that—is purposely indeterminate. The poem itself will never reveal its biographical secret, if it even has one; in this way it is like some of Emily Dickinson's more personally resonant poems. Perhaps the addressee of the dead letters is the closest of platonic friends; perhaps the reference carries a homoerotic overtone, as when Whitman speaks of his dear young "comrades"; perhaps the reference carries the suggestion of a distant God who is no longer present, who has moved "away." Or perhaps the recipient only exists as an imaginative trope, a figure (of speech) who never receives the letters, which are really only solitary cries anyway, soundings in the darkness. What matters is that the imaginary recipient—the beloved—is now far away. He is absent.

The introjection—the exclamation "alas!"—is a wonderful Hopkinsian touch. It parallels the exclamation at the close of Hopkins's Italian sonnet "God's Grandeur" where the Holy Ghost "over the bent / World broods with warm breast and with ah! bright wings." That marvelous "ah!" in the early poem has been transformed here into a regretful "alas!" Coming as it does before the final word of the octave, it freshens and focuses the feeling, and rivets us to the way the speaker registers his emotion. Such a touch gives the poem its individual stamp, its distinctive tone. One of the signal truths about Hopkins's work is that he always seems emotionally present in his poems.

The second part of this poem is filled with a painful self-loathing, a dark self-hatred. It spews out a terrible self-indictment as the speaker is mortified by his flesh, thrown back into his physical self. The rueful tone that infused the last line of the first stanza has now turned into the harsh self-judgment that marks the conclusive turning point in the poem. A great divide has been crossed. "I am gall, I am heartburn," he cries out, identifying himself as bile, as rancor and bitterness. He has seen himself reduced to something acrid, a burning sensation. He views himself as the horrifying physical manifestation of an inescapable body. It is not just a "decree" of God's, but His "most deep decree" that would have the self sentenced to its own rancid taste. The spiritual self has now become the "bones" that "built," the "flesh" that "filled," the "blood" that "brimmed" the curse. The alliterations well up in the speaker and, consequently, in the reader. One tastes the bile.

The progression is completed in the summary twelfth line: "Selfyeast of spirit a dull dough sours." I find this sentence something of a tongue twister, and when I first tried to memorize the poem I found that I kept stumbling over this awkward mouthful of words. And that is precisely the point, for the "selfyeast" of the spirit has been dulled and soured by the physical body. It cannot rise. In an earlier draft of this poem, Hopkins had written the line as "Selfyeast of spirit my selfstuff sours," but then, presumably, he saw the symbolic possibilities, the Christian overtone, of using the metaphor of bread. The body is the "dough" that keeps the "yeast" of the spirit from fulfilling itself.

The last lines of this poem have always struck me as curious, modest, and sympathetic; and yet I have often found myself resisting them. For years I consciously had to make an effort to remember them whereas the rest of the poem came to me naturally. This may be because the conclusion of the poem swerves toward a recognition of Hopkins's that cannot be my own. The poem mines its theological implications and makes a theological pronouncement I find hard to endorse. No matter. The recognition is characteristic of the spirit of this poet.

There is a play on the enjambed phrase "I see."

                              I see
The lost are like this, and their scourge to be
As I am mine, their sweating selves; but worse.

This has a visionary overtone since the speaker is still in an outer darkness. His recognition is spiritual. He enlarges on his own state, widening the panorama, as it were, and recognizes his kinship to "the lost." One can guess what this recognition must have cost him as a Jesuit priest, how painful it must have seemed. He suggests that to exist in hell is to be reduced to a body—a sweating self—that cannot be transformed by spirit. Rather than claiming his own suffering as the greatest of all possible sufferings, it's as if he has come to the far edge of suffering and discovered other people. He has looked through the abyss of self into an inferno where the permanently damned must suffer. His final recognition is out-ward—the suffering of others is "worse."

I am deeply moved by this poem of a tortured and emblematic in-somnia. No wonder then that in the next sonnet in this sequence Hop-kins cries out, "Patience, hard thing," and in the following one pleads:

> My own heart let me have more pity on; let
> Me live to my sad self hereafter kind,
> Charitable; not live this tormented mind
> With this tormented mind tormenting yet.

These lines are a casting out for comfort, a prayer for self-forgiveness, and I have found myself reciting them aloud in my own hard hours.

I have been teasing out the implications of two sturdily constructed poems which face up to an inner desolation. But now I want to turn to a poem in which the poet recognizes the tempting ensnarement of such inner desolation but self-consciously turns away from it. I first encoun-tered Nâzim Hikmet's "Some Advice to Those Who Will Serve Time in Prison" more than twenty years ago in *American Poetry Review*. I could soon place it in fuller context when I read it again as part of the section entitled "Poems from Prison" in Randy Blasing and Mutlu Konuk's groundbreaking translation from the Turkish, *Things I Didn't Know I Loved* (1975). The poem is dated May 1949, but it still feels, to me, as if the speaker is actually with us in the room. Or, more precisely, talking to someone else in the very next room. The poem has a startling intimacy. Like Whitman, who obviously influenced him, Hikmet can sometimes sound as if he is standing on a soapbox, but he can speak with an over-powering directness. His poems tremble with the presence of his living voice: "Who touches this touches a man."

Some Advice to Those
Who Will Serve Time in Prison
If instead of being hanged by the neck
     you're thrown inside
     for not giving up hope

in the world, in your country, and people,
       if you do ten or fifteen years
       apart from the time you have left,
you won't say
         "Better I had swung from the end of a rope like a
          flag"—
you'll put your foot down and live.
It might not be a pleasure exactly,
but it's your solemn duty
      to live one more day
         to spite the enemy.
Part of you may live alone inside,
      like a stone at the bottom of a well.
But the other part
      must be so caught up
      in the flurry of the world
      that you shiver there inside
    when outside, at forty days' distance, a leaf moves.
To wait for letters inside,
or to sing sad songs,
or to lie awake all night staring at the ceiling
      is sweet, but dangerous.
Look at your face from shave to shave,
forget your age,
watch out for lice,
      and for spring nights;
   and always remember
     to eat every last piece of bread—
also, don't forget to laugh heartily.
And, who knows,
the woman you love may stop loving you.
Don't say it's no big thing:
it's like the snapping of a green branch
            to the man inside.
To think of roses and gardens inside is bad,
to think of seas and mountains is good.
Read and write without rest,

and I also advise weaving
and making mirrors.
I mean, it's not that you can't pass
  ten or fifteen years inside,
          and more—
      you can,
      as long as the jewel
      on the left side of your chest doesn't lose its luster!
          May 1949
          (translated by Randy Blasing
          and Mutlu Konuk)

Hikmet's poem has an openhearted didacticism. It is voice-driven, meant
to sound as if someone is talking aloud, giving instructions on how to
feel in prison, and as such it is written in a conversational free-verse style.
The rhythm is informal; the dropped lines create an added level of
intensity and movement by isolating certain phrases, focusing parts of
sentences. This method of lineation isn't systematic the way that, say,
William Carlos Williams's triadic stanza tries to be systematic, but it is lo-
cally effective. Notice how the first two lines in the following sentence
create an equivalency whereas the next two lines suggest a progression.

It might not be a pleasure exactly,
but it's your solemn duty
          to live one more day
              to spite the enemy.

Hikmet's intuitive method of lineation is directive, like Ezra Pound's. It
is oddly just that the free verse of Hikmet's prison poems so closely re-
sembles that of *The Pisan Cantos*, which were written during Pound's in-
carceration at the end of the second World War. Both were written at
nearly the same moment in history. The fact that Hikmet was a commit-
ted Marxist and Pound a notorious fascist suggests that, whether traditional
or experimental, poetic means and methods have no intrinsic politics.

Hikmet's poem has a very specific addressee: those to whom some-
thing unjust is going to happen. Consider yourself addressed directly if
you're going to be spending time in prison for political reasons. Hikmet's

advice is meant literally and can be understood metaphorically. One notes that the title is addressed to a plurality (there will always be those who are going to be "spending time" in prison for believing in justice), but the poem itself is directed toward a singular "you." Once the prison doors shut, this speaker suggests, you're going to feel as if you're alone. The bars create a divide. The point of this so-called advice is to find ways for the incarcerated to avoid despair, to move beyond desolation and feel connected to the "outside." This poem is, among other things, a quirky commonsense instruction manual.

Hikmet called poetry "the bloodiest of the arts," and "Some Advice" is filled with the bitter certainty of a man who would spend some seventeen years in prison. The poem is filled with dark knowledge of what it takes to survive. He is not writing a "confessional" poem—that is, he is not detailing the horrors of his experience, or even exposing it so much as he is drawing conclusions from his experience. His authority is personal and absolute. He knows, for example, one can't afford to give in to desolation. He is against brooding about enclosed spaces, even beautiful ones like gardens, but supports dreaming of wild open spaces, like seas and mountains. He understands too well the temptations of sadness, the dangers of indifference, the healing power of laughter. Frank O'Hara wrote a kind of "I do this, I do that" poem (or so it was termed by Marjorie Perloff), and here Hikmet works up a "Don't do this, do that" kind of lyric. Cavafy's great poem "The God Abandons Antony" belongs to the same genre. It, too, is addressed to a listener—in this case Mark Antony—and by teaching him teaches us how to comport ourselves in the face of disastrous loss. Cavafy's insistence that Antony "listen with deep emotion" parallels Hikmet's insistence that the heart should keep its shine, even while both advise a certain kind of stoicism. Hikmet also puts me in mind of Hart Crane's struggle to find a ground for affirmation in response to the collective desolations of *The Waste Land*.

So many modern and contemporary poets are terrified of deep feeling, of seeming undefended and "sentimental." Many write as if it were desirable to refine out the emotional registers of the lyric. We live in a cool age. But I invoke Hikmet precisely for his emotional excesses, for writing an oracular human-sized poetry, for his toughness and unblushing sentiment, for calling the heart a jewel that should never lose its luster. He takes his place with César Vallejo and Miklós Radnóti and Cesare

Pavese: poets of the empathic imagination who feel their way into the lives of other people, who put their wild creative energies and tremendous learning at the service of a humanizing vision. Hikmet affirms human connection. He wants to praise because he knows what we are going to lose and he's determined to grieve about it *right now*. Hence the galvanizing conclusion of "On Living," an advancing, forward-looking planetary elegy:

> This earth will grow cold,
> a star among stars
>   and one of the smallest—
> a gilded mote on the blue velvet, I mean,
>   I mean *this,* our great earth.
> This earth will grow cold one day,
> not like a heap of ice
> or a dead cloud even,
> but like an empty walnut it will roll along
>   in pitch-black space ...
> You must grieve for this right now
> you have to feel this sorrow now,
> for the world must be loved this much
>   if you're going to say "I lived" ...
>   *(translated by Randy Blasing*
>   *and Mutlu Konuk)*

8

Poetry and History:
Polish Poetry after
the End of the World

In 1973, when I was twenty-three years old, I decided to stop in Warsaw during a year I was traveling in Europe. From that trip I remember one chilly gray dusk in particular when I walked through the neighborhood that had once been the Warsaw Ghetto. People were bustling home from work, but their activity only seemed to accentuate the eerie and even ghostly absence of all those missing persons, an annihilated people. One didn't need to travel to Auschwitz to feel guilty absence and palpable vacancy. That night I reread Czesław Miłosz's poems "A Poor Christian Looks at the Ghetto," "A Song on the End of the World," and "Dedication." This last poem was addressed to "You whom I could not save," and dated Warsaw, 1945. Its key stanza has thereafter set a standard of moral seriousness in poetry:

> What is poetry which does not save
> Nations or people?
> A connivance with official lies,
> A song of drunkards whose throats will be cut in a moment,
> Readings for sophomore girls.
> That I wanted good poetry without knowing it,
> That I discovered, late, its salutary aim,
> In this and only this I find salvation.

Miłosz's early postwar poems are all haunted by survivor's guilt, the poignancy of living after what was, for so many, the world's end. Poetry here becomes an offering to the dead, a form of expiation, a hope for redemption.

Reading the work of Zbigniew Herbert, Tadeusz Różewicz, and Wisława Szymborska—the half-generation after Miłosz—I soon discovered that all of postwar Polish poetry was similarly haunted by guilt, initiated in the apocalyptic fires of history. These writers shared an important collective experience, and the formative nature of that experience helped shape the spirit of their work. Born in the early 1920s, they grew up during one of the few periods of independence in Polish history, but they came of age during the terrible years of World War II. Poland lost six million people during the war, nearly one-fifth of its population, and the young writers felt the almost crushing burden of speaking for those who did not survive the German occupation. "I am twenty-four / led to slaughter / I survived," Różewicz wrote in "The Survivor." It was no boast. No wonder, then, that at the conclusion of "Dedication" Miłosz asks for the dead to free him:

> They used to pour millet on graves or poppy seeds
> To feed the dead who would come disguised as birds.
> I put this book here for you, who once lived
> So that you should visit us no more.

The war was such a traumatic event that for a new generation of Polish poets it called all moral and aesthetic values into question. Before the war, Polish poetry was mostly dominated by two groups: Skamander and the Kraków Vanguard (also known as the First Vanguard). The group of poets clustered around the magazine *Skamander* were vital Bergsonian traditionalists—lyric, tender, cosmopolitan—who believed said Miłosz, "unshakably in the sanctity of a good rhyme, in the divine origin of rhythm, in revelation through images born in ecstasy and through shapes chiseled by work." They were exuberant formal poets (I especially recommend the poetry of Julian Tuwim) but the war blew apart the optimistic premises of their program. The First Vanguard—Julian Przyboś is the best example—rejected the poetic techniques of Skamander, but shared their optimistic faith in the future of technological civilization.

The consensus of the young poets was that those who survived the war could never believe in that future again. Nor could they revert to traditional forms. They rejected the aesthetics of elaborate, ornamental, or sonorous language. It was as if poetry had to be reinvented again from the ground up. These poets thus foresaw the necessary relationship between poetry and history. They teach us what it means simultaneously to doubt poetry itself, and to put one's faith in it.

The major poets of postwar Poland all share a distrust of rhetoric, of false words and sentiments. "Try to understand this simple speech as I would be ashamed of another," Miłosz avows in "Dedication": "I swear, there is in me no wizardry of words." Różewicz was among the first to catch this mood in a naked, stripped-down poetry of drastic simplicity. Here is the beginning of his poem "In the Midst of Life":

> After the end of the world
> after death
> I found myself in the midst of life
> creating myself
> building life
> people animals landscapes
>
> This is a table I said
> this is a table
> on the table is bread a knife
> a knife is to cut bread
> people live on bread
>
> Man must be loved
> I studied night and day
> what must be loved
> I answered man
> *(translated by Magnus J. Krynski
> and Robert A. Maguire)*

Różewicz's brutal simplicity enacted his suspicion of all general ideas and philosophies.

After the war, Herbert, too, deliberately cultivated a cool, economical and antirhetorical style, dispensing with punctuation in his poems and eschewing grandiose effects—what one poem calls "the piano at the top of the Alps" and "the artificial fires of poetry." His early poems show "a rapacious love of the concrete," a strong fascination with inanimate objects, which he viewed as steadfast and immutable, unlike human beings. His concentration on objects was part of his determination to see things as they are, to give them their proper names. "At last the fidelity of things opens our eyes," he declares in "Stool." To the poet who suffered under, and had seen the collapse of, several shameful ideologies, his commitment to concrete particulars stands as a fundamental contrast and direct alternative to the cant and half-truths of human beings. Thus he asserts in his poem "Pebble": "The pebble / is a perfect creature / equal to itself / mindful of its limits," and "its ardour and coldness / are just and full of dignity." He confesses:

> I feel a heavy remorse
> when I hold it in my hand
> and its noble body
> is permeated by false warmth
>
>   —Pebbles cannot be tamed
>   to the end they will look at us
>   with a calm and very clear eye
>   (translated by Czesław Miłosz)

A radically understated style stands as a special corollary to the quest for things-in-themselves. Herbert has sought a cleansed language of what he calls "semantic transparency," the pristine word that holds against modern debasements of language.

Every major Polish poet shows an absolute distrust of any political creed or ideology. They had to come to this position, however, at their own rate, in their own ways. In 1949, socialist realism was imposed on Polish artists and, as Miłosz has written, "the world of Orwell ceased to be a literary fiction in Poland." The poets responded to authoritarian pressures in different ways. Some, like Miłosz, saw what was coming and went into exile. Others, like Herbert and Miron Białoszewski, chose internal exile or "writing for the drawer." Różewicz, who was already famous, and Szymborska, who was then virtually unknown, had a moment of believing in communism and tried to conform, writing stridently socialist realist poems. Those poems make discouraging reading today. Soon they understood that communism was a utopian fantasy and distanced themselves from its illusions. It wasn't until after the "thaw" of 1956—the year that censorship famously loosened its grip in Poland—that Szymborska, for example, truly hit her own note and started to become a major poet. Her third book, *Calling Out to Yeti*, reveals a fresh disillusion with Stalinist politics, a mordant humor, and deep skepticism. The figure of Yeti, the Abominable Snowman, is the book's central metaphor for Stalinism. Believing in communism is like believing in the Abominable Snowman; neither offers any human warmth or artistic comfort. "Notes from a Nonexistent Himalayan Expedition" ends:

> Yeti, we've got Shakespeare there.
> Yeti, we play solitaire
> and violin. At nightfall,
> we turn lights on, Yeti.
>
> Up here it's neither moon nor earth,
> Tears freeze.
> Oh Yeti, semi-moonman,
> turn back, think again!
>
> I call this to the Yeti,
> inside four walls of avalanche,
> stomping my feet for warmth
> on the everlasting
> snow.
> *(translated by Stanisław Barańczak
> and Clare Cavanagh)*

The snow here is very cold, very Siberian, but for the Snow Creature there would be no coming down to accommodate the vulnerability of actual human beings.

Ever since the fifties, Polish poets have struggled to keep human beings in full view. It's no easy task to preserve individual integrity. Miłosz writes in "*Ars Poetica?*":

> The purpose of poetry is to remind us
> how difficult it is to remain just one person,
> for our house is open, there are no keys in the doors,
> and invisible guests come in and out at will.
> *(translated by Czesław Miłosz*
> *and Lillian Vallee)*

I'm reminded how Aleksander Wat, a poet who belonged to the generation before Miłosz's and who could never forgive himself for his two- or three-year period of complicity with communism, of "moral insanity," considered the poet to be a fractured being aspiring to a lost unity and wholeness, a guilty prisoner wounded by memory and longing for freedom. He considered himself a poet not simply because he wrote poetry (what he called the "no-doubt meaningless fact of writing verses") but because he struggled toward transcendence of our tragic fragmentation, because he had a radiant platonic dream of being. As he says in *My Century:*

> But my life, oh, my life, had been a constant search for an enormous dream in which my fellow creatures and animals, plants, chimeras, stars, and minerals were in a pre-established harmony, a dream that is forgotten because it must be forgotten, and is sought desperately, and only sporadically does one find its tragic fragments in the warmth of a person, in some specific situation, a glance—in memory, too, of course, in some specific pain, some moment. I loved that harmony with a passion; I loved it in voices, voices. And then, instead of harmony, there was nothing but scraps and tatters. And perhaps that alone is what it means to be a poet.

For Wat, poems are scraps and tatters, fragments and notes, the jagged remnants of a dream, grief-stricken fallings away from perfection, the imaginings of a fallen creature in the presence of language.

Szymborska, Herbert, and Różewicz have, in some sense, refused the mantle of a poetry which could save nations or people. Each refuses a utopian dream of perfection. Each writes a poetry of sardonic individualism. Yet their poems also tend to shed light on common experiences. They understand something fundamental about our century. "See, how efficient it still is, / how it keeps itself in shape— / our century's hatred," Szymborska writes. And in "The Century's Decline" she declares, "Our twentieth century was going to improve on the others":

A couple of problems weren't going
to come up anymore:
hunger, for example,
and war, and so forth.

There was going to be respect
for helpless people's helplessness,
trust, that kind of stuff.

Anyone who planned to enjoy the world
is now faced
with a hopeless task.

Stupidity isn't funny.
Wisdom isn't gay.
Hope
isn't that young girl anymore,
et cetera, alas.

God was finally going to believe
in a man both good and strong
but good and strong
are still two different men.
(translated by Stanisław Barańczak
and Clare Cavanagh)

The radical accessibility of contemporary Polish poetry has sometimes bewildered advanced American readers who often miss the point that for these poets stylistic clarity is a form of ethics. One might say that the very clarity of this poetry is a response to ideological obfuscations, political double-talk.

Take, for example, Szymborska's poem "Children of Our Age." She takes a common assertion—"We are children of our age, / it's a political age"—and examines it until it begins to leak and then fall apart. She tries to find the human being—the human reality—obscured by the political dogma:

> Meanwhile, people perished,
> animals died,
> houses burned,
> and the fields ran wild,
> just as in time immemorial,
> and less political.
> *(translated by Stanisław Barańczak
> and Clare Cavanagh)*

Syzmborska's characteristic strategy is to run through all the ramifications of an idea to see what it will yield. Often she begins by seeming to embrace a subject and ends by undercutting it with a sharp, disillusioned comment. One key to her style may well be the way she works subversive variations on familiar rhetoric.

The best Polish poets are determined to speak in their own voices. They have mounted in their work a witty and tireless defense of individual subjectivity against collectivist thinking. At the same time they find it virtually impossible to ignore the catastrophic history of their country. "Politics is our destiny," Wat wrote, "a cyclone in whose eye we constantly are even though we take shelter in the frail craft of poetry." One might say that these poets are involuntary witnesses to such overwhelming events as World War II and the Holocaust, the bitter years of the Stalinist repression in Poland, the imposition of martial law in 1981. No writer can safely ignore the occupation of his or her own country. So, too, these writers share a communal sense of liberation over the October "thaw" of 1956, or the final fall of communism in the late 1980s. These historical events naturally impinge upon and inform their work. As Miłosz says in *The Witness of Poetry*:

One can say that what occurred in Poland was an encounter of a European poet with the hell of the twentieth century, not hell's first circle, but a much deeper one. This situation is something of a laboratory, in other words: it allows us to examine what happens to modern poetry in certain historical conditions.

I sense a deep and perhaps unresolvable tension, an ongoing dialogue, in the laboratory of Polish poetry. It takes place between the solitary singer and the larger community. On one hand, there is a strong expectation that the poet speaks on behalf of others. One might call this the prophetic function of poetry. On the other hand, there are compelling reasons, in Poland as elsewhere, for the poet to resist any public or ideological pressure to speak for anyone besides oneself. Even so, there is often a public dimension—a dimension of civitas—to this private speech. Herbert writes in "The Trial":

for so many months years I was composing the final speech
to God to the court to the world to the conscience
to the dead rather than the living

> (translated by John Carpenter
> and Bogdana Carpenter)

The basic dialectic of Polish poetry is set out in the title of Adam Zagajewski's fine book of essays, *Solidarity, Solitude.* "In Polish poetry there is always a dialogue between the individual and history," Zagajewski has said. "Every major Polish poet is opposed to collectivist thinking. Yet the individual is also in touch with what is general, impersonal, historical. The individual is under pressure to justify being an individual."

The individual is also under pressure to justify poetry itself. I'm reminded of Witold Gombrowicz's funny and cutting piece "Against Poets" which appears as an appendix to the first volume of his *Diary.* Gombrowicz especially objects to "this pharmaceutical extract called 'pure poetry,'" to any style that loses contact with direct human feeling and seems inherited from other poets: "The minute the poets lost sight of a concrete human being and became transfixed with abstract Poetry, nothing could keep them from rolling down the incline into the chasm of the absurd." Gombrowicz's challenge to the cult of pure poetry has resounded through the work of the postwar generation, and it has been taken up, and implicitly answered, by every major Polish poet from Miłosz to Zagajewski. The *ars poetica* has been necessary in Polish poetry because the poets have repeatedly been called upon to justify their art. The notion of *witnessing* is one such justification.

Polish poetry has often been called a poetry of witnessing, but that notion needs some refining and expanding. Polish poets themselves have often shown an ambivalence about being so-called "witnesses" to history. Miłosz called his Charles Eliot Norton Lectures at Harvard *The Witness of Poetry,* but he also wrote a letter to the *New York Review of Books* objecting to a praiseworthy review by A. Alvarez that called him a "witness." In Miłosz's view, the label narrowed the meanings of his poetry and implied that his poems were a kind of journalistic response to events. Miłosz's ambivalence points out that Polish poets are in some sense metaphysical poets forced to become historical ones. While they could not help being aware of the history inflicted upon them, they nevertheless have remained most keenly interested in exploring the nature of reality at even deeper levels, meditating on life's essences.

For example, Herbert, who is the most ironic, civilized, and classically conscious of poets (the exemplary personages in his poems tend to be figures such as Marcus Aurelius and Hamlet, Roman proconsuls and Greek gods), has spent virtually his entire adulthood in opposition to totalitarianism. He is a stubbornly idiosyncratic poet of isolation, disinheritance, and grief—what one critic terms "multilevel orphanhood." He is also a poet of "historical irony" (the phrase is Miłosz's), continually confronting his own experience and juxtaposing it with the experience of the past, seeking the grounds for what he has called "universal compassion." For all his professed love of the concrete, he isn't a phenomenological poet per se; on the contrary, he is supremely a poet of thought—self-questioning, philosophically self-conscious, a tragic post-Cartesian attracted to Erasmus. Many of his poems address the issues and problems of accurate description. As he puts it at the end of "Never About You," "Don't be surprised we don't know how to describe the world / and only speak to things affectionately by their first names." Herbert's poems often return to the textual and ethical problems involved in inscribing and psychologizing experience, in trying to write down the fluctuating external world and be faithful not only to what we know but also to what we don't know. Thus an "uncertain clarity" becomes the primary representative value even as he has pursued classical values, raising questions about the nature of nature, of philosophical truth, of suffering, of time, of God.

Like Herbert, Szymborska is a philosophically inflected poet who investigates large unanswerable questions with terrific élan and delicacy. Her poems—wise, funny, personal—have the sting of long experience. She comes at common experiences from her own angle: "Four billion people on this earth, / but my imagination is still the same," she confesses in "A Large Number": "It's bad with large numbers. / It's still taken by particularity." Like Herbert, Szymborska is also all too aware of how the world keeps escaping our various formulations about it: "But even a Dante couldn't get it right," she admits, "let alone someone who is not. / Even with all the muses behind me."

Szymborska meditates on huge general subjects such as hatred and true love and ranges from the mathematical concept of pi to the socialist ideal of Utopia to the joys of composing poetry. Characteristically a poem is made up of questions ("Plotting with the Dead") or of apologies, as in "Under One Small Star":

My apologies to chance for calling it necessity.
My apologies to necessity if I'm mistaken, after all.
Please, don't be angry, happiness, that I take you as my due.
May my dead be patient with the way my memories fade.
My apologies to time for all the world I overlook each second.
My apologies to past loves for thinking that the latest is the
    first.
Forgive me, distant wars, for bringing flowers home.
Forgive me, open wounds, for pricking my finger.
I apologize for my record of minuets to those who cry from
    the depths.

As this poem progresses the speaker keeps shifting from one category to another. She begs forgiveness from inanimate objects and even concepts, then from places and from groups of people—everything is anthropomorphized. She herself feels unequal to the world's sufferings and fears that by narrowing her focus on the world to make it manageable, she has trivialized it. But all viewpoints are incomplete, all efforts inadequate:

> My apologies to everything that I can't be everywhere at once.
> My apologies to everyone that I can't be each woman and each
>   man.

The poem's conclusion amounts to a small *ars poetica:*

> Don't bear me ill will, speech, that I borrow weighty words,
> then labor heavily so that they may seem light.
>
> > *(translated by Stanisław Barańczak*
> > *and Clare Cavanagh)*

Szymborska's notion of witnessing seems to involve extracting general truths from individual observations. Take her poem "Reality Demands":

> Reality demands
> that we also mention this:
> Life goes on.
> It continues at Cannae and Borodino,
> at Kosovo Polje and Guernica.
>
> There's a gas station
> on a little square in Jericho,
> and wet paint
> on park benches in Bila Hora.
> Letters fly back and forth
> between Pearl Harbor and Hastings,
> a moving van passes
> beneath the eye of the lion at Cheronea,
> and the blooming orchards near Verdun
> cannot escape
> the approaching atmospheric front.
>
> There is so much Everything
> that Nothing is hidden quite nicely.

Eventually, even the worst of destructions recedes:

> On tragic mountain passes
> the wind rips hats from unwitting heads
> and we can't help
> laughing at that.
> > (translated by Stanisław Barańczak
> > and Clare Cavanagh)

Szymborska's subject is how, despite catastrophes that defy the imagination, daily life goes on, forgetfulness seems to conquer memory, the world keeps mysteriously renewing itself. Reality demands, she suggests, that this, too, must be taken into account when we think about history.

Szymborska seems characteristic in the way she learned to use the specifics of the war experience to pose, and even generalize about, the nature of human experience itself. For example, her poem "Could Have," which has also been translated as "There But for the Grace," appears to be set in wartime Poland during the German occupation:

> It could have happened.
> It had to happen.
> It happened earlier. Later.
> Nearer. Farther off.
> It happened, but not to you.

> You were saved because you were the first.
> You were saved because you were the last.
> Alone. With others.
> On the right. The left.
> Because it was raining. Because of the shade.
> Because the day was sunny.

> You were in luck—there was a forest.
> You were in luck—there were no trees.
> You were in luck—a rake, a hook, a beam, a brake,
> > a jamb, a turn, a quarter inch, an instant.
> You were in luck—just then a straw went floating by.

As a result, because, although, despite.
What would have happened if a hand, a foot,
within an inch, a hairsbreadth from
an unfortunate coincidence.

So, you're here? Still dizzy from another dodge, close shave,
    reprieve?
One hole in the net and you slipped through?
I couldn't be more shocked or speechless.
Listen,
how your heart pounds inside me.

While the poem recalls the brutal uncertainty of the Nazi period, it also addresses the radical contingency of experience, the sheer dumb luck, that leads to one's survival. So, too, there is a sense of the vast distance between simple things ("a rake, a hook, a beam, a brake . . .") and how much life depends on them. Even the most innocuous objects can become sinister or hazardous, while ridiculous coincidence can account for one's survival. It's as if we're all actors in an unrehearsed slapstick comedy. But the poem ends on bitter irony, for the speaker has had her share of unwitting reprieves and ruefully pays for them with an incurably guilty conscience.

All Szymborska's poems take place on the edge of an abyss. It's the poetry of the close shave. And it's not only accidents we contend with, but history itself, with its hatreds and more deaths than we can count ("the impeccable executioner / towering over its soiled victim"). Against which: the imagination, the joy of writing.

In one of her signature poems Szymborska playfully investigates the nature of the poetic imagination. The title points not to the art of poetry, but to the joy—the *jouissance*—of writing, the deep pleasure of the activity itself. The poem alertly raises some basic questions about what is involved when a poet inscribes letters on a blank page. It muses about the relationship between words and things, and illuminates the character of poetic making.

The Joy of Writing
Why does this written doe bound through these written
    woods?

For a drink of written water from a spring
whose surface will xerox her soft muzzle?
Why does she lift her head; does she hear something?
Perched on four slim legs borrowed from the truth,
she pricks up her ears beneath my fingertips.
Silence—this word also rustles across the page
and parts the boughs
that have sprouted from the word "woods."

Lying in wait, set to pounce on the blank page,
are letters up to no good,
clutches of clauses so subordinate
they'll never let her get away.

Each drop of ink contains a fair supply
of hunters, equipped with squinting eyes behind their sights,
prepared to swarm the sloping pen at any moment,
surround the doe, and slowly aim their guns.

They forget that what's here isn't life.
Other laws, black on white, obtain.
The twinkling of an eye will take as long as I say,
and will, if I wish, divide into tiny eternities,
full of bullets stopped in mid-flight.
Not a thing will ever happen unless I say so.
Without my blessing, not a leaf will fall,
not a blade of grass will bend beneath that little hoof's full stop.

Is there then a world
where I rule absolutely on fate?
A time I bind with chains of signs?
An existence become endless at my bidding?

The joy of writing.
The power of preserving.
Revenge of a mortal hand.

(translated by Stanisław Barańczak
and Clare Cavanagh)

This poem begins with an author puzzling over what she has just written; indeed, the word "written," repeated twice, gets a certain amount of pressure: "Why does this *written* doe bound through these *written* woods?" This is not a rhetorical question but a genuine problem which the poem sets out to investigate. It suggests that the poem is not a setup, a construct thought up and worked out wholly in advance, but an ongoing process of listening and making. Why does this imaginary doe, as soon as it is inscribed, seem to take on a life of movement through an equally imaginary woods? And where is it going? No sooner does the writer place a doe in the woods than she has to answer a question of motivation. She finds herself leading the doe to water (to *written* water, of course), watching her lift up her head (in fear?), perched on legs just like ones the writer has observed on real does (they are, after all, "borrowed from the truth"). The poet sees a world come alive, as if cinematically, on the page. No sooner does she write the word "silence" than the word itself seems to rustle across the page (this is a delicious philosophical paradox) and part the particular boughs (the line mimics the action of parting) that have sprung forth from the general word "woods." This writer marvels at the creative process. She is astonished at every point by the way the words repeatedly blossom into things.

She is also humble before the process, well aware that the letters could come together in the wrong way, in the wrong formulation. How easy it would be for her to misspeak, to misrepresent, thereby trapping her doe, unwittingly trapping herself. In a drop of ink (this old-fashioned writer still writes by hand) there seem to be those who are capable of overpowering the poet and destroying her doe. She is well aware that words can be used malevolently, that the creator can be subject to overpowering political and historical forces. She knows because, historically speaking, she has seen the sword overpower the pen. Here the poem takes on the tinge of allegory—a more generalized and emblematic status—about a vulnerable doe and malevolent hunters. These hunters, it seems, are always poised to get their prey.

But in the fourth stanza the modest writer asserts her authorial priority—a full Joycean control—over her creation. Unlike so-called "real life," the laws of art obtain here. In this realm temporality can be suspended; another order of time comes into play. Here, for once, bullets can be stopped. Suddenly, consciousness and conscience prevail. The lyric poem becomes a stay against time.

The penultimate stanza steps back to ask three questions, not just about the poem at hand but about poetry in general. These questions are about the ontological status of the created work. She wants to know if there truly is a world, a time bound "with chains of signs," an existence she can entirely control. It does seem to her as if the author creates a realm subject to its own laws. The work of art becomes a universe unto itself.

The final three lines create a triple equivalence: "The joy of writing. / The power of preserving. / Revenge of a mortal hand." What is so arresting is the sudden shift from joy to power to revenge. Writing becomes a form of protest against the incontestable ravages of time. The poet takes revenge on mortality, defeating cruelty and saving what she can by thinking the unthinkable and presiding over her own creation. The joy of writing stands against the bitter knowledge of just how much of the world cannot be controlled outside the work of art. This is the art of poetry trying to kill time.

"Probably I am an ordinary middle-class / believer in individual rights, the word / 'freedom' is simple to me, it doesn't mean / the freedom of any class in particular," Adam Zagajewski writes in his poem "Fire." Zagajewski's development is especially instructive since he belongs to the generation after Szymborska, Herbert, and Różewicz, and thus he has inherited, and helped to articulate, the deep tension and ongoing dialogue in Polish poetry. He started out in the early 1970s writing under the sign of the newborn oppositional movement. He had a strong sense of the writer's social responsibility and a clear idea that "the collectivity (the nation, society, generations) is the chief protagonist and addressee of creative, artistic works." This phase of Zagajewski's work culminated in the work he edited with Julian Kornhauser, *The Unrepresented World* (1974). Since then he has increasingly given sway to another aspect of his nature, committing himself to the permanent values of art. Or as he puts it: "I have discovered there is also a 'metaphysical' part of myself that is rather anarchic—not interested in politics or history but in poetry and music."

Zagajewski has never forgotten the necessity of civitas, and yet he has also learned the fundamental value of privacy, the morality of speaking only for oneself. These rival claims on his attention have increasingly given sway to even deeper aesthetic and even metaphysical divisions. He is a poet of the most profound and compelling dualisms ("The world is torn. Long live duality! One should praise what is inevitable," he wryly proclaims) and there is a powerful dialectic operating in his work between reality and imagination, between history and philosophy, between the temporal and the eternal.

"Two contradictory elements meet in poetry: ecstasy and irony," Zagajewski writes in *Two Cities:* "The ecstatic element is tied to an unconditional acceptance of the world, including even what is cruel and absurd. Irony, in contrast, is the artistic representation of thought, criticism, doubt." Zagajewski has given weight to both ecstasy and irony, and yet his deepest impulse may be to go through history to praise the mysteries of—and beyond—the world.

"That day, infinity, as though in sheer fun, / assumed the form of a flock of sparrows, / and, changing shape, pirouetted over the grass," he writes in one poem ("That Day"); "I know only the mysteries are immortal," he confesses in a second ("Presence"); "I was impaled by sharp barbs of bliss," he concludes in a third ("Cruel"). Here is the beginning of his poem "The Bells":

We'll take refuge in bells, in the swinging bells,
in the peal, the air, the heart of ringing.
We'll take refuge in bells and we'll float
over the earth in their heavy casings.
            (translated by Renata Gorczynski,
            Benjamin Ivry, and C. K. Williams)

He rejoices in the power of wings and bells, of poetry, music, and art. "I'm truly not a child of the ocean," Zagajewski says about himself in his poem "Self-portrait," "but a child of air, mint and cello." Zagajewski is in some sense a pilgrim, a celebrant in search of the divine. He keeps getting called back to the world of historical ironies, of doubts, but he also keeps getting pulled toward the ecstatic acceptance of *everything.* He is "impaled by sharp barbs of bliss," his poems are filled with radiant moments of plenitude. They are spiritual emblems, hymns to the unknown, levers for transcendence.

———

One final example. In Zbigniew Herbert's poem "Mr. Cogito and the Imagination" there is a compelling list of those things that Mr. Cogito, Herbert's stand-in, would like to consider to the very end. It's a catalog of subject rhymes:

—Pascal's night
—the nature of a diamond
—the melancholy of the prophets
—Achilles' wrath
—the madness of those who kill
—the dreams of Mary Stuart
—Neanderthal fear
—the despair of the last Aztecs
—Nietzsche's long death throes
—the joy of the painter of Lascaux
—the rise and fall of an oak
—the rise and fall of Rome
> (translated by John Carpenter
> and Bogdana Carpenter)

Herbert wants to know about the victims of history, both individual and collective, but he also wants to know about the nature of religious faith and the miracle of nature. Compelled by the rage and madness of some that leads to the fear and despair of others, this catalog certainly points to the horrors of history. But he also wants to meditate on the mysteries of creation and the joys of artistic creativity. He concludes by paralleling the cycle of nature and the cycle of civilization. If this is witnessing, it is of a particularly philosophical kind.

I admire postwar Polish poetry for its unfashionable clarity, its democratic ethos, its commitment to an idiosyncratic individuality, its suspicion of absolutes and rejection of tyranny. I admire its humane values, its eminent sanity, its deep humility before the plenitude of the world. Each of these Polish poets has struggled to find an individual way to replace the nihilism that engulfed civilization after the end of the war. Miłosz has sought a ground for transcendence; Różewicz endorses what has been called a "qualified humanism"; Herbert stubbornly maintains an allegiance to "uncertain clarity"; Szymborska rejoices in what she calls "commonplace miracles" and the gaiety of art; Zagajewski becomes a rapturous skeptic, an ecstatic ironist. These poets try to tell the truth about human suffering, but they also seek to make meaning out of that suffering. Hence Miłosz's brave claim: "Human reason is beautiful and invincible." Here is a poetry that takes history into account even as it seeks to transcend history, to find the stability of truth.

9

Re: Form

The poet wants justice. The poet wants art. In poetry there can't be one without the other. The poet is Jeremiah crying out to the assembly to witness the folly unprecedented in both West (Cyprus) and East (Kedar) of a people who forsake the *fountain of living waters* for the stagnant water at the bottom of a leaky *cistern*. The prophet is wild, unsparing, oracular, ruthless. He thinks in metaphors (the fountain, the cistern), he communicates with lightning force. His irony is withering. And the meaning of his prophecy can only be captured and enacted through the faithful cadences of art. In "The Constant Symbol" Robert Frost points out:

> Jeremiah, it seems, has had his sincerity questioned because the anguish of his lamentations was tamable to the form of twenty-two stanzas for the twenty-two letters of the alphabet. The Hebrew alphabet has been kept to the twenty-two letters it came out of Egypt with, so the number twenty-two means as much form as ever.

The poetic word can only be delivered formally. The poet who wrote The Lamentations of Jeremiah (a series of poems mourning the desolation of Jerusalem and the sufferings of her people after the siege and de-

struction of the city and the burning of the Temple by the Babylonians)
needed all the art at his disposal.

The poet wants justice through language. Turn the American key
and here is William Carlos Williams declaring:

> It is difficult
> to get the news from poems
> yet men die miserably every day
> for lack
> of what is found there.

This excerpt from "Asphodel, That Greeny Flower," which gave Adri-
enne Rich the title for her recent notebooks on poetry and politics,
What Is Found There, suggests that poetry carries "news" or information
crucial to the populace. This is not the kind of service information char-
acteristically carried in newspapers, but it is a way of delivering us up to
our own spiritual lives and, therefore, to ourselves. Can we live without
such sustenance? It is difficult to get the "news" from poems because
that news can only be delivered poetically. Williams himself took drastic
American measures to remake the lyric. His poem, for example, is writ-
ten in the triadic or three-ply line that he developed as a mode of trans-
formative thinking. His message is that we live in a new world and that
we somehow need a form of poetry equal to that reality. It was his deep
conviction that

> unless there is
> a new mind there cannot be a new
> line, the old will go on
> repeating itself with recurring
> deadliness.
>
> *(Paterson)*

Williams struggled to find a "new mind" that would be released in the
service of a large and humane vision of America.

"New conditions of life germinate new forms of spiritual understand-
ing," Hart Crane declares in "General Aims and Theories." This key

modernist idea, that fresh or changing conditions ferment fresh forms, has had particular resonance in the New World, where it has become one of the signs of the American difference in art. I think of Pound's maxim "Make it new," or of Emerson's confident, resounding claim:

> For it is not metres, but a metre-making argument, that makes a poem—a thought so passionate and alive, that like the spirit of a plant or an animal, it has an architecture of its own and adorns nature with a new thing.

Emerson does not forget here that *poiēsis* means "making," and that the poet is first and foremost a maker. He calls for an art that is organic and crafted, that emerges with an architecture of its own. He does not forget what he deems "the instant dependence of form upon soul." This is a wondrously fresh idea.

"Mad Ireland hurt you into poetry," W. H. Auden famously decreed in his elegy for W. B. Yeats, and so, too, we might say that the madness of any country's brutality has wounded its poets into poetry. "I stand as a witness to the common lot, / survivor of that time, that place," Anna Akhmatova wrote in 1961. Instead of a preface to her epic poem "Requiem" (1935–1940), she offered the following emblematic anecdote:

> In the terrible years of the Yezhov terror I spent seventeen months waiting in line outside the prison in Leningrad. One day somebody in the crowd identified me. Standing behind me was a woman, with lips blue from the cold, who had, of course, never heard me called by name before. Now she started out of the torpor common to us all and asked me in a whisper (everyone whispered there):
> "Can you describe this?"
> And I said: "I can."
> Then something like a smile passed fleetingly over what had once been her face.

There is a terrible splendor imposed on the poet who says "I can describe this." Behind the poem in quest of justice, these lines from Shakespeare's *Antony and Cleopatra:*

> our size of sorrow,
> Proportion'd to our cause, must be as great
> As that which makes it.
>
> *(act 4, scene 15)*

I came across these lines again recently as the epigraph to a translation of the Argentinian poet Juan Gelman's selected poems, *Unthinkable Tenderness*. Gelman writes with terrific potency about the Disappeared, about those kidnapped and killed during Argentina's "Dirty War." Gelman himself went into political exile in 1975, when he was forty-five years old, and could not return to Argentina for thirteen years. In 1976, his only son, Marcelo, and seven-month-pregnant daughter-in-law, Claudia, were kidnapped and taken to a concentration camp known as Automotores Orletti, which the military sinisterly christened "The Garden." Each was twenty years old. His son was murdered but nothing is known of his daughter-in-law's fate, though she was almost certainly also murdered after giving birth to a child. They simply vanished. No one ever recovers from such a loss. The poet has a particular way of not recovering: "I have laid them out in my memory / to keep on searching for the light."

I take Gelman as an example because, as Eduardo Galeano writes, "Juan has committed the crime of marrying justice to beauty." He has dedicated his work "to the families of Argentina's Disappeared, especially the twice-orphaned Mothers of the Plaza de Mayo Linea Fundadora, and to all those forced to live in the shadow of absence and impunity, the lingering resonance of brutality." Gelman insistently keeps alive the memory of "dreams broken by reality" and "the bravery of so many" who are now "pieces scattered about beneath the country / little fallen leaves of fervor / of hope / of faith." Gelman's poetry is filled with the deepest sadness and grief, yet an odd hopefulness keeps breaking through. Lamentation about history keeps giving way to praise of the renewable universe. As Julio Cortázar wrote about Gelman: "He is a man whose family has been severed from him, who has seen his most beloved friends disappeared or killed, yet nobody has been able to kill in Juan the will to subvert the sum of this horror into an affirmative counterstrike, a creator of new life." Cortázar calls Gelman's poems "a permanent caress of words on unknown tombs."

That is a good description of many of the best political poems of our century. I think, for example, of Vahan Tekeyan's poems of the Armenian genocide; of the Spanish Civil War poet Miguel Hernández's haunting prison poems, especially his masterpiece "Lullaby of an Onion"; of Bertolt Brecht's World War II poems and Nelly Sach's Holocaust poems. I think of the Italian poet Cesare Pavese's testimonies to ordinary people in trouble, *Hard Labor,* and of Randall Jarrell's brave dramatic monologues from the point of view of overlooked middle-class women, "Next Day" and "The Woman at the Washington Zoo." I think of the many poems of indictment and summons, of land and liberty, collected in the Nigerian writer Wole Soyinka's breakthrough anthology, *Poems of Black Africa.*

What Soyinka says about the South African poet Dennis Brutus strikes me as especially instructive:

> What gives, for instance, the love poems of Dennis Brutus their raw, passionate desperation is the fact that they are just as much poems about love as they are poems of indictment—a word I prefer to "protest"—against the brutish environment from which such emotions are painfully wrenched, that they speak of integral refuge and outer defiance, hope and resolve, within one breath. Even when the poem emerges as essentially tender, its poignancy remains a yet more lacerating accusation.

It is a deeply political act to maintain an "unthinkable tenderness" and thus preserve the human feeling.

The poem of history has a deep commandment to remember. Read Primo Levi's poem "Shemá," which is based on the principal Jewish prayer "Hear, [*Shema*] O Israel: the Lord is our God, the Lord is One!" (Deuteronomy, 6:4–9).

You live secure
In your warm houses,
Who return at evening to find
Hot food and friendly faces:

Consider whether this is a man,
Who labours in the mud

Who knows no peace
Who fights for a crust of bread
Who dies at a yes or a no.
Consider whether this is a woman,
Without hair or name
With no more strength to remember
Eyes empty and womb cold
As a frog in winter.

Consider that this has been:
I commend these words to you.
Engrave them on your hearts
When you are in your house, when you walk on your way,
When you go to bed, when you rise.
Repeat them to your children.
Or may your house crumble,
Disease render you powerless,
Your offspring avert their faces from you.

(translated by Ruth Feldman
and Brian Swann)

The fury behind this "witnessing," this *remembering*, is immense. The poem puts a terrible curse upon anyone who forgets these people, this Adam and Eve. We must keep them from becoming anonymous victims, we must engrave their images on our hearts.

A political poem need not be a didactic poem. It's often a deeper poem that speaks to the communal from a position of self-division and estrangement. The West Indian poet Derek Walcott grew up in St. Lucia as a "divided child," a Methodist in an overwhelmingly Catholic country, a developing artist with a middle-class background and a mixed, African, English, and Dutch ancestry coming of age in a mostly black world, a backwater of poverty. Some of the dramatic tension in Walcott's work comes from the gap he has always had to cross to describe the people with whom he shares an island. Walcott has called himself "a mulatto of style" and increasingly has given voice to the contending languages and cultures operating inside him. For example, the Odyssean figure of Shabine in "The Schooner *Flight*" undoubtedly speaks for his creator when he uses the demotic and turns the language of colonial scorn into a source of pride:

> I'm just a red nigger who love the sea,
> I had a sound colonial education,
> I have Dutch, nigger, and English in me,
> and either I'm nobody, or I'm a nation.

Homer has become Walcott's tutelary spirit, and he mimics *The Odyssey* here by echoing that moment when Odysseus slyly deceives the Cyclops by calling himself "nobody." He is also asserting that this "nobody" is the culture's representative figure, "a nation." *Omeros,* Walcott's Caribbean reworking of *The Odyssey,* suggests that the task of the Homeric bard is to unearth lost lives and shattered histories but also to sing of a new people and a new hope.

A great deal of rage sometimes breaks loose in Walcott's work. He lashes out against racism; against those who have typed the poet as neither white nor black enough ("The first chain my hands and apologize 'History,'" Shabine says, "the next said I wasn't black enough for their pride"); against those who still view the Caribbean people as illegitimate and rootless ("There are no people there," the pamphleteer Froude wrote, "in the true sense of the word"); against the legacies of slavery and colonialism and "the incurable sore / of poverty"; against a venal middle class "who want a new art / and their artists dying in the old way"; against the "ministers of culture, ministers of development" who sold out the idea of a federation and have been eager to prostitute West Indian culture ("Adam had an idea. / He and the snake would share / the loss of Eden for a profit. / So both made the New World. And it looked good"). Shabine expresses this overwhelming rage when he warns

> all you best dread the day I am healed
> of being a human. All you fate in my hand,
> ministers, businessmen, Shabine have you, friend,
> I shall scatter your lives like a handful of sand,
> I who have no weapon but poetry and
> the lances of palms and the sea's shining shield!

Faced with such a devouring anger and bitter alienation, Walcott has often turned to the splendors of "a virginal, unpainted world" shining beyond the claims of history or politics. And he has kept in mind his abiding covenant. When Shabine anchors in Castries harbor in St. Lucia he can say with quiet pride:

> I have kept my own
> promise, to leave you the one thing I own,
> you whom I loved first: my poetry.

The Adamic task is finally a healing one since the poet overcomes history and turns back with reverence to his first realm.

The poet wants mercy. Open up *What Will Suffice,* a collection of poems and statements by contemporary poets on the art of poetry, and you hear Garrett Hongo's eloquent testament about his poem "Stay with Me":

> I wanted *mercy.* I wanted the universe to bend down and kiss its own creation, like a parent does to a child just after it's born, as if a pure tenderness were the expression of the world for itself. I wanted to believe that what was not given, *could* be given, that were a man or a woman to cry out for solace, that the world, for all its steel plants and tire factories, for all its liquor stores and razor wire, for all its buses that belched carcinogenic poisons and people who passed you by on the freeway who cursed you with their eyes; for all of that, I wanted to believe the heavens would still lay its soft wings of blessing upon you if you cried out in need. It was *aloha*—the breath of love upon your face.

The poet wants an unthinkable tenderness, mercy, justice. The poet wants art.

I'd like to look now at two radically American poems, a work song by Sterling Brown and an ode by Pablo Neruda, that return us to the ancient roots of poetic form in order to make it new. I'd like to contextualize them, and then offer something of the history of the forms they employ. These poems are eccentric and individualistic, but they also address the polis, the communal impulse, the collectivity. There is nothing about them that smacks of the court or the monarchy, they are opposed to all hierarchical models of society. Here are poems that give us the soul of participatory form. The poet wants art. The poet wants justice.

Reverberations of a Work Song

Sterling Brown's *Collected Poems* (1980) brings together three important books of poems: *Southern Road* (1932), one of the key books of American, and perhaps *the* key book of African American, poetry in the 1930s; *The Last Ride of Wild Bill* (1975), a uniquely narrative book of eight idiomatic literary ballads rewritten in African American terms out of the central tall-tale tradition of American literature; and *No Hiding Place*, a fierce, durable group of poems mainly completed in the late 1930s but which found no publisher and consequently had to wait some forty years to appear in print. Brown was not, as he has sometimes been treated, a minor satellite of the Harlem Renaissance, but a poet of comparable stature to Claude McKay and Countee Cullen and engaged in a different but parallel poetic revolution. As a young writer influenced by the poetical and social concept of the New Negro, energized by the sharp articulate writings of Alain Locke and W. E. B. DuBois, Brown turned his verbal gifts not to the urban life of his contemporaries but to exploring the social nature of the southern black experience in a sensitive folk idiom. As Langston Hughes experimented with jazz rhythms to render Harlem nightlife (at first in *Fine Clothes to the Jew* [1927] and later, with greater success, in *Montage of a Dream Deferred* [1951]), so Brown turned to folk forms like the blues, spirituals, and work songs to create an accurate, unsentimentalized, and dignified portrait of southern black life in the twentieth century. In the deceptively simple forms of his chosen folk idiom, Sterling Brown's poems successfully brought an unknown African American world into the realm of recorded history.

The operant formal influence on Brown's work was his radical reliance on both secular (blues, ballads, work songs) and sacred (spirituals) African American musical traditions. It was virtually unprecedented for Brown, who was from Washington, D.C., and educated at Williams

College and Harvard University, to turn his considerable intellectual resources to rural folk forms. But then, as Sterling Stuckey has said, Brown always had a sense of the connecting timbre, "a feel for reciprocity between past and present." That same feel was evidenced in his historical delineations and primary sourcebooks for black culture, *The Negro in American Fiction* (1937), *Negro Poetry and Drama* (1937), and *Negro Caravan* (1941).

In *Southern Road* Brown was both resurrecting and affirming the essential dignity of folk forms (and, consequently, of black slave and farm experience conveyed through them) and implicitly redefining a recognizably American aesthetic of the local. (I think of William Carlos Williams's idea of putting into his poems "the speech of Polish mothers.") Even more radically, Brown's poems were first written in dialect at a time when dialect was associated not with a vigorous living speech but with the mawkish sentimentality of the plantation and blackface minstrel traditions.

In his introduction to the first edition of *Southern Road*, James Weldon Johnson praised Brown for "adopting as his medium the common racy, living speech of the Negro in certain phases of *real* life," thus reversing his earlier opinion that dialect was "an instrument with but two complete stops, humor and pathos" (*God's Trombones*, 1927). Johnson's polemical objections were to parodic traditions which, as he said, "had but slight relation, often no relation at all, to *actual* Negro life." (Think of the excesses of Tin Pan Alley or the pseudofolk idiom of a poet like Vachel Lindsay.) What he discovered in Brown's poetry was both the denial and the dismantling of the exaggerated sentimentality of previous dialect tradition. *Southern Road* in effect rewrote and reformulated the nature of the black vernacular as it had been presented in American literature. By turning to an oral folk tradition as opposed to a written literary one, Brown's poetry called the written tradition into question and instead privileged the external immediacy of black life.

As he later put it in "A Son's Return: Oh, Didn't He Ramble":

I love Negro speech and I think it is rich and wonderful. It is not *dis* and *dat* and a split verb. But it is "Been down so long that down don't worry me," or it is what the spirituals had in one of the finest couplets in American literature: "I don't know what my mother wants to stay here for. This old world ain't been no friend to her."

By using his poetry as an instrument to redefine the character of black speech and song, Brown was also redefining the character of rural southern blacks, replacing geniality with fierce stoicism, ironic humor, and deep tragedy.

Now here is the title poem of *Southern Road:*

Southern Road
Swing dat hammer—hunh—
Steady, bo';
Swing dat hammer—hunh—
Steady, bo';
Ain't no rush, bebby,
Long ways to go.

Burner tore his—hunh—
Black heart away;
Burner tore his—hunh—
Black heart away;
Got me life, bebby,
An' a day.

Gal's on Fifth Street—hunh—
Son done gone;
Gal's on Fifth Street—hunh—
Son done gone;
Wife's in de ward, bebby,
Babe's not bo'n.

My ole man died—hunh—
Cussin' me;
My ole man died—hunh—
Cussin' me;

Ole lady rocks, bebby,
Huh misery.

Doubleshackled—hunh—
Guard behin';
Doubleshackled—hunh—
Guard behin';
Ball an' chain, bebby,
On my min'.

White man tells me—hunh—
Damn yo' soul;
White man tells me—hunh—
Damn yo' soul;
Got no need, bebby,
To be tole.

Chain gang nevah—hunh—
Let me go;
Chain gang nevah—hunh—
Let me go;
Po' los' boy, bebby,
Evahmo'...

This fictive prison song appears in a section called "Poetry in the Folk Manner" in Langston Hughes and Arna Bontemps's *Book of Negro Folklore* (1958). Brown contributed essays on spirituals and on the blues as folk poetry to this anthology, which contained a section of collected work songs, like this one:

Take This Hammer

Take this hammer—huh!
And carry it to the captain—huh!
You tell him I'm gone—huh!
Tell him I'm gone—huh!

If he asks you—huh!
Was I runnin'—huh!
You tell him I was flyin'—huh!
You tell him I was flyin'—huh!

If he asks you—huh!
Was I laughin'—huh!
You tell him I was cryin'—huh!
You tell him I was cryin'—huh!

The work song is a utilitarian form whose main function is to synchro-nize the efforts of workers who must move together as in a chain gang. A leader provides a strong rhythmic cue with two or three bars which are then answered by the ejaculatory word or words of moving workers. The rhythmic interaction and continual interplay create a call-and-response pattern, making music a *participatory* activity. The words are cre-ated in an improvisatory mode, known as "signifying"—or, as Henry Louis Gates Jr. designates it, "Signifyin(g)"—which Roger Abrahams calls "a technique of indirect argument or persuasion," "a language of implication." The singer creates a mask of address to the so-called "cap-tain," the white boss, and at the same time satirizes and undercuts that very voice, thus building morale by subversively talking back to power.

John and Alan Lomax's *Folk Song U.S.A.* (1947) gives a classic de-scription of a work song going at full swing:

> The hot southern sun shines down on the brown and glossy muscles of the work gang. The picks make whirling rainbow arcs around the shoulders of the singers. As the picks dig into the rock, the men give a deep, guttural grunt; their pent-up strength flows through the pick handle and they relax their bodies and prepare for the next blow.
>
> The song leader now begins—pick handle twirling in his palms, the pickhead flashing in the sun:
>
> *Take this hammo—Huh!*

The men grunt as the picks bite in together. They join the leader on his line, trailing in, one in harmony, one talking the words, another grunting them out between clenched teeth, another throwing out a high falsetto cry above the rest. On the final syllable, the picks are descending and again they bite a chip out of the rock and again there is a grunting exhalation of breath:

Carry it to my Captain—Huh!

The picks whirl up together in the sunlight and down again, they ring on the earth together, with maybe one or two bounding a couple of times in a sort of syncopation. When the leader comes to the third—

Carry it to my Captain

he holds on to the word "captain" as long as he can, looks around at the boss and grins; his buddies chuckle and relax for a moment, knowing he is giving them a little rest; then, "wham" the steel bites at the rock and the whole gang roars out the final line, so that the hill gives back the sound.

The way the gang responds to the leader here—one voice slipping in harmonically, another talking words, a third grunting them, a fourth lifting a falsetto cry over the rest—is a polyrhythmic variation on the West African call-and-response pattern. The song puts a tremendous claim on experience. Some folklorists have persuasively argued that the work song actually challenges the nature of work itself by changing the framework of the workers. The singer supplies the beat and relieves the tedium, transposing the space, creating a different relationship to time. In *Black Culture and Black Consciousness*, the historian Lawrence Levine argues:

> Secular work songs resembled the spirituals in that their endless rhythmic and verbal repetitions could transport the singers beyond time, make them oblivious to their immediate surroundings and create a state of what Wilfred Mellers has referred to as "ritualistic hypnosis." The chant then becomes, again in Mellers's words, "a positive rhythmic ecstasy rather than a negative numbing of pain."

The experience is time-stopping and becomes a medium of transcendence.

The lyric "Southern Road" resonates with a rich background context, a way of life which it evokes in its very rhythms, its call-and-response pattern. But because it is a written and not an oral poem, it removes the work song from its immediate social and historical context. The work song loses its primary function (no one ever thought "Southern Road" was going to be sung in the fields) and thus becomes non-utilitarian, a different kind of animal that behaves in an analogous but different way. Brown compensates by asking the poem to do a different kind of symbolic work. He inscribes the values of the work song. He creates a particular speaker with a particular history and textualizes the feeling of an individual testifying to a participating community. He models the relationship between the singer and the community. And he gives the poem a narrative or storytelling value. It has a lyric bluesy element.

In fact, if you change the lineation and drop the choral response you have a slightly foreshortened but otherwise classic three-line blues stanza:

> White man tells me damn yo' soul;
> White man tells me damn yo' soul;
> Got no need, bebby, to be tole.

The work song almost certainly contributed to the statement-and-response pattern of the blues, which retains elements of the field holler. Like the classical four-line ballad stanza, the blues form is a good vehicle for telling a story of any length, but it stages a different kind of drama through its repetitions. The blues have always retained a flexible style and structure, but have tended toward a twelve-bar tercet with an *aab* pattern. The first line establishes the premise and the scene; the second repeats (sometimes with slight variations) and hammers it in; the third line punches, develops, or turns it. Each line is an intact entity, each stanza a unit unto itself. Here's a traditional blues verse:

> I'm going to the river, take my rockin' chair,
> Goin' to the river, take my rockin' chair,
> If the blues overcome me, I'll rock on away from here.

Brown also imitates the blues form undisguised and to great effect in his three-part sequence "New St. Louis Blues." Here's the first stanza of part 2, "Tornado Blues," which shows how he works the imagery and the form:

> Black wind come a-speedin' down de river from de Kansas
>   plains,
> Black wind come a-speedin' down de river from de Kansas
>   plains,
> Black wind come a-roarin' like a flock of giant aeroplanes—

The blues are more highly personalized than the work song since the call-and-response pattern remains but the singer in essence answers and responds to himself or herself. In *Blues People,* Amiri Baraka (LeRoi Jones) persuasively argues that the form resonates with a powerful individual ethos that would have been alien to African society and thus shows a high degree of American acculturation. Thus the blues becomes a more characteristically American form of verbal art.

It's the voice of an individual testifying to the collective that I hear in "Southern Road." We know, for example, the speaker has got a "gal" on Fifth Street, a son who has disappeared for good, a wife having a baby, a father who died cursing him. He's not just a victim of white people alone, he participates in his own fate. Brown once said that he modeled the speaker on the character of Big Boy Davis, a traveling guitar player who is also the speaker in "Odyssey of Big Boy," a poem that begins with a singer's call for community with a race's folk heroes:

> Lemme be wid Casey Jones,
>   Lemme be wid Stagolee,
> Lemme be wid such like men
>   When Death takes hol' on me,
>   When Death takes hol' on me...

Brown reported that he first heard from Davis about John Henry, about Stagolee, about "The Ballad of the Bollweevil." The same guitar player stands at the center of "When de Saints Go Ma'ching Home," a poem in which the great spiritual becomes the vehicle for the singer to create his own "chant of saints." Rereading the three poems about Big Boy Davis I was reminded of something that William Williams said about Robert

Hayden: "His speakers confront their history as active participants in its making and not as distant onlookers bemoaning their isolation."

Brown also captures the fierce undercurrent of pain in the blues. As he put it, "Irony, stoicism, and bitterness are deeply but not lingeringly expressed." There's a tragic undertow to:

> Chain gang nevah—hunh—
> Let me go;
> Po' los' boy, bebby,
> Evahmo' . . .

The ellipsis at the end of this poem tells everything. It is heart stopping. This suffering feels like it is going to go on and on endlessly.

One of Sterling Brown's main poetic tasks was to show "the extra-ordinary in ordinary lives." Early on he was influenced both in his idiom and in his themes by the American common man mythology, descending from Emerson and Whitman to Edwin Arlington Robinson and Robert Frost. I think, for example, of Whitman's poem "A Song for Occupations" ("In the labor of engines and trades and the labor of fields I find the developments, / And find the eternal meanings"), of how he vows to put "the family kiss" on the right cheek of the cotton field drudge and the cleaner of privies, of how he remembers "The heave'e'yo of stevedores unloading ships by the wharves, / The refrain of the anchor lifters." Here is a passage from section 12 of "Song of My-self" where he closely follows the rhythmic movement of blacksmiths:

> Blacksmiths with grimed and hairy chests environ the anvil,
> Each has his main-sledge, they are all out, there is a great heat
>   in the fire.
>
> From the cinder-strew'd threshold I follow their movements,
> The lithe sheer of their waists plays even with their massive
>   arms,
> Overhand the hammers swing, overhand so slow, overhand so
>   sure,
> They do not hasten, each man hits in his place.

It seems to me that the work song generates or opens up naturally in the direction of a poetry that becomes *about* working, and here one thinks how Brown's notion of "the extraordinary in ordinary lives" has reverberated through the work of such contemporary poets as Michael Harper, Sherley Anne Williams, and Yusef Komunyakaa, of Garrett Hongo and Philip Levine, who has written the best postwar book of poems on the subject, *What Work Is*. These poets have a fierce commitment to the lost and failed, to the poor, the marginal, the refused. They take up Whitman's chant "Vivas to those who have failed!" Reading through two recent anthologies of poetry about work, *A Song of Occupations* and *Working Classics*, I started to feel that one of the main tasks of the poet in the late twentieth century who would write about the subject of work is to affirm a community of workers who no longer share a common transfiguring music. The poems mostly fail because they rely on a chopped-up prose that doesn't do any of the figural or rhythmic work of poetry itself.

"What else formerly went to rhythm?" Louise Bogan asks in her essay "The Pleasures of Formal Poetry":

> We think of certain tasks, the rhythm of which has become set. Sowing, reaping, threshing, washing clothes, rowing, and even milking cows go to rhythm. The variety of rhythm in sea chanties depends upon the variety of tasks on board a sailing ship, with the doing of which a sailor was confronted. Hauling up sail or pulling it down, coiling rope, pulling and pushing and climbing and lifting, all went to different rhythms; and these rhythms are preserved for us, fast or slow, smooth or rough, in sailors' songs.

"Southern Road" is an American poem that participates in a deeply rooted tradition we do well to remember. The work song has been found wherever there are Africans in the New World. It was probably first sung in the United States when people who were enslaved were landed and forced to work. The subsequent black work song—the song of woodcutters and fishermen, of rail and prison road gangs—summons up the group labor songs of the West Indies and West Africa. As the anthropologist Melville Herskovits explained:

This tradition, carried over into the New World, is manifest in the tree-felling parties of the Suriname Bush Negroes, the *combites* of the Haitian peasant, and in various forms of group labor in agriculture, fishing, house-raising, and the like encountered in Jamaica, Trinidad, the French West Indies, and elsewhere.

The African American work song traces back to Africa where music was always associated with dancing and with working.

So, too, the earliest indications of lyric activity, the Egyptian tomb inscriptions (ca. 2600 B.C.), also include the work songs of shepherds, fishers, and chair carriers. I'm reminded of Robert Graves's theory ("Harp, Anvil, Oar") that the rhythm of Anglo-Saxon poetry was based on the slow pull and push of the oar:

> Then I of myself/will máke this known
> That awhile I was held/the Héodenings' scop,
> To my duke most dear/and Déor was my name.

According to Graves, the function of the Nordic scop (an Old English name for a harpist and poet-singer who commanded full mastery of the complex oral-formulaic materials of old Germanic prosody) was twofold: the poet's first task was as a "shaper" of charms to protect the king and thus ensure prosperity for the kingdom, but, secondarily, to persuade "a ship's crew to pull rhythmically and uncomplainingly on their oars against the rough waves of the North Sea, by singing them ballads in time to the beat." The oldest meaning of the word *beat* is "to strike repeatedly," and thus it retains vestiges in poetry of that sense of repeated physical action.

Whereas Nordic versecraft was linked to the movement of the oar, the Irish tradition developed a technique of craftmanship based on the hammer and anvil. "When two hammers answer each other five times on the anvil—*ti-tum, ti-tum, ti-tum, ti-tum, ti-tum*—five in honour of the five stations of the Celtic year," Graves suggests, "there you have Chaucer's familiar hendecasyllabic line."

> A knight ther was, and that a worthy man
> That fro the timë that he first began
> To ryden out, he lovéd chivalrye....

By contrast, Greek verse is connected to the ecstatic beat of dancers moving around a sacred altar. It has been plausibly suggested, as W. H. Auden has pointed out, that Greek verse, which has a quantitative meter, has its origins in ritual or play, but that English verse, which has a qualitative meter, has its origins in the physical action of work. Both were embodied.

The word "ballad" derives from the Middle English *balade,* from Old French *ballade,* from Provençal *balada,* a dancing song. The etymology would have had special resonance for Graves in his description of the Nordic scop because he believed, as he put it in a short critical survey of the English ballad (1927), "When the word 'ballad' was adopted by English singers, though the association with dancing did not survive, there remained latent in it the sense of *rhythmic group action* whether in work or in play." It seems likely that the medieval ballad originated in religious ritual, conjoining narrative and dancing, performed by a choral leader and a group of participants who both sang and danced. The leader would have sung the main body of the tale and the chorus would have followed with the refrain. Thus it has a strong parallel with the secular work song.

The traditional British ballad may be defined as a short narrative song (a poem that tells a story) preserved and transmitted orally, and Graves was correct that it retains vestiges of archaic modes of ritual participation. He was incorrect in his idea that the ballad was collectively rather than individually composed, though, as Northrop Frye notes in *Anatomy of Criticism,* the ballad is "so close to the poem of community as to have led some scholars to believe that its origin was in communal composition." The individual singer of the traditional ballad, of "Sir Patrick Spens" or "The Twa Corbies" or "Lord Randall," stands in for the community, serving as the deputy of a public voice.

In traditional societies there were two main types of oral narrative poetry—epic and ballad—and both have oral formulaic elements. They are models of the fluid text, of fixity and flux, tradition and innovation. The epic is nonstanzaic (or stichic) and thus creates a strong sense of linear development, whereas the ballad, a much shorter form, is stanzaic and thus balances lyric and narrative elements. It slows down the narration. In his groundbreaking book *The Singer of Tales,* Albert Lord, following the lead of Milman Parry, demonstrates the connection between *The Iliad* and *The Odyssey* and the living epic tradition of Yugoslavia.

The epic singer brings together a powerful memory and a strong improvisatory technique, using formulaic phrases, lines and half lines, propulsive rhythms, stock descriptions, recurrent scenes and incidents, to build an epic tale in song and verse. The singer of tales could also apply those same skills to work songs and funeral chants. So, too, the ballad singer could use formulaic elements to pace the narrative action, to expand and condense the story line, to emphasize recurrent lyric elements even as the song is being recomposed.

Dialogue is the main vehicle of action for the folk ballad which has been scoured down by oral transmission to a masterpiece of rapid elliptical narration. There is very little description or analysis of the thoughts or feelings of the characters in the traditional ballad (as there is, say, in prose fiction).The listeners actively collaborate in the making of meaning, which only emerges in performance, as they supply the background scene and the underlying motivation. Indeed, both the epic and the ballad give us strong cases of an emergent poiēsis.

I suspect that isolated writers have always understood the power of this interactive relationship. The writer would maintain his or her freedom through writing (Northrop Frye defines the lyric as the form of literature in which the writer turns his back on the audience) but would nonetheless tap into this communal model. As Susan Stewart puts it: "The *writing* of oral genres always results in a residue of lost context and lost presence that literary culture . . . imbues with a sense of nostalgia and even regret" (*Crimes of Writing*). Certainly this desire helps explain the widespread popularity and recurrence of the written literary ballad for a couple of centuries, from Robert Burns and Sir Walter Scott to W. B. Yeats, W. H. Auden, and Graves himself; from Blake, Wordsworth, and Coleridge to Swinburne, Tennyson, and both Rossettis; from William Morris and Oscar Wilde to Thomas Hardy, Walter de la Mare, A. E. Housman, and Rudyard Kipling; from Louis MacNeice and Edwin Muir to Sterling Brown and Robert Hayden. The writer would transcend isolation, seeking thus to stand in as the expression of a primordial collective will. The ballad writer also tends to be in quest of an archaic way of knowing, and thus the very form of the ballad becomes a way of attaining what Daniel Hoffman calls "barbarous knowledge." Whitman loved Sir Walter Scott's collection of old ballads, *The Minstrelsy of the Scottish Border,* precisely because it seemed to take him back to the primitive roots of all poetry and thus offered a bardic model for his own "barbaric yawp." "Stop this day and night and you shall possess the origin of all poems," he wrote in "Song of Myself," where he tried to conjure up the earthly and divine origins of archaic poetry on behalf of a forward-looking democratic art. "Our heart is in the future," Pablo Neruda declared in a Whitmanesque line, "and our pleasure is ancient."

The origins of poetry are highly speculative. The earliest poetry recedes into the vast mist of centuries of oral tradition before writing inscribed, and thus transfixed, these texts. We do know that throughout history oral expression can and has existed without writing, but that writing has never existed without orality (Walter Ong). There is a strong continuity between oral and written verbal art forms. Writing immobilizes texts in visual space, allowing us to linger and internalize them, to scan them backwards and forwards, reread and study them. It creates a space for introspection. But it is fundamental to remember that all over the world peoples have considered words to have magical potency. The interaction between the singer and the group provides one strong model of participation in literary exchange. Writing removes us from such face-to-face communication. It calls us deeply to each other. The written ballad, the written blues, the written work song—all these forms model a particular kind of participatory relationship between the poet and the community. They are poems with stories and refrains. They use oral elements to empower the relationship between writer and reader. Perhaps we should speak more often of the *work* of poetry, the work that poetry does in rhythmically restructuring time. That restructuring is at the heart of the work song, which is one of the fountainheads of poetry itself.

Reverberations of an Ode

I first fell in love with Pablo Neruda's poetry through his cycle *Residence on Earth,* which he once called "a mass of almost ritualistic verses . . . with mystery and suffering, like those created by the poets of old." I responded to Neruda's radical disordering of the world, his profound sense of estrangement from everything around him, his ancient terrors and modern anxieties, his harsh surreal near-religious desolation. These were the poems of his *Season in Hell.*

I now love equally Neruda's Odes for their contagious exuberance and perpetual wonderment about the world. The three books of odes are a rapturous late companion, an answer, to the three disconsolate books of *Residence on Earth;* they are a mass of almost ritualistic verses with mystery and joyousness, like those created by the poets of old who were astonished by everything. The odes have dark political shadows, but they also carry the news of our abiding attachment to the earth. They renew us by making the ordinary world startlingly fresh and strange.

Neruda began to write the odes when he returned to Chile after years of wandering exile. He had finally completed the epic that he had been working on for fourteen years, *Canto general,* a cycle of 340 poems arranged in fifteen sections that comprise his "General Song" or "Song to All," a book that deserves to stand beside Hart Crane's *The Bridge* as a modern mythification of America, a fierce Whitmanesque chant to the New World. It's striking that Crane, too, was especially interested in the celebratory ode. Setting out to write *The Bridge* he asserted: "I feel myself quite fit to become a suitable *Pindar* for the dawn of the machine age."

When Neruda was invited by the editor of a Caracas newspaper, *El Nacional,* to contribute weekly articles, he accepted on the condition that the work appear in the news section and not in the literary supplement. The paper agreed. "This is how I published a long history of time, things, artisans, people, fruit, flowers, and life," Neruda said. The three books that came out in rapid succession—*Elemental Odes, New Elemental Odes,* and *Third Book of Odes*—were truly meant to be elemental, even elementary, to carry news of things from their birth onward, to accord material objects a life of their own, to estrange the familiar. The odes are long and lyrical poems of celebration. They are meant to be inclusive. "Nothing was to be omitted from my field of action," Neruda commented. The first poem, "The Invisible Man," is explicit both about the Orphic calling and the social urgency of the poet's task:

> what can I do,
> everything asks me
> to speak,
> everything asks me
> to sing, sing forever,
> everything is saturated with

dreams and sound,
life is a box
filled with songs, the box opens
and a flock
of birds
flies out
and wants to tell me something,
perching on my shoulders,
life is a struggle,
like an advancing river,
and men
want to tell me,
tell you,
why they struggle,
and, if they die,
why they die,
and I walk by and I haven't
time for so many lives,
I want
them all to live
through my life,
to sing through my song...
(translated by Margaret Sayers Peden)

The list of Neruda's subjects in the odes is dizzying. Nothing ordinary was alien to him, or ordinary for that matter—everything was magical in an inventory that celebrates a great physical absorption in the world. He wrote separate odes to tomatoes, artichokes, and onions, to Conger Chowder, to a large tuna in the market, to salt. He wrote brilliantly comical odes to his socks and to his suit. He wrote odes to his native birds, to lizards and bees, to seagulls, to light on the sea. He wrote an ode to the dictionary, to a stamp album, to a ship in a bottle, to a sleeping house and a village movie theater. He wrote an ode to a boy with a hare, to a woman gardening, to César Vallejo, to an aged poet. He wrote an ode to time and another to the earth, an "Ode for Everything." The odes are funny, fiery, and exultant, they are both savagely new and profoundly ancient.

For the past few centuries the Spanish *oda*, like the English and the French ode, has generally been considered "a celebratory poem of address in an elevated language written on an occasion of public importance" (Paul Fry, *The Poet's Calling in the English Ode*). Neruda eschews the elevated language, but his lyrics are celebratory poems of address which he insisted on calling "news," thus radically revising the notion of "public importance." They are odes. The word derives from the Greek *ōidē*, meaning "a poem intended to be sung," and thus it was virtually synonymous with the word *lyric*. It comes to us through its Latin form, *oda*. Indeed, the modern ode often freely intermingles Greek and Latin elements. It shows a dual inheritance from classical sources by combining the occasional, ecstatic character of the Greek Pindaric ode with the philosophical, reflective character of the Latin Horatian ode.

Greek odes were sung, Latin ones written. Neruda uses the word *cantar* throughout the odes—he would "sing" them as poets did in ancient Greece, but in truth "singing" has become a metaphor, like Catullus' *Carmina*. Neruda's odes create a sensation of frenzied speech, but the jagged short lines spiral downward and create a sinuous physical shape on the page. One critic has called the poems "a river of print flowing down the page"; a translator has suggested that Neruda intuitively "transported the physical contours of Chile to the printed page." These odes were *written*.

Greek lyrics, poems to be sung to the lyre, took either the form of monodies, sung by single persons, or choral odes, sung by choirs. Alcaeus and Sappho were two of the great monodists, Pindar the key exponent of the choral form. Pindar's triumphal poems of varying lengths were performed at Greek shrines or theaters to celebrate athletic victories. Pindar's odes from the fifth century B.C. are the first truly written narrative texts of any length. The poems were simultaneously sung and danced, though now the words are all that survive of the complete Pindaric experience. The Pindaric ode consists of three stanzas that mirror a musical dance pattern: strophe, antistrophe, epode. The strophe and antistrophe share the same metrical pattern and structure (the chorus in movement and countermovement); the epode has a different pattern (the chorus at rest). The movement of the verse is emotionally intense and highly exalted. Horace, demonstrating that he could be something of a Pindarist, wrote that Pindar's poetry was like a torrent rushing down rain-swollen from the mountains, overflowing its banks, boiling and roaring.

The scholar Kurt Schlüter has argued in *Die Englische Ode* for the evolution of the ode from the structure and occasion of the Greek and Latin cult hymns. It has a religious derivation and can be related to other public types of religious lyric: the Hebrew psalms, the Christian hymns, the Hindu Vedas. The cult hymn spins off into the panegyrical ode (a formal eulogistic composition intended as a public compliment) to a human intermediary, a mortal representative of the deity, often a hero or a king. The Pindaric ode focuses on the victorious athlete who has a symbolic connection to the god. It incorporates a mythology. And it called for ecstatic performance that communally reenacted the ritual of participation in the divine. I suspect this originary ritual of participation always shadows the later secular ode.

Horace's *Odes* (newly available to English-speaking readers in David Ferry's splendid recent translation) provides the second key classical model. The 103 short poems that comprise his four books of odes are the perfect exemplars of the Latin form. Horace adapted to Latin verse the complex meters of the Greek monodists (alcaics, sapphics, etc.). He replaced the irregular stanzas of the Pindaric ode with richly symmetrical arrangements. His poems tend to be well-balanced systems, thoroughly measured and paced, thoroughly written. Writing inscribes and monumentalizes. There is an obsession with absence, with the invisible presence of death in the written ode that wasn't there in its oral forebears. After Horace the poetic ode will seek an influx of Pindaric power to create a vessel that will outlast death. As Horace puts it at the end of the third book of *Odes:*

Today I have finished a work outlasting bronze
And the pyramids of ancient royal kings.
The North Wind raging cannot scatter it
Nor can the rain obliterate this work,
Nor can the years, nor can the ages passing.
Some part of me will live and not be given
Over into the hands of the death goddess.
                    (translated by David Ferry, 3:30)

Horace's technical range was astonishing (he was "the adroitest of makers," as W. H. Auden calls him in his poem "A Thanksgiving") and his tones widely various: one thinks of his high-spirited drinking songs, his lighthearted love poems, his saddened meditations on the transience of human life and the fleeting nature of happiness, the grave seriousness of his so-called "Roman Odes." Horace's odes tend to be personal rather than public, general rather than occasional, contemplative rather than frenzied. An ecstatic choral form has become a mode of individual speculation, a form of embodied intellection. The ode comes to occupy a different mental space. It holds the body in a different way. Coleridge was demonstrating how Horatian he longed to become when he characterized the ideal ode in a notebook entry:

> Peculiar, not far-fetched; natural, but not obvious; delicate, not affected; dignified, not swelling; fiery, but not mad; rich in imagery, but not loaded with it—in short, a union of harmony and good sense, of perspicuity and conciseness. Thought is the body of such an ode, enthusiasm the soul, and imagery the drapery.

Yet Coleridge also shows his Pindaric roots when he speaks of the *fusion* power of poetry, when he affirms that the poet "diffuses in tone and spirit the unity that blends, and (as it were) *fuses,* each into each, by that synthetic and magical power to which we have exclusively appropriated the name of Imagination."

The ode came into European literature in the fifteenth and sixteenth centuries with the rediscovery of classical forms. I wish I had space to give a full history of the intermingling fate of what came to be called the greater ode (Pindaric) and the lesser ode (Horatian) in English poetry. (Both John Heath-Stubbs and John Jump have written useful short handbooks to the ode.) One of my favorite poems of the seventeenth century is the first great imitation of Pindar in English, Ben Jonson's "To the Immortall Memorie and Friendship of That Noble Paire, Sir Lucius Cary and Sir H. Morison," wherein he indicated the stanzaic pattern of the strophe, antistrophe, and epode with the terms "turn," "counterturn," and "stand." For Jonson the actual physical dance form has become a form of mentation, a mental dance, and thus the Pindaric form takes on the dialectical structure of argument: thesis, antithesis, synthesis.

So, too, Andrew Marvell's imitation of Horace's Regulus ode in praise of Augustus is one of the great political poems of the seventeenth century, "An Horatian Ode upon Cromwell's Return from Ireland." Marvell's poem is a tragic panegyric, a lyric in which the conquering hero is also a tragic figure.

The ode always promises a certain elevated style. It reclaims its connection to the ancients. And it is haunted by the fact that the form once meant a poem sung to music. "And why not I . . . Th'old *Lyric* kind revive?" Michael Drayton asks in "To Himselfe and the Harpe," one of the first odes in English. He continues on to name his precursors: Pindar, Horace, and also Orpheus, Hermes, Amphion, even King David. He also brings in the bardic craftsmen of Celtic Britain:

> And diversly though strung,
> So anciently We sung
>   To it, that Now scarce known,
> If first it did belong
> To *Greece,* or it be our Own,

as well as ancient druids "imbrew'd with Gore, on Altars rude" and Irish and Welsh harpers:

> Th'old British bards, upon their Harps,
> For falling Flats, and rising Sharps,
>   That curiously were strung;
> To stir their Youth to Warlike Rage,
> Or their wild Fury to assuage,
>   In these loose Numbers sung.

The bardic craftsman used the very measure of his music to incite and console. This remembrance shadows the written ode where the rhythm and measure of the poem without musical accompaniment must still give the poem its lofty quality. The diction tends to lift it above speech toward song. This is precisely the ceremonial music that Neruda plays with and undermines in his sometimes comical odes even as he, too, would reclaim the druidic power of the old bards. As Robert Duncan writes in "A Poem Beginning with a Line by Pindar":

The light foot hears you and the brightness begins
god-step at the margins of thought,
      quick adulterous tread at the heart.
Who is it that goes there?
      Where I see your quick face
notes of an old music pace the air,
torso-reverberation of a Grecian lyre.

The form is shadowed by the ghostly memory of a song to a wild god.

In both English and Continental poetry the ode developed a life of its own with deep roots as a noble and grave poem on a theme of acknowledged importance. There are odes of speculation, odes *on* (Milton's "On the Morning of Christ's Nativity," Gray's delightful mock ode "Ode on the Death of a Favourite Cat Drowned in a Tub of Gold Fishes," Keats's "Ode on a Grecian Urn"), and odes of address, odes *to* (Ben Jonson's poem "Ode to Himself," Collins's "Ode to Evening," Keats's "Ode to a Nightingale"). The ode in English separated from its Pindaric roots ("If a man should undertake to translate *Pindar* word for word, it would be thought that one *Mad man* had translated *another,*" Abraham Cowley wrote), but never forgot the Pindaric dream of ecstatic participation, of standing beside oneself and becoming one with the divine. I follow Paul Fry's idea that the modern ode distinguishes itself from the hymn, the collective poem of praise or thanksgiving, that it "longs to participate in the divine, but it never participates communally, never willingly supplies a congregation with common prayer." The separation between the knower and the known in the ode creates a space for greater subjectivity and introspection, it speaks to an internal power that is different than a collective or communal power. I think of the rhapsodic dream, the celebration of internal power, that is Shelley's "Ode to the West Wind"; of Keats's obsession with fusion experiences, with an elusive unity identified with death, in what are probably the greatest odes in our language; of Wordsworth's "Intimations of Immortality" and Coleridge's desolate rejoinder "Dejection: An Ode"; of Allen Tate's ironic "Ode to the Confederate Dead" and W. H. Auden's highly ambivalent "Ode" (previously entitled "Which Side Am I Supposed to Be On?"); of Robert Pinsky's recent "To Television." The writer of odes walks a tightrope, balancing a criticism of society with an affirmation of the vatic vocation of the poet who speaks to deep-lying individual powers within all of us.

The idea of a formal poem of considerable length written in magniloquent language has had less currency in our time when poets have been rightly skeptical of using poetry as a vehicle for public utterance. Think of Mallarmé's insistence that "Official verse must be used only in crisis moments of the soul." So, too, as Octavio Paz says, "Poetry is always dissident." It is always individual. The lyric poem is in dialogue with the historical world. The writer of modern odes tends to stand somewhere between complete isolation and mystic communion. For example, Neruda goes a long way toward trying to heal the divide between people without entirely being able to break it down. Because the ode has been a highly ceremonial form (public, occasional, usually of considerable length) it was a radically assertive, Whitmanesque, and political gesture for Neruda to appropriate such a wide variety of daily objects and to remake the ode as a chronicle of daily life. One animating impulse was to mix the high and the low, the mundane and the grand, the concrete and the abstract, the local and the universal. A Catholic priest in Chile attacked Neruda's odes for being materialistic, Marxist, and anti-Christian. They are all these things, in a very pagan American way. They are engaged in a deep utopian quest for both natural and social unity. But there is a divide between nature and history.

Here is Neruda's "Ode to the Americas":

Oh, pure Americas,
ocean-guarded lands
kept
purple and intact,
centuries of silent apiaries,
pyramids and earthen vessels,
rivers of bloodstained butterflies,
yellow volcanoes
and silent peoples,
shapers of pitchers,
workers of stone.

Today, Paraguay, water-formed
turquoise, buried rose,
you have become a prison.
Peru, heart of the world,
eagles'
aerie,
are you alive?
Venezuela, Colombia,
no one hears
your happy voices.
What has become of
your silvery morning chorus?
Only the birds
of ancient plumage,
only the waterfalls,
display their diadems.
Prison bars have
multiplied.
In the humid kingdom of
fire and emerald,
between
paternal rivers,
each day
a new despot arises and with his saber
lops off mortgages and auctions your treasure.
Brother begins
to hunt brother.
Stray shots sound in the ports.
Experts arrive
from Pennsylvania,
the new
conquistadors,
meanwhile,
our blood
feeds
the putrid
plantations and the buried mines,

the dollars flow,
and
our silly young girls
slip a disk learning the dance
of the orangutan.
Oh, pure Americas,
sacred lands,
what sadness!
A Machado dies and a Batista is born.
A Trujillo remains in power.
So much room
for sylvan freedom.
Americas,
so much
purity, ocean
waters,
solitary pampas, dizzying
geography, why do
insignificant blood merchants
breed and multiply?
What is happening?
How can the
silence continue
interrupted
by bloodthirsty parrots
perched in the branches
of Pan-American greed?
Americas, assailed
by broadest expanse of foam,
by felicitous seas
redolent
of the pepper of the archipelagos,
dark
Americas,
in our orbit
the star of the people
is rising,

heroes are being born,
new paths being garlanded
with victory,
the ancient nations
live again,
autumn passes
in the most radiant light,
new flags
flutter on the wind.
May your voice and your deeds,
America,
rise free from your
green girdle,
may there be an end
to love imprisoned,
may your native dignity
be restored,
may your grain rise toward the sky
awaiting with other nations
the inevitable dawn.

   (translated by Margaret Sayers Peden)

Walter Holzinger's essay "Poetic Subject and Form in *Odas elementales*" points out that Neruda's ode marries a Pindaric tripartite structure to a utopian social doctrine. The first strophe (stanza 1) is set in the past, the antistrophe (stanza 2) set in the present. The epode turns to a hortatory future with the tonal shift and address to the "Americas, assailed." The ode is caught between celebrating the earthly beauty of the continent and criticizing its political divisions and realities, its regimes. Throughout the ode there is some ambivalence about whether Neruda is addressing the Americas as a geographical or as a political entity.

America began as a utopian idea. It represented a new world. Paz calls it "a victory for nominalism: the name engendered the reality." Neruda begins by celebrating a paradisaical America before the European invasions. He praises the ocean-protected lands, the pre-Columbian people integrated into those lands, the objects (pyramids and earthen vessels) they created. The image of the beehive ("centuries of silent apiaries") summons up the idea of a cooperative society in harmony with the world around it.

The second stanza, the antistrophe, stands as a foil to the first as Neruda calls up the individual countries—Paraguay, Peru, Venezuela, Colombia—and challenges the gap between the natural beauty and the historical reality. The image of prison bars is recurrent. He reproaches Latin Americans for letting their continent be plundered by new conquerors from the north. The pure Americas, sacred lands, are polluted by blood merchants. The countermovement concludes with an outraged rhetorical question ("How can the / silence continue...?") that stands as an outcry against "Pan-American greed."

The poem concludes by turning and envisioning a future beyond alienation. It calls upon the plural "Americas" to become one "America," to break a shameful collective silence and let its one voice be heard. He would restore dignity to the land. He calls upon the lands and the peoples to be reunited, offering up a dream of freedom.

Neruda's ode concludes with a fusion dream that would seal the historical divisions of the Americas. He would restore the continent to a sacred past that would also provide a new future. He writes as a social poet but recalls the religious role of the maker. Neruda's odes were written for a daily newspaper but they retain their ancient vestiges. In his *Memoirs* Neruda writes:

Poetry is a deep inner calling in man; from it came liturgy, the psalms, and also the content of religions. The poet confronted nature's phenomena and in the early ages called himself a priest, to safeguard his vocation.... Today's social poet is still a member of the earliest order of priests. In the old days he made his pact with the darkness, and now he must interpret the light.

10

A Shadowy Exultation

"Thence did I drink the visionary power," Wordsworth declares in Book 2 of *The Prelude*, "And deem not profitless those fleeting moods / Of shadowy exultation." It has been one of the key tasks of writers for the past two centuries to try to dramatize and unleash in their work "visionary power," to recall, recapture, and render—indeed, to create—"fleeting moods / Of shadowy exultation," those ecstatic or transcendental moments which Wordsworth elsewhere formulated as "spots of time." The early manuscripts of *The Prelude* indicate that Wordsworth's autobiographical masterpiece was initially conceived as a collection of just such "spots of time." They are the small spiritual cells around which the larger narrative organism eventually grew.

Similarly, as a young man James Joyce put together a manuscript collection of what he chose to call "epiphanies," thus employing a Christian theological term for an aesthetic experience. *Epiphany* means the manifestation of a god or spirit in the body, and the Christian epiphany is literally the manifestation of Christ to the Magi. Joyce secularized the theological term so that it came to mean a sudden revelation or manifestation of spiritual meaning, an insight or revelation of truth in the commonplace, a psychological and literary mode of perception. In *Stephen Hero*, the forerunner of *Portrait of the Artist as a Young Man*, Joyce's autobiographical hero, Stephen Daedalus, hears a fragment of conversation in the street that pierces through him; it affects him keenly enough "to afflict his sensitiveness very severely" and this experience in turn makes him think of "collecting many such moments together in a book of epiphanies." The forty epiphanies from Joyce's early manuscripts that have survived (in *Ulysses*, Stephen Dedalus ironically refers to his youthful epiphanies as "deeply deep") have now been published as *The Workshop of Daedalus*, and many of them read as a hybrid between dreamy late-nineteenth-century symbolist prose poems and quick naturalistic sketches for *Dubliners*. As in Wordsworth, these epiphanies are the spiritual cells which grow into the larger narrative and autobiographical work.

My subject here is these sudden spiritual manifestations as they occur in writing. How are these forceful moments when consciousness blazes into revelation psychologically "profitable," to adapt Wordsworth's term, and precisely how do they operate in context? And how does one create such an experience in words? What are the necessary literary strategies for introducing, embodying, and containing such threshold experiences?

The spiritual insight or luminous moment has often been considered the motivating pulse of lyric writing itself. It is "Within a Moment: a Pulsation of the Artery," Blake writes, when "the Poets Work is Done." Such key moments are by definition sudden, unexpected, revelatory, unconscious. They are breakthroughs that arise out of commonplace experiences. Shelley refers to "our best and happiest moments... arising unforeseen and departing unbidden." T. S. Eliot reintroduces a theological slant to the experience by referring to the moment of moments as a Christian incarnation, that instant in the rose garden in *Four Quartets*, for example, when the temporal and the timeless intersect. Alternatively, Ezra Pound's moment of moments was pagan, a "magic moment" of metamorphosis, a movement from the quotidian into the divine or permanent world. Indeed, Pound's definition of the image as "an intellectual and emotional complex in an instant of time" may be understood as a modernist reformulation of Wordsworth's "spots of time." Virginia Woolf referred to such sudden illuminations as "Moments of Being," and in *To the Lighthouse*, Lily Briscoe speaks of "little daily miracles, illuminations, matches struck unexpectedly in the dark." These daily miracles are akin to the philosopher Henri Bergson's concept of *durée* (pure duration) which proved so useful to Proust. In "On the Intensity of Psychological States," Bergson writes:

Our ideas and sensations succeed each other with increased rapidity ... Finally, in extreme joy, our perceptions and memories acquire an indefinable quality, comparable to heat or light, and so new, that at certain moments, returning upon ourselves, we experience an astonishment of being.

Such an astonishment was what Keats was referring to when he spoke in a letter about "coming continually upon the spirit with a fine suddenness."

In *The Prelude,* Wordsworth provides some emblematic formulations of the epiphanic experience. That experience—the arc from physical action to spiritual motion—is what Harold Bloom and other critics have defined as a "poetic crossing." I want to take a look at two such Wordsworthian moments in order to decipher precisely what happens in a poetic crossing. My first example comes from Book 2, entitled "School-Time."

> and I would stand
> If the night blackened with a coming storm,
> Beneath some rock, listening to notes that are
> The ghostly language of the ancient earth,
> Or make their dim abode in distant winds.

Here the place is grounded and established. The speaker is standing under the shelter of a large rock, only to be mysteriously changed by the approaching storm. One world is suppressed as another is encountered. We have a movement from one sense to another, from sight to sound, as the ear catches what the eye can no longer find. We are moving from eyesight to vision, to an interior music of pure duration. It is too dark to see but it *is* possible to detect the sounds of a profounder music. Everything about the experience is transitory and difficult to pin down. Notice that the language is "*ghostly*" and that it comes from a long way off, from "the *ancient* earth," that it makes its "*dim* abode in *distant* winds." The moods are fleeting and the exultation "shadowy."

> Thence did I drink the visionary power;
> And deem not profitless those fleeting moods
> Of shadowy exultation: not for this,

That they are kindred to our purer mind
And intellectual life; but that the soul,
Remembering how she felt, but what she felt
Remembering not, retains an obscure sense
Of possible sublimity, whereto
With growing faculties still growing, feeling still
That whatever point they gain, they yet
Have something to pursue.

The experience is troubling and difficult, nay impossible, to recall. He literally can't remember *what* he felt; that is, the content of the experience. All he remembers is *how* he felt. The experience creates a recurrent hole in the past, a gap in the autobiographical narrative. What *was* it he felt? He doesn't know. The loss is in turn compensated for by a hope for the future, by the "obscure sense / of possible sublimity." Here the adjective "obscure" parallels the words "ghostly," "dim," and "fleeting"; the potential sublimity stands in relation to the "ancient" earth, to "distant" winds, and to "shadowy" exultation. The compensation will come in writing a certain type of poetry. In Book 5 of *The Prelude,* Wordsworth writes that "Visionary power / Attends the motion of the viewless winds / Embodied in the mystery of words." Thus he hopes that the same visionary power he felt as a boy experiencing a coming storm will be the attendant power that will assist him at the birth of a new art. The growing faculties are what he aspires to, what he hopes will be embodied in the very poem we are reading.

Another passage illuminates the relationship between the epiphanic experience, in this case even more troubling and terrifying, and the growth of the poet's powers and his visionary imagination. In the Simplon Pass section of Book 6, "Cambridge and the Alps," Wordsworth interrupts his remembered account of a journey through the mountains.

Imagination—here the Power so called
Through sad incompetence of human speech,
That awful Power rose from the mind's abyss
Like an unfathered vapour that enwraps,
At once, some lonely traveller. I was lost;
Halted without an effort to break through;

But to my conscious soul I now can say—
"I recognize thy glory": in such strength
Of usurpation, when the light of sense
Goes out, but with a flash that has revealed
The invisible world, doth greatness make abode,
There harbours whether we be young or old.
Our destiny, our being's heart and home,
Is with infinitude, and only there;
With hope it is, hope that can never die,
Effort, and expectation, and desire,
And something evermore about to be.

What is terrifying about the experience for the protagonist is that his conscious mind is suspended as the light of sense literally goes out. Indeed, the experience demonstrates how radically unstable and indeterminate the self can be. His quotidian self, his ordinary social character, is obliterated. Why? Because his mind usurps the visible universe. Something arises from inside him, some "awful Power," which, as he says, we have weakly and inadequately labeled "Imagination," and blacks out the ordinary world. But with the loss of one world another is gained. The flash that usurps the visible world also reveals a second invisible world, profound and impalpable. This is the charismatic revelation that arises from the experience. Later, the conscious mind recognizes that the terrifying vapor that seems to arise from inside is a signal of destiny, of "our being's heart and home." The protagonist, or "I," has become a fresh character as a revitalized hero has usurped the old narrative and the original protagonist. This one lives with "infinitude." In Wordsworth, a higher or increased consciousness is what compensates for the loss of a naive or original relationship to nature. The experience is painful and costly, but also a sign of vocation. We can see from these passages, however, why Kant added terror as a crucial component of the sublime.

I have come to wonder if ecstatic experiences, technically speaking, are actually distinguishable from agonizing ones when it comes to lyric poetry. I think, for example, of Emily Dickinson and how the condition of pain operates in her work, She served as its celebrant even as she was its sufferer. She was a diagnostician exposing the various gradations of psychic extremity—from lesser hurts to fuller miseries to excruciating agonies. She wrote of the "imperial—Thunderbolt / That scalps your naked soul" and of having a "tomahawk" in her side. She said she sang to conquer fear. (As she put it to Higginson, "I had a terror—since September—I could tell to none—and so I sing as the Boy does by the Burying Ground—because I am afraid.") And yet she was fearless in the poetic risks she would take and the psychic dangers she would face down. Dickinson wasn't concerned with the originating causes of psychic pain (her poems are permanently severed from their literal sources in her life and will never fully reveal their autobiographical secrets), but she was preoccupied, even obsessed, with the nature of affliction itself. What we observe in her poems is how completely pain usurps consciousness, how it obliterates everything visible, destroying what is both near and far. It recoils from and surpasses ordinary chronology. It creates an enormous gap in experience, and it entirely colonizes the self. In this way diametrically opposed but equally extreme psychic states such as pain and ecstasy, despair and bliss, are comparable experiences because they both usurp and annihilate time. They create their own sense of eternity.

Here is poem number 967. Notice how pain radically widens the sense of ordinary time and then radically condenses it.

> Pain—expands the Time—
> Ages coil within
> The minute Circumference
> Of a single Brain—
>
> Pain contracts—the Time—
> Occupied with Shot
> Gamuts of Eternities
> Are as they were not—

And here is number 650. Pain in this poem is portrayed as nameless. It has neither origin nor destination. It is a kind of expanded present without borders or horizon, without any before or after. It is an eternal blankness that makes thinking discontinuous.

Pain—has an Element of Blank—
It cannot recollect
When it begun—or if there were
A time when it was not—

It has no Future—but itself—
Its Infinite contain
Its Past—enlightened to perceive
New Periods—of Pain.

And here is number 937. In this poem we see how pain destroys the se-
quential processes of thought itself. Such an agony is alienating. It is so
radically dislocating that it entirely splits the self off from itself and think-
ing becomes virtually impossible. The mind is left with its own psychic
fragments.

I felt a Cleaving in my Mind—
As if my Brain had split—
I tried to match it—Seam by Seam—
But could not make them fit.

The thought behind, I strove to join
Unto the thought before—
But Sequence ravelled out of Sound
Like Balls—upon a Floor.

What seems brilliant about this little eight-line poem is that Dickinson
creates a terrifying feeling of disorientation without actually disorienting
the reader. She creates a fiction of dislocation. We might say the author
of the poem is not only recalling but also scrupulously re-creating (re-
structuring) the way that pain creates a cleaving in the mind.

Here is number 599.

There is a pain—so utter—
It swallows substance up—
Then covers the Abyss with Trance—
So Memory can step

Around—across—upon it—
As one within a Swoon—
Goes safely—where an open eye—
Would drop Him—Bone by Bone.

Pain swallows everything. It creates an abyss and then covers that abyss with a kind of fantasy, a trance, so that memory can move across the bridge without falling into the destructive waters. Pain is so comprehensive that it takes over the self. What we need to survive such psychic trauma is what Dickinson calls "pyramidal nerve." The act of naming is for her restorative. She has faced the worst and returned to tell the tale. What we see in all these poems is Dickinson naming what would otherwise resist representation. It would be unspeakable because outside the experience of language. The poem becomes her way of speaking back. And we might say that such speaking back—the trance or swoon—is rhapsodic poetry itself.

In thinking about the nature and consequence of such extreme experiences, represented in poetry, I would now like to turn the wheel one more notch by introducing Freud's idea of the uncanny, and use that notion to illuminate two contemporary poems, Anthony Hecht's "A Hill" and Elizabeth Bishop's "In the Waiting Room." Freud provides us with a psychological explanation for ghostly, mysterious, and eerie experiences. These experiences are, in his terms, involuntary repetitions, compulsive unconscious returns. They occur when something revives repressed impulses in us. "The Uncanny," Freud writes, "is the name for everything that ought to have remained . . . hidden and secret and has become visible." Freud's account of epiphanic moments of rupturing intensity provides another aid in comprehending "the mind's abyss," experiences which minimize referentiality, call the ordinary social character into question, and destroy time.

Here is "A Hill":

In Italy, where this sort of thing can occur,
I had a vision once—though you understand
It was nothing at all like Dante's, or the visions of saints,
And perhaps not a vision at all. I was with some friends,
Picking my way through a warm sunlit piazza

In the early morning. A clear fretwork of shadows
From huge umbrellas littered the pavement and made
A sort of lucent shallows in which was moored
A small navy of carts. Books, coins, old maps,
Cheap landscapes and ugly religious prints
Were all on sale. The colors and noise
Like the flying hands were gestures of exultation,
So that even the bargaining
Rose to the ear like a voluble godliness.
And then, when it happened, the noises suddenly stopped,
And it got darker; pushcarts and people dissolved
And even the great Farnese Palace itself
Was gone, for all its marble; in its place
Was a hill, mole-colored and bare. It was very cold,
Close to freezing, with a promise of snow.
The trees were like old ironwork gathered for scrap
Outside a factory wall. There was no wind,
And the only sound for a while was the little click
Of ice as it broke in the mud under my feet.
I saw a piece of ribbon snagged on a hedge,
But no other sign of life. And then I heard
What seemed the crack of a rifle. A hunter, I guessed;
At least I was not alone. But just after that
Came the soft and papery crash
Of a great branch somewhere unseen falling to earth.

And that was all, except for the cold and silence
That promised to last forever, like the hill.

Then prices came through, and fingers, and I was restored
To the sunlight and my friends. But for more than a week
I was scared by the plain bitterness of what I had seen.
All this happened about ten years ago,
And it hasn't troubled me since, but at last, today,
I remembered that hill; it lies just to the left
Of the road north of Poughkeepsie; and as a boy
I stood before it for hours in wintertime.

"A Hill" begins by establishing a literal place—the epiphanic mode is always grounded in the quotidian world—and ironically announcing its Dantesque vision. The setting ("Italy, where this sort of thing can occur") and the ironic declaration about the vision ("I had a vision once"—it was "perhaps not a vision at all") allow the poet both to declare and project the approaching transcendental experience even as he defends himself against the grandiosity of the claim. The next part of the poem is necessarily mimetic, emphasizing the social realm ("I was with some friends") and the dailiness of life ("Books, coins, old maps, / Cheap landscapes and ugly religious prints / Were all on sale"). Slyly, however, there is a religious overtone to the dailiness (we are, after all, in Italy)—the colors and noise seem like "gestures of exultation" and even the bargaining rises to the ear "like a voluble godliness." This is the preparation and trigger to the experience. Nonetheless, there is still a radical break in the text as the visionary experience irremediably ruptures the temporal world:

> And then, when it happened, the noises suddenly stopped
> And it got darker...

Notice the cessation of sound and the sudden darkening (as in Wordsworth) as the social world dissolves, the world of colors and noise and other people. The protagonist is suddenly alone. The very emblem of culture, the great Farnese Palace, disappears and is replaced by an inexplicable, primordial image, a bare, mole-colored hill. The social and cultural worlds have been totally blanked out and replaced by something terrifyingly cold and silent. Unable to see, uncertain of precisely what is happening or where he is (he is lost in the dark woods), suspended in some unknown realm, the protagonist hears a loud noise that seems to be the crack of a rifle. He guesses it comes from a hunter and considers himself momentarily fortunate—here the weight of his isolation is hinted at—because at least he is not alone. But immediately he hears "the soft and papery crash / Of a great branch somewhere unseen falling to earth." He may only be listening to the crack of thunder and a branch falling, but what he senses is some gratuitous primal murder. The epiphanic moment—we might call it a downward or negative epiphany—is extended for another stanza as the protagonist is literally outside of time, experiencing an emptiness that promises to "last forever." The next stanza returns him to ordinary time: "Then prices came through, and fingers..." The syntax mirrors his restoration to the external social world. For over a week he is scared, and then he forgets or represses the experience. And it is now, at the conclusion of the poem, that he comes to a second epiphanic realization, the full knowledge of the previous vision which has taken a decade to reveal its true origin:

All this happened about ten years ago,
And it hasn't troubled me since, but at last, today,
I remembered that hill; it lies just to the left
Of the road north of Poughkeepsie; and as a boy
I stood before it for hours in wintertime.

Thus the Italian vision of the hill turns out to be a long-repressed memory from his New York childhood, what Freud calls an uncanny experience, a compulsive return and involuntary repetition. We are never told precisely what the hill means or represents, or what inside the house and inside himself drove him out to encounter it. We *are* told that he was literally entranced by that hill, that it represented something primary and basic for him, something profoundly compelling since he stood before it for hours in winter. It is a primal, inexplicable image that has arisen out of the "mind's abyss," that has been buried inside him all these years and can no longer be repressed. A vision has turned into a recollection, and we are left at the conclusion of the poem with the silent and mysterious gaze of the boy upon the hill, staring at it with a mixture of wonder and terror.

Elizabeth Bishop's "In the Waiting Room" dramatizes an epiphany of identity, a profound loss and realization of self, a painful memory of coming into self-consciousness. It enacts a child's sudden realization that she actually has a self, a singular and complex identity that simultaneously separates her from others and connects her to them. She is reexperiencing nothing less than some primary, original separation.

In Worcester, Massachusetts,
I went with Aunt Consuelo
to keep her dentist's appointment
and sat and waited for her
in the dentist's waiting room.

It was winter. It got dark
early. The waiting room
was full of grown-up people,
arctics and overcoats,
lamps and magazines.
My aunt was inside
what seemed like a long time
and while I waited I read
the *National Geographic*
(I could read) and carefully
studied the photographs:
the inside of a volcano,
black, and full of ashes;
then it was spilling over
in rivulets of fire.
Osa and Martin Johnson
dressed in riding breeches,
laced boots, and pith helmets.
A dead man slung on a pole
—"Long Pig," the caption said.
Babies with pointed heads
wound round and round with string;
black, naked women with necks
wound round and round with wire
like the necks of light bulbs.
Their breasts were horrifying.
I read it right straight through.
I was too shy to stop.
And then I looked at the cover:
the yellow margins, the date.

Suddenly, from inside,
came an *oh!* of pain
—Aunt Consuelo's voice—
not very loud or long.
I wasn't at all surprised;
even then I knew she was

a foolish, timid woman.
I might have been embarrassed,
but wasn't. What took me
completely by surprise
was that it was *me:*
my voice, in my mouth.
Without thinking at all
I was my foolish aunt,
I—we—were falling, falling,
our eyes glued to the cover
of the *National Geographic,*
February, 1918.

I said to myself: three days
and you'll be seven years old.
I was saying it to stop
the sensation of falling off
the round, turning world
into cold, blue-black space.
But I felt: you are an *I,*
you are an *Elizabeth,*
you are one of *them.*
Why should you be one, too?
I scarcely dared to look
to see what it was I was.
I gave a sidelong glance
—I couldn't look any higher—
at shadowy gray knees,
trousers and skirts and boots
and different pairs of hands
lying under the lamps.
I knew that nothing stranger
had ever happened, that nothing
stranger could ever happen.
Why should I be my aunt,
or me, or anyone?
What similarities—

boots, hands, the family voice
I felt in my throat, or even
the *National Geographic*
and those awful, hanging breasts—
held us all together
or made us all just one?
How—I didn't know any
word for it—how "unlikely"...
How had I come to be here,
like them, and overhear
a cry of pain that could have
got loud and worse but hadn't?

The waiting room was bright
and too hot. It was sliding
beneath a big black wave,
another, and another.

Then I was back in it.
The War was on. Outside,
in Worcester, Massachusetts,
were night and slush and cold,
and it was still the fifth
of February, 1918.

Bishop's poem begins, as poems in the epiphanic mode tend to do, by establishing a firm sense of locale, a recognizable setting, a clear narrative coherence. It is winter in Worcester, Massachusetts; the protagonist is waiting for her aunt in the public space of the waiting room at the dentist's office. She is surrounded by other people, all strangers, slightly bored (her aunt has been gone what seems a long time), glancing through a magazine (in a nice touch she boasts that she could read at the time). She is riveted by *National Geographic* photographs; indeed, she is shocked by terrifying images of "nature": a volcano spilling over, two explorers or hunters standing next to "a dead man slung on a pole," and, most shockingly, babies with pointed heads "wound round and round with string" and "black, naked women with necks / wound round and round with wire / like the necks of light bulbs." She is in effect stunned to see the women so exposed, irremediably—horrifyingly—marked by gender. She is glimpsing, to use a Freudian language, that which was not intended to be seen. Turning away, she looks at the cover of the magazine, as if to fix it in her mind, a marker of ordinary time, which she is about to leave. She is moving outside the yellow margins, as it were, outside the date, as she passes from external eyesight to internal vision:

> Suddenly, from inside,
> came an *oh!* of pain
> —Aunt Consuelo's voice—
> not very loud or long.

Notice the pun on the word *inside:* the voice is coming from inside the other room, apparently from Aunt Consuelo, but, also, surprisingly, as she discovers, from inside herself.

> What took me
> completely by surprise
> was that it was *me:*
> my voice, in my mouth.

She is experiencing what we have been calling a greater degree of interiorization. The crisis is that the self is an other, that "I—we—were falling, falling..." As she discovers that she is identical to her foolish aunt, the protagonist is falling outside the recognizable boundaries even as she tries to fix the date of the magazine in her head. She tries to hold on to the familiar world by telling herself (and us) that she is almost seven years old. She is unsuccessfully trying to cling to what she already knows, to keep from falling off the edges of experience. But she is free-floating now, losing her previous sense of gravity, moving past the known boundaries, creating an enormous hole in herself, in the narrative sequence of her life. She is intuiting that she is, in fact, a separate self, a named person to others, simultaneously "other" to herself, "one of *them*"—a female, a human being. In one sense she is still inside the waiting room, but in another she has floated into space: "I knew that nothing stranger / had ever happened," she says, "that nothing / stranger could ever happen." She is now meditating and commenting upon what is happening to her, she is puzzling it out for herself, trying to come to grips with the knowledge of having a self that seems both knowable and unknowable, both separate and familiar, that bears the stamp of uniqueness and commonality—family resemblance, the markings of gender. The radically modest and understated word *unlikely*, a very characteristic Bishop word, is literally accurate even as it suggests something of the inability of language to capture the intensity of experience. How unlikely, the poem reminds us, it is to be anyone at all. What a strange and specific constellation of factors comes together in the shaping of an identity. There is no answer to the question "How had I come to be here, / like them, and overhear / a cry of pain that could have / got loud and worse but hadn't?"

The next stanza prolongs the epiphanic experience for a final moment. The room is both too hot and too bright ("our perceptions and memories acquire an indefinable quality," Bergson wrote, "comparable to heat or light"). It is intensely physical and uncomfortable. It is as if she needs to hide from the intensity of what she is "seeing" even as the room seems to be sliding into primal darkness, a succession of waves. The lens is bright, the ground uncertain. Then the conclusion of the poem. Notice the word *then*, which in the epiphanic mode marks a turn (or return) to a different level of time.

> Then I was back in it.
> The War was on. Outside,
> in Worcester, Massachusetts,
> were night and slush and cold,
> and it was still the fifth
> of February, 1918.

Thus she turns from the intense brightness and heat of what she has experienced to the slush and cold of the external world. She has been "out of it" and now is "back in it"; that is, back in the wintry world where the war is still going on, where it gets dark early, and where the date has not changed. In one sense, nothing has changed, but in another sense, for her, everything has changed. She has both lost and reconstituted herself.

She returns to the outer dark where it is still February 5 with a painful self-awareness and knowledge of human identity, with a sense of the mysterious strangeness of life itself, with what W. B. Yeats calls "a new knowledge of reality."

The epiphanic moment always marks a crisis point in a work, a threshold experience. One notices how often, and how primitively, it is set off by the word *suddenly*. It is a moment of illumination that signals a dramatic turning point for the protagonist. The change is interiorized; under the pressure of insight one's mental landscape is irrevocably altered. Such moments are "visionary"; that is, they mark a crossover from one level of experience to another. There is a twofold risk or danger in trying to incorporate or contain the transcendental experience in writing. Since the epiphany is by definition triggered by an ordinary experience, one danger is that the writer will communicate the ordinariness and not the epiphany, thus getting stuck in concrete particulars, in an untransformed matter-of-factness. The other risk is that the ordinary experience will trigger what seems an inordinate or melodramatic response, what Keats calls "the egotistical manufacture of metaphysical importance upon trivial themes."

Epiphanic experiences exist outside ordinary time. They are atemporal. The consequences of such visionary experiences for time-bound narratives are profound. Most poems, for example, have both narrative and lyrical values: the impulse to tell a story, the impulse to sing. These impulses are not necessarily in harmony with each other. The point of narrative is to strengthen the bonds of consequence, the course of narrative is movement. Momentum is life itself since its goal is always to continue, to carry on, to create an unceasing flow of events. It is all motion and accretion. That is why E. M. Forster called narrative "the lowest and simplest of literary organisms." The goal of the lyric, on the other hand, is often to dramatize intense states of feeling. When Wordsworth decided in the "Preface" to the *Lyrical Ballads* "to let the feeling give importance to the action and situation, and not the action and situation to the feeling," he was in effect reversing the Aristotelian prescription for the primacy of action. He was lyricizing narrative (hence the title, *Lyrical Ballads*), loosening the relentlessness of narrative consequence in the interests of the higher bonds of emotion. Poems are lyrical precisely because they interrupt or interfere with narrative.

Epiphanies can't be held on to. "Don't allow the lucid moment to dissolve," Adam Zagajewski instructs himself in one poem. But such lucid moments inevitably *do* dissolve. "Clear moments are so short," he declares in another poem: "There is much more darkness." "For these are moments only, moments of insight," John Ashbery affirms in his poem "The Task." What is true about narrative poems is also true about long discursive poems of consciousness, such as Wallace Stevens's late poems or Ashbery's own humorously self-reflexive meditations. Ashbery is a poet who recognizes that the epiphany is a kind of death and, indeed, one way to read his long poems—"Self-Portrait in a Convex Mirror," or "Grand Gallop," or "A Wave," or the book-length *Flow Chart*—is as a continual postponement of epiphanies, a way of engaging consciousness to repeatedly hold off the concluding insight. As he puts it in "Self-Portrait":

> The locking into place is "death itself,"
> As Berg said of a phrase in Mahler's Ninth;
> Or, to quote Imogen in *Cymbeline,* "There cannot
> Be a pinch in death more sharp than this," for,
> Though only exercise or tactic, it carries
> The momentum of a conviction that had been building.

Ashbery's poems establish a pattern of opening up and closing down, of disclosure and concealment. They reveal, they reveil. They embrace "the charity of the hard moments," they welcome and embrace change. They are flow charts that repeatedly push back the locking into place that is "death itself."

The epiphanic moment is a radical attempt to defy the temporal order and dramatize an intense moment of monumental change. Such moments defy continuity. These intense recognitions create gaps or ruptures in the text. They move from the ordinary to some other extraordinary realm of experience in order to negate time itself. The experience is shockingly painful since it involves being separated from daily life and losing one's former self. The compensation is a new knowledge and consciousness. The everlasting splendor of dramatizing epiphanies may well be the mystery of communicating moments when the self is both lost and found.

11

Soul in Action

"To understand poetry," Federico García Lorca once said, "we need four white walls and a silence where the poet's voice can weep and sing." Lorca evokes the four white walls as an emblem of pure space, of an enclosure that separates us from the social realm and allows us the solitude to respond to the poet's voice. The four white walls are the poet's image of a primary shelter where one can experience a central simplicity. It must be a silent space because only in such silence can one listen to the words and daydream one's way back into the house of being.

Wallace Stevens meant something similar when he said, "Poetry is like prayer in that it is most effective in solitude and in the times of solitude as, for example, in the earliest morning" ("Adagia"). Poetry tries to get at something elemental by coming out of a silence and returning us—restoring us—to that silence. It longs to contact the mysteries; hence its kinship to prayer.

Lyric poetry is one of the soul's natural habitats. The poem of high spiritual attainment has the power, the almost magical potential, to release something that dwells deep within us. It taps into something that we otherwise experience haphazardly or at unlikely, decisive moments in our lives. Go to your bookshelf and take down a copy of Emerson's *Essays*. Turn to his piece "The Over-Soul," and you'll find him pointing to those odd, dramatic moments when we suddenly intuit something of the soul's elusive, defining epiphanic power:

> If we consider what happens in conversation, in reveries, in remorse, in times of passion, in surprises, in the instructions of dreams, wherein often we see ourselves in masquerade—the droll disguises only magnifying and enhancing a real element and forcing it on our distinct notice—we shall catch many hints that will broaden and lighten into knowledge of the secret of nature. All goes to show that the soul in man is not an organ, but animates and exercises all the organs; is not a function, like the power of memory, of calculation, of comparison, but uses these as hands and feet; is not a faculty, but a light; is not the intellect or the will, but the master of the intellect and the will; is the background of our being, in which they lie—an immensity not possessed and that cannot be possessed.

The soul, in Emerson's notion of it, has a radical coherence and authority. It is a light that shines "from within or from behind." I find that same light burning in lyric poetry. The poem surprises us in words by formally delivering a sense of overpowering spiritual immensity. It instills us with a feeling of what cannot be possessed, and it lets the soul have its way with us. The poem is a soul in action through words.

Here is a short poem by Walt Whitman, "A Clear Midnight," that has the soulfulness I am trying to articulate. It's a late and somewhat neglected work of Whitman's, the final poem in the section "From Noon to Starry Night" in the seventh edition of *Leaves of Grass* (1881). Whitman is well-known as our swaggering national bard, as an epic chanter of democracy, but, as this poem shows, he was also a delicate and tender solitary.

A Clear Midnight
This is thy hour O Soul, thy free flight into the wordless,
Away from books, away from art, the day erased, the lesson
    done,
Thee fully forth emerging, silent, gazing, pondering the themes
    thou lovest best,
Night, sleep, death and the stars.

I want to dwell in some detail over this short poem to suggest how it enacts its own spiritual motion. I also recall what Emerson said in his essay "The Poet" about a passage from Spenser: "Here we find ourselves suddenly, not in a critical speculation, but in a holy place, and should go very warily and reverently."

I want to proceed carefully because I'm aware that ever since the advent of modernism in the early part of the twentieth century the word *soul*, which Whitman's poem depends upon for its meaning, has seemed antiquated in poetry. For many it has felt like a concept whose usefulness waned along with the nineteenth century. Yet Gaston Bachelard was right to say in *The Poetics of Space* that "the word *soul* is an immortal word. In certain poems it cannot be effaced, for it is a word born of our breath." Bachelard refers to the fact that, as one nineteenth-century French dictionary put it, "the different names for the soul, among nearly all peoples, are just so many breath variations, and onomatopoeic expressions of breathing." The French word for soul, *âme*, derives from the Latin *anima*, which originally designated the breath of life. Whitman has given us one such breath of life in this short poem by vocalizing a profound commitment to the soul, to naming in the self what is essential and irreducible, permanent and beyond human limitation.

"A Clear Midnight" is about releasing the soul back into the universe and in this sense it has the character of an archaic or primitive poem with a nineteenth-century diction. It is also a romantic poem in the way, like other romantic poems, it points to a threshold or visionary experience. It makes a poetic crossing. We move in this poem past daylight into nighttime, past the temporal realm into a timeless one. And because the poem arcs away from the human toward the divine, it follows the trajectory of a prayer, offering a sense of spiritual release and liberation associated with godliness.

"A Clear Midnight" has such spaciousness that I have to remind myself the entire poem is only four lines long: one quatrain. The body of the poem consists of one sentence made up of forty-two words, none difficult to understand. How does it work? How does it achieve its feeling of compression and expansiveness?

First: "A Clear Midnight" is a simple title with significant import. The poem is set at a culminating hour in the nocturnal realm. At this hour, everything associated with the rest of the day must be let go. It is the witching hour, a haunted time. It is the time of a literal and poetic crossing. The midnight is clear, not cloudy or obscure, because the lyric itself is a clarifying action that represents a peak of spiritual lucidity. The soul, released, can see all the way to the stars.

"I believe in you my soul," Whitman declared in "Song of Myself," and it's the way he apostrophizes the soul in "A Clear Midnight" that gives the poem its spiritual tonality. Whitman also declares here that he *has* a soul, but instead of addressing that credible soul as a familiar "you," he addresses it more formally and even reverently as "thou," as something almost independent and sacred dwelling within himself. "This is thy hour O Soul," he says directly, capitalizing the noun "Soul," speaking as a contingent self releasing what is most primary within himself, freeing it from the interior where it has been hidden all day. The initial vocative "O" gives a certain loftiness to the address and, indeed, by speaking to the soul as a distinct entity he also celebrates its unalterable character. And here we cannot escape the fact that Whitman is directing and claiming his *soul* and not his mind (mentation) or heart (emotion). He is giving free rein to that designated spirit. The burden of the day has been lifted and the speaker feels a new authority in endorsing what is absolute and unchanging.

The soul in Whitman's poem is a little like a magical or imaginary bird: opaque by day, transparent by night. The true or essentialist self is unleashed in this poem. Another observation by Bachelard is also to the point: "A consciousness associated with the soul is more relaxed, less intentionalized than a consciousness associated with the phenomena of the mind. Forces are manifested in poems that do not pass through the circuits of knowledge" (*The Poetics of Space*). Hence Whitman tells his soul that this is the moment of its "free flight into the wordless"; that is, of its winged motion upward, its soaring into a mystic realm beyond language. It's the paradox of Whitman's poem (and the fate of all mystic poetry) that it must use words (the very ones we are reading) to point to and define a nonlinguistic experience. There is no free flight into the wordless that does not charge the words to transport us there.

This leads us to the directive of the second line: "Away from books, away from art, the day erased, the lesson done." It's striking that the speaker has spent his earlier hours with books and art, with what is beautiful, bound or framed, and humanly made, and now moves away from that experience toward something even more elemental. This is Whitman at his most Emersonian since it's implied that books and art—secondhand experiences—must now be transcended. I suppose another way to think about this is that the books and art have been preparing the soul for its liberation. And of course we only feel this particular arc toward spiritual freedom because it is enacted for us in print, in the work of art we are now encountering.

So, too, the day must be erased because it stands for earthly knowledge. Beneficial knowledge can be obtained during the day, but now that realm has disappeared so another can be attained. The word "erased" has associations with classes, with schoolroom learning, which in turn leads us to the last phrase in the line, "the lesson done." Whatever could be learned during a set period of instruction is completed now so another type of learning can take place: a schooling for the soul. One of the secondary meanings of the word *lesson* Whitman would have known: "A reading from the Bible or other sacred writing part of a religious service." That reading, too, must be put behind him so that the soul can school itself directly on naturalistic mysteries, on the themes it loves above all others.

The free-verse rhythm of Whitman's sentence, its almost biblical cadence, gives it a compressed but expanding feeling of a soul's emergence. There's a slow, stately, gradualist rhythm in the third line. This becomes evident when we isolate the line as a unit unto itself: "Thee fully forth emerging, silent, gazing, pondering the themes thou lovest best." The very length of this line as a unit of meaning gives it a trancelike quality, the sense of a content stretching beyond speech, beyond the social realm. The sense of forceful emergence is emphasized by the alliterative *f*s in the phrase "Thee fully forth." Note the slight caesura, a pause in the line, after the word "emerging." The word *caesura* derives from the Latin word *caedere*, "to cut," and this cutting takes place so we can pause and savor the experience of the soul's growth. Its release is silent (reverential, hushed), gazing (this sight is visionary because beyond what one could normally "see" during the day), and pondering (the soul weighs and deliberates, it touches a deeper depth than thought itself).

How revealing that the soul ponders the "themes" it loves best. *Themes* is a word saturated with literary connotations since it suggests a topic of discourse, a perception or idea expanded upon in a literary work.

The word has such resonance here because it suggests that a soul trying to go beyond poetry still expresses itself in terms compromised and elevated by poetry. Whitman cannot escape the reality that to be understood and communicated the soul's action must be translated into language.

In her useful book *The Symbol of the Soul from Hölderlin to Yeats*, Suzanne Nalbantian points out several aspects of the literary usage of the soul especially germane to Whitman's poem. She demonstrates, for example, how closely in classical philosophy and literature the soul was associated with the element of air; how obsessively in romantic poetry it was linked to the imagery of the bird; how often it was connected with the sky. These associations take nothing away from Whitman's poem, but they do show how deeply saturated it is in conventions of literary expression. The "soul" is a literary device for transcendence.

And it is a device that works. For no matter how many times I've read or recited the last line of "A Clear Midnight," I am always struck by its grandeur. There's a majestic quality to "night, sleep, death and the stars." The thinking is slightly more linear than it might initially seem since Whitman is creating a subtle progression; the order of these four words, these four mysteries, cannot in any way be altered or changed. Night leads to sleep, which in turn leads one to think of death, a familiar association in romantic poetry. It's the brilliance of the stars that gives the poem its final sense of luminosity. It's inconceivable to think of this particular poem ending on the darkness of the word *death*. For the soul must ponder something that stretches beyond death, something sparkling and lit up in the distance. Something radiant beyond time. Something that releases us into the eternal.

Whitman's poem exemplifies the correspondence between our inner and outer worlds. It is all about transport, about the imagination in cooperation and harmony with the universe. Whitman seems to address his soul to achieve that harmony. This is a dramatic utterance, but it is also a conjuration. Whitman is playing a magician to his own soul on our behalf. The real addressee of the incantation is the reader who exists on the distant horizon of the poem. I cannot help but feel that one part of the poem's meaning is that the reader, too, has an imperishable soul. The poem wants to trigger that soul to dwell on the eternal. It would release something wordless and equivalent in any of us who read it.

Sometimes, late at night, I'll read "A Clear Midnight" and feel something within me beginning to stir. The words spur me in the direction of the Mysteries. I recite the poem over to myself like a prayer and feel its themes inhabiting me. I put down my book. For a moment I pause in the doorway to listen to the sound of others sleeping near me. I breathe deeply. Then I go outside and ponder the stars.

"Life is a spell so exquisite that everything conspires to break it," Emily Dickinson said. One reason I like staying up to read long after everyone else has gone to sleep is that in the middle of the night not much conspires to break that spell. I like the dark hour when the secular world recedes and consciousness is loosened for poetic reverie. I have called the poem a soul in action through words because I want to suggest that lyric poetry provides us with a particular means of spiritual transport.

Here is a poem by Wallace Stevens that has something of the same spiritual poise as "A Clear Midnight," a poem Stevens especially admired. "The House Was Quiet and the World Was Calm" first appeared in *Transport to Summer*. It was written in what J. V. Cunningham calls Stevens's "quiet plain style."

The house was quiet and the world was calm.
The reader became the book; and summer night

Was like the conscious being of the book.
The house was quiet and the world was calm.

The words were spoken as if there was no book,
Except that the reader leaned above the page,

Wanted to lean, wanted much most to be
The scholar to whom his book is true, to whom

The summer night is like a perfection of thought.
The house was quiet because it had to be.

The quiet was part of the meaning, part of the mind:
The access of perfection to the page.

And the world was calm. The truth in a calm world,
In which there is no other meaning, itself

Is calm, itself is summer and night, itself
Is the reader leaning late and reading there.

Stevens's poem is so fulfilling because it doesn't merely report the activity of reading deep into the night; it actually dramatizes and re-creates the feeling of the experience. Notice, for example, how at one moment the fictive reader merges with his chosen text ("the reader *became* the book"), the words coming to him seemingly unmediated by the printed letters on the page, the physical object of the book itself ("the words were spoken *as if* there was no book"). But at another moment he feels himself hovering over that very book ("the reader *leaned* above the page"). Reading is re-created here as a physical activity and mental action. An act of attention. A quest. The fulfillment of a desire.

"The House Was Quiet and the World Was Calm" is a poem of spiritual attainment that locates and focuses the transaction between the reader, the book, the house, the night, and the world. It's as if all the terms are algebraically lined up. The poem establishes a correspondence between the inner realm of the house and the outer one of the cosmos. The quietness of the dwelling and the calmness of the universe are a kind of subject rhyme. This is a twofold proposition: the house was quiet *and* the world was calm. The poem has to be set at night because it suppresses the ordinary or quotidian world and creates a world of autonomous solitude. It has to be a summer night because summer is the season of plenitude, of fulfillment.

It's striking that the reader becomes a scholar in the fourth stanza of the poem, because the scholar is one of Stevens's Emersonian figures for the poet. Stevens elsewhere calls the poet "the scholar of one candle." He says, "Poetry is the scholar's art." How compelling that the poetic quester in this poem—the pilgrim in search of a vivid transference—is not so much the writer as the reader. The reader wants to transform himself into "The scholar to whom his book is true"; that desire is made most emphatic by the slow mouthful of words "wanted much most to be." That desire leads to an even greater one for this scholar wants to be the one "to whom / The summer night is like a perfection of thought."

He wants the night to become akin to an utter realization of mind and, indeed, "a perfection of thought" puts one in mind of the divine.

So, too, the book the reader studies becomes the emblem of a spiritual meditation. It's as if through the contemplative act the scholar and the book merge with the night to become the form of its substantiation. The silence (of house, of the mind) is causal: it makes possible "The access of perfection to the page." That access, the possibility of perfect expression, is one of the spiritual goals of the romantic lyric.

"The House Was Quiet and the World Was Calm" enacts a satisfying transport to summer. *Transport* means to carry from one place to another, but it also means to enrapture. This particular transport moves on the wheels of eight beautifully balanced and modulated two-line stanzas. These stanzas, with their faint echoes of the heroic couplet, create a sense of deep stillness and calm movement, of stately rhythm and meditative repose. The stillness is reinforced when the sentence and the line coincide, as in the title, which also serves as the refrain. The refrain itself creates a sense of musical recurrence, of circularity. The enjambed or carry-over lines emphasize an almost ritual progression forward. Note, too, how the poem moves from the past into the present tense. This gives a sense of achieved immediacy to the conclusion.

The iterated last lines have a chantlike quality, an incantatory fullness:

And the world was calm. The truth in a calm world,
In which there is no other meaning, itself

Is calm, itself is summer and night, itself
Is the reader leaning late and reading there.

These lines suggest there is no symbolic truth beyond the immanent truth of the world in and of itself at a perfect moment. (The phrase "itself is" is reiterated three times.) Yet they also have a feeling of transcendental plenitude, of spiritual embodiment and realization. The feeling is created by the sonorousness of the language, a sonorousness so complete it is difficult to disentangle. I hear the consonants quietly recurring—the *w*s and *c*s in one line—

And the *w*orld *w*as *c*alm. The truth in a *c*alm *w*orld

the *r*s and *l*s in another—

Is the *r*eader *l*eaning *l*ate and *r*eading the*r*e.

So, too, I hear the vowels calmly lining up—the *e*s and *a*s coming to-gether in the "*r*eader *lea*ning and *rea*ding." I also hear those reiterated *i*s and *s*s in "*I*t*s*elf *is*." The overall effect of the repetitions seems musical. "Music falls on silence like a sense," Stevens writes, "a passion that we feel, not understand."

"The House Was Quiet and the World Was Calm" gives us access through a third-person center of consciousness to a reader's mind in a state of complete receptivity. It lets part of the mind rise and creates ac-cess to a realm of the mind that isn't antagonized. It re-creates that con-sciousness for us and thus gives refreshment. I would call this a poem of the spirit because it triggers a vital principle or animating force within the poem. And that, too, is part of the meaning, part of the passion that is felt. One might speculate that the poem itself is only fully realized when the reader of Wallace Stevens's poem becomes like the reader *within* his poem, reading late and leaning there, perhaps even pondering the themes the soul loves best: night, sleep, death and the stars.

I have been trying to show how Stevens's poem, like Whitman's, creates what Rilke called "outer standstill and inner movement." These poems suspend normative time and arrest temporality. They refuse social im-pingement by erasing the noise of the day and welcoming the stillness of night, thereby creating a sense of deepening interiority which I am asso-ciating with the emergent soul. "The Soul achieves—Herself," Emily Dickinson writes (number 383). And:

> The Soul's Superior instants
> Occur to Her—alone—
> When friend—and Earth's occasion
> Have infinite withdrawn—
> *(number 306)*

In Dickinson's terms the withdrawal from the occasional world is a nec-essary prelude to spiritual disclosure.

Dickinson imaginatively employs a transcendental idiom in her poems, and that's one of the reasons she returns so often to the figure of the soul. In *The Passion of Emily Dickinson*, Judith Farr points out that Dickinson speaks of the *soul* or *souls* 141 times in her poems. One could make a wonderful little anthology of Dickinson's images of the soul. Some of these images bear traces of Jonathan Edwards's sermons, or Emerson's essays, or the Protestant hymns of her childhood. Others are all her own. She writes of the soul as a lost boat, an internal lamp, a storm within, an emperor; she characterizes her soul numb and her soul ripening, her soul entombed and her soul released, her soul as an adventure unto itself. She writes of "The Cellars of the Soul" and the "electric gale" of that same soul, and thus the soul becomes the image for her plunges into the psychological depths as well as a sign of her flight to the celestial heights. She asks, "Dare you see a Soul *at the White Heat?*" She speaks of the soul admitted to itself as a site of "polar privacy" and "Finite infinity." She directs her soul to "Take thy risk." It is characteristic of her always to sever the soul from the power of the collective and scandalously reclaim it for the autonomous self.

Seven of Dickinson's poems start off with declarative assertions about the soul. I take number 683 as my example:

The Soul unto itself
Is an imperial friend—
Or the most agonizing Spy
An Enemy—could send—

Secure against its own—
No treason it can fear—
Itself—its Sovereign—of itself
The Soul should stand in Awe—

This is a poem of logical definition about the soul alone, the soul "unto itself" and thus cut off from others. It gives an acute anatomy of the deepest internal division within the self: Dickinson was nothing if not extreme. The soul could be defined here as a compression, or condensation, of the self: distilled to its true essence. The quintessential self, the "Essential Me." Dickinson powerfully defines what it means to face oneself at ground level, presenting it in the form of a single alternative: either the soul is a royal friend or a traitorous enemy. There is nothing between these extremes. Dickinson has clearly experienced both alternatives, but she presents that felt experience in terms of a logical proposition, an impersonal lyric. The speaker of the poem, the lyrical "I," is inferred, not given. Experience is not delineated so much as interpreted and generalized, the poem summary.

Almost all of Dickinson's poems are examples of "compactness compacted" (to borrow Marianne Moore's description of Louise Bogan's verse). This one consists of a mere thirty-seven words arranged in eight lines divided into two quatrains. There's only one rhyme for emphasis ("friend"/"send"). There's not a single period in the poem, and thus the sentence comes to no final or conclusive stopping point, though the dashes create hesitations and interruptions at the ends of lines as well as within two of the lines. For example, the rhythm of the first two lines is smooth, whereas the dashes at the close of the third line and in the middle of the fourth line roughen the rhythm to match the rougher content. So, too, the dashes in the penultimate line create an emphatic pause and therefore give special sovereignty to the word "Sovereign." Here as elsewhere, the dashes create what Susan Howe calls "Hush of hesitation for breath and for breathing."

There is not a wasted word in this little poem or, for that matter, a wasted capital letter. The phrase "imperial friend" is lowercase and, since Dickinson uses capital letters *very* frequently in her poems, it's striking that "imperial friend" is lowercase. The word "imperial" is well chosen because it suggests a friend of supreme authority, an emperor. I assume the word "friend" is not capitalized because Dickinson sought a secular term for an inner harmony—the soul's harmonious relationship to itself. The soul's self-connection is regal not divine. Godlike, perhaps, but not God. Yet I cannot help but feel that the friend is therefore outweighed by the opposition; after all, the nouns "Spy" and "Enemy" are both capitalized. So, too, this is not just any spy, but "the most agonizing" one, a devilishly superlative traitor who betrays from within. Dickinson has sought and found a figure for what the self does against itself. It's evident she was painfully familiar with the experience of self-laceration, acute self-punishment. She may even have taken a certain pride in facing the hardest psychological truths and not turning away ("I like a look of

Agony," she confesses, "because I know it's true"). She could not abide social falseness.

Since this is a poem about a singular divide within the self it is formally divided into two equal parts. The second half of the poem presents the image of a house or fortress secure against insurrection. The image of a dwelling that cannot be breached points to Dickinson's self-imposed exile, her reclusion indoors, which was at times quasi-celestial, at times prisonlike. Freedom within confinement was one of her key subjects. So was attainment by renunciation. The penultimate line—"Itself—its Sovereign—of itself"—creates a kind of standstill within the poem as it rhetorically insists that the soul recognizes no external reign but its own.

This poem is dated 1862, one of the great years of Dickinson's writing life, and it takes civil war as its metaphor for inner spiritual division. Here, as everywhere, Dickinson grants power not to the society at large ("The Soul selects her own Society— / Then—shuts the Door"), but to the self having it out with itself. In February 1863 Dickinson enclosed this poem along with a letter to Thomas Wentworth Higginson after she read in the *Springfield Republican* that he had departed to lead his regiment in South Carolina. It seems to be a terse and complex act to send a poem toward the front that insists on the complete integrity of the self, that suggests an emperor resides within, that notes how the soul has paramount or supreme authority over itself. The country of this poem is a spiritual aristocracy.

The last line of the poem is isolated and majestic. It is also directive.

The Soul should stand in Awe—

"Awe" is the splendid word here. The sound of the word itself circles and fills the mouth with the feeling of awe. Awe is an emotion mingled with reverence, dread, and wonder inspired by something majestic or sublime. It is a radical move for Dickinson to take a word usually associated with the sublime, with the stunned feeling one has before an immense natural force or landscape (think of those luminist paintings of Niagara Falls or the Grand Canyon) and to apply it to an interior realm. The act of standing in awe: this is an experience of existential grandeur of outer paralysis and inner spiritual transport. (*Transport* was one of Dickinson's favorite words, and her manuscripts show, as Harold Bloom points out, that she used it almost interchangeably with "rapture" and "terror.") Awe bears traces of the holy. It is both rapturous and terrifying because it puts one in the space of the transcendental, the world beyond, and thus also in the presence of death. "No man saw awe," Dickinson wrote in a late poem. It is fateful. The soul that stands in awe experiences a sense of root or radical wonder, an astonishment before the depths and heights that seem to be opening up within. It stands wordless on the edge of time, the brink of death. It has its own brilliant sparks of the divine.

The feeling in the poems I have been discussing by Whitman, Stevens, and Dickinson may seem a little dated, a little elusive and alien to us now because our lives are so speeded up we have almost lost the capacity for stillness, for solitary contemplation. We have almost lost the word *soul* as a figure of deep spiritual essence outside the terms of organized religion. When we lose a word we also lose its meaning. The depletion in our vocabulary leads to a dire loss of soulfulness. And it signals our increasing inability to employ language to go beyond the daylight mind. We still need to read for "soul-culture."

In a splendid essay about stillness in fiction published in *DoubleTake* magazine, Charles Baxter writes:

So, finally, we arrive at wonder, which, for me, is at the bottom level, the ground floor, of stillness. Wonder is at the opposite pole of worldliness, just as stillness is at the opposite pole from worldly action. Wonder puts aside the known and accepted, along with sophistication, and instead serves up an intelligent naiveté.

That's beautifully put. It does take an intelligent naiveté, a knowing innocence, to give oneself up to the experience of literature. Wonder puts us in a state of astonishment before the strangeness of the world. It teaches us to dwell in uncertainties before great mysteries. With characteristic riddling acuity, Emily Dickinson wrote:

Wonder—is not precisely Knowing
And not precisely Knowing not—
A beautiful but bleak condition
He has not lived who has not felt—

The lyric poem rejuvenates the capacity for wonder within us. We cannot live what we cannot feel. It instills the culture of the soul back into us. And it speaks to what Stevens calls "the substance in us that prevails." It gives us the precise words for a clear midnight. For a reader leaning late and reading there. For a soul in transit, a soul in awe.

12

"To the Reader at Parting"

Read these poems to yourself in the middle of the night. No one knows precisely how or why it was that sometime in the seventh or sixth century B.C. the ancient Greeks began to write down poems, thus inaugurating what we now think of as lyric poetry. Writing instigates a different kind of possibility in poetry. It invites a different and more sustained kind of attention to language. As the classicist Denys Page explains:

> The use of writing enabled the poet to make the word, rather than the phrase, the unit of composition; it assisted him to express ideas and describe events outside the traditional range; it gave him time to prepare his work in advance of publication, to premeditate more easily and at greater leisure what he should write, and to alter what he had written.

Writing allows for revision, for rethinking, for rereading. Writing transforms the dynamic relationship of a live performer and an audience to a relationship that is more removed, more private and, ultimately, more intimate. Writing widens the space for individual feeling, for paradoxical emotion, for self-interrogation, for second thoughts, for confession. There is always an element of secrecy and the occult in the relationship between the writer and the reader. The poem is an apparatus that requires a collusion. It is a message in a bottle.

I have said that metaphor is at the very heart of lyric poetry. It entails an interaction, a transference. Anne Carson explains that "The English word 'symbol' is the Greek word *symbolon* which means, in the ancient world, one half of a knucklebone carried as a token of identity to someone who has the other half. Together the two halves compose one meaning. A metaphor is a species of symbol. So is a lover."

Here is Aristophanes in Plato's *Symposium:*

Each one of us is but the *symbolon* of a human being—sliced in half like a flatfish, two instead of one—and each pursues a neverending search for the *symbolon* of himself.

Each of us is riven in half. Each of us is a seeker in quest of fulfillment. Desire for the other means we are not entirely sufficient, not entirely whole unto ourselves. We need each other. There is no poetry without desire. A lover in quest of the beloved is one half of a knucklebone. A writer and a reader are each one half of a knucklebone separated from each other and brought together through an intermediary, an imaginative act of attention, a poem.

I have been arguing throughout this book for a participatory poetics, which I take to be a radically democratic and egalitarian idea as well as a loving and agonistic literary one. "The reader will always have his or her part to do," Whitman declared, "just as much as I have mine." We make meaning together, we wrestle with what we read and talk back to it, we become more fully ourselves in the process. We activate the poem inside us by engaging it as deeply as possible, by bringing our lives to it, our associational memories, our past histories, our vocabularies, by letting its verbal music infiltrate our bodies, its ideas seep into our minds, by discovering its pattern emerging, by entering the echo chamber which is the history of poetry, and most of all, by listening and paying attention. *Attentiveness is the natural prayer of the soul.*

I have tried to listen hard and pay close attention to individual poems, but also to take poets at their word about the nature of poetry itself, which can set even the nothingness strutting. I have taken seriously what, in an autobiographical letter to Paul Verlaine, Stéphane Mallarmé calls "the Orphic explanation of the Earth which is the sole task of the poet." I have also found in the writing of this book that I need always to stay with the body of the poem in speaking about poetry. I physically and spiritually can't bear to be away from the poems themselves, which I have let guide me in how they should be read. There seems to me great intellectual dignity in staying in the affective realm, in being pulled into the deepest experience of reading poetry. It is an initiation, what Coleridge calls "a willing suspension of disbelief." I would have us remember that Philip Sidney said he wanted from poetry "a heart-ravishing knowledge." The brilliant Nicaraguan poet Rubén Darío confessed:

> I thought that the poetic element was not the word in its phonic value, nor color, nor line, nor a complex of sensations, but a deep pulsing of spirit: what the soul supplies, if it does supply anything; or what it says, if it says anything, when aroused to response by contact with the world.

I like the idea of a poetry that seeks to alleviate human suffering and to preserve the human image. I like the simple dignity of Auden's idea that poems are personlike. When I read a poem deeply I enter a world of threshold and engagement that still bears traces of the holy. I am taking a path that still vibrates with a sacred air. The encounter is unprecedented—the text has certain incitements, the reader certain experiences. Our desire and need for each other is mutual. It is when as a reader I encounter and interiorize the poem, when I ingest it, dreaming it and letting it dream its way into me, that I can feel the Orphic enchantment, the delirium and lucidity, the swoon of poetry.

"Poetry may be this or it may be that," Robert Desnos wrote, "but it shouldn't necessarily be this or that... except delirious and lucid." I note that Desnos, the most openhearted of French surrealist poets, asserted this in "Reflections on Poetry," which he made in January 1944, just one month before he was arrested by the Gestapo and tortured for his participation in the French Resistance. The stakes were high. But then the stakes are always high in lyric poetry because the poet is writing against disappearance, staving off death, going beyond death. In his essay "The Poet and These Times," Hugo von Hofmannsthal said about the poet: "It is as if his eyes had no lids." And that's how I am made to see when I read the deepest poems.

Everything depends on the reciprocity, the strange interrelationship between the poet, the poem, and the reader.

Here is a story about the essential gift of poetry. In an essay called "Childhood and Poetry" Pablo Neruda links an odd event from his boyhood to the affirmative impulses of lyric poetry itself. Neruda grew up in Temuco, a far outpost in southern Chile. He remembers playing in the backyard behind the family house and suddenly discovering a hole in a fence board:

> I looked through the hole and saw a landscape like that behind our house, uncared for, and wild. I moved back a few steps, because I sensed vaguely that something was about to happen. All of a sudden a hand appeared—a tiny hand of a boy about my own age. By the time I came close again, the hand was gone, and in its place there was a marvelous white sheep.
>
> The sheep's wool was faded. Its wheels had escaped. All of this only made it more authentic. I had never seen such a wonderful sheep. I looked back through the hole but the boy had disappeared. I went into the house and brought out a treasure of my own: a pinecone, opened, full of odor and resin, which I adored. I set it down in the same spot and went off with the sheep.
>
> I never saw either the hand or the boy again. . . .

Neruda carefully goes on to link this episode to the origin of his poetry, to the humane impulses of the lyric. "To feel the love of people whom we love is a fire that feeds our life," he says.

> But to feel the affection that comes from those whom we do not know, from those unknown to us, who are watching over our sleep and solitude, over our dangers and our weaknesses—that is something still greater and more beautiful because it widens out the boundaries of our being, and unites all living things.
>
> That exchange brought home to me for the first time a precious idea: that all of humanity is somehow together . . .

It won't surprise you then that I attempted to give some-
thing resiny, earthlike, and fragrant in exchange for human
brotherhood. . . .

That is the great lesson I learned in my childhood, in the
backyard of a lonely house. Maybe it was nothing but a game
two boys played who didn't know each other and wanted to pass
to the other some good things of life. Yet maybe this small and
mysterious exchange of gifts remained inside me also, deep and
indestructible, giving my poetry light.

Neruda dreams of the imagination as an intimate medium of exchange,
an affectionate gift passed between strangers in the solitary backyard of a
now-lost house. He implies that the task of the imagination may well be
to protect the vulnerability of others, "watching over our sleep and soli-
tude." Robert Bly, who quotes this story in the introduction to his trans-
lation of Neruda's *Selected Poems,* suggests that Neruda consciously rejected
the linkage between poetry and sickness. Instead, Neruda affirmed the es-
sential healthiness of poetry, asking us to treat the lyric as a gift freely
given and taken. To the outside world, in the practical realm of utility and
commerce, this gift may seem worthless—a miniature sheep, a fragrant
pinecone—but for the interior world, in the hidden realm of our affective
lives, it is curiously deep and renewing. Something that might seem frag-
ile—a group of words arranged on a page—turns out to be indestructible.

And now here is Whitman's late poem "To the Reader at Parting."
Whitman's desire for his poems—his advocacy on their behalf—was
tremendous. He knew that his leaves needed to be planted in fertile soil,
that his poems required unusually sympathetic readers if they were going
to have a future at all. Thus he boldly sought those readers. He would
touch them directly if he could. He was unembarrassed about affection-
ately addressing unknown readers as "comrades," about (metaphorically)
embracing each stranger—each one of us—as a familiar, about imagin-
ing the exchange between poet and reader as a form of creative love. I
am touched by the playful tenderness, the poignance, with which he says
good-bye to the reader. I leave this short poem as a last enactment—a
fleeting final gesture—of the affectionate, vehement, and soulful partic-
ipation that is the heart of lyric exchange.

To the Reader at Parting

Now, dearest comrade, lift me to your face,
We must separate awhile—Here! take from my lips this kiss;
Whoever you are, I give it especially to you;
So long!—And I hope we shall meet again.

The Glossary
and the Pleasure of the Text

The devices work the magic in poetry, and a glossary gives names to those devices. It unpacks them. I believe its purpose is to deepen the reader's initiation into the mysteries of poetry. Here is a repertoire of poetic secrets, a vocabulary, some of it ancient, that proposes a greater pleasure in the text, a deeper level of enchantment.

accent The vocal stress or emphasis placed on certain syllables in a line of verse. From the Latin *accentus,* meaning "song added to speech."
SEE ALSO *meter.*

alexandrine A twelve-syllable poetic line used primarily in French poetry until the advent of vers libre (free verse) in the nineteenth century. The six strong accents of the English alexandrine give it a particularly drawn-out feeling. Alexander Pope evokes what he criticizes in the second line of this couplet:

> A *needless Alexandrine* ends the Song,
> That like a wounded Snake, drags its slow length along.

SEE ALSO *free verse, hexameter, vers libre.*

allegory From the Greek *allēgoria* from *állos* ("other") and *-ēgorein* ("to speak"), that is, "speaking otherwise." An allegory is a story operating on two levels simultaneously. The narrative acts as an extended metaphor with a primary or surface meaning that continually discloses a secondary or representational meaning. The two levels provide a parallel experience: one entertains; the other instructs.

The characters in an allegory are often personifications, that is, abstract ideas incarnated as persons. There is a one-to-one correspondence between what they are and what they mean. Think of the characters Death, Fellowship, Good-Deeds, and Beauty in the medieval morality play *Everyman,* or the characters Christian, Faithful, and Mr. Worldly Wiseman in Bunyan's *Pilgrim's Progress.* Think of the surrealist André Breton's characterization of reverie:

> Reverie...a magical young girl, unpredictable, tender, enigmatic, provocative, from whom I never seek an explanation of her escapades.

The characters of the great allegories go beyond merely representing their designated vices and virtues; they become them.

We are in the range of allegory whenever a writer explicitly indicates the relationship of the image to the precept. As Northrop Frye puts it, "A writer is being allegorical whenever it is clear that he is saying 'by this I *also* (allos) mean that'" (*Anatomy of Criticism*). The hero of an allegory is also a cipher or a designated figure for the reader since it's understood that the action takes place in the mental landscape of the audience. Allegory is a distinctive form. It treats the story as a means to an end and channels our affective responses.

Allegory is a method of critical analysis as well as a literary model. Critics interpret works allegorically when they perceive coherent analogies behind living characters and abstract ideas (hence psychoanalytic criticism). In *The Well Wrought Urn* (1947), Cleanth Brooks allegorizes the poems he explicates insofar as they become "parables about the nature of poetry." Frye suggests in *Anatomy of Criticism* (1957) that all criticism is covert allegorizing. For a theoretical study and application, see Angus Fletcher's instructive *Allegory: The Theory of a Symbolic Mode* (1964).

SEE ALSO *metaphor, personification.*

alliteration   The audible repetition of consonant sounds at the beginning of words or within words. Listen to the *m*s and *d*s in Gerard Manley Hopkins's striding, strutting, ecstatic evocation of a kestrel in "The Windhover":

> I caught this morning morning's minion, king-
> dom of daylight's dauphin, dapple-dawn-drawn Falcon...

Alliteration is part of the sound stratum of poetry. It predates rhyme and takes us back to the oldest English and Celtic poetries. Alliterative meter was the principal organizing device in Anglo-Saxon poetry and continued to resound through the fourteenth century, as in the opening line of *Piers Plowman:*

> In a somer season, whan soft was the sonne...

The repetitive *s*s here tie four words together and urge their interaction upon us. Alliteration can reinforce preexisting meanings (summer season) and establish effective new ones (soft sun). A device of phonic echoes, of linked initial sounds, alliteration reverberates through most of the poetries of the world.

SEE ALSO *assonance, consonance.*

allusion   A passing or indirect reference to something implied but not stated. The writer refers to something the reader will presumably recognize—a historical or fictional character, a specific place, a particular event or series of events, a religious or mythological story, a literary or artistic work. Allusion is a compact between writer and reader, a means of summoning a shared world or tradition, a way of packing a work with meaning. Thus Dante alludes throughout *The Inferno* to Virgil's *Aeneid*, especially the sixth book that charts Aeneas's descent into the underworld, even as Virgil alludes to Homer's *Odyssey*, especially Book 11 where Odysseus pours libations to the unnumbered dead and gathers the shades at the edges of the known world.

Throughout the history of poetry the song of Orpheus (according to Greek mythology, Orpheus's song was so enchanting that all the animals and even the rocks and trees gathered to listen) has been alluded to as the ideal of poetic creation. "When there is poetry, / it is Orpheus singing," Rilke writes in *The Sonnets to Orpheus.*

analogy   A resemblance between two different things, frequently expressed as a simile. William Blake talks back to ecclesiastical authority with this satirical analogy from "Proverbs of Hell": "As the caterpillar chooses the fairest leaves to lay her eggs on, so the priest lays his curse on the fairest joys."

The reader participates in the making of an analogy by probing the resemblance, teasing out its implications, testing the proposition against lived experience. It is the reader who decides to what extent Paul Valéry's analogy is true when he says that poetry is to prose as dancing is to walking.

SEE ALSO *simile.*

anapest   A metrical foot consisting of three syllables, two unaccented followed by one accented, as in the words "ĭn ă wár." It was originally a Greek martial rhythm and often creates a galloping sense of action, as in these lines from the beginning of Lord Byron's "The Destruction of Sennacherib":

> Thĕ Ăssýr|iăn cắme dŏwn|lǐke ă wólf|ŏn thĕ fóld,
> Ănd hǐs có|hŏrts wĕre gleám|ĭng ĭn púr|plĕ ănd góld;
> Ănd thĕ sheén|ŏf thĕir spéars|wăs lǐke stárs|ŏn thĕ séa,
> Whĕn thĕ blúe|wăve rŏlls níght|lў ŏn deép|Gălĭlée.

SEE ALSO *foot, meter.*

anaphora   From the Greek, meaning "a carrying up or back." The repetition of the same word or words at the beginning of a series of phrases, lines, or sentences. The words accumulate mysterious power and resonance through repetition. Anaphora serves as an organizing poetic strategy for long lists or catalogs, and the piling up of particulars is itself a joyous poetic activity, a way of naming and claiming the world. For example: open almost any page of *Leaves of Grass* and you immediately encounter Whitman's anaphoric method, his ecstatic iterations. Here is an excerpt from "A Broadway Pageant":

> For I too raising my voice join the ranks of this pageant,
> I am the chanter, I chant aloud over the pageant,
> I chant the world on my Western sea,
> I chant copious the islands beyond, thick as stars in the sky,
> I chant the new empire grander than any before, as in a vision it comes to me,
> I chant America the mistress, I chant a greater supremacy,
> I chant projected a thousand blooming cities...

antiphon   A song, hymn, or poem in which two voices or choruses respond to one another in alternate verses or stanzas, as is common in verses written for religious services. Antiphonal poetry has the quality of call and response, of liturgy. In George Herbert's "Antiphon (1)," for example, the chorus begins:

> Let all the world in ev'ry corner sing,
> *My God and King.*

The leader or minister calls back:

> The heav'ns are not too high,
> His praise may thither fly:
> The earth is not too low,
> His praises there may grow.

And the congregation responds again:

> Let all the world in ev'ry corner sing,
> *My God and King.*

antistrophe   The middle section of a classical ode, following the strophe and preceding the epode. The structure of the classical ode is based on the odes of Pindar, who adapted this characteristic pattern from the songs chanted by the chorus in Greek drama. The chorus moved to the left during the strophe and to the right during the antistrophe.
SEE ALSO *epode, ode, strophe.*

The Glossary / 267

apostrophe   From the Greek, meaning "to turn away." The poet turns away from the audience to address a God or gods, the muse, a dead or absent person, a natural object, a thing, an imaginary quality or concept. Anything can be addressed. Chaucer playfully addresses his purse, "Complaint to His Purse"; Anne Bradstreet addresses a book she has written, "The Author to Her Book"; John Donne speaks to the sun, "The Sun Rising." Think of the fervor with which Blake cries out, "O Rose thou art sick!" ("The Sick Rose") or the ritualistic formality with which Shelley calls out, "O wild West Wind, thou breath of Autumn's being" ("Ode to the West Wind") or the unhinged grief with which Tennyson proclaims, "Ring out, wild bells" (*In Memoriam*). Apostrophe seems to take us back to the realm of magic ritual, to the archaic idea that the dead can be contacted and propitiated, the absent recalled, the inanimate and nonhuman formally humanized and invoked, called upon for help.

SEE ALSO *invocation*. Jonathan Culler offers a helpful essay on apostrophe in *The Pursuit of Signs* (1981).

ars poetica   "Poetry is the subject of the poem," Wallace Stevens declared, and the ars poetica is a poem that takes the art of poetry—its own means of expression—as its explicit subject. It proposes an aesthetic. Self-referential, uniquely conscious of itself as both a performance and a treatise, the great ars poetica embodies what it is about.

Horace's *Ars Poetica* is our first known poem on poetics and the fountainhead of the tradition. Horace introduces himself as both poet and critic in what was probably his final work (between 19–18 B.C.), a combination of the formal epistle and the technical treatise. It is, among other things, an eloquent defense of freedom at a time when freedom was imperiled in Rome. Horace speaks of art and ingenuity, of the poet's need to fuse unity and variety, of the poet's dual function to delight and to be useful (*dulce* and *utile*). He wittily defends the usefulness of artistic constraints and the necessity for artistic freedom, and he writes on behalf of both the writer and the reader, the poet and the audience: "it is not enough for poems to be beautifully crafted, let them be attractive and drive as they wish the audience's emotion,...if you want me to weep, you must first yourself feel grief, only then will I share the pain of your disasters." Horace also speaks of the sacred role of poets in earlier times.

An anthology of the ars poetica would include Pope's "Essay on Criticism," the exemplary treatise of the Enlightenment; passages from Wordsworth's *Prelude*, which traces the growth of the poet's mind, and from Whitman's "Song of Myself" ("I speak the pass-word primeval...I give the sign of democracy"); Emily Dickinson's poem number 1129 ("Tell all the Truth but tell it slant—"); Wallace Stevens's "Of Modern Poetry"; and Hugh MacDiarmid's "The Kind of Poetry I Want" ("A poetry that takes its polish from a conflict / Between discipline at its most strenuous / And feeling at its highest"). It would include Marianne Moore's adversarial ars poetica "Poetry" ("I, too, dislike it") and Czesław Miłosz's conditional "*Ars Poetica?*" ("The purpose of poetry is to remind us / how difficult it is to remain just one person").

The ars poetica, like the defense of poetry, becomes a necessary form when poetry is called into question and freedom is endangered.

To gauge the ongoing vitality of the form, see Christopher Buckley and Christopher Merrill's useful anthology, *What Will Suffice: Contemporary American Poets on the Art of Poetry* (1995).

assonance   The audible repetition of vowel sounds within words encountered near each other. From the Latin *assonare*, meaning "to answer with the same sound." Listen to the interplay of vowels in these lines from Alfred Tennyson's "The Lotos-Eaters":

And round about the keel with faces pale,
Dark faces pale against that rosy flame,
The mild-eyed melancholy Lotos-eaters came.

Assonance is an aural device, a form of internal vowel play that pleases the ear with little help from the eye, and sets up an echo chamber within a poem. SEE ALSO *alliteration, consonance.*

aubade   A dawn song expressing the regret of parting lovers at daybreak. ("Ah God! Ah God! that dawn should come so soon!") The earliest European examples date from the end of the twelfth century (the Provençal and German equivalents are *alba* and *Tagelied*), but the dawn song is found in nearly all early poetries. Chaucer gives a splendid example in Book 3 of *Troilus and Criseyde*. It begins when Criseyde hears the cock crow and then continues on for fourteen additional stanzas:

"Myn hertes lif, my trist, and my plesaunce,
That I was born, allas, what me is wo,
That day of us moot make disseveraunce!
For tyme it is to ryse and hennes go,
Or ellis I am lost for evere mo!
O nyght, allas! Why nyltow over us hove,
As long as whan Almena lay by Jove?"

The aubade recalls the joy, the communion, of two lovers joined together in original darkness. It remembers the ecstasy of union. But it also describes a parting at dawn, and with that parting comes the dawning of individual consciousness; the separated, or daylit, mind bears the grief or burden of longing for what has been lost.

Augustan   One of the high moments in poetry: the period of Horace, Virgil, and Ovid under the Roman emperor Augustus (27 B.C.–A.D. 14). The term also describes the literature of Britain during the first half of the eighteenth century, including works by Alexander Pope and Jonathan Swift, which reflect such neoclassical virtues as balance and decorum, but also display a scathing wit and scapular wisdom, a rage against encroaching unreason.

ballad   The traditional British ballad is a narrative song (a poem that tells a story) preserved and transmitted orally. It unfolds in four-line stanzas (quatrains) and customarily alternates four- and three-stress lines, the second and fourth lines rhyming. Here is the opening of "Earl Brand":

Rise up, rise up, my seven brave sons,
    And dress in your armour so bright;
Earl Douglas will hae Lady Margaret awa
    Before that it be light.

The ballad, a form of great antiquity, has been built up and scoured down by oral transmission to a work of eloquent simplicity. It often opens abruptly, focuses on a single, crucial episode, and moves decisively—dramatically—toward a tragic conclusion. Dialogue carries the story and the narration is rapid, elliptical, and impersonal, though it retains vestiges of ritual participation. The individual singer stands in for the community, serving as the deputy of a public voice. The high degree of repetition is mnemonic, the refrain a way of creating and discharging intense emotion.

The written literary ballad echoes the spirit, and often the language and form, of the traditional folk ballad. It emerged at the end of the eighteenth century as a viable and widely practiced subgenre. The ballad especially appealed to the romantic poets—one thinks of Wordsworth and Coleridge's *Lyrical Ballads* (1798)—because it is an authentically popular form practiced by ordinary people, because of its "medieval" subject matter and "Gothic" taste, because it calls up deep feeling in the audience. The literary ballad perhaps always resonates with nostalgia for a lost oral poetry. It has had powerful appeal for poets from the nineteenth century onward, and one could make a splendid anthology of twentieth-century literary ballads in English, including works by W. B. Yeats, Thomas Hardy, A. E. Housman, Robert Graves, Edwin Muir, and W. H. Auden. See James Kinsley, ed., *The Oxford Book of Ballads* (1969).

SEE ALSO *incremental repetition, refrain.*

bard   The word *bard* originally referred to the ancient Celtic order of minstrel-poets who composed verses celebrating the laws and heroic achievement of the people, of chiefs and warriors. The bards carried necessary information and underwent rigorous technical training in order to tell the tale of the tribe.

The professional literary caste of the bardic order in Ireland lasted from the thirteenth to the seventeenth century. It was serious business to become a bard and serve the prince, and the training period could extend for as long as twelve years. In *The Book of Irish Verse,* John Montague says that one way of describing the training is as "seven winters in a dark room," and quotes an early eighteenth-century memoir:

> Concerning the poetical Seminary or School . . . it was open only to such as were descended of Poets and reputed within their Tribes . . . The Structure was a snug, low Hut, and beds in it at convenient Distances, each within a small Apartment. . . . No windows to let in the Day, nor any Light at all us'd but that of Candles, and these brought in at a proper Season only . . . The reason of laying the Study aforesaid in the Dark was doubtless to avoid the Distraction which Light and the variety of Objects represented thereby commonly occasions.

The poets who came through this strict regimen created poems that sometimes let deep emotion break through their virtuoso technique. Some of their most poignant poems that have come down to us are ones that mourn the passing of their order.

In his essay "The Poet" Emerson wrote, "The ancient British bards had for the title of their order, 'Those who are free throughout the world.' They are free, and they make free." In "Merlin 1" he wrote:

> Great is the art,
> Great be the manners, of the bard.

Since the eighteenth century the term *bard* has often been used as a synonym for *poet.* One legacy of the bardic order is to preserve language, another to embody imaginative freedom. The creative use of technical poetic skill and wide literary and cultural knowledge makes for our greater freedom. Hence Emerson's dual claim that the poets are "liberating gods" and "America is a poem in our eyes." The poet offers us a thought schooled by intuition, an emotion deeper than thought, a soulfulness deeper than emotion. Such archaic ways of knowing go all the way down to the roots of being. "But trust my instinct," Robert Frost says jauntily in "To a Thinker," arguing reasonably against excessive reason, "I'm a bard."

beat   The main rhythmic pulse in metrical verse. Sometimes called *ictus,* sometimes called *stress.* The oldest meaning of the word *beat* is "to strike repeatedly," and thus it carries the memory—the vestiges—of repeated physical action.

blank verse   Unrhymed (hence "blank") iambic pentameter. The five-beat, ten-syllable line—a line of great flexibility and scope—was established in English between the fourteenth and sixteenth centuries, its emergence coterminous with the rise of Renaissance humanism. Blank verse was first employed by Surrey in his translation of Virgil and later became the standard form of the Elizabethan theater. Milton used blank verse in *Paradise Lost* to liberate poetry from the "bondage" of rhyme, thus establishing and confirming it as the pattern with the greatest equilibrium in English.

It has been estimated that three-fourths of all English poetry is written in blank verse. This suggests that blank verse is the modal pattern in English, the pattern closest to natural speech, and therefore, as Allen Grossman puts it, "the form speech takes when it depicts the speech of persons in social situations." Blank verse has most often been used—from Shakespeare's plays to Frost's dramatic monologues—to evoke the spoken word, to create a speaker in a dramatic situation.

SEE ALSO *dramatic monologue, iambic pentameter, meter.*

blues   A secular form of African American folk song. Sung solo, the blues often express a deep stoic grief and despair, a dark mood of lamentation, but also a wry and ribald humor, a homemade political philosophy, a proverbial wisdom. In the black community the blues have traditionally been contrasted to spirituals, a sacred form, and thus likened to devil's music. "You can bury my body down by the highway side / So my old devil spirit can catch a Greyhound bus and ride." (The *Oxford English Dictionary* informs us that the color blue was associated with the devil as early as the sixteenth century, hence the expression "blue devils.")

The blues were first arranged, scored, and published early in the twentieth century, but have their roots in much earlier work songs, field hollers, group seculars, sacred harmonies. The blues have retained a flexible style and structure, but classically tend toward a twelve-bar, three-line stanza with an *aab* rhyme pattern: a couplet stretched to three lines. The first line establishes the premise and scene, the second repeats (sometimes with slight variations) and hammers it in. This allows the singer to emphasize and modify the first line while improvising the next one. The third line punches, develops, or turns the premise. Each line is an intact entity, each stanza a complete unit.

> I'm goin' to the river, take my rockin' chair,
> Goin' to the river, take my rockin' chair,
> If the blues overcome me, I'll rock on away from here.

The trick to singing the blues is to flatten the third, fifth, and seventh notes of the major scale, thus creating the "blue notes." Here is a durable vocal art, a living tradition, a foundational form, a shaping influence on American music, such as jazz and rock and roll. The blues have also been a major influence on African American written poetry as well, from Langston Hughes and Sterling Brown to Michael Harper and Yusef Komunyakaa.

SEE A. X. Nicholas, ed., *Woke Up This Mornin': Poetry of the Blues* (1973).

caesura   From the Latin *caedere,* meaning "to cut"; a pause in the poetic line. For example, there is a caesura after the semicolon in the first line and after the comma in the second line of this sonnet by William Wordsworth:

The world is too much with us; late and soon,
Getting and spending, we lay waste our powers:

SEE ALSO *meter, sonnet.*

canzone   A term referring to various kinds of medieval Provençal and Italian lyric poems, usually on the subject of love. Petrarch established (and perfected) the canzone as a form comprising five- or six-line stanzas and a concluding envoi (half stanza). Dante composed a maddeningly difficult form of the canzone—an unrhymed poem which uses the same five end words in each of the five twelve-line stanzas, intricately varying the pattern. There is also a five-line envoi (a *tornata*) that uses all five of the words. This form of the canzone has been keenly employed in our time by W. H. Auden, L. E. Sissman, James Merrill, Anthony Hecht, and Marilyn Hacker. John Hollander explains two versions of the traditional canzone by enacting them in his ingenious handbook, *Rhyme's Reason* (1981).

carmen   The Latin word *carmen*, which means "song" or "lyric" (Catullus's *Carmina*), has especially attracted English poets because of its closeness to the word *charm*. In older Latin texts it also means a magic formula, an incantation to make things happen. Horace uses it in the *Odes* to suggest divine inspiration, the song of the poet as a vehicle of the muse.

SEE ALSO *charm, incantation.*

chant   The term *chant* (from the Latin *cantare*, "to sing") has multiple meanings. It may refer to any song or melody; it may denote the particular melody to which a psalm or canticle is sung; it may refer to the actual psalm or canticle itself; it may suggest any religious recitative with a refrain. The Gregorian plainsong (*cantus firmus*) is the most influential form of religious chant. Here is a strange chant, a pantheistic fragment, usually dated to the sixth century and attributed to Amergin, the chief bard of the Milesians and first poet of Ireland:

> *The Mystery*
>
> I am the breeze breathed at sea,
> I am the wave woven of ocean,
> I am the soft sound of spume,
> I am the bull of the seven battles,
> I am the cormorant upon the cliff,
> I am the spear of the sun striking,
> I am the rose of the fairest rose.
> I am the wild bull of war,
> I am the salmon stroking the flood,
> I am the mere upon the moor,
> I am the rune of rare lore,
> I am the tooth of the long lance,
> I am He who fired the head.
>
> Who emblazons the mountain-meeting?
> Who heralds the moon's marches?
> Who leads the sun to its lair?
> I am the Word, I am the Eye,

"The Mystery" is a rune, a Celtic incantation, with a deep archaic power.

Chanting also refers to a way of reciting a poem, giving it liturgical emphasis that is something between speaking and singing. W. B. Yeats, for example, had elaborate ideas about how his poems should be chanted aloud. Chanting is a stylized mode of recitation that subordinates the musical element to the verbal one. It gives verse an oracular quality. I'm put in mind of the many oral epic poets who composed and chanted their poems aloud: of the Greek rhapsodists and the Celtic bards, of the Old English scops and the Scandinavian skalds, of the French trouvères and jongleurs. There are still *guslari* (minstrels) in Bosnia, Serbia, and Macedonia, who compose and recite—who *chant*—heroic poems aloud to the accompaniment of a one-stringed fiddle. This is called a "gusla," hence their name. SEE ALSO *bard, rhapsodist, scop, skald, troubadour.*

charm   A spell or incantation (a word, a phrase, a verse, a song) spoken or sung to invoke and control supernatural powers. Charms, which are universally known, are among the earliest forms of recorded written literature. They carry the resonance of magic rites in archaic cultures. The Old English charms (against wens, against the theft of cattle, for taking a swarm of bees, for a land remedy) stand as some of the first written works in our language. (See Burton Raffel and Alexandra H. Olson's anthology, *Poems and Prose from the Old English,* 1998.)

Charms can be used for positive or negative ends, to ward off the spirit of evil or invoke it, to destroy an enemy or attract a beloved, to enchant objects, to ensure good luck with supranormal power. Here is the beginning of a charmed and charming poem by Thomas Campion:

> Thrice tosse these Oaken ashes in the ayre,
> Thrice sit thou mute in this inchanted chayre;
> Then thrice three times tye up this true loves knot,
> And murmur soft; shee will, or shee will not.

SEE ALSO *incantation, spell.*

conceit   An elaborate figure of speech comparing two extremely dissimilar things. A good conceit discovers or creates a surprisingly apt parallel between two otherwise unlikely things or feelings. It is an arresting mental action that draws attention to the issue—the artificial process—of figuration. "Shall I compare thee to a summer's day?" Shakespeare famously asks in a sonnet that goes on to develop and extend the analogy. The process invites the reader to participate in the making of the analogy, in playfully developing and extending it.

There are two main types of conceit. The *Petrarchan conceit,* borrowed from Italian poetry, compares the beloved to a rose, the sun, a statue, a summer day. Shakespeare employs these conceits even as he satirizes them in the first eight lines of Sonnet 130:

> My mistress' eyes are nothing like the sun;
> Coral is far more red than her lips' red;
> If snow be white, why then her breasts are dun;
> If hairs be wires, black wires grow on her head.
> I have seen roses damasked, red and white,
> But no such roses see I in her cheeks;
> And in some perfumes is there more delight
> Than in the breath that from my mistress reeks.

In his essay "The Metaphysical Poets," T. S. Eliot defined the *metaphysical conceit* as the elaboration "of a figure of speech to the furthest stage to which ingenuity can carry it."

Since its ingenious employment by the metaphysical poets in the seventeenth century, the conceit has often been associated with poems about erotic love or the most intense spiritual or sensual experiences. In this famous example from John Donne's "A Valediction: Forbidding Mourning" he compares two lovers to the two complementary legs of a compass:

> If they be two, they are two so
> As stiffe twin compasses are two,
> Thy soule the fixt foot, makes no show
> To move, but doth, if the'other doe.
>
> And though it in the center sit,
> Yet when the other far doth rom,
> It leanes and hearkens after it,
> And growes erect, as that comes home.
>
> Such wilt thou be to mee, who must
> Like th'other foot, obliquely runne;
> Thy firmness draws my circle just,
> And makes me end, where I begunne.

SEE K. K. Ruthven, *The Conceit* (1969).

SEE ALSO *analogy, metaphor, simile*.

concrete poetry   A poem of visual display, a form of spatial prosody. Each concrete poem presents itself in a different physical shape—a lyric typed out to look like a typewriter, the word *SHRINK* printed in gradually smaller letters, and so forth. All written poems have a spatial dimension, but the concrete poem foregrounds the visual configuration (how a poem looks) and pushes the pictorial boundaries of poetry.

Concrete poetry became an international movement in the 1950s, but the desire to bring together literary and visual impulses into a shaped poem is very ancient. Guillaume Apollinaire coined the term *Calligrammes*, but he was in truth delivering a lively avant-garde manifestation of what was once known as *technopaignia* or *pattern poetry*, verses arranged in distinctive shapes on the page.

The most powerful concrete poems still follow the example of Renaissance figure poems where the words are arranged to form a perceivable design on the page that mimics what the poem is about.

For examples, see Emmett Williams, ed., *An Anthology of Concrete Poetry* (1967).

SEE ALSO *pattern poetry*.

consonance   The audible repetition of consonant sounds in words encountered near each other whose vowel sounds are different, as when W. H. Auden presses the consonants from "rider to reader" and from "farer to fearer" and from "hearer to horror" in the last stanza of "'O where are you going?'" It is a way of enforcing relation. Listen to the letters *f* and *l* woven through these lines from Wilfred Owen's "Insensibility":

> The front line withers.
> But they are troops who fade, not flowers
> For poets' tearful fooling:
> Men, gaps for filling:
> Losses, who might have fought
> Longer; but no one bothers.

SEE ALSO *alliteration, assonance.*

couplet   Two successive lines of poetry, usually rhymed (*aa*). The couplet has been an el-
emental stanzaic unit—a couple, a pairing—as long as there has been written rhyming po-
etry in English. It can stand as an epigrammatic poem on its own, a weapon for aphoristic
wit, as in Pope's "Epigram Engraved on the Collar of a Dog which I gave to his Royal
Highness":

> I am his Highness' Dog at Kew;
> Pray tell me Sir, whose Dog are you?

The couplet also serves as an organizing pattern in long poems (Shakespeare's "Venus and
Adonis," Marlowe's "Hero and Leander"), or part of a larger stanzaic unit. It stands as the
pithy conclusion to the ottava rima stanza (*abababcc*), the rhyme royal stanza (*ababbcc*), and
the Shakespearean sonnet (*ababcdcdefefgg*).

The rhyming iambic pentameter or five-stress couplet—later known as the *heroic cou-
plet*—was introduced into English by Chaucer in "The Prologue to the Legend of Good
Women" (1386), in imitation of French meter, and employed for most of *The Canterbury
Tales.* It was taken up and used with great flexibility by the Tudor and Jacobean poets and
dramatists (especially Shakespeare, Marlowe, Chapman, and Donne) and then permanently
stamped, and perhaps perfected, as a neoclassical form by Dryden, Pope, and Johnson.

So, too, the octosyllabic or four-stress couplet, probably based on a common Latin
meter, became a staple of English medieval verse (such as *The Lay of Havelok the Dane*),
then was virtually reinvented by Samuel Butler in his mock-heroic satire *Hudibras,* whose
couplets became known as "Hudibrastics," and raised to a higher power by Milton
("L'Allegro" and "Il Penseroso"), Marvell ("To His Coy Mistress"), and Coleridge
("Christabel").

We call a couplet *closed* when the sense and syntax come to a conclusion or strong pause
at the end of the second line, thus giving a feeling of self-containment and enclosure, as in
the first lines of "To His Coy Mistress":

> Had we but world enough, and time,
> This coyness, Lady, were no crime.

We call a couplet *open* when the sense carries forward past the second line into the next
line or lines, as in the beginning of Keats's *Endymion:*

> A thing of beauty is a joy for ever:
> Its loveliness increases; it will never
> Pass into nothingness, but still will keep
> A bower quiet for us, and a sleep
> Full of sweet dreams...

All two-line stanzas in English carry the echo—the vestigial memory—of closed or open
couplets, which have a rudimentary genius.

SEE ALSO *enjambment, end-stopped line, meter, stanza.*

dactyl   A metrical foot consisting of three syllables, one accented syllable followed by two
unaccented ones, as in the word *timelessly.* It means "finger" in Greek. Tennyson's "The
Charge of the Light Brigade" employs it, as do many nursery rhymes, the earliest poems we

learn by heart. Here is the dactyllic opening of Thomas Hardy's haunting poem "The Voice": "Wŏmăn mŭch| mĭssed, hŏw yoŭ| cáll tŏ mĕ,| cáll tŏ mĕ."

SEE ALSO *foot, meter.*

dada   Surrealism grew directly out of the flamboyantly self-conscious and joyously ni-hilistic movement known as *dada,* which began in the Café Voltaire in Zurich in 1916 when a group of young writers and artists (including Tristan Tzara, Hans Arp, Richard Huelsen-beck, Hugo Ball, Emmy Hennings, and Sophie Taeuber) decided to shower their contempt on the decadent values of bourgeois society and the moral insanity of World War I. The word *dada,* chosen at random from a dictionary, is baby talk for "hobbyhorse" in French. The dadaists' favorite word was *nothing,* and there is a wildly subversive, childlike energy in their manifestos, sound poems, simultaneous lyrics, noise music, and provocative public spectacles aimed at destroying rational logic, social restraints and conventions, traditional art and literature. Dada was subsumed by surrealism and formally laid to rest in a mock funeral service in Paris in 1923, though there have been reported sightings wherever nonsense thrives and the spirit of anarchy reigns. For a comprehensive collection of dada poetry, see Willard Bohn, ed., *The Dada Market* (1993).

SEE ALSO *surrealism.*

dramatic monologue   "Everything written is as good as it is dramatic," Robert Frost declared in the preface to his play, *A Way Out.* Poems become dramatic when we get the sensation of someone speaking, when we hear a poem, in Frost's words, "as sung or spoken by a person in a scene—in character, in a setting."

A *monologue* presents a single person speaking alone—with or without an audience, as in a prayer or a lament. ("But a monologue is not the same as talking to oneself," Paul Goodman writes in *Speaking and Language:* "it is more like a daydream.") A dramatic mono-logue presents an imaginary or historical character speaking to an imaginary listener or au-dience, as in Robert Browning's superb poems "Andrea del Sarto," "My Last Duchess," and "The Bishop Orders His Tomb at St. Praxed's Church." Browning termed such poems "dramatic lyrics."

The speaker of the dramatic monologue is decidedly *not* the author, and thus the poem requires a high degree of impersonation. It enacts the displacement of the poetic self into another being. The utterance tends to take place in a specific situation at a critical moment, the speaker addresses and sometimes interacts with one or more auditors (this is revealed by what the speaker *says*), and the speaker reveals his or her character to the reader. The dra-matic monologue imagines a speaker into being over the course of a poem, and we collab-orate in the construction of that self. It engages us in the very act of poetic making and reminds us that the poem is always an artificial utterance.

Many poets have explored and exploited the possibilities of the dramatic monologue over the past 150 years—from Tennyson ("Ulysses") and Browning ("Fra Lippo Lippi") to Yeats (Crazy Jane poems), Eliot ("The Love Song of J. Alfred Prufrock," which gives us what Hugh Kenner calls "a name plus a voice"), and Frost (*North of Boston*). (In E. A. Robinson's favorite poem of his own, "Rembrandt to Rembrandt," one phase of the painter's soul converses with another through the surface of his mirror.) One could make a wonderful anthology of American dramatic monologues from midcentury onward, begin-ning with the Middle Generation, Robert Lowell, John Berryman, Elizabeth Bishop, and Randall Jarrell (who so poignantly crossed genders in some of his best poems), highlighting the work of Richard Howard (whom Harold Bloom calls the Robert Browning of our time) and marching forward to include recent pieces by Frank Bidart (from *In the Western*

Night), Louise Glück (from *The Wild Iris*), Norman Dubie (from *In the Dead of the Night*), David St. John (from *Study for the World's Body*), Nicholas Christopher (from *Desperate Characters*), and S. X. Rosenstock (from *United Artists*).

For a helpful exploration of the form, see Robert Langbaum, *The Poetry of Experience* (1957).

duende   (Spanish: "lord of the house"). A figure out of Andalusian folklore, the duende was traditionally considered a trickster figure, something like the Yiddish dybbuk, but the great Spanish poet Federico García Lorca uses it as a metaphor for the demonic inspiration of art. García Lorca calls the duende "a mysterious power which everyone senses and no philosopher explains." Every art, every country, is capable of duende. It is a power (not a work), a struggle (not a thought). It seems to come up from the earth, it means a radical change in forms, it signals a closeness to death. "All that has black sounds has duende." It means something like inspiration in the presence of death.

Duende exists for readers and audiences as well as for writers and performers. "The magical property of a poem is to remain possessed by duende that can baptize in dark water all who look at it, for with duende it is easier to love and understand, and one can be *sure* of being loved and understood."

Read García Lorca's speech, "Play and Theory of the Duende," in his splendid book of prose pieces, *Deep Song and Other Prose* (1980).

elegy   A poem of mortal loss and consolation. The word *elegy* derives from the Greek *elegeia* or "lament." It was among the first forms of the ancients, though in Greek literature it refers to a specific verse form as well as the emotions conveyed by it. Any poem using the particular meter of the *elegiac couplet* was termed an elegy. Here are two lines from Longfellow's "Elegiac Verse":

> So the Hexameter, rising and singing, with cadence sonorous,
>   Falls; and in refluent rhythms back the Pentameter flows.

There were elegies, chanted aloud and traditionally accompanied by the flute, on love (amatory complaints) and war (exhortatory martial epigrams) as well as death. But, as Peter Sacks puts it, "behind this array of topics there may have lain an earlier, more exclusive association of the flute song's elegiacs with the expression of grief."

Since the sixteenth century the elegy has designated a poem mourning the death of an individual (as in W. B. Yeats's "In Memory of Major Robert Gregory") or a solemn meditation on the passing of human life (as in Gray's "Elegy Written in a Country Churchyard"). The elegy does what Freud calls "the work of mourning." It ritualizes grief into language and thereby makes it more bearable. The great elegy touches the unfathomable and originates in the unspeakable, in unacceptable loss. It allows us to experience mortality. It turns loss into remembrance and delivers an inheritance. It opens a space for retrospection and drives a wordless anguish, wordless torment, toward the consolations of verbal articulation, verbal ceremony.

The sense of overwhelming loss that powers the poetry of lamentation seems to exist in all languages and poetries. One finds it in ancient Egyptian, in Hebrew, in Chinese, in Sanskrit, in Zulu. . . . A profound grief is formalized as mourning, as in Lamentations 2:10:

> The elders of the daughter of Zion sit upon the ground, *and* keep silence: they have cast up dust upon their heads; they have girded themselves with sackcloth: the virgins of Jerusalem hang down their heads to the ground.

The poetry of intense grief and mourning, such as the Lamentations of Jeremiah or David's lament for Saul and Jonathan, has its roots in religious feeling and ritual. The process, the action of mourning, of doing something to pass on the dead, thus clearing a space between the dead and the living, has residual force in the ceremonial structure of the elegy.

Classical antiquity had several literary vehicles for the formal expression of deep sorrow. The *dirge* was a song of lament deriving from the Greek *epicedium,* a mourning song sung over the body of the dead. The *threnody* was a Greek "wailing song" sung in memory of the dead. Originally a choral ode, it evolved into the *monody* (Greek: "alone song"); that is, an ode sung by a single actor in a Greek tragedy or a poem mourning someone's death. Milton described "Lycidas" (1638), a poem inspired by the death of Edward King, as a monody; Matthew Arnold also termed "Thyrsis" (1866), a lament for Arthur Clough, a monody.

These two poems, along with Spenser's "Astrophel" (1586), a lament for Sidney, and Shelley's "Adonais" (1821), a lament for Keats, belong to a subspecies of the tradition called the *pastoral elegy*. The laments of three Sicilian poets writing in Greek—Theocritus (third century B.C.), Moschus (second century B.C.), and Bion (second century B.C.)—inspired the pastoral conventions of the later English elegy. These highly elaborated conventions (the invocation to the muse, the representation of nature in the lament, the procession of mourners, and so forth) become the formal channel of mourning. "The elegy follows the ancient rites in the basic passage from grief or darkness to consolation and renewal" (Sacks). The pastoral conventions are dropped in a poem such as Tennyson's *In Memoriam* (1850), his heartbroken book on the death of Arthur Hallam, but the ritualistic feeling remains. There is a sense of lineage and inheritance in Swinburne's hieratic Baudelairean elegy for Baudelaire, "Ave atque Vale" ("a mourning musical of many mourners"), and Hardy's Swinburnean elegy for Swinburne, "A Singer Asleep." The dignified formality opens out into elegies commemorating a public figure, such as Whitman's beautiful poem for Abraham Lincoln, "When Lilacs Last in the Dooryard Bloom'd," and W. H. Auden's "In Memory of Sigmund Freud" ("to us he is no more a person / now but a whole climate of opinion"). It empowers the elegy for a friend who is also a public figure, such as García Lorca's "Lament for Ignacio Sánchez Mejías," one of the great elegies of our century.

Coleridge was thinking of the elegy as a departicularized form, a poem with a certain meditative mood or style, a certain kind of sadness, when he described it as "the form of poetry natural to the reflective mind." The definition of the elegy as a serious reflection on a serious subject applies to the so-called "Anglo-Saxon elegies," some of the earliest poems in the English tradition, such as "The Wanderer" and "The Seafarer," which are poems of great personal deprivation shading off into mediations on mutability and petitions for divine guidance and consolation. This sense of the elegy carries forward through Thomas Nashe's "A Litany in Time of Plague," Samuel Johnson's "Vanity of Human Wishes," Gray's "Elegy Written in a Country Churchyard," Edward Young's *Night Thoughts,* and Rilke's masterpiece, *Duino Elegies*.

The sense of a highly self-conscious dramatic performance, of a necessary and sometimes reluctant reentry into language, continues to power the elegy in our century, but the traditional consolations of the elegy—the very comforts of the genre—have often been called into question. For example, Thomas Hardy radicalizes the genre by speaking from a position of uncompromising isolation in his superbly formal but emotionally unsheltered elegies for his dead wife, *Poems of 1912–13.* Think, too, of Wilfred Owen's ironically titled "Dulce et Decorum Est" and his poems "Greater Love" and "Anthem for Doomed Youth"

("What passing-bells for those who die as cattle?"), of Isaac Rosenberg's "Dead Man's Dump" and Edward Thomas's "Tears" ("It seems I have no tears left"), of Edith Sitwell's "Dirge for the New Sunrise" and Dylan Thomas's "A Refusal to Mourn the Death, by Fire, of a Child in London."

The American elegist in particular seems to suffer from a "polar privacy" (Dickinson), a dark sense of isolation, of displacement from the traditional settings of grief and the consolations of community ("I, with no rights in this matter, / Neither father nor lover," Theodore Roethke writes in "Elegy for Jane"). This is accompanied by a more naked experience of grief. A saving and even ceremonial formality still helps Allen Tate's "Ode to the Confederate Dead" (whose true subject is solipsism), James Merrill's *The Changing Light at Sandover,* Amy Clampitt's "A Procession at Candlemas," Charles Wright's *The Southern Cross,* Richard Howard's deeply aggrieved elegies for dead friends. How many dead paternities stalk like ghosts through the precincts of American poetry. One thinks of Dickinson ("Burgler! Banker—Father!") and Plath ("Daddy, daddy, you bastard, I'm through"), of Robert Lowell (*Life Studies*), Philip Levine (*1933*), and Sharon Olds (*The Father*), of mournful poems to the father by James Agee, John Berryman, Stanley Kunitz, Stanley Plumly, William Matthews, Garrett Hongo, Li-Young Lee, Alberto Rios. I have been moved over the years by William Meredith's memorial poems to his beloved friends in poetry, by Robert Hayden's "Elegies for Paradise Valley," by L. E. Sissman's self-elegies (*Night Music*), by Ellen Bryant Voigt's poems on her dead parents, by Arthur Smith's elegies for his wife (*Elegy on Independence Day*), by Judith Hall's meditations on her relationship to her dead mother (*Anatomy, Errata*), by Susan Wood's elegies for dead female precursors, by Mark Doty's heartbreaking elegies for a lover dying, a lover who has died, of AIDS (*My Alexandria*), by Larry Levis's posthumous collection, *Elegy*. These poems continue to ask, as W. H. Auden writes in his elegy "At the Grave of Henry James," "What living occasion can / Be just to the absent?"

SEE Peter Sacks, *The English Elegy* (1985).

enjambment   The carryover of one line of poetry to the next without a grammatical break. A run-on or *enjambed* line is the alternative to an end-stopped line. Enjambment creates a dialectic of hesitation and flow. The lineation bids the reader to pause at the end of each line even as the syntax pulls the reader forward. This creates a sensation of hovering expectation. Milton called enjambment "sense variously drawn out from one verse to another."

Here is a stanza from William Carlos Williams's poem "To a Poor Old Woman" in which he breaks down a sentence three times in order to present an old woman sensuously eating plums. The first and fourth lines are end-stopped, the middle lines are enjambed:

> They taste good to her.
> They taste good
> to her. They taste
> good to her

Each line break emphasizes something different (that the plums taste good to *her,* that they taste *good,* that they *taste*) and the lineation is a signpost to the meaning.

SEE ALSO *end-stopped line.*

end-stopped line   A poetic line in which a natural grammatical pause (such as the end of a phrase, clause, or sentence) coincides with the end of a line. An end-stopped line is the alternative to an *enjambed,* or run-on, line. The end-stopped line gives the sensation of a whole syntactical unit, and this gives it an additional rhetorical weight and authority. The effect is increased when each end-stopped line concludes with an emphatic punctuation mark, as in the first eight lines of "The Starlit Night," an ecstatic sonnet by Gerard Manley Hopkins:

> Look at the stars! look, look up at the skies!
> O look at all the fire-folk sitting in the air!
> The bright boroughs, the circle-citadels there!
> Down in dim woods the diamond delves! the elves'-eyes!
> The grey lawns cold where gold, where quickgold lies!
> Wind-beat whitebeam! airey abeles set on a flare!
> Flake-doves sent floating forth at a farmyard scare!
> Ah well! it is all a purchase, all is a prize.

SEE ALSO *enjambment.*

envoi   (or **envoy**) A "send-off." The half stanza that concludes certain French forms, such as the sestina. The troubadours liked to call their envoys *tornados* (returns). The envoy is a final return to the subject, a conclusive summing up, a clever sending off.

SEE ALSO *sestina, troubadour.*

epic   A long narrative poem, exalted in style, heroic in theme. The earliest epics all focus on the legendary adventures of a hero against the backdrop of a historical event: think of the Trojan War and Odysseus's action-packed journey home in the Homeric epics *The Iliad* and *The Odyssey;* the territorial battles of a warrior culture in the Anglo-Saxon epic *Beowulf;* or the preservation of city (and a civilization) in the Babylonian *Gilgamesh.* These epics have their roots in early oral traditions and carry key cultural information. They seem to be the written versions of texts long sung and retold, composed and recomposed by many epic singers over time, all telling the tale of a tribe.

The singer of tales brings together a powerful memory and strong improvisatory technique, using formulaic phrases, lines, and half-lines; propulsive rhythms; stock descriptions; recurrent scenes and incidents, to build a tale with encyclopedic range and cyclical action. "The cyclical form of the Classical epic is based on the natural cycle," Northrop Frye explains. "The cycle has two main rhythms: the life and death of the individual, and the slower social rhythm which, in the course of years . . . brings cities and empires to their rise and fall."

Ezra Pound called the epic "a poem including history." Literary epics—one thinks of Virgil's *Aeneid,* Dante's *Divine Comedy,* Spenser's *Faerie Queene,* Milton's *Paradise Lost*— adopted many of the conventions and strategies of the traditional epic, even though they are written poems meant to be read rather than oral ones intended to be told and sung. Byron satirizes the epic apparatus he employs in this stanza from *Don Juan.*

> My poem's epic, and is meant to be
> Divided in twelve books; each book containing,
> With Love, and War, a heavy gale at sea,
> A list of ships, and captains, and kings reigning,
> New characters; the episodes are three:
> A panoramic view of Hell's in training,
> After the style of Virgil and of Homer,
> So that my name of Epic's no misnomer.

All in all, as Jorge Luis Borges writes, "the epic is one of the necessities of the human mind." SEE Paul Zumthor's chapter on epic in *Oral Poetry: An Introduction* (1990).

epiphany   From a Greek word meaning "to appear." An epiphany is a sudden spiritual manifestation, a luminous or visionary moment. Epiphany means the manifestation of a god or spirit in the body, and the Christian epiphany is literally the manifestation of Christ to the Magi. James Joyce secularized the term so that it came to mean a sudden manifestation of spiritual meaning, an unexpected revelation of truth in the commonplace, a psychological and literary mode of perception. The epiphany is akin to what Wordsworth called "spots of time" and Virginia Woolf termed "moments of being." It is a moment out of time.

   See Ashton Nichols, *The Poetics of Epiphany* (1987); M. H. Abrams's valuable chapters (7 and 8) on the subject in *Natural Supernaturalism* (1971); and Robert Langbaum's insightful chapter on the epiphanic mode in Wordsworth and modern literature in *The Word from Below* (1987).

epode   From the Greek, meaning "after-song," and referring to the third section of a classical ode, which differs in meter from the first two sections, the strophe and the antistrophe. SEE ALSO *antistrophe, ode, strophe.*

feminine rhyme   (also called double rhyme) A rhyme of two syllables, the first stressed and the second unstressed (*trances/glances*). The double rhyme has often been employed for light verse, as when Lewis Carroll playfully riffs through the opening stanza of "Rules and Regulations":

> A short direction
> To avoid dejection
> By variations
> In occupations,
> And prolongation
> Of relaxation,
> And combinations
> Of recreations
> And disputation
> On the state of the nation
> In adaptation
> To your station,
> By invitations
> To friends and relations,
> By evitation
> Of amputation,
> By permutation
> In conversation,
> And deep reflection
> You'll avoid dejection.

SEE ALSO *masculine rhyme, rhyme.*

foot   A group of syllables forming a metrical unit. The poetic foot is a measurable, conventional unit of rhythm. It is a useful abstraction since there are no poetic feet in nature, few pure examples of any of the standard feet in English verse. "For that matter," as Hugh Kenner puts it, "you will never encounter a round face, though the term is helpful. . . . The term 'iambic foot' has the same sort of status as the term 'round face.'"

The most common feet in English versification are:

iamb: a pair of syllables with the stress on the second one, as in the word *adóre.*
trochee: a pair of syllables with the stress on the first one, as in the word *árdor.*
dactyl: a triad consisting of one stressed syllable followed by two unstressed ones, as in the word *rádiant.*
anapest: a triad consisting of two unstressed syllables followed by one stressed one, as in the words *in a bláze.*
spondee: two equally stressed syllables, as in the word *ámén.* It is the most common syllabic variation or substitution.

Here is Coleridge's witty illustrative poem "Metrical Feet":

Trŏchĕe trĭps frŏm lōng tŏ shōrt;
From long to long in solemn sort
Slōw Spōndēe stālks; strŏng fōot! yet ill able
Ēvĕr tŏ cŏme ŭp wĭth Dāctўl trĭsŷllăblĕ.
Īambĭcs mārch frŏm shŏrt tŏ lōng;—
Wĭth ă lēap ănd ă bōund thĕ swĭft Ānăpæsts thrŏng;

SEE ALSO *anapest, dactyl, iamb, meter, spondee, trochee.* See also the discussion of *accentual-syllabic meter* under the entry for *meter.*

free verse   A poetry of organic rhythms, of deliberate irregularity, improvisatory delight. Free verse is a form of nonmetrical writing that takes pleasure in a various and emergent verbal music. "As regarding rhythm," Ezra Pound wrote in the first imagist manifesto (1912): "to compose in the sequence of the musical phrase, not in sequence of a metronome." Free verse is often inspired by the cadence—the natural rhythm, the inner tune—of spoken language. It possesses visual form and uses the graphic line to differentiate itself from prose. "The words are more *poised* than in prose," Louis MacNeice writes in *Modern Poetry* (1938); "they are not only, like the words in typical prose, contributory to the total effect, but are to be attended to, in passing, for their own sake." The dream of free verse is for every poem to have an originary verbal music that hits the depths of feeling. Jorge Luis Borges wrote that "Beyond its rhythm, the typographical appearance of free verse informs the reader that what lies in store for him is not information or reasoning but emotion."

The term *free verse* is a literal translation of *vers libre,* which was employed by French symbolist poets seeking freedom from the stranglehold of the alexandrine. It has antecedents in medieval alliterative verse, in highly rhythmic prose (think of those three-page sentences in *Moby Dick*), in Milton's liberated blank-verse lines and verse paragraphs. But the greatest antecedent is the King James Version of the Psalms and the Song of Songs, based in part on the original Hebrew cadences. The rhetorical parallelism and expansive repetitions of the Hebrew Bible inspired Christopher Smart, who created his own canticles of praise in *Jubilate Agno,* and William Blake, whose long-lined visionary poems have the power of prophetic utterance, and Walt Whitman, the progenitor of American free verse, who hungered for a line large enough to express the totality of life:

My voice goes after what my eyes cannot reach,
With the twirl of my tongue I encompass worlds and volumes of worlds.

Speech is the twin of my vision, it is unequal to measure itself...

Whitman's breathtaking Adamic rhythms are a direct influence on Gerard Manley Hopkins's long-lined metrical experiments and William Carlos Williams's exercises in a new measure, the three-ply line and the variable foot, on C. K. Williams's rangy inclusive cadences and Charles Wright's rich development of a two-part dropped line, a Whitmanesque line with an additional rhythmic (and spatial) thrust. They are a repressed influence on T. S. Eliot, who in some ways initiated modern poetry with the iambic-based free-verse rhythms of "The Love Song of J. Alfred Prufrock," and Ezra Pound, whose poem "The Return" W. B. Yeats praised as the "most beautiful poem that has been written in the free form, one of the few in which I find real organic rhythms." Some of Whitman's international progeny are Apollinaire (France), Pessoa (Portugal), García Lorca (Spain), Vallejo (Peru), Neruda (Chile), Paz (Mexico), Borges (Argentina), Martí (Cuba), Darío (Nicaragua). So, too, Whitman stands behind the improvisatory free-verse rhythms of such poets as Langston Hughes, Philip Levine, and Michael Harper, all of whom are influenced by jazz, and such New York poets as Frank O'Hara, John Ashbery, and James Schuyler, all of whom are influenced by abstract expressionism. Indeed, jazz and action painting are two good American analogues for free verse in our century.

Blank verse offers the normative line in English poetry, the line closest to actual speech (as both Wordsworth and Frost perceived), and so one tends to feel that lines extending well beyond five beats and ten syllables are also going beyond the parameters of oral utterance, or over them, beyond speech itself. The long lines widen the space for reverie, they have a dreamlike associativeness, as in the early poems of W. B. Yeats. Or else they radiate an oracular feeling of prophetic utterance, as in Smart and Blake and D. H. Lawrence (England), or in Muriel Rukeyser, Allen Ginsberg, Gerald Stern, Allen Grossman, Dave Smith, T. R. Hummer (United States). In contrast, when we read lines much shorter than iambic pentameter we tend to feel something has been taken away, something is attenuated or missing. This sense of a poem being less than, or going under, speech works well for poems of clipped loss, such as those in Robert Creeley's *For Love,* or Louise Glück's *The Triumph of Achilles,* or for poems that seek what the imagists called "direct treatment of the thing." We feel that the clutter, the dead wood, has been cleared away to create a clean, well-lit space for the imagist poems of T. E. Hulme, F. S. Flint, and H.D., or the objectivist works of George Oppen, Charles Reznikoff, and Louis Zukofsky. Poems with drastically reduced lines aspire to be lyrics of absolute concentration, rhythmic economy.

As the length of the lines varies in free-verse poems, so the reader participates in the working—the making—of poetic thought. The free-verse poem fits no mold, it has no accepted prosody, no preexistent pattern. The reader supplies the verbal speeds, intonations, emphasis. Or as Frank O'Hara says: "You just go on your nerve." For a useful introduction to the subject, see Charles Hartman, *Free Verse* (1980).

SEE ALSO *blank verse, prose poem, vers libre.*

haiku   A Japanese poetic form usually consisting, in English versions, of three unrhymed lines of 5, 7, and 5 syllables. The haiku emerged as a separate form in the sixteenth century, partially because of Bashō's brilliant work (see *Narrow Road to the Far North*), but has its roots in the Middle Ages, or earlier, in the classic poetic form of the *tanka* (five lines of 5, 7, 5, 7, 7 syllables) and the *renga* (linked verse: a collaborative poem composed in alternation according to elaborate rules by a small group of poets).

The haiku, invariably written in the present tense, almost always refers to a season or time of day, focuses on a natural image, captures the essence of a moment. Its goal: a sudden insight or spiritual illumination.

See Hiroaki Sato and Burton Watson's anthology of Japanese poetry: *From the Country of Eight Islands* (1981) and Robert Hass's *The Essential Haiku* (1994).

hendecasyllabics   Lines of eleven syllables. The term *hendecasyllable* usually refers to the precise metrical line used by the ancient Greek poets and perfected by the Latin poet Catullus. It later became the standard verse line of Italian poetry, exploited brilliantly by Dante in the *Divine Comedy* and Petrarch in his sonnets. It is relatively rare in English, though Tennyson experimented with lines "All composed in a meter of Catullus."

hexameter   A six-foot metrical line, as when Shelley writes: "In profuse strains of unpremeditated art" ("To a Skylark"). The classical dactylic hexameter reached its pinnacle in Greek and Latin epic poetry (*The Iliad, The Odyssey, The Aeneid*). It was successfully adapted to German and Russian poetry (by Goethe and Pushkin, among others), but, despite many experiments, has never found a natural place in French, English, or American poetry. The dactylic hexameter is to classical verse what iambic pentameter is to English-language poetry. Coleridge wittily discriminates between them in "Ovidian Elegiac Metre":

> In the hexameter rises the fountain's silvery column;
> In the pentameter aye falling in melody back.

SEE ALSO *alexandrine, dactyl, foot, iambic pentameter, meter.*

hymn   From the Greek *hymnos:* "song in praise of a god or hero." In the ancient classical world, odes were composed in honor of gods and heroes and chanted or sung at religious festivals and other ceremonial occasions. One thinks of the ringing hexameters of the so-called Homeric hymns, of the splendid hymns of Callimachus (ca. 305–ca. 240 B.C.), and the Orphic hymns chanted by initiates in the Orphic mysteries.

Songs in praise of gods and heroes became in Christianity "Praise of God in song." Hymns as scriptural texts came into the church in the fourth century (early examples include the nativity song "*Gloria in excelsis*" and the three Gospel canticles) and have been part of devotional services ever since. Latin hymns were written throughout the Middle Ages.

Isaac Watts (1674–1748) wrote modern hymns that have a radiant clarity and take great joy in God's created world. He envisioned the promised land, as on a clear day, and dramatically adapted the psalms to his own purposes, as when he "translated the scene of this psalm—67—to Great Britain":

> Sing to the Lord, ye distant lands,
>> Sing loud with solemn voice;
> While British tongues exalt his praise,
>> And British hearts rejoice.

Charles Wesley (1707–1788) had an uncanny gift for transposing and adapting Holy Scriptures into memorable metrical verses. His hymns have a potent rhetoric and powerful devotional urgency. He brought a stately grace to the hymnal stanza, as in this passage from Psalm 17:

> Hear him, ye deaf; his praise, ye dumb,
>> Your loosened tongues employ;
> Ye blind, behold your Saviour come,
>> And leap, ye lame, for joy!

The hymnal stanza, also known as common measure, is traditionally the same as the ballad stanza, but has the stricter rhythms and rhymes (*abab*) found in the hymnal.

In her essay "Lyric Possession" Susan Stewart explains that "The phrase *common meter* joins with the terms from music, *common measure* and *common time*, to signify the two pulses to a measure, $\frac{4}{4}$ rhythm, under which the entire musical system is coordinated and out of which variations proceed. The coordination of song and the coordination of social life under a common temporal framework emphasize integration and solidarity."

The hymn has accrued terrific liturgical importance as a source of communal devotion. Think, then, of what it meant for Emily Dickinson to fracture the common measure, thus invoking the hymn tradition and responding to—remaking—its communal nature with a radical individuality of her own. We hear the distinctiveness—the imposition—of her voice against a traditional nineteenth-century social and religious backdrop.

See Donald Davie, ed., *New Oxford Book of Christian Verse* (1982) and J. R. Watson's excellent study, *The English Hymn: A Critical and Historical Study* (1937).

SEE ALSO *ballad, ode, psalm.*

iamb   A two-syllable metrical foot, the first unstressed, the second stressed, as in the word unknown. It is an upbeat followed by a downbeat, an alternation. The ancients considered iambic rhythm close to ordinary speech. It is by far the most typical foot in English because it fits the natural stress pattern of English words and phrases. It functions, as Pope puts it, "To wake |the soul |by tender strokes |of art."

SEE ALSO *foot, iambic pentameter, meter.*

iambic pentameter   A five-stress decasyllabic line. This line, established by Chaucer for English poetry, was energized when English attained a condition of relative stability. It is the traditional formal line closest to the form of our speech and thus has been especially favored by dramatists ever since Marlowe, whose *Tamburlaine* (1587) inaugurated the greatest Elizabethan drama, and Shakespeare, who used it with astonishing virtuosity and freedom. Milton showed just how supple and dignified the pentameter line could be in *Paradise Lost:*

> Of Man's First Disobedience, and the Fruit
> Of that Forbidden Tree, whose mortal taste
> Brought Death into the World, and all our woe,
> With loss of *Eden,* till one greater Man
> Restore us, and regain the blissful Seat,
> Sing, Heav'nly Muse...

The iambic pentameter line was strategically employed by most of the great nineteenth-century English poets, from Wordsworth and Coleridge to Browning and Tennyson. It puts us near the spoken word, and it was given a distinctly American stamp in the ringing cadences of Robert Frost, Wallace Stevens, and Hart Crane, all of whom extended the romantic lineage in the twentieth century.

SEE ALSO *blank verse, meter.*

image   (collective noun: imagery) The image, which Wyndham Lewis calls the "primary pigment" of poetry, relates to the visual content of language. It speaks to our capacity to embody meaning through words. It is a sudden salience in language.

The *Princeton Encyclopedia of Poetry and Poetics* defines the image as "the reproduction in the mind of a sensation produced by a physical perception." It has a sensuous element, a mental component. Cleanth Brooks and Robert Penn Warren define it as "the representation in poetry of any sense experience" (*Understanding Poetry*), whereas another handbook characterizes it as "a mental picture evoked by the use of metaphors, similes, and other figures of speech." These are then the two bases for its definition: the image is sensuous ("I give you my sprig of lilac"); the image is figurative ("The star my departing comrade holds and detains me"). The literal literally bubbles over into the symbolic:

> All over bouquets of roses,
> O death, I cover you over with roses and early lilies,
> > (Walt Whitman, "When Lilacs Last
> > in the Dooryard Bloom'd")

Ezra Pound offered a one-sentence definition: "An 'Image' is that which presents an intellectual and emotional complex in an instant of time." He added: "It is the presentation of such a 'complex' instantaneously which gives the sense of sudden liberation; that sense of freedom from time limits and space limits; that sense of sudden growth, which we experience in the presence of the greatest works of art." The image here becomes a moment of revelation, of apprehended truth. This is the prevailing aesthetic device of the imagist movement. (See William Pratt's anthology *The Imagist Poem*, 1963.)

The poetic image is always delivered to us through words. It passes through the circuits of language. Poetry engages our capacity to make mental pictures ("This is the forest primeval"), but it also taps a place in our minds that has little to do with direct physical perceptions ("Heard melodies are sweet," Keats writes, "but those unheard / Are sweeter"). There are poetic images that give us the remembrance of things past ("When to the sessions of sweet silent thought / I summon up remembrance of things past"), that summon up the memory of the dead. Think of the opening of Yeats's "In Memory of Major Robert Gregory":

> Now that we're almost settled in our house
> I'll name the friends that cannot sup with us
> Beside a fire of turf in th'ancient tower,
> And having talked to some late hour
> Climb up the narrow winding stair to bed:
> Discoverers of forgotten truth
> Or mere companions of my youth,
> All, all are in my thoughts to-night being dead.

There are images that have the character of daydreams, of dreaming consciousness, and images that have the hallucinatory power of fevers and dreams.

The literary theorist Christopher Collins contends that since every literary image is also a mental image and since every mental image is a representation of an absent entity, then the imagination itself is a poiesis, a making-up, an act of free play for both the writer and the reader. The reader participates in the creation of imagery through what Coleridge calls "the willing suspension of disbelief."

For a consideration of the image as a picture made out of words, see C. D. Lewis, *The Poetic Image* (1947). For a consideration of the image as a deeper entity, as a flare-up of being into imagination, see Gaston Bachelard, *The Poetics of Space* (1964). For a key reading of the romantic and modern reinvention of the image, see Frank Kermode, *The Romantic Image* (1957). For an advanced theoretical discussion, see Christopher Collins, *Reading the Written Image* (1991).

SEE ALSO *simile, metaphor, trope,* and *symbol.*

incantation   A formulaic use of words to create magical effects. *Incantation* derives from a Latin word meaning "to consecrate with charms or spells," and, indeed, charms, spells, and conjurations all employ the apparatus of sympathetic magic. Incantations, whether spoken or chanted, are characteristic of archaic poetries everywhere, which have always employed the power of repetition to create enchantment.

Here is a statement from "The Song of Amergin," which was, as Robert Graves has pointed out, "said to have been chanted by the chief bard of the Milesian invaders as he set his foot on the soil of Ireland, in the year of the world 2736 (1268 B.C.)":

> Invoke, People of the Sea, invoke the poet, that he may compose
>   a spell for you.
> For I, the Druid, who set out letters in Ogham,
> I, who part combatants,
> I will approach the rath of the Sidhe to seek a cunning poet
>   that together we may concoct incantations.
> I am a wind of the sea.

SEE ALSO *charm, spell.*

incremental repetition   This term, coined by Francis Gummere in *The Popular Ballad* (1907), describes one of the key rhetorical devices of the ballad form. It refers to the repetition of succeeding stanzas with small substitutions or changes. The refrain, modified each time it is repeated, takes on additive power even as the changes in crucial words build, develop, and heighten the suspenseful dramatic situation, as in the traditional Scottish ballad "Lord Randal":

> "What d'ye leave to your mother, Lord Randal, my son?
> What d'ye leave to your mother, my handsome young man?"
> "Four and twenty milk kye: mother, mak my bed soon,
> For I'm sick at the heart, and I fain wad lie down."
>
> "What d'ye leave to your sister, Lord Randal, my son?
> What d'ye leave to your sister, my handsome young man?"
> "My gold and my silver; mother, mak my bed soon,
> For I'm sick at the heart, and I fain wad lie down."

SEE ALSO *ballad, refrain.*

invocation   An apostrophe asking a god or goddess, asking the muse, for inspiration, especially at the beginning of an epic, as when John Milton calls out at the beginning of *Paradise Lost,* "Sing, Heavenly Muse." The invocation recognizes that there is an uncontrollable aspect of art, that poetry is never entirely at the dispensation of the poet's conscious will or intellect. It is helpless without an element of mania, an element of the demonic or the irrational or the unconscious. Thus the invocation becomes a plea for an uncontrollable power, a prayer for creativity.

SEE ALSO *apostrophe, epic, muse.*

kenning   A standard phrase or metaphoric compound used in Old Norse and Old English poetry as a poetic circumlocution for a more familiar noun. In *Beowulf,* for example, the human body is called *banhus* ("bone house"), a ship is termed *saewudu* ("sea wood"), and the sea is named *swanrud* ("swan road") and *windgeard* ("home of the winds").

lyric   The short poem has been practiced for at least 4,500 years. It is one of the necessary forms of human representation, human speech, one of the ways we invent and know ourselves. It is as ancient as recorded literature. It precedes prose in all languages, all civilizations, and it will last as long as human beings take pleasure in playing with words, in combining the sounds of words in unexpected and illuminating ways, in using words to convey deep feeling and perhaps something even deeper than feeling. The lyric poem immerses us in the original waters of consciousness, in the awareness, the aboriginal nature, of being itself.

The Greeks defined the lyric as a poem to be chanted or sung to the accompaniment of a lyre (*lyra*). It has its origins, like Egyptian and Hebrew poetry, in religious feeling and practice. The first songs were most likely written to accompany occasions of celebration and mourning. Prayer, praise, and lamentation are three of the oldest impulses in poetry. Aristotle distinguished three generic categories of poetry: epic, drama, and lyric. This evolved into the traditional division of literature into three generic types or classes, dependent upon who is supposedly speaking in a literary work:

> *epic* or *narrative:* in which the narrator speaks in the first person, then lets the
>   characters speak for themselves;
> *drama:* in which the characters do all the talking;
> *lyric:* uttered through the first person.

The lyric, which offers us a supposed speaker, a person to whom we often assign the name of the author, shades off into the dramatic utterance ("All poetry is of the nature of soliloquy," John Stuart Mill writes), but has always been counterposed to the epic. Whereas the speaker of the epic stands in as the deputy of a public voice, a singer of tales narrating the larger tale of the tribe, the lyric offers us a solitary singer or speaker singing or speaking on his or her own behalf. Ever since Sappho, the lyric poem has created a space for personal feeling. It has introduced a subjectivity and explored our capacity for human inwardness. The intimacy of lyric—and the lyric poem is the most intimate and personally volatile form of literary discourse—stands against the grandeur of epic. It asserts the value and primacy of the solitary voice, the individual feeling.

The definition of the lyric as a poem to be sung held until the Renaissance, when poets routinely began to write their poems for readers rather than composing them for musical presentation. The words and the music separated. Thereafter, lyric poetry has retained an associational relationship to music. It exists in the region between speech and song. Its cadences and sound patterns, its tonal variations and rhythms, all show its melodic origins (hence Yeats's title *Words for Music, Perhaps*). But writing offers a different space for poetry. It inscribes it in print and thus allows it to be read, lingered over, reread. Writing fixes the evanescence of sound and holds it against death. It also gives the poem a fixed visual as well as an auditory life. With the advent of a text, the performer and the audience are physically separated from each other. Hence John Stuart Mill's idea that "eloquence is *heard;* poetry is *overheard*," and Northrop Frye's notion that the lyric is "a literary genre characterized by the assumed concealment of the audience from the poet." Thereafter, the lyric becomes a different kind of intimate communiqué, a highly concentrated and passionate form of communication between strangers. It delivers on our spiritual lives precisely because it gives us the gift of intimacy and interiority, of privacy and participation. Perhaps the asocial nature of the deepest feeling, the "too muchness" of human emotion is what creates the space for the lyric, which is a way of beating time, of experiencing duration, of verging on infinity. SEE ALSO *dramatic monologue, epic.*

masculine rhyme   A rhyme on a terminal syllable (*Pan* / *man*). The commonest kind of rhyme, masculine or single-syllable rhyme is contrasted to feminine or multisyllabic rhyme. The one-syllable rhyme makes emphatic connection, it creates a force field of relation—as when this anonymous sixteenth-century poet declares in "To Her Sea-Faring Lover":

> Alas! say nay! say nay! and be more so dumb,
> But open thou thy manly mouth and say that thou wilt come:

SEE ALSO *feminine rhyme, rhyme.*

metaphor   A figure of speech in which one thing is described in terms of another—as when Whitman characterizes the grass as "the beautiful uncut hair of graves." The term *metaphor* derives from the Greek *metaphora*, which means "carrying from one place to another," and a metaphor transfers the connotations of one thing (or idea) to another. Metaphor is a device for seeing—for experiencing—one thing in terms of another. It says A equals B (Life is a dream). A transfer of energies, a mode of energetic relation, of interpenetration, a matter of identity and difference. A collision, or a collusion, in the identification of unlike things. There is something dreamlike in it. Kenneth Burke calls this "perspective by incongruity" (*Permanence and Change*, 1954). Robert Frost says, "There are many other things I have found myself saying about poetry, but the chiefest of these is that it is metaphor, saying one thing and meaning another, saying one thing in terms of another, the pleasure of ulteriority" ("The Constant Symbol").

In *The Philosophy of Rhetoric* (1936), I. A. Richards distinguishes the two parts of a metaphor by the terms *tenor* and *vehicle*. The tenor stands for what is being talked about. It is the subject. The vehicle stands for the way it is being talked about and carries the weight of the comparison. When Macbeth says that "life is but a walking shadow," "life" is the tenor and "walking shadow" is the vehicle.

One philosophical tradition maintains that there is no logical difference between metaphors and similes. Metaphors are considered literal comparisons with the explicit "like" or "as" suppressed. Another tradition, the one to which I belong, holds that there is a radical difference (or should be) between saying that A is *the same as* B and saying that A is *like* B. ("I am crossing the word *like* out of the dictionary," Mallarmé declared.) Metaphor works by condensation and compression, simile by discursiveness and digression.

Metaphor works by a process of interaction. It draws attention to the categories of language, and it crosses them. The language of poetry, Shelley writes in his *Defence of Poetry,* is "vitally metaphorical; that is, it marks the before unapprehended relations of things and perpetuates their apprehension." Shelley suggests that the poet creates relations between things unrecognized before, and that new relations create new thoughts and thus revitalize language. That's why he claimed that "Poets are the unacknowledged legislators of the world."

It is my contention throughout this book that the reader actively participates in making meaning through metaphor, in thinking through the conjoining—the relation—of unlike things. Meaning emerges as an intimate collaborative process between writer and reader.

The literature on metaphor is massive. To begin: Max Black, *Models and Metaphors* (1962), Terence Hawkes, *Metaphor* (1972), Sheldon Sacks, ed., *On Metaphor* (1979).

SEE ALSO *metonymy, simile, trope.*

meter   The word *meter* derives from the Greek term *métron*, meaning "measure." Meter is a way of describing rhythmic patterning in poetry, of keeping time, of measuring poetic language. Meter marks a poem as verse, as a made thing, a work of art. As Barbara H. Smith writes in *Poetic Closure* (1968):

> Meter serves . . . as a frame for the poem, separating it from a "ground" of less highly structured speech and sound. . . . Meter is the stage of the theater in which the poem, the representation of an act of speech, is performed. It is the arena of art, the curtain that rises and falls as well as the music that accompanies the entire performance.

The first pleasures of meter are physical and intimately connected to bodily experience—to the heartbeat and the pulse, to breathing, walking, running, lovemaking. The meter of a poem can slow us down or speed us up, it can focus our attention or hypnotize us. Imagine you have gone down to the ocean in the early morning. You stand in the water and feel the waves breaking against the shore. You watch them coming in and going out. You feel the push and pull, the ebb and flow, of the tide. The waves repeat each other, but no two waves are exactly the same. Every wave is the same wave *with a difference*. Think of those waves as the flow of words washing across the lines and sentences of a poem. To measure the rhythmic pattern of those waves is to establish its meter. It is something you are observing, but also something you are experiencing. As I. A. Richards puts it in *Principles of Literary Criticism* (1952):

> Its effect is not due to our perceiving a pattern in something outside us, but to our becoming patterned ourselves. With every beat of the metre a tide of anticipation in us turns and swings, setting up as it does extraordinarily extensive reverberations. We shall never understand metre so long as we ask, "Why does temporal pattern so excite us?" and fail to realise that the pattern itself is a vast cyclic agitation spreading all over the body, a tide of excitement pouring through the channels of the mind.

I have a fondness for the old term *numbers* for metrical units, as in Pope's line, "I lisp'd in Numbers, for the Numbers came." Meter has to do with beating out time, with counting and naming. The terminology of metrics is problematic because it is borrowed from classical languages and applies only imperfectly to English. I have avoided it whenever possible in this book. Still, there are readers who find metrical analysis an important constitutive feature of poetic meaning, and it is useful for all readers of poetry to know the four generally distinguishable metrical systems.

• *pure accentual meter:* This system, which we all recognize from nursery rhymes, measures only the number of stressed or accented syllables in each line. Accentual meter is the basis of most Germanic poetries. English poetry began in a pure accentual meter. The standard line throughout the Old and Middle English periods consists of four accents with a strong medial pause (see *caesura*) and a pattern of repetitive consonants (see *alliteration, consonance*), as in this line from Ezra Pound's version of the ninth-century poem "The Seafarer":

> Waneth the watch, but the world holdeth.

The fifteenth-century poet John Skelton came up with a version of accentual meter called *Skeltonics,* Coleridge experimented with pure accentual verse in "Christabel," and Gerard Manley Hopkins developed a creative form of it he called "sprung rhythm," his most important metrical discovery.

• *pure syllabic meter:* This system measures only the number of syllables in each line. It pays no attention to accentuation. Some languages are accent-timed, such as German and English, whereas other languages are syllable-timed, such as French and Japanese. Pure syllabic verse is an alien import into English and always has an imposed air. It has an experimental feeling because it frustrates and works against what Paul Fussell calls "our own Anglo-Saxon lust for stress."

Marianne Moore is the great practitioner of syllabics in our century. Her compositions in verse—she was reluctant to call them "poems"—make the syllable a visible particle of language. It's as if she broke words down into their constituent parts and held them up to the light before reassembling them. This gives a scrupulously observed, slightly clinical feeling to her measures.

> The Fish
>
> wade
> through black jade.
>   Of the crow-blue mussel shells, one keeps
>   adjusting the ash heaps;
>   opening and shifting itself like
>
> an
> injured fan.

Moore intermingles her line lengths and each stanza repeats the syllabic pattern exactly. The syllabics are used contrapuntally to the rhythm of the phrase, and the poem has the precision of an X ray.

• **quantitative meter:** This system measures duration—the time it takes to pronounce a syllable—rather than contrasting stresses or accents. Sanskrit, Greek, and Latin meters were all quantitative. The foot in classical prosody was something like a musical measure. Syllables were long or short, and one long syllable took the same length of time it took to utter two short ones. Robert Bridges experimented interestingly with quantitative meters, but applying durational values to English verse has generally failed because English is such a heavily accented language. Our speech falls naturally into a pattern of stresses. It was only when classical feet were replaced with pairs or triads of stressed and unstressed syllables that meter began to have any applicability to the evolution of English poetry.

• **accentual-syllabic meter:** This system counts both the number of accents and the number of syllables in each line. Rhythm results from the interplay between them. Accentual-syllabic meter comprises the main tradition of English poetry from the late sixteenth century to the early twentieth century. It is traditionally discussed as a sequence of *feet.* Each foot consists of a nucleus of one stressed syllable and one or two unstressed syllables. The main feet in English versification are the *iamb, trochee, dactyl,* and *anapest.* (See the entry under *foot* for the definition of these terms.)

A meter is determined by the prevailing accentual pattern (iambic, trochaic, dactylic, anapestic) plus the number of feet per line: *monometer* (one); *dimeter* (two); *trimeter* (three); *tetrameter* (four); *pentameter* (five); *hexameter* (six); *heptameter* (seven); *octometer* (eight).

The native four-beat rhythm, which is rooted in the Old English line, has an inescapable feeling of symmetry, and our language falls into it naturally. It establishes the rhythm of ballads and hymns, of most folk, rock and roll, and rap songs. The very reason that iambic pentameter became the preferred meter in our language is that, as Derek Attridge observes in *The Rhythms of English Poetry,* "it is the only simple metrical form of manageable length which escapes the elementary four-beat rhythm, with its insistence, its hierarchical structures, and its close relationship with the world of ballad and song."

It has been estimated that three-fourths of all English poetry from Chaucer to Frost has been written in rhymed or unrhymed iambic pentameter. It was the modal line in English for over three hundred years—the meter that Chaucer used for most of *The Canterbury Tales,* Spenser employed for *The Faerie Queene,* Shakespeare used with great versatility through most of his plays, Milton needed for his epics, Pope used judiciously for nearly all his verse, Wordsworth used with great flexibility in *The Prelude,* Robert Browning carried through *The Ring and the Book,* Yeats, Frost, Stevens, and Crane re-created for many of their greatest poems.

Every meter has accrued a history and that history haunts later usages. It becomes part of its conscious and unconscious associations, its meanings and memories.

For an enjoyable guide to English verse, see John Hollander's *Rhyme's Reason* (1981), in which he illustrates each scheme, form, and pattern of English verse with a witty, self-descriptive example. For two excellent studies, see Derek Attridge's *The Rhythms of English Poetry* (1982) and Paul Fussell's *Poetic Meter and Poetic Form* (1979).

SEE ALSO *ballad, blank verse, hymn, iambic pentameter, rhythm,* and the entries for individual feet: *anapest, dactyl, iamb, spondee,* and *trochee.*

metonymy   (From the Greek meaning "change of name.") A figure of speech that replaces or substitutes the name of one thing with something else closely associated with it. We say, "the pen is mightier than the sword" (and mean that writing is more powerful than warfare). We say "Homer says" rather than "In *The Iliad* it is written" (and thus substitute the name of an author for his work).

Metonymy strategically employs concrete, tangible, or corporeal terms to convey abstract, intangible, or incorporeal states, as when we speak of "the heart" and mean "the emotions." It's a way of embodying emotive and spiritual experiences. "If you trail language back far enough," Kenneth Burke explains, "you'll find all our terms for 'spiritual' states were metonymic in origin."

Synecdoche, the most crucial kind of metonymy, substitutes the name of a part for that of a whole (e.g., hired hand for worker). Burke argues that "all such conversions imply an integral relationship, a relationship of convertibility between the two terms."

In his insightful essay "The Four Master Tropes," Burke goes on to argue for the synecdochic nature of ancient metaphysical doctrines:

> The "noblest synecdoche," the perfect paradigm or prototype for all lesser usages, is found in metaphysical doctrines proclaiming the identity of "microcosm" and "macrocosm." In such doctrines, where the individual is treated as a replica of the universe, and vice versa, we have the ideal synecdoche, since microcosm is related to macrocosm as part to whole, and either the whole can represent the part or the part can represent the whole.

The metonym and the metaphor are complementary figures. Whereas a metaphor establishes a radical likeness between two different things ("my heart is a thirsty black handkerchief"), a metonym establishes a contiguous or associative relationship between them ("Heart cries, 'No'"). It is a form of associative or representational thinking. The linguist

Roman Jakobson famously extended the field of complementary figures, metaphor and metonym, to encompass dreams, myths, psychoanalysis, types of aphasia, and so forth. Metonymy and metaphor offer the creative reader two different ways of organizing experience, of making meaning.

For guidance, see Kenneth Burke, *A Grammar of Motives* (1945).

SEE ALSO *metaphor, trope.*

mimesis   The Greek word for "imitation" and a key term in aesthetics since Aristotle asserted in the *Poetics* that tragedy is the imitation of an action. Mimesis has come to mean "representation," especially in terms of verisimilitude. We call a work "mimetic" or "realistic" when it gives the semblance of truth, the illusion of transparency, the sense of fidelity to an external reality. See Erich Auerbach's classic work, *Mimesis* (1953).

muse   A source of poetic inspiration. Each of the nine Greek goddesses, daughters of Zeus and Mnemosyne (or Memory), traditionally presided over an activity or art: Calliope (epic poetry); Clio (history); Erato (love poetry); Euterpe (lyric poetry); Melpomene (tragedy); Polyhymnia (songs of praise to the gods); Terpsichore (dancing); Thalia (comedy); Urania (astronomy, i.e., cosmological poetry).

The invocation to the muse ("Sing, goddess...") acknowledges the need for an inspiring spirit. Poetry is never entirely at the dispensation of the poet's conscious will or intellect, and whoever calls out, "Help me, O Heavenly Muse" advertises a dependence on a force beyond the intellective powers. Hence this invocation of the chorus at the beginning of Shakespeare's *Henry V:*

> O! for a Muse of fire, that would ascend
> The brightest heaven of invention...

The sacred muse (the phrase is Spenser's) is the spirit of creativity, and thus inspires reverence or awe. Such a beloved has uncanny powers. Wallace Stevens invoked her as the "inexplicable sister of the Minotaur," Robert Graves exalted her as the resplendent White Goddess. Louis MacNeice remembers that "the Muse will never / Conform to type."

SEE ALSO *invocation.*

negative capability   John Keats coined this term in a letter to his brothers George and Thomas (December 21, 1817). He wrote:

> several things dove tailed in my mind, and at once it struck me what quality went to form a Man of Achievement, especially in Literature, and which Shakespeare possessed so enormously—I mean *Negative Capability,* that is when man is capable of being in uncertainties, Mysteries, doubts, without any irritable reaching after fact and reason.

In another letter (October 27, 1818), Keats wrote that

> The poetical Character itself...has as much delight in conceiving an Iago as an Imogen....A Poet is the most unpoetical of any thing in existence; because he has no Identity—he is continually in for—and filling some other Body.

Keats describes the selfless receptivity he considers necessary for the deepest poetry. He exults in the poetic capacity for total immersion, for empathic release, for entering into whatever is being described.

octave   The first eight lines of an Italian or Petrarchan sonnet. The octave, or octet, is followed by the last six lines, the *sestet*. The octave can also refer to any eight-line poem or stanza, as in the dramatic opening of W. B. Yeats's "Among School Children":

> I walk through the long schoolroom questioning;
> A kind old nun in a white hood replies;
> The children learn to cipher and to sing,
> To study reading-books and history,
> To cut and sew, be neat in everything
> In the best modern way—the children's eyes
> In momentary wonder stare upon
> A sixty-year-old smiling public man.

Yeats employs *ottava rima* here, an eight-line stanza in iambic pentameter rhyming *abababcc*. The pattern unfolds as six interlocking lines followed by a climactic couplet. The Italian poets (Boccaccio, Pulci, Tasso) especially favored this aristocratic and symmetrical stanza for narrative and epic verse. It was imported to England by Wyatt, flourished during the Renaissance, and was brilliantly deployed by Byron in his mock epic *Don Juan* (a poem "meant to be a little quietly facetious upon everything"). Here Byron sends up some classic ancestors:

> Ovid's a rake, as half his verses show him,
> > Anacreon's morals are a still worse sample,
> Catullus scarcely has a decent poem,
> > I don't think Sappho's Ode a good example,
> Although Longinus tells us there is no hymn
> > Where the Sublime soars forth on wings more ample;
> But Virgil's songs are pure, except that horrid one
> Beginning with "*Formosum pastor Corydon.*"

SEE ALSO *sestet, sonnet, stanza.*

ode   A celebratory poem in an elevated language on an occasion of public importance or on a lofty universal theme. Think of Tennyson's ceremonial "Ode on the Death of the Duke of Wellington" and of Keats's partly rhapsodic, partly forlorn "Ode to a Nightingale" ("Thou wast not born for death, immortal Bird!"). The word *ode* derives from the Greek *ōidē*, a poem intended to be sung, and thus was virtually synonymous with the word *lyric*. It comes to us through its Latin form, *oda*. The modern ode, which freely intermingles Greek and Latin elements, represents the claiming of an obligation, some inner feeling rising up in urgent response to an outer occasion, something owed.

Greek lyrics took either the form of *monodies*, sung by single persons, or *choral odes*, sung by groups. Alcaeus ("Ode to Castor and Polydeuces") and Sappho ("Ode to Aphrodite") were unsurpassed monodists, Pindar the key exponent of the choral form. Simultaneously sung and danced, the Pindaric ode consists of three stanzas that mirror a musical dance pattern: strophe, antistrophe, epode. The strophe and antistrophe share the same metrical pattern and structure (the chorus in movement and countermovement); the epode has a different pattern (the chorus at rest). The Pindaric ode, which has its roots in religious rites, called for an ecstatic performance that communally reenacted the ritual of participation in the divine. The movement of the verse is emotionally intense and highly exalted.

Horace perfected the Latin form. He adapted the complex meters of Greek monodists to Latin verse, and replaced the irregular stanzas of the Pindaric ode with symmetrical arrangements. Horace's odes tend to be personal rather than public, general rather than occasional, contemplative rather than frenzied.

The English ode begins with Ben Jonson's 1629 "To the Imortall Memorie and Friendship of That Noble Paire, Sir Lucius Cary and Sir H. Morison," a self-conscious attempt to create an exact equivalent for Pindar's complicated stanzaic form. The Horatian model was represented by Andrew Marvell's outstanding political poem of the seventeenth century, "An Horatian Ode upon Cromwel's Return from Ireland." In both English and Continental poetry the ode developed a life of its own with deep roots as a poem on a theme of acknowledged importance. There are odes of speculation, odes *on* (Milton's "On the Morning of Christ's Nativity," Gray's delightful mock ode "Ode on the Death of a Favourite Cat, Drowned in a Tub of Gold Fishes") and odes of address, odes *to* (Dryden's "To the Pious Memory of the Accomplished Young Lady, Mrs. Anne Killigrew," Shelley's rhapsodic "Ode to the West Wind," Keats's culminating "To Autumn," and Schiller's magisterial "Ode to Joy," transformed by Beethoven in the final movement of the Ninth Symphony). The idea of a formal poem of considerable length written in an elevated language has had less currency in modern times, but has sometimes been revitalized as in, say, Hölderlin's mystical odes or in Pablo Neruda's wildly energetic three books of odes on daily subjects.

For a helpful introduction, see John Heath-Stubbs, *The Ode* (1969), and for a more advanced study, Paul Fry, *The Poet's Calling in the English Ode* (1980).

SEE ALSO *antistrophe, epode, lyric, strophe.*

onomatopoeia   (Greek: "name making") The formation and use of words which imitate sound (such as *blare, crash, dip, flare, growl, hum, jeer, knock, lick, murmur, nip, purr, quack, rustle, swish, thud, veer, wallop, yell, zoom*). Listen to what Shakespeare does with animal sounds in this exchange from *The Tempest:*

> Hark, hark.
>   Bow-wow!
> The watch-dogs bark.
>   Bow-wow!
> Hark, hark, I hear
> The strain of strutting Chanticleer
>   Cry, "cock-a-diddle-dow!"

Onomatopoeia is a form of name making, of phonic symbolism. It is a poetic device that creates verbal texture by weaving sounds through lines. It physicalizes Pope's dictum that "the sound must seem an echo to the sense." In poetry, Thomas Lux writes in his poem "Onomatopoeia," "the sound, the noise of the sound, is/the thing."

ottava rima   SEE *octave.*

panegyric   A public speech or poem in praise of an individual, a group of people, or a public body. Pindar's odes have been loosely characterized as panegyrics. After the third century B.C. the panegyric was generally recognized as a specific poetic type (a formal eulogistic composition intended as a public compliment), which persisted until the Renaissance. The panegyric may have led to a form of public flattery about which we are now rightly skeptical, but it most likely has its roots in religious practice, in the Greek and Latin cult hymns. Behind it persists one of the most long-standing and permanent impulses in poetry: to praise.

parallelism   (Greek: "side by side") The correspondence between two parts of an utterance (a phrase, a line, a verse) through syntactic and rhythmic repetition. Parallelism is a constitutive device—a basic aesthetic principle—in oral and archaic poetries. One thinks of the oral-formulaic strategies of the early epics, of chants, charms, and spells, of incantatory prayers. It is the central device of biblical Hebrew poetry, as in these lines from Psalm 96:

> Let the heavens rejoice, and let the earth be glad;
>> let the sea roar, and the fulness thereof.
>> Let the field be joyful, and all that *is* therein: then
> shall all the trees of the wood rejoice.

The buildup of parallel lines often creates a feeling of intense emotion—of incantation, of litany, of exaltation. It instills a reverence. This complex device of synthesis and accumulation (there are repetitions, for example, based on identity, on antithesis, on complementary meaning) has been wondrously explored in the ecstatic poetry of Christopher Smart and William Blake. It is at the heart of Walt Whitman's ecstasies and of the work of his free-verse progeny, D. H. Lawrence, Theodore Roethke, Allen Ginsberg.

Here is Gerard Manley Hopkins's account of the necessary role of parallelism in the structure of poetry:

> The artificial part of poetry . . . reduces itself to the principle of parallelism. . . . But parallelism is of two kinds necessarily . . . the first kind . . . is concerned with the structure of verse—in rhythm, the recurrence of a certain sequence of syllables, in metre, the recurrence of a certain sequence of rhythm, in alliteration, in assonance and in rhyme. Now the force of this recurrence is to beget a recurrence or parallelism answering to it in the words or thought and, speaking roughly, . . . the more marked parallelism in structure . . . begets more marked parallelism in the words and sense. . . . To the [other] kind of parallelism belong metaphor, simile, parable, and so on, where the effect is sought in likeness of things, and antithesis, contrast, and so on, where it is sought in unlikeness.

SEE ALSO *anaphora.*

pathetic fallacy   A phrase invented by John Ruskin in *Modern Painters* (1856) to describe the attribution of human characteristics to inanimate objects. To illustrate his point Ruskin quoted from Charles Kingsley's "The Sands of Dee":

> They rowed her in across the rolling foam—
> The cruel, crawling foam.

"The foam is not cruel, neither does it crawl," Ruskin wrote:

> The state of mind which attributes to it these characters of a living creature is one in which the reason is unhinged by grief. All violent feelings . . . produce in us a falseness in all our impressions of external things, which I would characterize as the "Pathetic Fallacy."

What was for Ruskin a derogatory term, a morbid romantic and Victorian phenomenon, has been a central poetic device of archaic and tribal poetries everywhere, which view the natural world as alive in all its parts. Think of the pathetic fallacy as empathic feeling for the overlooked world. This projection of feeling has also flourished as a strain in epic poetry from Homer onward, as a feature of prophetic poetry from the major and minor prophets of the Hebrew Bible to Smart and Blake, Coleridge and Shelley, Whitman and Crane... It emerges whenever poets testify to, or dream of, the natural world saturated with psyche.

pattern poetry   A form of spatial prosody, pattern poetry (or *technopaignia*) offers verses as visual arrangements on the page. The impulse to display poetry in concrete shapes is ancient, and pattern poems have been found in Greek, Latin (*carmen figuratum:* "shaped poem"), Hebrew, Chinese, Sanskrit, ancient Persian, and in most of the modern European languages. The pattern poem (that is, the poem shaped like an altar, an egg, a pair of wings) promotes itself as a hybrid, a combination of verbal and visual art. It concretizes the relationship between content and form, and invites—challenges—the reader to perceive the relationship between the shape and the theme.

Unlike some concrete poems, the pattern poem always creates a relationship between the design and the meaning. (Two exemplary postwar collections are John Hollander's *Types of Shape,* 1969, and May Swenson's *Iconographs,* 1970.) The pictorial lyric displays itself as a metaphor: it says, *I am something else.* The reader is a viewer interacting with the shape, the viewer is a reader exploring the relationship between subject and object, content and form.

For a useful history, see Dick Higgins, *Pattern Poetry: Guide to an Unknown Literature* (1987). SEE ALSO *concrete poetry.*

persona   The mask or character—the voice—created by the speaker or narrator in a literary work. In Latin *persona* means "the mask (a false face of clay or bark) worn by actors in the ancient classical theater." The term *dramatis personae* (the characters in a play) derives from *persona,* as does the word *person.* The concept of persona originates in magical thinking, in archaic rituals where masks are independent beings that possess the ones who assume them. The poetic move into personae has a quality of animism; it embodies the displacement of the poet's self into another existence, a second self.

In "A General Introduction for My Work," W. B. Yeats said that the poet "never speaks directly as to someone at the breakfast table, there is always a phantasmagoria." The term *personae* refers to all forms of this phantasmagoria, from the narrators in Chaucer's *Canterbury Tales* to the unidentified autobiographical speakers in Emily Dickinson's lyrics (Dickinson called the speaker in her poems a "supposed person") and Stevie Smith's poems to the characters in Robert Browning's dramatic monologues. Creating a persona is a way of staging an utterance. There is always a difference between the writer who sits down to work and the author who emerges in the text. One contention of this book is that selfhood is a constructive process in poetry. It depends on collaboration, something created between writer and reader. SEE ALSO *dramatic monologue.*

personification   The attribution of human qualities to inanimate objects, to animals or ideas, as when Sylvia Plath engenders the moon as female ("The Moon and the Yew Tree") or Philip Sidney apostrophizes it:

> With how sad steps o Moone, thou climb'st the skies,
>   How silently, and with how wanne a face,

We personify poetic terms when we define rhymes as "masculine" or "feminine." Person-
ification has sometimes been thought a quirky or marginal poetic activity, but it may be
central to the Orphic function of the poet, who, as Emerson said, "puts eyes and tongues
into every dumb and inanimate object."

Personification has special purpose as the basis for allegory. Think, for example, of those
medieval morality plays in which characters are named "Lust" or "Hope," thus indicating
that general ideas, and not individual people, are being dramatized. For an advanced theory
of this term, see James J. Paxson, *The Poetics of Personification* (1994).

SEE ALSO *allegory, pathetic fallacy.*

poem   A made thing, a verbal construct, an event in language. The word *poiesis* means
"making," and the oldest term for the poet means "maker." The *Princeton Encyclopedia
of Poetry and Poetics* points out that the medieval and Renaissance poets used the word *makers,*
as in "courtly makers," as a precise equivalent for *poets.* (Hence William Dunbar's "Lament
for the Makers.") The word *poem* came into English in the sixteenth century and has been
with us ever since to denote a form of fabrication, a verbal composition, a made thing.

William Carlos Williams defined the poem as "a small (or large) machine made of
words." (He added that there is nothing redundant about a machine.) Wallace Stevens char-
acterized poetry as "a revelation of words by means of the words." In his helpful essay
"What Is Poetry?" the linguist Roman Jakobson declared:

> Poeticity is present when the word is felt as a word and not a mere representation of
> the object being named or an outburst of emotion, when words and their composi-
> tion, their meaning, their external and internal form, acquire a weight and value of
> their own instead of referring indifferently to reality.

Ben Jonson referred to the art of poetry as "the craft of making." The old Irish word
cerd, meaning "people of the craft," was a designation for artisans, including poets. It is cog-
nate with the Greek *kerdos,* meaning "craft, craftiness." Two basic metaphors for the art of
poetry in the classical world were carpentry and weaving. "Whatsoever else it may be,"
W. H. Auden said, "a poem is a verbal artifact which must be as skillfully and solidly con-
structed as a table or a motorcycle."

The true poem has been crafted into a living entity. It has magical potency, ineffable
spirit. There is always something mysterious, something inexplicable in a poem. It is an
act—an action—beyond paraphrase because what is said is always inseparable from the way
it is being said. A poem creates an experience in the reader that cannot be reduced to any-
thing else. Perhaps it exists in order to create that aesthetic experience. Octavio Paz main-
tained that the poet and the reader are two moments of a single reality.

poetic crossing   The movement within a poem from one plane of reality to another, as
when Dante crosses over from the earthly realm to the infernal regions in *The Inferno.* It re-
quires the blacking out of the quotidian world and the entrance into another type of con-
sciousness, another kind of reality. For an exploration of the consequences of a poetic
crossing in one poet, see Harold Bloom's study, *Wallace Stevens: The Poems of Our Climate*
(1976).

SEE ALSO *epiphany.*

poetic license   Poetry frees words and disturbs our ordinary usage of language. Some-
times it departs from agreed-upon rules of pronunciation or diction or syntax; it departs
from the tyranny of "fact." "This poeticall license is a shrewde fellow," George Gascoigne

wrote: "it maketh words longer, shorter, of mo sillables, of fewer, newer, older, truer, falser; and, to conclude, it turkeneth [alters] all things at pleasure."

John Dryden defined poetic license as "the liberty which poets have assumed to themselves, in all ages, of speaking things in verse which are beyond the severity of prose."

See chapter 3, "Varieties of Poetic License," in Geoffrey N. Leech, *A Linguistic Guide to English Poetry* (1969).

poetics The systematic doctrine or theory of poetry. The term derives from Aristotle (*Poetics*), who defined it as dealing with "poetry itself and its kinds and the specific power of each." Poetics investigates the distinguishing features of poetry—its branches, its governing principles, its technical resources, the nature of its forms, etc. The study of the nature of poetry has broadened in modern usage to refer to the general theory of literature, of literariness. Thus it becomes possible to speak of "structuralist poetics" or "the poetics of prose."

poetry A magical, mysterious, inexplicable (though not incomprehensible) event in language. The great Argentine writer Jorge Luis Borges believed that "Poetry is something that cannot be defined without oversimplifying it. It would be like attempting to define the color yellow, love, the fall of leaves in autumn." Borges liked Plato's designation of the poet as "that light substance, winged and sacred."

Poetry precedes prose in all literatures and there has probably never been a culture without it. The word *poesie* entered English in the fourteenth century and begat *poesy* (as in Sidney's "The Defence of Poesy," ca. 1582) and *posy,* a motto in verse. *Poetrie* (from the Latin *poetria*) entered fourteenth-century English vocabulary and evolved into our *poetry.* There have been many attempts by poets over the centuries to account for this mysterious, ancient, and necessary instrument of our humanity.

Sir Philip Sidney said that poetry is "a representing, counterfetting, a figuring foorth: to speak metaphorically: a speaking picture: with this end, to teach and delight."

Coleridge called poetry "that synthetic and magical power, to which we have exclusively appropriated the name of imagination."

Wordsworth famously called poetry "the spontaneous overflow of powerful feelings.. recollected in tranquillity." (John Stuart Mill followed up Wordsworth's emphatic emphasis on overflowing emotion when he wrote that poetry is "feeling confessing itself to itself in moments of solitude.")

Shelley joyfully called poetry "the record of the best and happiest moments of the happiest and best minds." He said that poetry "redeems from decay the visitations of the divinity in man."

Matthew Arnold narrowed the definition to "a criticism of life."

Gerard Manley Hopkins characterized it as "speech framed... to be heard for its own sake and interest even over and above its interest of meaning."

Marianne Moore formulated poetry as "imaginary gardens with real toads in them."

Robert Frost said wryly that "Poetry provides the one permissible way of saying one thing and meaning another."

Robert Graves thought of it as a form of "stored magic," André Breton as a "room of marvels."

Howard Nemerov said that poetry is simply "getting something right in language."

Heather McHugh writes that "The place of poetry is nothing less than the place of love, for language; the place of shifting ground, for human song; the place of the made, for the moving."

One supposition of this book is that poetry is a verbal transaction between a writer and a reader. I concur with the Australian poet Les Murray when he says that "poetry exists to provide the poetic experience." It exists on behalf of both reader and writer. Borges, too, affirms that poetry "is the poetic act when the poet writes it, when the reader reads it, and it always happens in a slightly different manner." We cannot know poetry by any intrinsic properties of poetry itself, but by our contact with it. It has an intensity which cannot be denied.

Emily Dickinson wrote in a letter:

> If I read a book [and] it makes my whole body so cold no fire can ever warm me I know *that* is poetry. If I feel physically as if the top of my head were taken off, I know *that* is poetry. These are the only way I know it. Is there any other way.

A. E. Housman wrote in *The Name and Nature of Poetry* (1933):

> A year or two ago, in common with others, I received from America a request that I would define poetry. I replied that I could no more define poetry than a terrier can define a rat, but that I thought we both recognized the object by the symptoms which it provokes in us. One of these symptoms was described in connection with another object by Eliphaz the Termanite: "A spirit passed before my face: the hair of my flesh stood up." Experience has taught me, when I am shaving of a morning, to keep watch over my thoughts, because, if a line of poetry strays into my memory, my skin bristles so that the razor ceases to act. This particular symptom is accompanied by a shiver down the spine; there is another which consists in a constriction of the throat and a precipitation of water in the eyes; and there is a third which I can only describe by borrowing a phrase from one of Keats's last letters, where he says, speaking of Fanny Brawne, "everything that reminds me of her goes through me like a spear."

prose poem   A composition printed as prose which names itself poetry. The prose poem takes advantage of its hybrid nature—it avails itself of the elements of prose (what Dryden called "the other harmony of prose") while foregrounding the devices of poetry. The French writer Aloysius Bertrand was one of the first to establish the prose poem as a minor genre in *Gaspard de la nuit* (1842), a book which influenced Baudelaire's *Petits poèmes en prose* (1869). Baudelaire dreamed of creating "a poetic prose, musical without rhyme or rhythm, supple and jerky enough to adapt to the lyric movements of the soul, to the undulations of reverie, to the somersaults of conscience." Baudelaire's prose poems—along with Rimbaud's *Les Illuminations* (1886) and Mallarmé's *Divagations* (1897)—created a mixed musical form (part social, part transcendental) that has been widely and internationally practiced in the twentieth century. The evidence is available in Michael Benedikt, ed., *The Prose Poem: An International Anthology* (1976).

psalm   A sacred song or hymn. The term generally refers to the Hebrew poems in the biblical Book of Psalms, which *The Oxford Companion to Music* calls "the oldest and the greatest book of songs now in use anywhere in the world." The psalms have been traditionally ascribed to King David, but David seems to be a composite author ensuring the formal integrity of poems composed over a period of more than five hundred years. Some seem to go as far back as the ninth and tenth centuries B.C. The earliest manuscripts date from the ninth century in Hebrew, from the fourth century in Latin, and from the second century in Greek when the *Book of Psalms*, spliced together from at least four previous collections, took final form. The Hebrew heading of the complete psalter found in several early manuscripts (a psalter is a collection of psalms) is a word meaning "the book of praises," and the psalms are ancient liturgical praise poems with terrific performative power.

> MAKE a joyful noise unto the LORD, all ye lands.
>
> Serve the LORD with gladness: come before his presence with singing.
>
> Know ye that the LORD he *is* God: *it is* he *that* hath made us, and not we ourselves; *we are* his people, and the sheep of his pasture.
>
> (Psalm 100:1–3)

In his essay "A Folk Inferno," the Australian poet Les Murray describes the psalms when he writes that "Unlike poetries of formula and definition, the celebratory doesn't presume to understand the world...and so leaves it open and expansive, with unforeclosed potentials."

The psalms have been a tremendous sourcebook for Western poets. As Donald Davie writes in the introduction to his splendid anthology *The Psalms in English,* "Through four centuries there is hardly a poet of even modest ambition who does not feel the need to try his hand at paraphrasing some part of Scripture, most often the psalms." One legacy of the psalms is what Coburn Freer calls "joyful religious play."

> All people that on earth do dwell,
>> Sing to the Lord with cheerful voice:
> Him serve with mirth, his praise forth tell,
>> Come ye before him, and rejoice.
>> (translated by William Kethe, 1561)

Donald Davie's anthology *The Psalms in English* (1996) consists of the finest English translations since the Reformation as well as poems meditating on David the psalmist. A useful analysis of the psalms can be found in S. E. Gillingham's *The Poems and Psalms of the Hebrew Bible* (1994).

pun   A form of wordplay. A figure of speech that depends upon a similar sound and disparate meaning. The pun may involve (1) the use of a word with two or more meanings; (2) a similarity of meaning of two words spelled differently but pronounced the same; (3) two words spelled and pronounced almost alike but with different meanings. Since the early eighteenth century, the pun has sometimes been condescended to as a "low species of wit" (Noah Webster), but the device has appeared in all literatures and seems to be as old as language itself.

A good pun releases the multiple energies in words. It can be a kind of holy fooling, as in Christopher Smart and Gerard Manley Hopkins. In *Romeo and Juliet* the dying Mercutio declares, "Ask for me to-morrow, you shall find me a grave man." Dorothy Parker writes of the unimpaired "poetical feats" of the romantic poets, "Byron and Shelley and Keats" ("A Pig's-Eye View of Literature"). In this stanza from "A Hymne to God the Father," John Donne puns both on his own name (done, Donne) and on the word *Son* (meaning both Christ and the sun):

> I have a sinne of feare, that when I have spunne
>> My last thred, I shall perish on the shore;
> Sweare by thy selfe, that at my death thy sonne

Shall shine as he shines now, and heretofore;
And, having done that, Thou hast done,
I feare no more.

For more on the pun, see Jonathan Culler, ed., *On Puns: The Foundation of Letters* (1988).

quatrain   A four-line stanza. The quatrain—used as a unit of composition in longer poems and as a complete utterance unto itself—is probably the most common stanzaic form in the world. It has the power of heavy stone, of sturdy buildings and rooted trees. It has the adaptability of workers everywhere. It has great antiquity and travels well between languages and countries. Thus it is the staple of the English ballad and the Latin hymn, the Malay pantun, the Russian chastushka, the German Schnadehüpfel. It exists in a variety of rhyme schemes and meters, formal variations. Here one thinks of alcaics and sapphics (named after two of the greatest early Greek lyricists), of the heroic quatrain (also known as the *elegiac stanza*, used in Gray's "Elegy Written in a Country Churchyard"), of the *In Memoriam* stanza (so-called for its adept use in Tennyson's *In Memoriam*), and the Omar Khayyám stanza (from Edward Fitzgerald's loose adaptation of the Persian original):

A Book of Verses underneath the Bough
A Jug of Wine, a Loaf of Bread—and Thou
Beside me singing in the Wilderness—
Oh, Wilderness were Paradise enow!

Each form of the quatrain has its own way of treating the stanza as a solid block of meaning, a rectangular place of indwelling. Each has its own distinctive measure, distinctive music. Here is a famous anonymous poem that was found, along with its music, in an early sixteenth-century manuscript:

Westron wynde when wylle thow blow
The small rayne down can Rayne
Cryst yf my lowe were in my Armys
And I yn my bed A gayne

SEE ALSO *ballad, hymn, stanza.*

quintet   A stanza of five lines. Also called a *quintain,* it appears in various forms, from the clever English *limerick* (which rhymes *aabba* and thus relies on a principle of return) to the classical Japanese *tanka* (composed in lines containing 5, 7, 5, 7, 7 syllables). A wildly inventive mask of insanity energizes the conventional "mad song," as in this anonymous example from a sixteenth-century "Tom o' Bedlam" song:

I know more than Apollo,
For, oft when he lies sleeping,
I behold the stars
At bloody wars
And the wounded welkin weeping,

There seems to be something a little beyond reason, something emotionally excessive in punching past the symmetrical quatrain. Thus the possibilities of five unfold: Edmund Waller joins a three-line stanza to a couplet (*ababb*) in "Go, Lovely Rose"; Sidney employs the common rhyme scheme (*ababa*) in his enjoyable "Eleventh Song"; Wyatt utilizes an interlocking pattern (*aabab*) in "The Lover Complaineth the Unkindness of His Love," the last stanza of which concludes:

> Now cease, my lute, this is the last
> Labour that thou and I shall waste,
> And ended is that we begun.
> Now is this song both sung and past,
> My lute, be still, for I have done.

SEE ALSO *quatrain, stanza*.

refrain   A phrase, a line, or a group of lines recurring at intervals during a poem, often at the ends of stanzas (as in Shakespeare's nonsense refrain from *Much Ado about Nothing*, "hey nonny, nonny").

A refrain can be as short as a single word, it can appear irregularly or as a partial rather than a complete repetition (when it tends to be called a *repetend*), it can be as long as an entire stanza (when it is called a *burden*). The refrain is a universal device of archaic and tribal poetries, and indeed, reiterated words and phrases may stand at the origin of poetic practice. The refrain functionally accompanies communal labor, dance, and song (it is called a *chorus* because it allows everyone to join in) and perhaps evokes its distant ancestry in collective life. Refrains can be found in *The Egyptian Book of the Dead* and the Hebrew Bible, in Greek and Latin poetry, in Provençal and Renaissance verse, in English and Scottish ballads ("hey nonny, nonny").

Repetition is one of the crucial unifying elements in poetry. The refrain is a way of marking time, of timing poems. It can build and accrue meaning, whether by exact repetitions that change meaning in each new context ("Nevermore") or by undergoing slight modulations in a process called *incremental repetition* (as in Trumbull Stickney's splendid poem "Mnemosyne"). As John Hollander puts it in "Breaking into Song: Some Notes on Refrain": "Refrains are, and have, memories—of their prior strophes or stretches of text, of their own preoccurrences, and of their own genealogies in earlier texts as well" (*Melodious Guile*, 1988). Refrains are haunted by circularity, by turnings and recurrences ("hey nonny, nonny").

SEE ALSO *incremental repetition*.

rhapsodist (or **rhapsode**), **rhapsody**   In ancient Greece a rhapsodist was an itinerant minstrel who composed and recited epic poetry aloud. Some material was memorized, some improvised. The word *rhapsody* means "stitch song" in Greek, and a rhapsode "stitched together" various strands of heroic material. A rhapsody originally referred to the section of epic literature sung by a rhapsode. Later it came to mean an intensely emotional literary work, an ecstatic poetic utterance, as in Sir William Watson's "Hymn to the Sea":

> While, with throes, with raptures, with loosing of bonds, with unsealings,
> Arrowy pangs of delight, piercing the core of the world,
> Tremors and coy unfoldings, reluctances, sweet agitations,
> Youth, irrepressibly fair, wakes like wondering rose.

Such contemporary books of poems as Gerald Stern's *Lucky Life* (1977), Robert Hass's *Praise* (1979), and Susan Mitchell's *Rapture* (1992) all remember, even at our late date, the rhapsodic impulse in poetry.

rhyme   Rainer Maria Rilke called rhyme "a goddess of secret and ancient coincidences." He said that "she comes as happiness comes, hands filled with an achievement that is already in flower." Rhyme has the joyousness of discovery, of hidden relations uncovered, as if by accident. Rhyme is a form of relationship and connection, of encounter and metamorphosis. Rhyme occurs, Joseph Brodsky said, "when one thing turns into another without changing its substance, which is sound." It creates a partnership between words, lines of poetry, feelings, ideas. (Gerard Manley Hopkins called rhyming words "rhyme fellows.") There is something charged and magnetic about a good rhyme, something both unsuspected and inevitable, something utterly surprising and unforeseen and yet also binding and necessary. It is as if the poet had called up the inner yearning of words to find each other.

Rhyme foregrounds the sounds of words as words. It functions as a marker signaling the end of a rhythmic unit. It is mnemonic:

> Red sky at night, sailor's delight
> Red sky at morning, sailors take warning.

Two different kinds of rhyme capture two different portents here: one joyful, the other dangerous.

There is a pleasure in the sound of words coming together, in the pulse and beat, the rhythm of their conjoining. ("The chances of rhyme are like the chances of meeting—/ In the finding fortuitous, but once found, binding," Charles Tomlinson writes in his poem "The Chances of Rhyme.") There was systematic rhyming in ancient Chinese, Sanskrit, Arabic, Norse, Provençal, and Celtic languages, but the origins of rhyme in English are mysterious since, as the great prosodist George Saintsbury once declared, no one really knows quite how or why or when rhyme actually entered our language. The word *rhyme* was spelled *rime* until the seventeenth century.

Rhyme is a device based on the sound identities of words. It is repetition with a difference. It involves the inner correspondence of end sounds in words or in lines of verse. W. N. Ewer writes in "The Chosen People":

> How odd
> Of God
> To choose
> The Jews.

This is an example of *exact rhyme* (also called *complete, full, perfect, true,* or *whole rhyme*) since the initial sounds are different, but all succeeding sounds are identical (How odd / of God / To leaven / Heaven). A rhyme that concludes a line, as here, is also called an *end rhyme*, whereas a rhyme that occurs within a line is called an *internal rhyme* (Red sky at *night*, sailor's *delight*"). A one-syllable rhyme is called *masculine* (*Oh/no*), a two-syllable rhyme *feminine* (as when Stevie Smith rhymes *epileptic* and *skeptic* and John Crowe Ransom *Plato* and *potato*). A three-syllable rhyme (*wittily/prettily*) is called *triple rhyme*. When the same words line up as a rhyme two or more times it is called *identical rhyme,* as in Jorge Luis Borges's "Ars Poetica":

> To see in death sleep, and in the sunset
> A sad gold—such is poetry,
> Which is immortal and poor. Poetry
> Returns like the dawn and the sunset.
>   (translated by W. S. Merwin)

One key way of making the sounds of words relate to each other and coincide is through *slant rhyme* (as when W. B. Yeats rhymes *houses* and *faces* at the opening of "Easter, 1916"), which is also called *approximate, half, imperfect, near, oblique,* or *partial rhyme*. Slant rhyme includes assonance (when the vowels of two stressed syllables sound similar: *love/have*) and consonance (when the consonants sound alike but the vowels differ: *love/leave*). Dickinson, Yeats, and Wilfred Owen were all masters of half rhyme, which often feels modern to us, perhaps because of its slight sense of dissonance and dislocation, but in fact was used in medieval Icelandic verse. Slant rhyme offers the pleasures of novelty and imperfection, of affinity and difference.

Rhyme helps to define and individuate a line of poetry even as it links it to another line or lines. Rhyme creates in the reader a sense of interaction between words and lines. In "One Relation of Rhyme to Reason" (1954), W. K. Wimsatt suggests that every rhyme invites the reader to consider semantic as well as sound similarities. Thus rhymes create both acoustic and logical linkages. The reader participates by feeling the weight of the rhyming words, by forging the meaning of their connections, by teasing out the implications of words coming together and identifying each other as partners. Emerson gives a wonderful sense of the boldness of rhyme in a notebook entry from June 27, 1839:

> *Rhyme*—Rhyme; not tinkling rhyme, but grand Pindaric strokes, as firm as the tread of a horse. Rhyme that vindicates itself as an art, the stroke of the bell of a cathedral. Rhyme which knocks at prose and dullness with the stroke of a cannon ball. Rhyme which builds out into Chaos and old night a splendid architecture to bridge the impassable, and call aloud on all the children of morning that Creation is recommencing. I wish to write such rhymes as shall not suggest a restraint, but contrariwise the wildest freedom.

See Samuel Daniel's brilliant *A Defence of Ryme, against a Pamphlet Entitled Observations in the Art of English Poesie* (1603). For a lively discussion, see Donald Wesling, *The Chances of Rhyme: Device and Modernity* (1980).

SEE ALSO *assonance, consonance, feminine rhyme, masculine rhyme.*

rhyme scheme A characteristic pattern of rhymes. As a shorthand for representing a rhyme scheme, each different rhyme is assigned a different letter. Thus a pair of couplets is designated *aabb*, a quatrain alternating rhymes is represented *abab*, and so forth.

The rhyme scheme embodies the emergence, the delivery, of meaning in a poem. It is an abstraction blooded. Think of the winding staircase of Dante's terza rima, which rhymes *aba, bcb, cdc,* etc. (you are always going forward while glancing backward), or the logical development of the Shakespearean sonnet, which rhymes *abab, cdcd, efef, gg,* and carries in its body the rhetorical argument of love. Some rhyme schemes repeat the same words in complex arrangements, as in the sestina, whereas others repeat entire lines, as in the villanelle.

The term *rhyme scheme* suggests that the rhyme organizes the structure of a poem. It simultaneously opens up and concludes the sense. It is an ordering, an offering, a binding together.

SEE ALSO *couplet, quatrain, sestina, sonnet, terza rima, villanelle.*

rhythm The word *rhythm* derives from a Greek word meaning "flow." Rhythm is sound in movement. It is related to the pulse, the heartbeat, the way we breathe. It rises and falls. It takes us into ourselves; it takes us out of ourselves. It differentiates us; it unites us to the cosmos.

Rhythm is the combination in English of stressed and unstressed syllables that creates a feeling of fixity and flux, of surprise and inevitability. Rhythm creates a pattern of yearning and expectation, of recurrence and change. It is repetition with a difference. "Repetition in word and phrase and in idea is the very essence of poetry," Theodore Roethke writes ("Some Remarks on Rhythm"). Renewal is "the pivot of lyricism," as Marina Tsvetaeva puts it, comparing the lyrical element to the waves of the sea: "The wave always returns, and always returns as a different wave" ("Poets with History and Poets without History"). I would say with Robert Graves that there is a rhythm of emotion in poetry that conditions the musical rhythm, the patterned energy, the mental bracing and relaxing which comes to us through our sensuous impressions. Rhythm is poetry's way of charging the depths, hitting the fathomless. It is oceanic.

The poem is a muscular and composed thing. It moves like a wave and hypnotizes words into phrases, phrases into lines, lines into stanzas. As readers we simultaneously produce and perceive poetic rhythm. "Rhythm is not measure, or something that is outside us," Octavio Paz writes, "but we ourselves are the ones who flow in the rhythm and rush headlong toward 'something.'" That "something" is a place where we are always arriving, an immanent revelation. "The purpose of rhythm," W. B. Yeats says, "is to prolong the moment of contemplation, the moment when we are both asleep and awake, which is the one moment of creation" ("The Symbolism of Poetry"). Rhythm is a means of re-creating that singular moment of creation, a way of participating in pure time, originary time. It is our immersion in temporality and our transcendence over it.

For a helpful study, see Derek Attridge, *Poetic Rhythm: An Introduction* (1995). For powerful claims, see Robert Hass's essay "Listening and Making" in *Twentieth Century Pleasures* (1984) and Octavio Paz's chapter on rhythm in his splendid defense of poetry, *The Bow and the Lyre* (1973).

scop   An Anglo-Saxon minstrel-poet, attached to the court of a chieftain or king, who both composed his own poems and sang or recited the traditional compositions of others. The scop is akin to the Celtic (Welsh) bard, the Gaelic (Irish) fili, and the Scandinavian skald.

SEE ALSO *bard, skald.*

septet   The seven-line stanza, of varying meter and rhyme, has been utilized by a large number of English poets from Chaucer and Lydgate to William Morris and John Masefield. It magically thrives. It has an odd extra punch—a piercing last line—that moves past the symmetry of any even-numbered stanza. Here is a breathtaking stanza from Thomas Nashe's "A Litany in Time of Plague":

> Beauty is but a flower
> Which wrinkles will devour;
> Brightness falls from the air;
> Queens have died young and fair;
> Dust hath closed Helen's eye.
> I am sick, I must die.
>   Lord, have mercy on us!

The most historically interesting fixed form of the seven-line stanza is *rhyme royal,* an iambic pentameter stanza rhyming *ababbcc,* which was employed with great dignity by Chaucer in *Troilus and Criseyde* and by Shakespeare in "The Rape of Lucrece." Something in the lucky number seven seems to lead to desperation or comedy. W. H. Auden uses it with great panache in "Letter to Lord Byron." Here are two stanzas that self-consciously consider the form:

I want a form that's large enough to swim in,
    And talk on any subject that I choose,
From natural scenery to men and women,
    Myself, the arts, the European news:
    And since she's on a holiday, my Muse
Is out to please, find everything delightful
And only now and then be mildly spiteful.

Ottava rima would, I know be proper,
    The proper instrument on which to pay
My compliments, but I should come a cropper;
    Rhyme-royal's difficult enough to play.
    But if no classics as in Chaucer's day,
At least my modern pieces shall be cheery
Like English bishops on the Quantum Theory.

sestet   The subdivision or last six lines of an Italian sonnet, following the first eight lines, the octave. It is also applied somewhat indiscriminately (along with the terms *sexain, sixain, sextain, sextet,* and *hexastich*) to the different varieties of the six-line stanza, such as the sestina and the so-called "Venus and Adonis" stanza (iambic pentameter: rhyming *ababcc*) named after Shakespeare's poem. Robert Burns mastered the Scottish stanza, a form found in medieval Provençal poems and in miracle plays of the Middle Ages, to such a degree that it came to be called the Burns stanza, or Burns meter. (The Burns stanza intermingles two rhymes and meters: it rhymes *aaabab;* lines 1, 2, 3, and 5 are tetrameter, lines 2 and 6 are dimeter.) Notice how the first three lines build to a crescendo which is then punctuated by the punch of the fourth line and the epigrammatic cut of the sixth one. Here are three central stanzas from "Epistle to John Lapraik, an Old Scottish Bard":

What's a' your jargon o' your schools,
Your Latin names for horns an' stools;
If honest nature made you fools,
        What sairs your grammars?
Ye'd better ta'en up spades and shools,
        Or knappin'-hammers

A set o' dull, conceited hashes,
Confuse their brains in college classes!
They gang in stirks, and come out asses,
        Plain truth to speak;
And syne they think to climb Parnassus
        By dint o' Greek!

Gie me ae spark o' Nature's fire,
That's a' the learning I desire;
Then tho' I drudge thro' dub an' mire
        At pleugh or cart,
My Muse, though hamely in attire,
        May touch the heart.

SEE ALSO *sestina, stanza.*

sestina   The sestina, an intricate verse form created and mastered by the Provençal poets, is a thirty-nine-line poem consisting of six six-line stanzas and one three-line envoi (or "send-off"). The six end words are repeated in a prescribed order, as end words in each of the subsequent stanzas. The concluding tercet brings together all six of the end words. The numerological scheme, which once may have had magical significance, has the precision and elegance of musical (or mathematical) form:

> stanza one: 1, 2, 3, 4, 5, 6
> two: 6, 1, 5, 2, 4, 3
> three: 3, 6, 4, 1, 2, 5
> four: 5, 3, 2, 6, 1, 4
> five: 4, 5, 1, 3, 6, 2
> six: 2, 4, 6, 5, 3, 1
> envoi: 5, 3, 1 or 1, 3, 5

Arnaut Daniel is credited with inventing the sestina, a form widely practiced by other Provençal poets as well as by Dante and Petrarch. Sir Philip Sidney put the form to good use in *Arcadia* (1590). The sestina has had particular fascination for Victorian and modern poets, perhaps because it generates a narrative even as it circles back on itself and recurs like a song. My own anthology of late nineteenth- and twentieth-century examples would begin with Swinburne's remarkable feat, "The Complaint of Lisa," a rhyming double sestina with twelve twelve-line stanzas and a six-line envoi. It would include examples by Rudyard Kipling and Edmund Gosse, by Ezra Pound and W. H. Auden, by Elizabeth Bishop ("Sestina"), John Ashbery ("Farm Implements and Rutabagas in a Landscape"), Alan Ansen ("A Fit of Something Against Something"), Donald Justice ("Here in Katmandu"), Donald Hall ("Sestina"), Anthony Hecht ("The Book of Yolek"), Marilyn Hacker ("Untoward Occurrence at Embassy Poetry Reading"), Donald Revell ("Near Rhinebeck"), and Deborah Digges ("Hall of Souls"). James Cummins adapts the form to American popular culture in his first book, *The Whole Truth* (1986), which consists entirely of twenty-five sestinas revolving around the characters in the Perry Mason television series. Here the Provençal form indecorously meets the hackneyed detective story and shimmers with comic life.

simile   The explicit comparison of one thing to another, using the word *as* or *like*—as when Robert Burns writes:

> My love is like a red, red rose
> That's newly sprung in June:
> My love is like the melodie
> That's sweetly play'd in tune.

The essence of simile is similitude; it is likeness and unlikeness, urging a comparison of two different things. A good simile depends on a certain heterogeneity between the elements being compared. "You smell of time as a Bible smells of thumbs," the Irish poet Mebdh McGuckian writes, thus comparing the odor that clings to someone aging to the smell imprinted on a holy book that has been paged through by hundreds of people over the years.

Similes are comparable to metaphors, but the difference between them is not merely grammatical, depending on the explicit use of *as* or *like*. It is a difference in significance, in kind. Metaphor asserts an identity. It says "A poem is a meteor" (Wallace Stevens); it says A equals B and in doing so relies on condensation and compression. By contrast, the simile is a form of analogical thinking. It says: "Poetry is made in a bed like love" (André Breton); it says A is *like* B and thereby works by opening outward. There is a digressive impulse in similes that keeps extending out to take in new things. "The embrace of poetry like the embrace of flesh" (Breton).

The simile asserts a likeness between unlike things, it maintains their comparability, but it also draws attention to their differences, thus affirming a state of division. When Shakespeare asks, "Shall I compare thee to a summer's day?" he draws attention to the issue, the artificial process, of figuration. The reader participates in making meaning through simile, in establishing the nature of an unforeseen analogy, in evaluating the aptness of unexpected resemblance.

SEE ALSO *analogy, metaphor, trope.*

skald   (or scald) This Old Norse word for a poet is generally applied to Norwegian or Icelandic court poets from the ninth to the thirteenth centuries. Longfellow introduces "The Saga of King Olaf":

> Legends that once were told or sung
> In many a smoky fireside nook
> Of Iceland, in the ancient day,
> By wandering Saga-man or Scald...

sonnet   The fourteen-line rhyming poem was invented in southern Italy around 1235 or so ("Eternal glory to the inventor of the sonnet," Paul Valéry declared) and has had an astonishingly durable life ever since. The word *sonnet* derives from the Italian *sonetto*, meaning "a little sound" or "a little song," but the stateliness of the form belies the modesty of the word's derivation. The sonnet is a small vessel capable of plunging tremendous depths. It is one of the enabling forms of human inwardness.

Something about the spaciousness and brevity of the fourteen-line poem seems to suit the contours of rhetorical argument, especially when the subject is erotic love. The form becomes a medium for the poet to explore his or her capacity to bring together feeling and thought, the lyrical and the discursive.

The meter of the sonnet tends to follow the prevalent meter of the language in which it is written: in English, iambic pentameter; in French, the alexandrine; in Italian, the hendecasyllable. The two main types of sonnet form in English are the *English* or *Shakespearean sonnet* (so-called because Shakespeare was its greatest practitioner), which consists of three quatrains and a couplet usually rhyming *abab, cdcd, efef, gg,* and the *Italian* or *Petrarchan sonnet* (so-called because Petrarch was its greatest practitioner), which consists of an octave (eight lines rhyming *abbaabba*), and a sestet (six lines rhyming *cdecde*). Italian readers coined the term *volta* (or "turn") to refer to the rhetorical division and shift between the opening eight lines and the concluding six.

The Petrarchan sonnet probably developed out of the Sicilian *strambotto,* a popular song form consisting of two quatrains and two tercets. The sonnet was widely practiced throughout the later Middle Ages by all the Italian lyric poets, especially the *stilnovisti*—Guinizelli, Cavalcanti, and Dante, who used it to reinvent the love poem as a medium of quasi-religious devotion to a beloved lady, a *donna.* (Giosuè Carducci wrote that Dante gave the sonnet "the movement of cherubim, and surrounded it with gold and azure air.")

Petrarch's 317 sonnets to Laura are a kind of encyclopedia of passion. (Shelley called them "spells which unseal the inmost enchanted fountains of the delight which is the grief of love.") The Petrarchan sonnet invites an asymmetrical two-part division of the argument.

Its rhyming is impacted and it tends to build an obsessive feeling in the octave which is let loose in the sestet. "One of the emotional archetypes of the Petrarchan sonnet structure," as Paul Fussell puts it, "is the pattern of sexual pressure and release."

Sir Thomas Wyatt and the Earl of Surrey imported the Petrarchan form into England early in the sixteenth century. Surrey later established the rhyme scheme *abab, cdcd, efef, gg*. George Gascoigne described this new version of the sonnet in 1735:

> Sonnets are of fourteene lynes, every lyne conteyning tenne syllables. The first twelve do ryme in staves of foure lynes by crosse metre, and the last two ryming together do conclude the whole.

"SHAKE-SPEARE'S SONNETS. Neuer before imprinted" appeared in 1609, and these 154 sonnets comprise one of the high-water marks of English poetry. The Shakespearean sonnet invites a more symmetrical division of thought into three equal quatrains and a summarizing couplet. It is well-balanced, well-suited to what Rosalie Colie calls Shakespeare's "particularly brainy, calculated incisiveness." The form enables a precision of utterance and freedom of forensic argument. It also offers more flexibility in rhyming, which is crucial since Italian is so much richer in rhyme than English. (Nonetheless, "Ryme is no impediment to his conceit," Samuel Daniel wrote in a 1603 defense of rhyme, "but rather giues him wings to mount and carries him, not out of his course, but as it were beyond his power to a farre happier flight.") The poet using this highly reasonable, toughly reasoning form can also create wild disturbances within the prescribed form. This seems to work especially well for closely reasoned and ultimately highly unreasonable and even obsessional subjects, like erotic love.

Over the centuries poets have proved ingenious at reinventing—reinscribing—the formal chamber of the sonnet. The Elizabethan poet Edmund Spenser developed an interlacing version of the sonnet called the *link* or *Spenserian sonnet*. It interlinks rhymes and concludes with a binding couplet (*abab, bcbc, cdcd, ee*). The Miltonic sonnet retains the octave rhyme scheme of the Petrarchan sonnet, but doesn't turn at the sestet and varies its rhyme scheme, thus opening up the form. Milton further extended the form in a *tailed sonnet,* composed of twenty lines. He turned the sonnet away from love to occasional and political subjects ("When the Assault Was Intended to the City," "On the Late Massacre in Piedmont").

The sonnet was virtually extinct after 1650 until the romantic poets revitalized it. How much poorer English poetry would be without Wordsworth's "Composed upon Westminster Bridge, September 3, 1802" and Keats's "On First Looking into Chapman's Homer" and Shelley's "Ozymandias." So, too, in France the sonnet was revived by Gautier and Baudelaire and further developed by Mallarmé, Rimbaud, and Valéry. George Meredith lengthened the traditional sonnet to sixteen lines in his startling fifty-poem sequence about the breakup of his marriage, *Modern Love* (1862). Gerard Manley Hopkins, whose so-called terrible sonnets are masterpieces of despair, also invented a form he called a *curtal sonnet*—literally, a sonnet cut short to ten and a half lines, such as "Pied Beauty" which ends with a simple directive: "Praise him." Hopkins also experimented with metrics in "Spelt from Sibyl's Leaves" ("the longest sonnet ever made"), which employs eight-stress lines and begins:

> Earnest, earthless, equal, attuneable, ǀ vaulty, voluminous, . . . stupendous
> Evening strains to be tíme's vást, ǀ womb-of-all, home-of-all, hearse-of-all night.

One thinks of Verlaine's "inverted" sonnets and Rupert Brooke's "Sonnet Reversed" (1911), which send up the tradition of idealized love, of Robert Frost's one-sentence sonnet "The Silken Tent" and W. H. Auden's sonnets about A. E. Housman, Arthur Rimbaud, and Edward Lear, a form used equally well by Jorge Luis Borges, who wrote wonderful sonnets about Ralph Waldo Emerson and Walt Whitman ("Emerson" and "Camden 1892"). There are five edgy, almost hallucinatory one- and two-sentence sonnets in Denis Johnson's *The Incognito Lounge* (1982). John Hollander's *Powers of Thirteen* (1983) employs a variety of the sonnet form that consists of thirteen unrhymed lines of thirteen syllables each ("a thirteen by thirteen," he calls it, in which "the final line, uncoupled, can have the last word"). Mona Van Duyn's *Firefall* (1983) includes a series of beguiling short poems she calls "minimalist sonnets" along with a few she baptizes (oxymoronically) "extended minimalist sonnets." "Of all the forms," she writes, "the sonnet seems most available to poets for deconstruction." In his poem "Post-Coitum Tristesse: A Sonnet," Brad Leithauser cleverly strips down the form to fourteen rhyming syllables (one per line) and, in so doing, takes the love poem all the way back to a sigh ("Hm..."). No wonder Borges said that "there is something mysterious about the sonnet."

There is a sense of permanence and fragility, of spaciousness and constriction, about the sonnet form that has always had poets brooding about it, as in John Donne's well-known lines from "The Canonization":

> We'll build in sonnets pretty roomes;
> As well a well wrought urne becomes
> The greatest ashes, as halfe-acre tombes...

Poets have written a number of stylish sonnets about the sonnet itself. The form becomes the muse of these poems, which include Wordsworth's "Nuns Fret Not" and "Scorn Not the Sonnet"; Keats's "On the Sonnet" ("Let us find out, if we must be constrain'd / Sandals more interwoven and complete / To fit the naked foot of poesy"); Edwin Arlington Robinson's "Sonnet"; Robert Burns's joyous meditation on the quintessential *fourteen-ness* of the sonnet form, "A Sonnet upon Sonnets" ("Fourteen, a sonateer thy praises sings / What magic mys'tries in that number lie!"); and Dante Gabriel Rossetti's peerless prefatory sonnet to *The House of Life,* which begins

> A sonnet is a moment's monument,—
> Memorial from the Soul's eternity
> To one dead deathless hour....

Every great sonnet is itself a moment's monument to the form itself. As Northrop Frye wrote about the Shakespearean sonnet, "The true father or shaping spirit of the poem is the form of the poem itself, and this form is a manifestation of the spirit of poetry." See Michael Spiller, *The Development of the Sonnet* (1992).

sonnet cycle   The sonnet tends to be a compulsive form, and the sonnet cycle (or *sequence*) consists of a series of sonnets on a particular theme to a particular person. Love is often the obsessive theme of this petition for emotional recognition. The great advantage of the cycle is that it allows the poet to record every aspect and mood of the experience, to explore feeling in detail, and to analyze the progress of attachment, the ups and downs of the affair. Yet each individual sonnet maintains its energy and integrity. Thus the cycle combines the rhetorical intensity of the short poem with the thematic scope of the long poem or story.

Some key early examples: Dante's *Vita nuova* (1293), which has extensive prose links; Petrarch's *Canzoniere* or *Rime* (1360), a sequence of 317 sonnets and 40 other poems in praise of one woman, Laura; Ronsard's *Amours* (1552–1584); Sidney's quasi-narrative *Astrophel and*

Stella (1591): "My Muse may well grudge at my heart's heav'nly joy"; Spenser's *Amoretti* (1595); Shakespeare's *Sonnets* (1609): "Who will believe my verse in time to come?"; and Donne's Holy Sonnets (1633).

There were no British sonnets before about 1530 and very few after 1650 until the romantic revival of the form. Some key romantic and postromantic examples of the sequence: Wordsworth's *Ecclesiastical Sonnets* (1822); Rossetti's *The House of Life* (1881): "A sonnet is a coin: its face reveals / The soul,—its converse, to what Power 'tis due"; Elizabeth Barrett Browning's popular *Sonnets from the Portuguese* (1850); Dylan Thomas's ten-part "Altarwise by Owl-Light" (1936), which William York Tindall called "obscurely magnificent in sound and shape"; W. H. Auden's "Sonnets from China" (1938); Geoffrey Hill's "Funeral Music" (1968); and Seamus Heaney's "Glanmore Sonnets" (1979).

One specialized version of the sonnet sequence is the *crown of sonnets*, which consists of seven interlocked poems. The final line of each lyric becomes the first line of the succeeding one, and the last line of the seventh sonnet becomes the first line of the opening poem. The whole is offered as a crown (a panegyric) to the one addressed. The repetitions and linkages within the larger circular structure are well suited to obsessional reiterations of supplication and praise. A crowning fervent example is the opening sequence of Donne's Holy Sonnets, which begins and ends with the line "*Deigne at my hands this crown of prayer and praise.*" For a fine recent example, see J. D. McClatchy's *Kilim* (1987), a tapestry set against the terrorist violence of the Middle East.

In our century poets have also revitalized the sonnet sequence by revising and inverting some of its key generic conventions regarding gender. One thinks of the eleven explicitly homoerotic *Sonnets of Dark Love* that García Lorca composed in 1935, or of how the American female lyricists of the 1920s (Elinor Wylie, Edna St. Vincent Millay, and others), most of whom have been written out of modernist literary histories, radicalized the traditional subject of the sonnet and the sonnet sequence by making the female speaker a ravenous lover—the authorizing presence—in quest of the beloved. So, too, such poets as Edwin Morgan (*Glasgow Sonnets,* 1972) and Tony Harrison (*From the School of Eloquence,* 1978) have used a tough-minded vernacular to deploy the sonnet as a site of class conflict.

In our time many poets have used the sonnet sequence as a vehicle to regain some of the scope and territory of prose fiction. One thinks of Gwendolyn Brooks's "The Womanhood" (1949), which intermingles sonnets with ballads and other poems, and James Merrill's witty masterpiece of childhood, "The Broken Home" (1966), of John Berryman's "Sonnets to Chris" (1947, 1966), which trace an ecstatic, edgy adulterous affair ("The original fault was whether wickedness / was soluble in art"), and Robert Lowell's three books of highly personal unrhymed sonnets, *Notebook* (1969), *For Lizzie and Harriet* (1973), and *The Dolphin* (1973). "Even with this license, I fear I have failed to avoid the themes and gigantism of the sonnet," Lowell wrote. Thus the intensity and spaciousness of the form continues to incite poets.

spell   An incantation or charm designed to produce magical effects. "It is exceedingly well / To give a common word the *spell*," the eighteenth-century poet Christopher Smart writes, punning on the word *spell*. Tribal peoples everywhere have believed that the act of putting words in a certain rhythmic order has magical potency, a power released when the words are chanted aloud.

SEE ALSO *charm, chant, incantation.*

spondee   A poetic foot consisting of two equally accented syllables, as in the word he*́*artbe*́*at. Spondees create an emphatic stress, a hammer beat, but seldom control an entire rhythm in English. The first, third, and fifth lines are spondaic in this anonymous nursery rhyme:

One, two
Buckle my shoe;
Three, four,
Shut the door;
Five, six,
Pick up sticks...

Since stress is always relative in English, there may be no perfect spondee.
SEE ALSO *foot, meter.*

stanza   The natural unit of the lyric: a group or sequence of lines arranged in a pattern. A stanzaic pattern is traditionally defined by the meter and rhyme scheme, traditionally considered repeatable throughout a work.

The word *stanza* means "room" in Italian—"a station," "a stopping place"—and each stanza in a poem is like a room in a house, a lyric dwelling place. Each has an identity, each a structural place in the whole. As the line is a single unit of meaning, so the stanza comprises a larger rhythmic and thematic sequence, a larger emotional unit. It's a basic division comparable to the paragraph in prose, but more discontinuous, more insistent as a separate melodic and rhetorical unit. In written poems stanzas are separated by white space, and this division on the printed page gives the poem a visible pattern, a particular visual reality. But the fact that *stave* is another name for stanza also suggests its early associations with song.

A stanza may be any length. A stanza of uneven length and irregular pattern—of fluid form—is sometimes called a *verse paragraph*. The *monostich* is a stanza—a whole poem—consisting of just one line. (The Spanish form the *mote* or *glosa* is a single line containing a complete thought.) After that, there is the *couplet* (two-line stanza); *tercet* (three-line stanza); *quatrain* (four-line); *quintet* (five-line); *sestet* (six-line); *septet* (seven-line); and *octave* (eight-line). There are stanzas named after the individual poets, such as the *Spenserian stanza* (the nine-line pattern Spenser invented for *The Faerie Queene* and Shelley adopted for *The Revolt of Islam,* not because he considered it a "finer model of poetical harmony than the blank verse of Shakespeare and Milton, but because in the latter there is no shelter for mediocrity; you must either succeed or fail"). Each stanza has its own distinctive features, its own music, its own internal history that informs and haunts later usage.
SEE ALSO *meter, rhyme, strophe* and *couplet, tercet, quatrain, quintet, sestet, septet, octave.*

stichic   A stichic poem is composed as a continuous sequence of lines without any division of those lines into regular stanzas. It is contrasted to strophic organization where the lines are patterned in stanzas. *Paradise Lost, The Prelude,* and *Four Quarters* are stichic; *The Faerie Queene,* "Ode to a Nightingale," and "Asphodel, That Greeny Flower" are strophic. If subdivided at all, the blocks of a stichic poem are called stanzas of uneven length or verse paragraphs. The tendency toward stichic verse is particularly strong in narrative and descriptive poetry, in long poems (such as A. R. Ammons's *Tape for the Turn of the Year,* 1965, John Ashbery's *Flow Chart,* 1991, and W. S. Merwin's *The Folding Cliffs: A Narrative of 19th-Century Hawaii,* 1998) with the wide sweep of prose.
SEE ALSO *stanza, strophe.*

strophe   A term for stanza or verse paragraph. A poem is traditionally considered strophic when its lines are arranged into stanzaic patterns (stichic when not). The word *strophe* (from the Greek for "turning") originally applied to the opening section (and every third succeeding section) of the Greek choral ode, which the chorus chanted while moving across the stage. This movement was followed by the antistrophe, an identical countermovement, and an epode, recited while the chorus was standing still.

SEE ALSO *ode, stanza, stichic.*

surrealism   The convulsive phenomenon known as *dada* was revitalized and transformed into the more durable movement of surrealism in France in the 1920s. The term *surréaliste* was coined by Guillaume Apollinaire in 1917 to suggest a dramatic attempt to go beyond the limits—the limitations—of an agreed-upon "reality." André Breton used the term *surrealism* ("superrealism" or "above reality") in 1924 in the first of three surrealist manifestoes. ("I believe in the future resolution of these two states, dream and reality, which are seemingly so contradictory, into a kind of absolute reality, a *surreality.*")

The surrealists were apostles of what Breton called "beloved imagination." They hungered for the marvelous and believed in the revolutionary power of erotic desire and "mad love," of dreams, fantasies, hallucinations. They freed the mind from the shackles of rational logic and explored the subterranean depths, the deeper reality, of the unconscious, the night mind. They cultivated a condition of lucid trance or delirium and experimented with automatic writing—that is, writing attempted without any conscious control, as under hypnosis. (W. B. Yeats conducted similar experiments with George Hyde-Lees after their marriage in 1922, and these séances eventuated in *A Vision.*) The surrealists believed in the possibilities of chance, of emotion induced by free association and surprising juxtapositions, as when Lautréamont had called something "Beautiful as the chance meeting, on a dissection table, of a sewing machine and an umbrella."

The surrealists were scandalized by the repressiveness of society, and thus scandalized society in return. They wanted to change the human condition. A practical, political dimension entered the movement in 1925, linking economic revolution with mental liberation (priority was always given to mental experiments), and a problematic relationship developed with the Communist party which never quite flowered into a full-scale alliance. The surrealists' goal was inner freedom. As André Breton put it in the second manifesto (1929):

> The idea of surrealism tends simply to the total recuperation of our psychic forces by a means which is no other than a vertiginous descent within ourselves, the systematic illumination of hidden places, the progressive darkening of all other places, the perpetual rambling in the depths of the forbidden zone.

The surrealists reiterated their faith in love, liberty, and the arts. (Robert Desnos called one work *La liberté ou l'amour!*; Paul Éluard entitled another *L'amour la poésie*).

The major surrealists in poetry: André Breton, Louis Aragon, Robert Desnos, Paul Éluard, Philippe Soupault, Benjamin Peret. In the visual arts: Man Ray, Picabia, de Chirico, Masson, Tanguy, Ernst, Dali. In film: Luis Buñuel. In theater: Antonin Artaud. Breton acknowledged that surrealism was the "prehensile tail" of romanticism. The surrealists recognized their ongoing debts to the Marquis de Sade (1740–1814) and Gérard de Nerval (1808–1855), who first used the term *supernaturalism,* to Charles Baudelaire and Stéphane Mallarmé, who considered the poet a magician, to Rimbaud, Apollinaire, and Freud.

Surrealism dissolved as a cohesive movement in the late 1930s, but the United States benefited from the wartime presence—the cultural transfusion—of some of the leading surrealists. In a broad sense, surrealism means a love of dreams and fantasies, a taste for strange marvels and black humor, an eagerness to take the vertiginous descent into the self in quest of the secret forces of the psyche, a faith in the value of chance encounters and free play, a belief in the liberating powers of eros, of beloved imagination.

For primary material, see André Breton's *Manifestoes of Surrealism* (1969). A good overview of the movement is Maurice Nadeau's *The History of Surrealism* (1965). A good anthology of translations from the French poets is Michael Benedikt's *The Poetry of Surrealism* (1974). To gauge some of the effects in our language, see Edward B. Germain, ed., *English and American Surrealist Poetry* (1978).

SEE ALSO *dada, romanticism.*

symbol   The word *symbol* derives from the Greek verb *symballein,* meaning "to put together," and the noun *symbolon,* meaning "mark," "emblem," "token," or "sign." In the classical world the *symbolon* was a sign of agreement, a concrete object that represented a pledge. It was a half coin or half of a knucklebone carried by one person as a token of identity or a mark of obligation to someone holding the other half. Each represented a whole. When the two halves were rejoined they composed one knucklebone, a complete meaning.

Broadly speaking, a symbol is anything that signifies, or stands for, something else. Dr. Johnson defines it as "that which comprehends in its figure a representation of something else." Thus a dove is both a graceful bird *and* a universal symbol of peace. A rose is both a literal flower ("A rose is a rose is a rose," Gertrude Stein reminds us in a famous tautology) *and* the most commonly used floral symbol in the West.

Words are symbols. They are also textured entities. In poetry it's critical to remember that a *rose* is first of all a one-syllable, four-letter noun with a specific sound that ovals the mouth when you say it aloud. It has an acoustic impact, as when Wordsworth seals it as a rhyme in his "Intimations" ode:

> The Rainbow comes and goes,
> And lovely is the Rose . . .

The rose here is a word that stands for a literal flower, but it is also something more, something else, like the transient rainbow. (The loveliness of Wordsworth's rose also alludes to the emblematic nature of the flower in Waller's well-known seventeenth-century poem "Go, Lovely Rose" and echoes the anonymous fourteenth-century lyric "Of a rose, a louely rose, of a rose is al myn song.") The literal and the literary symbolic work together in a poem. A poet writing about the beauty of a single rose can also give us a whiff, an intimation, of eternity. ("The greatness of a poem does not depend on the magnitude of its theme," García Lorca explained in a lecture on Góngora: "The form and fragrance of just one rose can be made to render an impression of eternity.") We bring to our reading of a poem all the symbolic connotations and meanings available to us, but the symbol should first be understood in terms of how it works as a device within a poem itself. Then we can see, for example, how in a series of symbolist poems in the 1890s Yeats was writing about the scent, shape, and petaled beauty of a rose even as he employed it as a major Rosicrucian and alchemical symbol, a sign of the eternal purity of love.

The *Princeton Encyclopedia of Poetry and Poetics* summarizes that in literary usage a symbol refers to "a manner of representation in which what is shown (normally referring to something material) means, by virtue of association, something *more* or something *else* (normally referring to something immaterial)." How a thing can be both itself and something else is one of the great mysteries of poetry. In poetry, a symbol offers a surplus of resonance, of significance, since a poem can have great suggestive power, like a dream. It can also have the strange precision of a dream, what Baudelaire termed "evocative bewitchment" and Yeats called "indefinable and yet precise emotions." In "The Symbolism of Poetry" (1900) Yeats called these lines by Burns, which he altered slightly in memory, "perfectly symbolical":

> The white moon is setting behind the white wave,
> And Time is setting with me, O!

Yeats said:

> Take from them the whiteness of the moon and of the wave, whose relation to the
> setting of Time is too subtle for the intellect, and you take from them their beauty.
> But, when all are together, moon and wave and whiteness and setting Time and the
> last melancholy cry, they evoke an emotion which cannot be evoked by any other
> arrangement of colours and sounds and forms. We may call this metaphorical writ-
> ing, but it is better to call it symbolical writing.

SEE ALSO *allegory, symbolism.*

symbolism   Initially called *"idealism,"* symbolism was a central literary movement that
thrived in France between the 1870s and the 1890s. The leading symbolist poets, Paul Ver-
laine, Arthur Rimbaud, and Stéphane Mallarmé, along with the key figures Jules Laforgue
and Tristan Corbière, were at the forefront of the modern poetic tradition. The symbolist
poets opposed all forms of naturalism and realism. They craved a poetry of suggestion rather
than direct statement and treated everything in the external world as a condition of soul.
They sought to repress or obfuscate one kind of reality, the quotidian world, in order to
attain a more permanent reality, a world of ideal forms and essences. They believed that a
magical suggestiveness (what Rimbaud termed *l'alchimie du verbe*) could best be achieved by
fusing images and senses (see *synaesthesia*) and bringing poetry as close as possible to music.
Thus Verlaine's poem "Art poétique" advocates "music before everything." (Walter Pater
formulated a parallel doctrine when he asserted that "all art constantly aspires towards the
condition of music.")

Baudelaire was one of the chief progenitors of the movement. His sonnet "Correspon-
dances" (in *Les Fleurs du mal*, 1857) envisioned nature as a "forest of symbols" and suggested
a correspondence between the phenomenal world and the ideal one. (Rimbaud followed
Baudelaire and anticipated the surrealists when he posited that "The poet makes himself *a
seer* by a long, immense, and reasoned *derangement* of all the senses.") Correspondence was
achieved through heightened concentration on the symbol, which had what Maeterlinck
called a *"force occulte."*

In 1891, Mallarmé defined symbolism:

> To name an object is to suppress three-quarters of the delight of the poem, which
> consists in the pleasure of guessing little by little; to *suggest* it, that is the dream. It is
> the perfect use of this mystery that constitutes the symbol: to evoke an object, grad-
> ually in order to reveal a state of the soul, or, inversely, to choose an object and from
> it identify a state of the soul, by a series of deciphering operations.... There must al-
> ways be enigma in poetry.

Enigma widens the space for daydreaming. It loosens the intellect and invites poetic reverie,
readerly imagination.

The symbolist movement reverberated around the globe. Everywhere it initiated poets
into its mysteries. The *Princeton Encyclopedia of Poetry and Poetics* lists some of the key figures
it influenced: W. B. Yeats, Arthur Symons, Oscar Wilde, Ernest Dowson, and George
Russell (Æ) in the British Isles; Stefan George and Rainer Maria Rilke in Germany; Hugo
von Hofmannsthal in Austria; Innokenty Annensky, Alexander Blok, and Andrey Bely in

Russia; Antonio Machado, Juan Ramón Jiménez, and Jorge Guillén in Spain; Rubén Darío in Nicaragua; T. S. Eliot, Ezra Pound, Amy Lowell, Hilda Doolittle (H.D.), Hart Crane, e. e. cummings, and Wallace Stevens in the United States.

Whoever believes in the occult or spiritual power of the poetic Word is an heir to the symbolists.

For two key texts, see Arthur Symons, *The Symbolist Movement in Literature* (1899), and Edmund Wilson, *Axel's Castle* (1931).

synaesthesia   A blending of sensations; the phenomenon of describing one sense in terms of another. The specific term dates only to the late nineteenth century, but the device may be as old as literature itself. Thus *The Iliad* compares the voices of aged Trojans to the "lily-like" voices of cicadas; *The Odyssey* evokes the "honey-voice" of the Siren; the Bible refers to "seeing" a voice and "tasting" the word of God.

Baudelaire popularized the notion of synaesthesia with his compelling idea that "the sounds, the scents, the colors correspond" ("Correspondances"). In his poem "Vowels," Rimbaud famously assigned colors to each of the vowels:

> Black A, white E, red I, green U, blue O—vowels,
> Some day I will open your silent pregnancies...
>   (translated by Paul Schmidt)

tercet   A verse unit of three lines. The tercet was historically defined as three lines containing rhyme, but the meanings of words change, and most contemporary poets use it as the name for any three-line stanza, with or without rhyme. It thus becomes a synonym for *triplet*, a word that seems to be becoming antiquated.

There are many kinds of three-line stanzas. One thinks of three lines ending with the same rhyme word, as in this lovely stanza from Robert Herrick's "Upon Julia's Clothes":

> Whenas in silk my Julia goes,
> Then, then, methinks, how sweetly flows
> That liquefaction of her clothes.

The interlocking three-line stanzas of terza rima are called tercets, as are the three-line stanzas in the villanelle. William Carlos Williams exploited the tercet as a kind of descending staircase in many of his best poems, such as "To Elsie" and "Asphodel, That Greeny Flower."

The tercet has never been as widely employed as the couplet and the quatrain, but it seems distinctive because each stanza has a beginning, a middle, and an end. The number three also has magical residue.

SEE ALSO *terza rima, villanelle.*

terza rima   A verse form of interlocking three-line stanzas rhyming *aba, bcb, cdc,* etc. The form was invented by Dante Alighieri for *The Divine Comedy,* using the hendecasyllabic (eleven-syllable) line common to Italian poetry. Rhyming the first and third lines gives each tercet a sense of temporary closure; rhyming the second line with the first and last lines of the next stanza generates a strong feeling of propulsion. The effect is both open-ended and conclusive, like moving through a series of interpenetrating rooms or going down a set of winding stairs: you are always traveling forward while looking back.

Shelley's "The Triumph of Life" is the finest English poem ever written in the form. The first eight lines capture its spiraling motion:

Swift as a spirit hastening to his task
Of glory and of good, the Sun sprang forth
Rejoicing in his splendor, and the mask

Of darkness fell from the awakened Earth—
The smokeless altars of the mountain snows
Flamed above crimson clouds, and at the birth

Of light, the Ocean's orison arose,
To which the birds tempered their matin lay.

trochee   A metrical foot of two syllables, the first stressed, the second unstressed, as in the word *lúcky̆*. The trochee starts with a downbeat, as in the word *poet*. (There are two trochees in the title of the Scottish poet Hugh MacDiarmid's autobiography *Lucky Poet*.) Here are two four-beat, rhyming trochaic lines from J. V. Cunningham's poem "With a Copy of Swift's Works":

> Underneath this pretty cover
> Lies Vanessa's, Stella's lover.

Longfellow's "Song of Hiawatha" is a celebrated example of extended trochaic meter, an insistent rhythm that encourages chanting.

Since the sixteenth century the trochee, the opposite of the iamb, has been mostly employed to provide emphasis, substitution, and variation, in normative iambic lines, as in Milton's companion poems "L'Allegro" and "Il Penseroso." It is the foot of reversal.

SEE ALSO *foot, iamb, iambic pentameter, meter.*

trope   A figure of speech. A way of extending the meaning of words beyond the literal. *Turn* is an older English word for trope, and tropes have the capacity to turn—to change and deepen—our sense of words and things. They can radically alter our sense of language and experience, and thus of ourselves. It's commonly said that figurative language—saying one thing and also meaning another—is an important resource for poetry, but in truth it is much more than that because it is at the heart of poetic thinking.

The master tropes, including metaphor, simile, and synecdoche, have been considered and taught for at least twenty-five centuries. *Metaphor*, the most crucial and widely employed type of trope, creates a radical likeness, an imaginary identity, between different things, as when Shelley says "a poet is a nightingale." *Simile* is the explicit comparison between two different things, using the word *as* or *like*, as when Wordsworth declares, "I wandered lonely as a cloud." *Synecdoche*, a form of metonymy, substitutes the name of one thing with something else closely associated with it, as when we say "the heart" and mean "the emotions" ("be quiet, heart!" Paul Goodman cries out when he sees "the Lordly Hudson"). Christopher Marlowe employs a synecdoche in *Doctor Faustus* when he asks

> Was this the face that launched a thousand ships
> And burnt the topless towers of Ilium?

The Russian poet Andrey Bely used both a simile and a metaphor when he informed the younger Marina Tsvetaeva, "A poet has to be condemned to poetry like a wolf to his howling, but you're a bird that keeps on singing."

Tropes depend on a collaborative interpretive process between writer and reader. They depend on personal impressions and interpretations which readers discover and experience for themselves.

SEE ALSO *metaphor, metonymy, personification, simile.*

troubadour   The troubadours (their name derives from a Provençal word meaning both "to find" and "to invent") were poets who traveled from one court to another and flourished in Southern France, northern Italy, and Spain between 1100 and 1350. They are akin to trouvères (court poets who thrived in northern and central France during the twelfth and thirteenth centuries), jongleurs (itinerant minstrels, jugglers, and acrobats who entertained at the courts of medieval France and Norman England), and minnesingers (wandering lyricists who flourished in Germany between the twelfth and fourteenth centuries).

The troubadours, some of whom were known by name (Arnaut Daniel, Bertran de Born), wrote amorous poems of stunning technical virtuosity, and were largely responsible for the phenomenon of courtly love. They had a powerful influence over the development of the European love lyric. See Frederick Goldin, trans. and ed., *Lyrics of the Troubadours and Trouvères: An Anthology and a History* (1973).

SEE ALSO *aubade, sestina.*

ubi sunt   A Latin phrase ("where are ... ?") used as the opening line or refrain in a great number of medieval Latin poems. The poet used the motif to catalog the names of those dead and gone, meditating on the fragility of beauty and transitoriness of life. François Villon's "Ballade des dames du temps jadis" is the greatest medieval example. Its famous refrain line

> Mais où sont les neiges d'antan?

was rendered into English by Dante Gabriel Rossetti as

> But where are the snows of yester-year?

in his translation of "The Ballad of Dead Ladies." The *ubi sunt* theme recurs in Edgar Lee Masters's *Spoon River Anthology* and in Robert Hayden's splendid "Elegies for Paradise Valley."

vatic   The word *vatic*, which means inspired with the power of prophecy, derives from the Latin term *vates* ("prophet"). From earliest times, the poet has often been considered a visionary, a divinely inspired prophet or seer, a *vates*. There was a class of Gaulish druids called *vates*. The vatic impulse is signaled in poetry whenever a poet speaks in a prophetic voice beyond the social realm—as when Shelley calls out to the west wind, "Be thou, Spirit fierce, / My spirit! Be thou me, impetuous one!" ("Ode to the West Wind") or D. H. Lawrence testifies, "Not I, not I, but the wind that blows through me!" ("Song of a Man Who Has Come Through").

verse   A metrical composition. The word *verse* is traditionally thought to derive from the Latin *versus*, meaning a "line," "row," or "furrow." It may alternately derive from the Latin *vertere*, "to turn." Verse is metrical writing (see *meter*). The poet disturbs language, arranging words into lines, into rows, turning them over, turning them toward each other, shaping them into patterns. Metrical writing is a way of charging sound, of energizing syllables and marking words, of rhythmically marking time. Such formal writing is markedly and perhaps even metaphysically different from prose. "Verse," Sir Philip Sidney wrote, "being in its selfe sweete and orderly, and being best for memory, the only handle of knowledge, it must be in jest that any man can speak against it."

Verse has been generally distinguished from prose, but it has also sometimes been differentiated from poetry. Thus Sidney also spoke of verse as

> being but an ornament and no cause to poetry, since there have been many most excellent poets that never versified, and now swarm many versifiers that need never answer to the name of poets. . . . It is not rhyming and versing that maketh a poet— no more than a long gown maketh an advocate, who though he pleaded in armour should be an advocate and no soldier.

Sidney was intent on distinguishing genuine poetry from its facsimile, true poets from mere dabblers, necessary words from ornamental ones, and yet I always get a minor jolt when poets use the term *verse* in a negative or somewhat derogatory way. It is unworthy of them. It is not the fault of *verse*, of metrical composition, that it has been misused. J. V. Cunningham gets an ironic pleasure in claiming for himself the lesser practice in "For My Contemporaries":

> How time reverses
> The proud in heart!
> I now make verses
> Who aimed at art.

The poet is a maker and verse a demanding art of its own. ("Making verse is not easy," Cunningham slyly acknowledges.) The formal deliverance of poetry gives it ceremonial authority, a way of inhabiting and marking us.

The term *versification* refers to the techniques, principles, and practice of composing verse. *Prosody* is the systematic study of versification. Sidney also acknowledged that "the senate of poets hath chosen verse as their fittest raiment."

The term *verse* is also used to refer to a single line of poetry, or to a single stanza, especially of a hymn or song. The poetic line on its own immediately announces its difference from prose. It creates its own visual and verbal impact, it declares its self-sufficiency as a unit of meaning, an act of attention. Paul Claudel called the fundamental line "an idea isolated by blank space." I would call it "words isolated by blank space" because the words can go beyond the idea, they can plunge deeper than thought. I open an anthology of English poetry and copy out this verse:

> Brightness falls from the air.

For a useful collection of essays, see Harvey Gross, ed., *The Structure of Verse: Modern Essays on Prosody* (1979).

versicle   This liturgical term can mean (1) a short sentence said or sung antiphonally (that is, in a call-and-response pattern); (2) a small verse; (3) a single verse of the Psalms or Bible; (4) a short or lone metrical line.

vers libre   French: "free verse." A radical innovation of French poetry dating to the 1870s, when the classically ordered language of traditional poetry began to break down. One strong impulse of vers libre was to rupture strictly prescribed metrical patterns and rules, especially to break the authoritarian stranglehold of the conventional twelve-syllable alexandrine verse line which dominated French poetry from the mid-seventeenth century onward. (The alexandrine was invented in the twelfth century and still circulates in the bloodstream of anyone classically educated in French poetry.) In the poetry of Verlaine and Corbière, Rimbaud and especially Laforgue (one of the first to translate Whitman into French), a symmetrical prosody gives way to the irregular surges and pauses of a new rhythm, a new music. The poets who investigated vers libre sought a fresh, emergent, asymmetrical lineation, a verbal music suited to a distinct subject matter. The dream of vers libre: every poem its own originary music ideally suited to its subject. The French practice of vers libre, especially the work of Laforgue, had terrific impact on T. S. Eliot, Ezra Pound, D. H. Lawrence, William Carlos Williams, and others, and thus greatly affected the development of free verse in English in our century.

SEE ALSO *free verse*.

villanelle   A French form codified in the sixteenth century, the villanelle has its roots in Italian folk song and was originally associated with pastoral verse (the name derives from *villa*, "a farm" or "country house"). It consists of nineteen lines divided into six stanzas—five tercets and one quatrain. The first and third lines become the refrain lines of alternate stanzas and the final two lines of the poem. They rhyme throughout, as do the middle lines of each stanza. The entire poem then builds around two repeated lines and turns on two rhymes.

The villanelle entered English poetry in the nineteenth century as a form of light verse (there are pleasurable examples by Andrew Lang, Oscar Wilde, W. E. Henley, and others), but it has had a more majestic life in our century. Many modern and contemporary poets have intuited how the compulsive returns of the villanelle could be suited to a poetry of loss ("The art of losing isn't hard to master"), to a poetry speaking up against loss ("Do not go gentle into that good night"). One could make a fine anthology of American villanelles, including ones by Edwin Arlington Robinson ("The House on the Hill"), Theodore Roethke ("The Waking"), Elizabeth Bishop ("One Art"), James Merrill ("The World and the Child"), Weldon Kees ("Five Villanelles"), Richard Hugo ("The Freaks at Spurgin Road Field"), Howard Nemerov ("Equations of a Villanelle"), Donald Justice ("In Memory of the Unknown Poet, Robert Boardman Vaughn"), Mark Strand ("Two de Chiricos"), Marilyn Hacker ("Villanelle"), Michael Ryan ("Milk the Mouse"), Deborah Digges ("The Rockettes"), and William Olsen ("Hereafter").

SEE ALSO *refrain*.

wit   The ability to make quick, clever connections with verbal deftness, to perceive the likeness in unlike things, relating incongruities and thus awakening the intelligence. The *Princeton Encyclopedia of Poetry and Poetics* makes clear that wit is a term with a long critical history. Aristotle treated it as the ability to make apt comparisons and also as a form of "well-bred insolence." Classical rhetoricians generally used it to mean "cleverness" or "ingenuity." To the Renaissance the word meant "intelligence" or "wisdom." During the seventeenth century, wit was associated with the metaphysical poetry of John Donne and others and identified with the ability to create stunning and far-fetched figures of speech. Reacting against the mode, Dr. Johnson attacked Abraham Cowley for "heterogeneous ideas . . . yoked by violence together," a criticism that would later be considered a compliment.

Once viewed as an essential feature of poetry, wit was defined by the philosopher Locke as "the Assemblage of Ideas, and putting those together with quickness and variety." Dryden characterized wit as "sharpness of conceit," thereby emphasizing the shared self-consciousness between the poet and the reader. Pope contrasted "true wit," guided by judgment, with mere fanciful writing:

True wit is Nature to advantage dressed,
What oft was thought, but ne'er so well expressed.

The romantic poets, rebelling against the association of wit with reason and common sense, used the concept of imagination to designate the ability to invent and perceive relations, and wit was degraded to a form of levity, from which it has never entirely recovered. In rediscovering the metaphysical poets, T. S. Eliot also revived the concept of wit, which he described in an essay on Andrew Marvell as a "tough reasonableness beneath the slight lyric grace."

The meaning of wit should come full cycle. From Anne Bradstreet to May Swenson, James Merrill, William Matthews, and Billy Collins, there have always been American poets who have understood that ingenuity—a clever act of intelligence—is not opposed to, but can serve, deep feeling in poetry.

SEE ALSO *conceit.*

work song   The song to accompany work is an oral phenomenon, a highly fluid, rhythmic, and utilitarian form of verse that is very ancient. Tomb inscriptions from Egypt (circa 2600 B.C.) include work songs for shepherds, fishermen, and chairmen. The earliest French lyrics, which were called *chanson de toile* and date from the twelfth century, were short poems to accompany needlework and tapestry weaving. It has been plausibly theorized that the rhythm of Anglo-Saxon poetry was based on the slow pull and push of the oar, whereas the Irish tradition developed a rhythm based on the pounding of hammer and anvil. If so, then English verse, which has a qualitative meter, has its origins in the physical action of work. Whenever the rhythm of certain tasks has become set—sowing, reaping, threshing, washing clothes, milking cows, rowing, hauling and pulling down sail, and so forth—then there are accompanying work songs which preserve those rhythms.

African traditional poetry includes songs to accompany such occupations as canoe paddling, milling of rice, marching, and nursing children. The call-and-response pattern of these songs carried over to the New World in the form of field hollers and other songs improvised by people forced into slavery, in the lyrics of woodcutters and fishermen, of rural and prison road gangs. In the African American work song a leader provides a strong rhythmic cue with two or three bars which are then answered in the ejaculatory word or words of moving workers. The rhythmic interaction makes both poetry and music a participatory activity.

Some folklorists have persuasively argued that the work song actually challenges the nature of work by changing the framework of the workers. The singer supplies a beat and relieves the tedium, transposing the space, creating a different relationship to time. The rhythm of the words—the work that poetry does—actively restructures time. It induces a kind of ritualistic hypnosis, a rhythmic ecstasy.

A Reading List
and the Pleasure of the Catalog

This is a list of the poets, of the works, cited in the main body of the text. It is not a definitive bibliography but a record of what has most immediately, most urgently, called out to me in the writing of this book. The word *bibliography* derives from a Greek word meaning "book writing." It is related to *bibliolatry* ("book worship"), *bibliomancy* ("divination by book"), *bibliomania* ("book madness"), and *bibliophile* ("book lover"). All testify to the irrational hold of books over us. W. H. Auden said that reading the critic W. P. Ker granted him "the vision of a kind of literary 'All Souls Night' in which the dead, the living and the unborn writers of every age and in every tongue were seen as engaged upon a common, noble and civilizing task." A bibliography is a list of books on a given subject, but it is also a dream of alliance, a bringing together of minds, an odd catalog of praise. It holds out the promise of greater knowing, of knowledge passed on, of deeper initiation into deeper mysteries.

AFRICA
Poems of Black Africa (ed. Wole Soyinka)
Nigeria
Soyinka, Wole
Mandela's Earth and Other Poems
Senegal
Senghor, Léopold Sédar
The Collected Poetry
South Africa
Brutus, Dennis
A Simple Lust: Selected Poems

ANCIENT NEAR EAST
The Ancient Egyptian Pyramid Texts (trans. Raymond Oliver Faulkner)
Gilgamesh (trans. David Ferry)
The Hebrew Bible
The Psalms in English (ed. Donald Davie)

ASIA
Japan

The Essential Haiku: Versions of Bashō, Buson, and Issa (ed. and trans. Robert Hass)
One Hundred Poems from the Japanese (ed. Kenneth Rexroth)

Bashō

> Bashō and His Interpreters: Selected Hokku with Commentary (trans. Makoto Uedo)

China

> Five T'ang Poets: Wang Wei, Li Po, Tu Fu, Li Ho, Li Shang-Yin (trans. David Young)
>
> The Works of Witter Bynner: The Chinese Translations (ed. James Kraft)

AUSTRALIA

Murray, Les

> The Rabbiter's Bounty: Collected Poems
>
> A Working Forest: Selected Prose

CENTRAL AND SOUTH AMERICA

> Twentieth-Century Latin American Poetry: A Bilingual Anthology (ed. Stephen Tapscott)

Argentina

Borges, Jorge Luis

> Selected Poems, 1923–1967 (ed. Norman Thomas di Giovanni)

Gelman, Juan

> Unthinkable Tenderness: Selected Poems (trans. Joan Lindgren)

Brazil

> An Anthology of Twentieth-Century Brazilian Poetry (ed. Elizabeth Bishop and Emanuel Brasil)

Andrade, Carlos Drummond de

> Travelling in the Family: Selected Poems (ed. Thomas Colchie and Mark Strand)

Chile

Neruda, Pablo

> Canto General (trans. Jack Schmitt)
>
> Neruda and Vallejo: Selected Poems (ed. Robert Bly)
>
> Selected Odes of Pablo Neruda (trans. Margaret Sayers Peden)
>
> Selected Poems (ed. Nathaniel Tarn)
>
> Twenty Love Poems and a Song of Despair (trans. W. S. Merwin)
>
> Memoirs (trans. Hardie St. Martin)
>
> Walter Holzinger, "Poetic Subject and Form in Odas elementales," in Pablo Neruda (ed. Harold Bloom)

Mexico

> Mouth to Mouth: Poems by Twelve Contemporary Mexican Women (ed. Forrest Gander)

Paz, Octavio

> Collected Poems, 1957–1987 (ed. Eliot Weinberger)
>
> The Bow and the Lyre (trans. Ruth L. C. Simms)

Nicaragua

Darío, Rubén

> Selected Poems (trans. Lysander Kemp)

Peru

Vallejo, César

> *The Complete Posthumous Poetry* (trans. Clayton Eshleman and José Rubia Barcia)
> *Human Poems* (trans. Clayton Eshleman)
> *Neruda and Vallejo: Selected Poems* (ed. Robert Bly)
> *Trilce* (trans. Clayton Eshleman)

CLASSICAL GREEK AND LATIN

> *The Greek Anthology and Other Ancient Epigrams: A Selection in Modern Verse Translations* (trans. Peter Jay)

Alcaeus

> *Three Archaic Poets: Archilochus, Alcaeus, Sappho* (trans. Anne Pippin Burnett)

Catullus

> *The Poems of Catullus* (trans. Charles Martin)

Homer

> *Homer in English* (ed. George Steiner)
> *The Iliad* (translations by Alexander Pope; Richmond Lattimore; Robert Fagles)
> *The Odyssey* (translations by Robert Fitzgerald; Robert Fagles)
> *War Music* (trans. Christopher Logue)

Horace

> *The Art of Poetry* (trans. Burton Raffel)
> *The Odes of Horace* (trans. David Ferry)

Ovid

> *The Erotic Poems* (trans. Peter Green)
> *The Metamorphoses of Ovid* (translations by Allen Mandelbaum; David Slavitt)
> *Ovid's Poetry of Exile* (trans. David Slavitt)

Pindar

> *The Odes of Pindar* (trans. C. M. Bowra)

Sappho

> *Poems and Fragments* (trans. Guy Davenport)
> *Sappho: A Garland* (trans. Jim Powell)
> *Sappho: A New Translation* (trans. Mary Barnard)

Virgil

> *The Aeneid* (trans. Robert Fitzgerald)

EUROPE

> *Modern European Poetry in Translation* (ed. Willis Barnstone)

Armenia

Tekeyan, Vahan

> *Sacred Wrath: The Selected Poems of Vahan Tekeyan* (trans. Diana der Hovanessian and Marzbed Margossian)

Austria

Bachmann, Ingeborg

> *In the Storm of Roses* (trans. Mark Anderson)
> *Songs in Flight* (trans. Peter Filkins)

Hofmannsthal, Hugo von
  Poems and Verse Plays (ed. Michael Hamburger)
  Selected Prose (trans. Mary Hottinger and Tania and James Stern)
Trakl, Georg
  Selected Poems (trans. Christopher Middleton)
  Song of the West: Selected Poems of Georg Trakl (trans. Robert Firmage)
  Twenty Poems (trans. James Wright and Robert Bly)

Czech Republic
Orten Jiří
  Elegies (trans. Lyn Coffin)

England
  Poems and Prose from the Old English (trans. Burton Raffel)
  Poets of the English Language, vols. 1–5 (ed. W. H. Auden and Norman
    Holmes Pearson)
Auden, W. H.
  Collected Poems
  The Dyer's Hand and Other Essays
  The Enchafèd Flood
  Forewords and Afterwords
Beowulf (anonymous)
  Beowulf: A New Translation (trans. Burton Raffel)
Blake, William
  The Complete Poetry and Prose of William Blake (ed. David V. Erdman)
Brontë, Emily
  The Complete Poems of Emily Jane Brontë (ed. C. W. Hatfield)
Browning, Robert
  The Complete Poetical Works of Robert Browning (ed. Horace E. Scudder)
Byron, Lord George Gordon
  The Complete Poetical Works (ed. Jerome McGann)
Campion, Thomas
  The Essential Campion (ed. Charles Simic)
Carew, Thomas
  The Poems of Thomas Carew
Carroll, Lewis
  Selected Poems (ed. Keith Silver)
Chaucer, Geoffrey
  The Canterbury Tales
  Troilus and Criseyde (ed. R. A. Shoaf)
Clare, John
  Selected Poems and Prose (ed. Eric Robinson and Geoffrey Summerfield)
Coleridge, Samuel Taylor
  Poetical Works (ed. Ernest Hartley Coleridge)
  Biographia Literaria (ed. James Engell and W. Jackson Bate)
de la Mare, Walter
  Collected Poems of Walter de la Mare
Donne, John
  The Complete Poetry of John Donne (ed. John T. Shawcross)

Douglas, Keith
    Collected Poems
Drayton, Michael
    Selected Poems of Michael Drayton
Empson, William
    Collected Poems
    Seven Types of Ambiguity
    The Structure of Complex Words
Graves, Robert
    New Collected Poems
    Collected Writings on Poetry
    The English Ballad: A Short Critical Survey
    On English Poetry
    The White Goddess: A Historical Grammar of Poetic Myth
Gray, Thomas
    Thomas Gray and William Collins: Poetical Works
Hardy, Thomas
    The Complete Poems of Thomas Hardy
Herbert, George
    The Complete English Poems
Hopkins, Gerard Manley
    Poems and Prose (ed. W. H. Gardner)
Housman, A. E.
    The Collected Poems of A. E. Housman
    Selected Prose
Hughes, Ted
    New Selected Poems: 1957–1994
Johnson, Samuel
    The Complete English Poems
    W. Jackson Bates, *Samuel Johnson*
    James Boswell, *Boswell's Life of Johnson*
Jonson, Ben
    The Complete Poems
Keats, John
    The Poems of John Keats (ed. Jack Stillinger)
    Letters
    W. Jackson Bate, *John Keats*
    Charles Brown, *The Life of John Keats*
Kipling, Rudyard
    The Complete Verse
Larkin, Philip
    Collected Poems
Lawrence, D. H.
    The Complete Poems
    Studies in Classic American Literature
Marvell, Andrew
    The Complete Poems

Milton, John
  The Complete English Poetry of John Milton
Morris, William
  The Poems of William Morris
Muir, Edwin
  Collected Poems: 1921–1958
  An Autobiography
  The Estate of Poetry
Owen, Wilfred
  The Complete Poems and Fragments
Raleigh, Sir Walter
  The Poems of Sir Walter Raleigh
Rossetti, Christina
  The Complete Poems of Christina Rossetti
Rossetti, Dante Gabriel
  The Essential Rossetti (ed. John Hollander)
Sassoon, Siegfried
  Collected Poems, 1908–1956
Shakespeare, William
  The Narrative Poems (ed. Maurice Evans)
  The Sonnets and A Lover's Complaint (ed. John Kerrigan)
  J. B. Leishman, *Themes and Variations in Shakespeare's Sonnets*
Shelley, Percy Bysshe
  Poetical Works (ed. Thomas Hutchinson)
  A Defence of Poetry
Sidney, Sir Philip
  The Poems of Sir Philip Sidney
  A Defence of Poetry
Smart, Christopher
  Selected Poems (ed. Karina Williamson and Marcus Walsh)
  W. F. Stead, *Rejoice in the Lamb: A Song from Bedlam*
Smith, Stevie
  Collected Poems
Swinburne, Algernon
  The Poems of Algernon Swinburne
Tennyson, Alfred, Lord
  Tennyson: A Selected Edition (ed. Christopher Ricks)
Traherne, Thomas
  Centuries, Poems, and Thanksgivings
Vaughan, Henry
  George Herbert and Henry Vaughan
Wilde, Oscar
  The Poems and Fairy Tales of Oscar Wilde
  De Profundis and Other Writings
Wordsworth, William
  Poems in Two Volumes (ed. Jared R. Curtis)

The Prelude: A Parallel Text
Literary Criticism of William Wordsworth

France

    Random House Book of Twentieth-Century French Poetry (ed. Paul Auster)

Apollinaire, Guillaume
    Alcools (trans. Donald Revell)
    Calligrammes (trans. Anne Hyde Greet)
    Selected Writings (trans. Roger Shattuck)

Aragon, Louis
    Une vague de rêves

Baudelaire, Charles
    Les Fleurs du mal: The Complete Text of the Flowers of Evil (trans. Richard Howard)
    Twenty Prose Poems (trans. Michael Hamburger)

Breton, André
    Selected Poems of André Breton (trans. Kenneth White)
    Manifestoes of Surrealism (trans. Richard Seaver and Helen R. Lane)
    What Is Surrealism? Selected Writings of André Breton (ed. Franklin Rosemont)

Char, René
    Selected Poems of René Char (ed. Mary Ann Caws and Tina Jolas)

Desnos, Robert
    The Selected Poems of Robert Desnos (trans. Carolyn Forché and William Kulik)
    The Voice (trans. William Kulik with Carole Frankel)

Éluard, Paul
    Selected Poems (trans. Gilbert Bowen)
    Uninterrupted Poetry: Selected Writings (trans. Lloyd Alexander)

Mallarmé, Stéphane
    Collected Poems (trans. Henry Weinfield)
    Selected Letters of Stéphane Mallarmé (ed. Rosemary Lloyd)
    Gordon Millan, *A Throw of the Dice: The Life of Stéphane Mallarmé*

Ponge, Francis
    Selected Poems (ed. Margaret Guiton)

Rimbaud, Arthur
    Arthur Rimbaud: Complete Works (trans. Paul Schmidt)

Tzara, Tristan
    "Approximate Man" and Other Writings (trans. Mary Ann Caws)

Valéry, Paul
    The Art of Poetry (trans. Denise Folliot)
    Paul Valéry: An Anthology (trans. James R. Lawler)

Germany

Benn, Gottfried
    Prose, Essays, Poems (ed. Volkmar Sanders)

Brecht, Bertolt
    Poems, 1913–1956 (ed. John Willett and Ralph Manheim, with cooperation of Erich Fried)

Celan, Paul
>   *Breathturn* (trans. Pierre Joris)
>   *Last Poems* (trans. Katharine Washburn and Margret Guillemin)
>   *The Poems of Paul Celan* (trans. Michael Hamburger)
>   *Collected Prose* (trans. Rosemarie Waldrop)
>   John Felstiner, *Paul Celan: Poet, Survivor, Jew*
Goethe, Johann Wolfgang von
>   *Selected Poems* (ed. Christopher Middleton, trans. Michael Hamburger)
Heine, Heinrich
>   *The Complete Poems of Heinrich Heine: A Modern English Version* (trans. Hal Draper)
>   Ernst Pawel, *The Poet Dying: Heinrich Heine's Last Years in Paris*
Hölderlin, Friederich
>   *Hymns and Fragments* (trans. Richard Sieburth)
Rilke, Rainer Maria
>   *The Book of Images* (trans. Edward Snow)
>   *Duino Elegies and The Sonnets to Orpheus* (trans. A. Poulin, Jr.)
>   *New Poems* (1907) (trans. Edward Snow)
>   *New Poems: The Other Part* (1908) (trans. Edward Snow)
>   *The Selected Poetry of Rainer Maria Rilke* (trans. Stephen Mitchell)
>   *Uncollected Poems* (trans. Edward Snow)
>   *Letters to a Young Poet* (trans. M. D. Herter Norton)
>   *The Notebooks of Malte Laurids Brigge* (trans. Stephen Mitchell)
>   Ralph Freedman, *Life of a Poet: Rainer Maria Rilke*
Sachs, Nelly
>   *O the Chimneys* (trans. Michael Hamburger)

Greece
>   *Modern Greek Poetry: From Caváfis to Elýtis* (trans. Kimon Friar)
Cavafy, Constantine
>   *Collected Poems* (trans. Edmund Keeley and Philip Sherrard)
Seferis, George
>   *Collected Poems* (trans. Edmund Keeley and Philip Sherrard)
>   *A Poet's Journal: Days of 1945–1951* (trans. Athan Anagnostopoulus)

Hungary
>   *Modern Hungarian Poetry* (ed. Miklós Vadja)
József, Attila
>   *Winter Night* (trans. John Bátki)
Radnóti, Miklós
>   *Clouded Sky* (trans. Steven Polgar, Stephen Berg, and S. J. Marks)

Ireland
>   *The Book of Irish Verse: Irish Poetry from the Sixth Century to the Present* (ed. John Montague)
Beckett, Samuel
>   *Collected Poems in English and French*
>   *Proust*
Boland, Eavan
>   *An Origin Like Water: Collected Poems, 1961–1987*

Object Lessons: The Life of the Woman and the Poet in Our Time
Grennan, Eamon
  Relations: New and Selected Poems
Heaney, Seamus
  Seeing Things
  The Government of the Tongue: Selected Prose, 1978–1987
  Opened Ground: Selected Poems, 1966–1996
  Preoccupations: Selected Prose, 1968–1978
  The Redress of Poetry
  The Rattlebag: An Anthology of Poetry (editor, with Ted Hughes)
MacNeice, Louis
  The Collected Poems of Louis MacNeice
  Modern Poetry: A Personal Essay
Yeats, William Butler
  The Poems of W. B. Yeats
  The Autobiography of W. B. Yeats
  Essays and Introductions
  Explorations
  Mythologies

Italy

Campana, Dino
  Orphic Songs (trans. Charles Wright)
Cavalcanti, Guido
  The Complete Poems (trans. Marc A. Cirigliano)
Dante Alighieri
  The Divine Comedy (ed. Charles Singleton)
  The Inferno of Dante: A New Verse Translation (trans. Robert Pinsky)
  La vita nuova: Poems of Youth (trans. Barbara Reynolds)
Francis of Assisi, Saint
  Francis and Clare: The Complete Works (trans. R. Armstrong and Ignatius C.
    Brady)
Levi, Primo
  Collected Poems (trans. Ruth Feldman and Brian Swann)
Leopardi, Giacomo
  A Leopardi Reader (trans. Ottavio Mark Casale)
  Leopardi: Selected Poems (trans. Eamon Grennan)
Montale, Eugenio
  Collected Poems, 1920–1954 (trans. Jonathan Galassi)
  The Second Life of Art: Selected Essays of Eugenio Montale (trans. Jonathan Galassi)
Pavese, Cesare
  Hard Labor (trans. William Arrowsmith)
Petrarch, Francesco
  Petrarch's Songbook (trans. James Wyatt Cook)

Poland

Postwar Polish Poetry: An Anthology (ed. Czesław Miłosz)
Białoszewski, Miron
  A Memoir of the Warsaw Uprising (trans. Madeline Levine)

Gombrowicz, Witold
"Against Poets," in *Diary*, Volume One (trans. Lillian Vallee)
Herbert, Zbigniew
Mr. Cogito (trans. John and Bogdana Carpenter)
Report from the Besieged City and Other Poems (trans. John and Bogdana Carpenter)
Selected Poems (trans. Czesław Miłosz and Peter Dale Scott)
Barbarian in the Garden (trans. John and Bogdana Carpenter)
Still Life with a Bridle: Essays and Apocryphas (trans. John and Bogdana Carpenter)
Miłosz, Czesław
The Collected Poems, 1931–1987
Provinces: Poems, 1987–1991 (trans. Czesław Miłosz)
The Captive Mind (trans. Jane Zielonko)
The History of Polish Literature
Native Realm: A Search for Self-Definition (trans. Catherine S. Leach)
The Witness of Poetry
Różewicz, Tadeusz
"The Survivor" and Other Poems (trans. Magnus J. Krynski and Robert A. Maguire)
Szymborska, Wisława
Poems New and Collected, 1957–1997 (trans. Stanisław Barańczak and Clare Cavanagh)
Wat, Aleksander
With the Skin: Poems of Aleksander Wat (trans. Czesław Miłosz and Leonard Nathan)
My Century: The Odyssey of a Polish Intellectual (trans. Richard Lourie)
Zagajewski, Adam
Canvas (trans. Renata Gorczynski, Benjamin Ivry, and C. K. Williams)
Mysticism for Beginners (trans. Clare Cavanagh)
Tremor: Selected Poems (trans. Renata Gorczynski)
Solidarity, Solitude: Essays (trans. Lillian Vallee)
Two Cities: On Exile, History, and the Imagination (trans. Lillian Vallee)

Portugal
Pessoa, Fernando
Fernando Pessoa & Company: Selected Poems (trans. Richard Zenith)
Poems of Fernando Pessoa (trans. Edwin Honig and Susan M. Brown)

Russia
Akhmatova, Anna
Poems of Akhmatova (trans. Stanley Kunitz and Max Hayward)
Selected Poems (trans. Richard McKane; D. M. Thomas)
Twenty Poems (trans. Jane Kenyon and Vira Sandomirsky)
My Half-Century: Selected Prose (ed. Ronald Meyer)
Sam Driver, *Anna Akhmatova*
Brodsky, Joseph
A Part of Speech
To Urania

Less Than One: Selected Essays

On Grief and Reason: Essays

Mandelstam, Osip

Fifty Poems (trans. Bernard Meares)

Selected Poems (trans. Clarence Brown and W. S. Merwin)

Stone (trans. Robert Tracy)

The Complete Critical Prose (trans. Jane Gary Harris and Constance Link)

Nadezhda Mandelstam, *Hope Abandoned* (trans. Max Hayward)

Nadezhda Mandelstam, *Hope Against Hope: A Memoir* (trans. Max Hayward)

Pasternak, Boris

Selected Poems (trans. Jon Stallworthy and Peter France)

Safe Conduct: An Early Autobiography and Other Works (trans. Alec Brown)

Tsvetaeva, Marina

Selected Poems (trans. Elaine Feinstein)

Art in the Light of Conscience: Eight Essays on Poetry by Marina Tsvetaeva (trans. Angela Livingstone)

A Captive Spirit: Selected Prose (trans. J. Marin King)

Scotland

Scottish Love Poems: A Personal Anthology (ed. Antonia Fraser)

Burns, Robert

Poems and Songs

MacDiarmid, Hugh

Collected Poems of Hugh MacDiarmid

Lucky Poet: A Self-Study in Literature and Political Ideas

Selected Essays of Hugh MacDiarmid

Spain

Roots and Wings: Poetry from Spain, 1900–1975 (ed. Hardie St. Martin)

García Lorca, Federico

Collected Poems (ed. Christopher Maurer)

Lorca and Jiménez: Selected Poems (trans. Robert Bly)

Poet in New York (trans. Greg Simon and Steven F. White)

Deep Song and Other Prose (trans. Christopher Maurer)

Hernández, Miguel

Selected Poems (trans. Timony Baland)

Jiménez, Juan Ramón

Selected Writings of Juan Ramón Jiménez (trans. H. R. Hays)

Lorca and Jiménez: Selected Poems (trans. Robert Bly)

John of the Cross, Saint

Poems (trans. John Frederick Nims)

Sweden

Tranströmer, Tomas

Tomas Tranströmer: Selected Poems, 1946–1987 (ed. Robert Hass)

Turkey

Hikmet, Nâzim

Human Landscapes (trans. Randy Blasing and Mutlu Konuk)

Selected Poetry (trans. Randy Blasing and Mutlu Konuk)

Wales

The Oxford Book of Welsh Verse in English (ed. Gwyn Jones)
Thomas, Dylan
Collected Poems

INDIA AND PAKISTAN

An Anthology of Urdu Verse in English (trans. David Matthews)
Faiz, Faiz Ahmed
The Rebel's Silhouette (trans. Agha Shahid Ali)

MIDDLE EAST

Modern Poetry of the Arab World (ed. Abdullah al-Udhari)
The Penguin Book of Hebrew Verse (ed. T. Carmi)

Israel

Amichai, Yehuda
Amen (trans. Yehuda Amichai and Ted Hughes)
Love Poems: A Bilingual Edition
Selected Poems (trans. Assia Gutmann and Harold Schimmel)
The Selected Poetry of Yehuda Amichai (trans. Chana Bloch and Stephen Mitchell)
Yehuda Amichai: A Life of Poetry, 1948–1994 (trans. Benjamin and Barbara Harshaw)
Ravikovitch, Dahlia
The Window: New and Selected Poems (trans. Chana Bloch and Ariel Bloch)

NORTH AMERICA

Canada

The New Oxford Book of Canadian Verse in English (ed. Margaret Atwood)
Carson, Anne
Glass, Irony, and God
Eros the Bittersweet: An Essay
Ondaatje, Michael
The Cinnamon Peeler: Selected Poems

United States

American Poetry: The Nineteenth Century, vols. 1 and 2 (ed. John Hollander)
Coming to Light: Contemporary Translations of the Native Literatures of North America (ed. Brian Swann)
Every Shut Eye Ain't Asleep: An Anthology of Poetry by African Americans Since 1945 (ed. Michael S. Harper and Anthony Walton)
The Open Boat: Poems from Asian America (ed. Garrett Hongo)
The Vintage Book of Contemporary American Poetry (ed. J. D. McClatchy)
Ammons, A. R.
Garbage
Glare
Selected Poems, 1951–1986
Set in Motion: Essays, Interviews, and Dialogues

Ashbery, John
  Flow Chart
  Selected Poems
Berg, Stephen
  New and Selected Poems
  The Steel Cricket: Versions, 1958–1997
Berryman, John
  Collected Poems, 1931–1971
  The Dream Songs
  The Freedom of the Poet
  Paul Mariani, *Dream Song: The Life of John Berryman*
Bidart, Frank
  Desire
  In the Western Night: Collected Poems 1965–1990
Bishop, Elizabeth
  The Collected Poems, 1927–1979
  The Collected Prose
  One Art: Letters
Bogan, Louise
  The Blue Estuaries: Poems, 1923–1968
  A Poet's Alphabet: Reflections on the Literary Art and Vocation
Bottoms, David
  Armored Hearts: Selected and New Poems
Bradstreet, Anne
  The Complete Works of Anne Bradstreet
Brooks, Gwendolyn
  Selected Poems
Brown, Sterling
  The Collected Poems of Sterling A. Brown
  Negro Caravan
  The Negro in American Fiction
  Negro Poetry and Drama
Christopher, Nicholas
  The Creation of the Night Sky
  Desperate Characters: A Novella in Verse and Other Poems
  5° and Other Poems
Clampitt, Amy
  The Collected Poems of Amy Clampitt
Collier, Michael
  The Neighbor
  The Wesleyan Tradition: Four Decades of American Poetry (editor)
Crane, Hart
  The Complete Poems
  O My Land, My Friend: The Selected Letters of Hart Crane
Cullen, Countee
  My Soul's High Song: The Collected Writings of Countee Cullen

cummings, e. e.
  Complete Poems, 1904–1962
Cunningham, J. V.
  The Collected Poems and Epigrams of J. V. Cunningham
  The Collected Essays of J. V. Cunningham
Dickinson, Emily
  The Complete Poems
  Emily Dickinson: Selected Letters
  Judith Farr, *The Passion of Emily Dickinson*
  Susan Howe, *My Emily Dickinson*
  Richard B. Sewall, *The Life of Emily Dickinson*
Digges, Deborah
  Late in the Millennium
  Rough Music
Doty, Mark
  Atlantis
  My Alexandria
  Sweet Machine
Duncan, Robert
  Selected Poems
Eliot, T. S.
  Collected Poems, 1909–1962
  *The Waste Land: A Fascimile and Transcript of the Original Drafts Including the
    Annotations of Ezra Pound* (ed. Valerie Eliot)
  On Poetry and Poets
  Selected Prose of T. S. Eliot (ed. Frank Kermode)
Emerson, Ralph Waldo
  Collected Poems and Translations (Library of America)
  Emerson in His Journals (ed. Joel Porte)
  Emerson's Literary Criticism (ed. Eric W. Carlson)
  Essays: First and Second Series (Library of America)
  Robert Richardson, *Emerson: The Mind on Fire*
Frost, Robert
  Collected Poems, Prose, and Plays (Library of America)
Ginsberg, Allen
  Selected Poems, 1947–1995
Gluck, Louise
  Meadowlands
  The Triumph of Achilles
  The Wild Iris
  Proofs and Theories: Essays on Poetry
Grossman, Allen
  The Ether Dome and Other Poems: New and Selected, 1979–1991
  The Long Schoolroom: Lessons in the Bitter Logic of the Poetic Principle
  The Sighted Singer: Two Works on Poetry for Readers and Writers
Hahn, Susan
  Confessions

Harper, Michael
    Images of Kin: New and Selected Poems
    A Chant of Saints: A Gathering of Afro-American Literature, Art, and Scholarship
        (editor, with Robert Stepto)
Hass, Robert
    Human Wishes
    Praise
    Sun Under Wood
    Twentieth Century Pleasures: Prose on Poetry
Hayden, Robert
    Collected Poems
    Collected Prose
Hecht, Anthony
    Collected Earlier Poems
    Flight among the Tombs
    Millions of Strange Shadows
    The Transparent Man
Hoffman, Daniel
    Hang-Gliding from Helicon: New and Selected Poems, 1948–1988
    Barbarous Knowledge: Myth in the Poetry of Yeats, Graves, and Muir
Hollander, John
    Selected Poems
    Types of Shape
    The Figure of Echo: A Mode of Allusion in Milton and After
    Melodious Guile: Fictive Pattern in Poetic Language
    Rhyme's Reason: A Guide to English Verse
    The Work of Poetry
Hongo, Garrett
    The River of Heaven
    Yellow Light
    Volcano: A Memoir of Hawai'i
Howard, Richard
    Fellow Feelings
    Like Most Revelations
    Lining Up
    Misgivings
    No Traveller
    Two-Part Inventions
    Alone with America: Essays on the Art of Poetry in the United States since 1950
    Untitled Subjects
Hughes, Langston
    The Collected Poems of Langston Hughes
    The Book of Negro Folklore (editor, with Arna Bontemps)
Hummer, T. R.
    Walt Whitman in Hell
Jarrell, Randall
    The Complete Poems

Randall Jarrell's Letters: An Autobiographical and Literary Selection (ed. Mary Jarrell)
    Poetry and the Age
    The Third Book of Criticism
Johnson, James Weldon
    God's Trombones
Justice, Donald
    New and Selected Poems
Kees, Weldon
    Collected Poems
Kinnell, Galway
    Selected Poems
Komunyakaa, Yusef
    Neon Vernacular: New and Selected Poems
Kunitz, Stanley
    Passing Through: The Later Poems, New and Selected
    Selected Poems, 1928–1958
    A Kind of Order, A Kind of Folly: Essays and Conversations
Lee, Li-Young
    The City in Which I Love You
    Rose
Levine, Philip
    The Mercy
    New Selected Poems
    What Work Is
    The Bread of Time: Toward an Autobiography
Lowell, Robert
    Selected Poems
    Collected Prose
Macdonald, Cynthia
    Living Wills: New and Selected Poems
    I Can't Remember
McClatchy, J. D.
    Ten Commandments
    Twenty Questions
    The Vintage Book of Contemporary World Poetry (editor)
Meredith, William
    Effort at Speech: New and Selected Poems
Merrill, James
    The Changing Light at Sandover
    A Scattering of Salts
    Selected Poems, 1946–1985
    A Different Person: A Memoir
Merwin, W. S.
    The Folding Cliffs: A Narrative of Nineteenth-Century Hawaii
    Selected Poems

Travels
The Vixen
Moore, Marianne
The Complete Poems of Marianne Moore
The Complete Prose of Marianne Moore
The Selected Letters of Marianne Moore
Nye, Naomi Shihab
Words Under the Words: Selected Poems
O'Hara, Frank
The Collected Poems of Frank O'Hara
Marjorie Perloff, *Frank O'Hara: Poet Among Painters*
Olds, Sharon
The Dead and the Living
The Father
The Wellspring
Pinsky, Robert
The Figured Wheel: New and Collected Poems, 1966–1996
Poetry and the World
The Situation of Poetry: Contemporary Poetry and Its Traditions
The Sounds of Poetry: A Brief Guide
Plath, Sylvia
Collected Poems
Poe, Edgar Allan
Poetry and Tales (Library of America)
Essays and Reviews (Library of America)
Pound, Ezra
The Cantos
Selected Poems
Translations
ABC of Reading
The Letters of Ezra Pound, 1907–1941
Literary Essays of Ezra Pound
Ransom, John Crowe
Selected Poems
The World's Body
Rich, Adrienne
An Atlas of the Difficult World: Poems 1988–1991
Dark Fields of the Republic: Poems 1991–1995
The Fact of a Doorframe: Poems Selected and New, 1950–1984
Blood, Bread, and Poetry: Selected Prose, 1979–1986
What Is Found There: Notebooks on Poetry and Politics
Robinson, Edwin Arlington
Selected Poems (ed. Robert Faggen)
Roethke, Theodore
The Collected Poems of Theodore Roethke
On the Poet and His Craft: Selected Prose of Theodore Roethke

Straw for the Fire: From the Notebooks of Theodore Roethke, 1943–1963
(ed. David Wagoner)
Rukeyser, Muriel
Out of Silence: Selected Poems
Schuyler, James
Selected Poems
Schwartz, Delmore
Selected Poems (1938–1958): Summer Knowledge
Selected Essays of Delmore Schwartz (ed. Donald A. Dike and David H. Zucker)
Sexton, Anne
Selected Poems
Simic, Charles
Hotel Insomnia
Jackstraws
Selected Poems, 1963–1983
Walking the Black Cat
A Wedding in Hell
Dime-Store Alchemy: The Art of Joseph Cornell
Orphan Factory: Essays and Memoirs
Another Republic: Seventeen European and South American Writers (editor, with
Mark Strand)
Sissman, L. E.
Night Music: Poems by L. E. Sissman
Stern, Gerald
This Time: New and Selected Poems
Stevens, Wallace
Collected Poetry and Prose (Library of America)
Charles Berger, *Forms of Farewell: The Late Poetry of Wallace Stevens*
Harold Bloom, *Wallace Stevens: The Poems of Our Climate*
James Longenbach, *Wallace Stevens: The Plain Sense of Things*
Stewart, Susan
The Forest
The Hive
Crimes of Writing: Problems in the Containment of Representation
On Longing: Narratives of the Miniature, the Gigantic, the Souvenir, the Collection
Strand, Mark
Blizzard of One
The Continuous Life
Dark Harbor
Selected Poems
Tate, Allen
Collected Poems, 1919–1976
Voigt, Ellen Bryant
Kyrie
The Lotus Flower
Two Trees

The Flexible Lyric
Warren, Robert Penn
New and Selected Poems, 1923–1985
Selected Essays
Whitman, Walt
Poetry and Prose (Library of America)
Walt Whitman: The Measure of His Song (ed. Jim Perlman, Ed Folsom, and
Dan Campion)
Walt Whitman and the World (ed. Gay Wilson Allen and Ed Folsom)
Wilbur, Richard
New and Collected Poems
Responses: Prose Pieces, 1953–1976
Williams, C. K.
A Dream of Mind
Flesh and Blood
Poems, 1963–1983
The Vigil
Poetry and Consciousness
Williams, Sherley Anne
Give Birth to Brightness
The Peacock Poems
Williams, William Carlos
Collected Earlier Poems
Collected Later Poems
Paterson
The Autobiography of William Carlos Williams
In the American Grain
Selected Essays
Winters, Yvor
Collected Poems
Wood, Susan
Campo Santo
Wright, Charles
Black Zodiac
Chickamagua
Country Music: Selected Early Poems
The World of the Ten Thousand Things: Poems, 1980–1990
Wright, James
Above the River: The Complete Poems
Collected Prose

WEST INDIES
Cuba
Martí, José
José Martí: Major Poems (trans. Elinor Randall)
On Art and Literature: Critical Writings (trans. Elinor Randall)

Martinique
　　Césaire, Aime
　　　　The Collected Poetry (trans. Clayton Eshleman and Annette Smith)
St. Lucia
　　Walcott, Derek
　　　　The Bounty
　　　　Collected Poems, 1948–1984
　　　　Omeros
　　　　The Antilles: Fragments of Epic Memory

COLLECTIONS OF POETS WRITING ABOUT POETRY
　　　　Routledge Anthology of Poets on Poetry: Poetic Responses to English Poetry from Chaucer to Yeats (ed. David Hopkins)
　　　　The Poet's Work: Twenty-nine Masters of Twentieth-Century Poetry on the Origins and Practice of Their Art (ed. Reginald Gibbons)
　　　　Claims for Poetry (ed. Donald Hall)

CRITICISM
　　　　Princeton Encyclopedia of Poetry and Poetics
　　Abrahams, Roger
　　　　Deep Down in the Jungle: Negro Narrative Folklore from the Streets of Philadelphia
　　Alter, Robert
　　　　The Art of Biblical Poetry
　　Aristotle
　　　　Poetics
　　Bachelard, Gaston
　　　　The Poetics of Reverie
　　　　The Poetics of Space
　　　　The Psychoanalysis of Fire
　　Baldassari, Anne
　　　　Picasso and Photography: The Dark Mirror
　　Baraka, Amiri (LeRoi Jones)
　　　　Blues People
　　Barfield, Owen
　　　　Poetic Diction: A Study in Meaning
　　Barish, Jonas
　　　　The Antitheatrical Prejudice
　　Barkan, Leonard
　　　　The Gods Made Flesh: Metamorphosis and the Pursuit of Paganism
　　Barthes, Roland
　　　　A Barthes Reader (ed. Susan Sontag)
　　　　A Lover's Discourse: Fragments
　　　　The Pleasure of the Text

Baxter, Charles
  "Stillness," in *Burning Down the House: Essays in Fiction*
Benjamin, Walter
  Illuminations
  Reflections
Bergson, Henri
  "On the Intensity of Psychological States," in *Essai sur les données immédiates de la conscience*
Bloom, Harold
  Agon: Towards a Theory of Revisionism
  Poetics of Influence: New and Selected Criticism
  Poetry and Repression: Revisionism from Blake to Stevens
  The Western Canon: The Books and School of the Ages
Brooks, Cleanth
  The Well Wrought Urn: Studies in the Structure of Poetry
Buber, Martin
  I and Thou
Burke, Kenneth
  A Grammar of Motives
  Language as Symbolic Action: Essays on Life, Literature, and Method
  Permanence and Change: An Anatomy of Purpose
  A Rhetoric of Motives
Calvino, Italo
  Six Memos for the Next Millennium
Cameron, Sharon
  Lyric Time: Dickinson and the Limits of Genre
Cohen, Ted
  "Metaphor and the Cultivation of Intimacy," in *On Metaphor* (ed. Sheldon Sacks)
Culler, Jonathan
  On Puns: The Foundation of Letters (editor)
  The Pursuit of Signs: Semiotics, Literature, Deconstruction
Donoghue, Denis
  Ferocious Alphabets
Du Bois, W. E. B.
  Writings (Library of America)
Eliade, Mircea
  Shamanism: Archaic Techniques of Ecstasy
Finnegan, Ruth
  Oral Poetry: Its Nature, Significance, and Social Context
Freud, Sigmund
  "Beyond the Pleasure Principle" in *The Standard Edition of the Complete Psychological Works of Sigmund Freud*, vol. 18
  "Mourning and Melancholia," in *Standard Edition*, vol. 14
  "The Uncanny" in *Standard Edition*, vol. 17
Fry, Paul
  The Poet's Calling in the English Ode

Frye, Northrop
   Anatomy of Criticism
Gates, Henry Louis, Jr.
   The Signifying Monkey: A Theory of African-American Literary Criticism
Goodman, Paul
   Speaking and Language: Defence of Poetry
Halperin, David
   One Hundred Years of Homosexuality and Other Essays on Greek Love
Hampl, Patricia
   Burning Bright: An Anthology of Sacred Poetry (editor)
Harrison, Jane
   Epilegomena to the Study of Greek Religion
   Themis: A Study of the Social Origins of Greek Religion
Heath-Stubbs, John
   The Ode
Heidegger, Martin
   Poetry, Language, Thought
Heraclitus, of Ephesus
   Heraclitus: Fragments (trans. T. M. Robinson)
Herskovits, Melville
   The American Negro: A Study in Racial Crossing
Higgins, Dick
   Pattern Poetry: Guide to an Unknown Literature
Highet, Gilbert
   The Classical Tradition: Greek and Roman Influences on Western Literature
Hillman, James
   The Dream and the Underworld
Iser, Wolfgang
   Act of Reading: A Theory of Aesthetic Response
Jump, John
   The Ode
Kenner, Hugh
   The Pound Era
Kermode, Frank
   An Appetite for Poetry
   Forms of Attention
   The Romantic Image
Levine, Lawrence
   *Black Culture and Black Consciousness: Afro-American Folk Thought from Slavery
      to Freedom*
Locke, Alain
   The New Negro
Lomax, John and Alan
   Folk Song U.S.A.
Longenbach, James
   Modern Poetry after Modernism

Longinus
    On the Sublime
Lord, Albert
    The Singer of Tales
Lowth, Bishop Robert
    Lectures on the Sacred Poetry of the Hebrews (De sacra poesi Hebraeorum)
Maritain, Jacques
    Creative Intuition in Art and Poetry
Marvel, Ik
    Reveries of a Bachelor: Or a Book of the Heart
Mellers, Wilfred
    *Music in a New Found Land: Themes and Developments in the History of American
        Music*
Mill, John Stuart
    Dissertations and Discussions, vol. 1
Nadeau, Maurice
    The History of Surrealism
Nalbantian, Suzanne
    The Symbol of the Soul from Hölderlin to Yeats: A Study in Metonomy
Ong, Walter
    Orality and Literacy: The Technologizing of the Word
Page, Denys
    "Entretiens sur l'antiquité classique," *Archilique,* vol. 10
Parry, Milman
    The Making of Homeric Verse: The Collected Papers of Milman Parry
Pascal, Blaise
    Pensées
Plato
    Collected Dialogues (ed. Edith Hamilton and Huntington Cairns)
Poincaré, Henri
    "Mathematical Creation" in *The Creative Process* (ed. Brewster Ghiselin)
Richards, I. A.
    The Philosophy of Rhetoric
    Practical Criticism: A Study of Literary Judgment
    Principles of Literary Criticism
Ruskin, John
    The Literary Criticism of John Ruskin
Sacks, Peter
    The English Elegy: Studies in the Genre from Spenser to Yeats
Said, Edward
    Beginnings: Intention and Method
Santayana, George
    Essays in Literary Criticism
Sapir, Edward
    Language: An Introduction to the Study of Speech
Sartre, Jean-Paul

"What Is Literature?" and Other Essays

Schiller, Friedrich von
  Naive and Sentimental Poetry and On the Sublime: Two Essays

Seneca
  Letter XLIX "On the Shortness of Life" in *Ad Lucilium Epistulae Morales,*
    vol. 1, The Loeb Classical Library (trans. Richard M. Gummere)

Schlüter, Kurt
  Die Englische Ode

Shklovsky, Victor
  "Art as Technique" in *Russian Formalist Criticism* (ed. L. T. Lemon and
    M. J. Reiss)

Smith, Barbara Herrnstein
  Poetic Closure: A Study of How Poems End

Spiller, Michael
  The Development of the Sonnet: An Introduction

Weil, Simone
  The Simone Weil Reader (ed. G. Panichas)

Welsh, Andrew
  Roots of Lyric: Primitive Poetry and Modern Poetics

Wimsatt, W. K.
  The Verbal Icon: Studies in the Meaning of Poetry

Zumthor, Paul
  Oral Poetry: An Introduction

Permissions

Index

For Discussion

1. Hirsch suggests that even the greatest poems are incomplete without readers. What role do you think the reader really plays in a poem?

2. Why do you think so many people (even people who rarely read for pleasure) turn to poems on ritual occasions, such as weddings and funerals? What, if anything, does this tell us about the need for poetry?

3. Consider this radical statement by Emily Dickinson. Is there any way to know poetry except by contact?

> If I read a book [and] it makes my whole body so cold no fire can ever warm me I know *that* is poetry. If I feel physically as if the top of my head were taken off, I know *that* is poetry. These are the only way I know. Is there any other way.

4. Consider Hirsch's discussion of reading Emily Brontë's poem "Spellbound" as a child and then his later reading of the poem as an adult (pp. 61–66). Can you think of any experiences you had with poetry as a child? Do you think your reading of those poems would be different today?

5. In discussing Elizabeth Bishop's poem "One Art" (pp. 32–33), list a few of the things you've lost, and arrange them so that the magnitude of each loss increases. Are these losses "hard to master"? Do you feel as if any of them "will bring disaster"? How *do* we come to terms with loss (do rituals help?) and is there anything to be gained in finding these losses, these feelings, organized by a poetic structure, such as a villanelle?

6. Have you ever loved an animal unreasonably? If you had to make a list of your pet's no doubt extraordinary attributes, as Christopher Smart does in writing about his cat Jeoffry (pp. 66–69), how would you make it interesting to others? What do you think of the strategy of parallelism that Smart employs?

7. What do you think happened to the two lovers in Yehuda Amichai's poem "A Pity. We Were Such a Good Invention" (p. 90)? Who are "they"? How can two lovers become an invention, "an aeroplane made from a man and wife"?

8. Read Guittone d'Arezzo's poem aloud as best you can in Italian as well as in English (p. 96). How does it make you feel? What do you think of the obsessive repetition of the word "gioi" ("joy") in this poem? Is it an effective translation?

9. Read two love poems aloud, say, Paul Éluard's "Lady Love" (p. 94) and Robert Desnos's "The Voice of Robert Desnos" (pp. 100–101). Do you find these voices seductive? Can words alone inspire affection or recall lost love?

10. Anna Akhmatova writes about the simple gesture of putting her left glove on her right hand in her poem "Song of the Last Meeting" (pp. 116–17). How much meaning does this gesture have?

11. How should we respond when we become aware that we are losing something we prize deeply? Constantine Cavafy's poem "The God Abandons Antony" (p. 136) gives Antony specific advice on how to behave, on what to do. What do you think of the counsel?

12. Miklós Radnóti's "Postcards" (pp. 146–50) were written under the most dire and extreme circumstances imaginable. Do the circumstances of how the poems were written change their meaning for you? If you had just one hour to write something by flashlight in the middle of the night, what would be your last communiqué to the world? Would poetry be your chosen vehicle?

13. Consider the nature of the things that Mr. Cogito would like to consider to the very end in Zbigniew Herbert's poem "Mr. Cogito and the Imagination" (p. 190). List some of the things you would never tire of thinking about.

14. Have you ever had an uncanny experience, such as the one Anthony Hecht describes in "A Hill" (pp. 233–34)? How does it change the poem when we discover that the hill in question was not a vision but a memory?

15. Elizabeth Bishop's "In the Waiting Room" (pp. 236–39) dramatizes a child's first consciousness of having a self. What does she learn about the self? Would your own recognitions be any different?

16. How would you characterize the soul in Walt Whitman's poem "A Clear Midnight" (p. 245)? How would you characterize it in Emily Dickinson's poem number 683 (p. 254)? Is it still possible for us to use the word "soul"? What are the "themes" that your own spirit would most love to ponder?

17. Jorge Luis Borges said, "Poetry is something that cannot be defined without oversimplifying it. It would be like attempting to define the color yellow, love, the fall of leaves in autumn." Is Borges right? Can poetry ever be defined without oversimplifying it?